THE WILD FLOWERS OF GUERNSEY

The Wild Flowers of Guernsey

with notes of the frequencies of all species recorded for the Channel Islands

DAVID McCLINTOCK

COLLINS
ST JAMES'S PLACE, LONDON

For La Société Guernesiaise, in appreciation of what its members, and those of the National Trust of Guernsey, do for the island

Maps by Deirdre Yuill

First published 1975

ISBN 0 00 219369 8

Made and Printed in Great Britain by
William Collins Sons & Co Ltd Glasgow

Contents

CONTENTS

Introduction

THE best is the enemy of the good. I trust this account of the Wild Flowers of Guernsey may be deemed good: best it is not. It is just some of the information I have come across about the at all wild flowers of a rich and charming island. Since a fresh book on the subject was long overdue, and there was no one else available to write it, I said late in 1967 that I would try to set out what had become known. In the event, more than a little has since been added to old as well as to more recent knowledge. My aim has been to interest and stimulate a wide variety of people.

I have been visiting Guernsey for 28 years now, but have never spent more than 13 days on end there. Indeed my total is only some 185 days during all these years (148 of them since 1967), and in the earlier visits I had no thoughts of writing a book. Those who have tried will know the great extra difficulties of not being on the spot to check this, see that and note changes of all sorts, or cover the area at all seasons. I seem always to be finding places I have never been to before. Marquand, the author of the last *Flora*, which came out in 1901, wrote that, after working assiduously for seven years at the flora of the island, he calculated it would have required seven years more of steady work to accomplish what he aimed at. Seven years more! – and after living in the island for seven years with nothing to distract him from his beloved natural history. Instead I have had six months scrappily spread over more than a quarter of a century, far from all the time being available for natural history. One of the distractions has been the warmth of Guernsey hospitality, shown me by so many people, which I have very much enjoyed and appreciated!

So time, or lack of it, is one reason why this book may not be all I would have wished it to be. Inevitably it deals only with the so-called higher plants, but the great, the to me lamentable, gap is the absence of ecological information, which should explain and expand the bare facts of distribution. Ecology is still a jargon word to most people, but nevertheless the subject is of supreme importance. It deals with how plants of all sorts and sizes and animals of all sorts and sizes live together, who eats what, what affects what, why this is here and not there, the fascinating competition and checks of life in the wild, all reacting, ever-changing and developing. I have made certain lists of plants, habitat studies, which are a very small start in this direction and are available in the archives of the Société Guernesiaise.

But a book such as this should ideally freely refer to such facts as which caterpillars or other larvae use which food plants in the island – not necessarily the same as elsewhere. The author should have looked more than he did at the whitish tunnels between the top and bottom layers of leaves where leaf miner grubs make their homes, many species of miner being confined to one species or group of plants, each mining in its distinctive fashion and easy to observe and collect. Then there are the very numerous other insects, thrips, psyllids, black and white flies, aphids, coccids and so on, which live in or on the roots, stems, leaves, flowers or fruits of plants, and the rusts and other microfungi, bacteria and viruses, some equally host-specific, some of them described as new to science from

Guernsey. I collected some notes on these, but they were so chancy and inexpert that I felt they would give an unbalanced effect and so were best left out.

My friends the bird observers could tell us which seed-eating birds eat which seeds and when, and which birds have other effects on the vegetation or are chiefly to be seen in certain terrain, or nest in certain sorts of vegetation or what their preferences are for nesting material, or which, usually (always?), garden, plants they may attack, and students of mammals should tell us the same. The chemically and geologically minded could tell us of the soils and rocks, the better to understand the distribution of certain plants; and the meteorologists the effects of climate, above all the extremes of climate, and of micro-climate, that of small areas. Historians too, of man and his economics, of vegetation and agriculture, and horticulture indeed, should be adding to this picture. All these different branches of knowledge are needed to give a satisfactorily rounded account of the wild flowers of Guernsey. To try to remedy in a small way this defect, there are in the Appendix sources of data on other features of the island's natural history. Some of these may have little or no effect on its wild flowers, but it seemed worth making the list as complete as possible, for no comparable record has been published for seventy years.

At least the next writer on this subject should have in this book a reliable set of facts on which to build further. I have tried by my phrasing to indicate when I consider a record good, and when it is based on a specimen, which impliedly I will have seen. There is a note on the cards for each species kept by the Société of all specimens we have come across of Guernsey plants, so they can be checked if the identification is doubted.

Here I might refer to the magnificent project, now well under way, of the island's colour photography club 'Spectrum', to record in colour all the island's wild flowers. Nothing like this has been attempted elsewhere, and its value will be immense. The leader in this enterprise is John Bichard, but several other members of the club have also done useful work this way of the extremely high standard for which it is internationally known. Sincere thanks are due to them.

In my search for records, I have used a vast number of sources. I am particularly indebted to Douglas Simpson's *Bibliographical Index to the British Flora* of 1960, which has led me to many valuable facts, which in turn have led to others. I am grateful to him, not only for his *Index*, which he published at his own expense, but for other personal help too. To supplement what was found in the field, I have sought specimens, with very varying amounts of thoroughness and success, in the most likely herbaria, chiefly those at Kew, the British Museum (Natural History), Edinburgh, Oxford, Cambridge, Birmingham, Harrow and St Peter Port, with sallies into a dozen others. Who is to say what has inevitably been missed in the continued absence of any sort of index or record of what is in most such collections, information buried and undiscoverable except by chance and luck – and I have had my share of this. From this and other sources I compiled a list of people who had collected plants in the island or made other records, and they total nearly 500. Details of them are in the archives.

In addition to the cards which are kept for each species, the Société has mapping cards, 1000 distribution maps on cards based on them, and the archives of letters and other documents relating to the island's wild flowers. These should substantiate statements and quotations given in this book. For the better learning of the distribution of the plants, records were kept on cards for each of the 79 squares covering the island on the standard Ordnance Survey 3 in. to 1 mile map with the 1966 grid – not the 1934 one. There are also separate cards for each of the off-islands, however small. These have formed the basis for the general recording and were much used by the field meetings, of which more anon.

There is so much to learn about Guernsey and its flowers that one could go on working happily at this indefinitely. But, genuinely fond as I am of the island, I have had many other calls and duties, quite apart from a full-time commercial job. Consequently there was a hard limit to what I could do, despite all the attractive lines of research and investigation I kept on coming across. I said therefore in 1967 that I would draw the line at the end of 1970, and meanwhile did all I could to collect records. By far the most important activity was to get field meetings in the island of the botanical societies, the Botanical Society of the British Isles and the Wild Flower Society, in conjunction with the Société. These were well attended, and gave a fillip and made discoveries which would have been totally impossible for one person alone, and much is due to them.

Indeed I did not expect quite the quantity of good finds that were made, which showed that the Guernsey Flora was even more underworked, and even richer and more interesting than had been realised. It must be almost, if not quite (Jersey is the rival), second to none in our islands. Two such field meetings, each representing some 200–250 man-days, covered all, or almost all, the squares on the island, which has always suffered from being unevenly searched. But repeating the fine haul of the first year in the second argued that there must be still more to find, and that to write a Flora on the basis solely of what had happened to be seen by then must be incomplete. So the final date was extended by another year and a third meeting held in 1971. This still made useful discoveries, but gave reason to believe that fewer new important discoveries lurked unrevealed. Time will show, but time prevented another extension and, as it proved, the task of writing up the findings and clearing endless loose ends needed more than another year, above all because of competing commitments.

Records in this book are up to the end of 1973, with the advantage of emendation during the completion of the text in 1974. That there are, always will be, good records to be made, I do not doubt. As the flora will always be changing, so will there always be more to watch and report, new finds, new frequencies and distributions, and new pleasures.

There are some details I ought to refer to.

I have treated identically nearly every species and subspecies ever claimed from the island. Marquand wrote that in a local Flora every known record should be recognised in some way and either confirmed, questioned or rejected: none should be ignored. Indeed some of the records here set out may be, almost certainly are, erroneous, some of them are suspect, some of them planted by human hands, some mere garden throw-outs. But there must always be an honest difference of opinion as to which of these to include in any account such as this, and which to downgrade or omit. It seemed to me the fairest way was to include them all, with the evidence, and allow the reader to form his own opinion. 'Extinct' is a dangerous word, and who is to say which single casual may not start a large population? Square brackets have been used only for purely garden plants of special Guernsey interest, which any keen plantsman should want to know about.

Another matter is the treatment of the lower categories of botanical classification, varieties and forms – my views on what these should cover are in the *Guide to the Naming of Plants* published by the Heather Society in 1969. Many such names have been used for Guernsey plants, but many of these are uncertain in their value, or application, or in the priority of rival names for apparently the same taxon (taxon is a modern word for any group of plants of uncertain status). I have therefore mentioned only those which seemed to me of some importance. All the rest are on the cards for their species, where the inquirer may learn of them. Variation is the life-blood of plant and animal life and is a large and profitable field for study which I hope the next writer will enlarge on, and show the relevance of the variation in Guernsey to Guernsey conditions.

Length is a bugbear – there always seems so much to include. I have taken various steps to curb myself. One was, alas, to omit the list nearly 400 strong, with their dates, of those who had helped with this book; but the galley proof of this is preserved in the archives. To all this throng, past and present, much is owed: indeed without their cumulative work this book would have been thin. The list was made in appreciation of, and gratitude for, their multifarious contributions. Another exclusion was the gazetteer of place names indexed to the map. Comments I have generally limited to facts observed in Guernsey or made on plants from there. I have also sometimes used curt comments, such as 'common', although I intend no discourtesy to the plants in question. Indeed the commonest ones deserve to have their success explained. Usually I have repeated nothing from Marquand's *Flora*, unless it is directly relevant to my account of the species or the matter under discussion. Some of his statements, notably first records, need correcting, when it will probably be done by implication, e.g. by giving a first record I would not otherwise have mentioned, for I rate the value of many of them low. Hence the constant reference to Gosselin's collections, which Marquand never saw. But this not repeating most of Marquand's data has meant leaving out, for example, the interesting information he gives for most species in its closing sentences. It will often be only by taking his account with this one that the fullest picture will emerge, or readers can appreciate the extent of the additions etc. in this present work. Nevertheless this book stands on its own and for most purposes should condense adequately our knowledge. Plants may be considered to have been British 'natives' in our era, unless their area of origin is given; and habitats as usually given in Floras unless mentioned otherwise.

English names have been given priority because this book is meant to appeal to as many people as possible. I tried to use those in the *Recommended List of English Names of Wild Plants* in its 1969 version, except when these were patently inapposite. The Latin names were minutely checked by J. E. Dandy, and I have immensely appreciated the detailed care he gave, even to the vexed matter of capital initials for specific epithets, which he personally would now never use. Partly because of this special trouble of his, and partly because I believe that their use adds character and accuracy to these, often ancient, names, I have used them, where appropriate, throughout. I consider this no pedantry, but rather that invariably to use small initials smacks of easy-going slovenliness. Guernsey-French names were a puzzle – how to spell them, how precise they were and how much still in use – happily Marquand's forecast that the language would now be extinct has proved far from true. Those I give have been culled from various sources, but are based on Marquand's own paper of 1905, and have been discussed with Mrs Marie de Garis, and others, to whom I am most grateful. She is the main author of *Le Dictiounnaire Angllais-Guernesiais* of 1967 and its '*Supplement*' of 1973.

Then there is the last sentence under each species – J.A.S.H. This tries to summarise the recorded distribution and frequency in the other groups of the Archipelago. These notes need considering with the topography of the island concerned, e.g. the absence of sand, nowadays at any rate, in Sark, and their size – Jersey 45, Guernsey 24.4, Alderney 3, Sark 1.6 and Herm 0.5 square miles. The data for Jersey I have gone through at length with Frances le Sueur – and who could help better? I thank her most specially, and for constant good collaboration and kindness over many years. The numerous references to species seen there for the last time between 1924 and 1931 are based on superb specimens of practically all the plants ever claimed from Jersey, and others too, which were, *mirabile dictu*, collected from there then by Brother Louis-Arsène (1875–1959). Mrs le Sueur was convinced all were genuinely wild. The data for the other islands may be more fallible. They are based on the *Check-lists* she and I produced which were published in the *Transactions* of the Société Guernesiaise for 1960 (Herm, including Jethou and its other satellite islets), 1962 (Sark, including Brechou of which I have written a *Flora* for its tenant, which has been in galley since 1969) and 1964 (Alderney, including Burhou), modified by subsequent information. But there is much more work to do in these other parts of the Bailiwick of Guernsey, and some absences may be more apparent than real. To complete the distribution in the Archipelago, a note is put in brackets of all other species which have been recorded for the other islands but not, yet, for Guernsey. The flora of the whole of the Channel Islands is therefore epitomised here. AM, AGM and FCC refer to the Royal Horticultural Society's Award of Merit, Award of Garden Merit and First Class Certificate. HCC to its Horticultural Colour Chart 1939/42.

No book such as this could, or should, be produced by one person unaided. I could not have done it without help from many people, past and present: surely no other Flora has had the benefit of so much expert assistance. But at the risk of being invidious, I must single out a few. First perhaps come Nigel and Jennifer Jee, who have given me the warm company of their home and family for many weeks and in addition have kept the card index, mounted specimens and done much else. Peter Girard, Nigel's recent predecessor as President of the Société, has also been a firm friend and helper – but who has not? The kindness that not only I but all those who came on the three field meetings met, has been unfailing. Even so, I must add the names of Rosemary de Sausmarez, lover of the minute and a great finder-out of historical facts; Bridget Elliott of the sharp eyes, who also did good work with the mapping cards – she is now at the Natural History Museum in London and, since 1974, Mrs Ozanne; Mary Burridge, who organised the field meetings and, like her husband Bill, has long been a staunch friend and able natural historian; and Patience Ryan, who emerged late with unbounded and able enthusiasm and produced the maps on which many of the assessments of distribution are based. Mrs Burridge and Mrs Ryan are two of the artists who have given their services to this book, thus greatly embellishing it. The others, all also Guernsey people, are Mary Blad, Zenia Davies, Roy Fenna, Yvonne Houston, Peter Howitt and Jasmine Torode. In addition, the photograph for the jacket was taken by yet another inhabitant of Guernsey, John Bichard already referred to. The practical support of the Bailiff and Jurats of the Royal Court has been very much appreciated, and so has the ready assistance of the staffs of the Guille-Allès and Priaulx libraries. Many other people are mentioned in the text for their special contributions, but I would like to end with the name of Hon. Lewis Palmer, Luly to so many, who endeared himself to all in his three short years in the island and in that time did such a power of good for its flowers of all sorts. All these, and many others, have helped make this book. My thanks are full, and very sincere.

Bracken Hill,
Platt, Kent
July 1974

DAVID MCCLINTOCK

'The Botany of the Channel Islands is worthy of a closer comparative study than it has yet received, and would amply repay the philosophical naturalist, able to view in their natural relations all the natural groups, and their bearing on physical geography and geology.'

D. T. Anstead. 1862

'There are few localities where natural history could be studied to greater advantage than here.'

A. Leipner. 1888

'The island is a perfect paradise for lovers of natural history.'

T. Green. 1893

'Une excursion dans les Iles Anglo-Normandes est toujours une aubaine pour un botaniste.'

A. Chevalier. 1933

All still true!

The Flowers of Guernsey

GUERNSEY, the second largest of the Channel Islands, the Iles de la Manche of Iles Anglo-Normandes in French, is geographically part of the continent or Europe. They are grouped with France in *Flora Europaea*, for their flowers have a greater affinity with those of Normandy and Brittany than with those of most of England. Several indeed show adaptation to Mediterranean conditions by dying down at the approach of summer. Add to this the varied terrain and the equable climate (mean temperature about 57°, rainfall 36 inches, and no air pollution) and its special interest to naturalists will be obvious.

Visitors from the Continent have been rare. Indeed the Channel Islands are too often in a natural history limbo, considered by the British to be part of the Continent and by the French to be part of Britain. Consequently they tend to get left out of books on both sides of the Channel. This is much to be regretted, for the French, especially from the neighbouring provinces, find surprises and interest in these islands, not only from their ancient Norman connections, but from the differences in their floras, because plants rare or unknown on the opposite coasts may do well here.

The number of different species of plants wild on Guernsey is remarkable. In the *Atlas of the British Flora*, which appeared in 1962, the average marked for each ten kilometre square of the National Grid – that is some 38 square miles – was about 400. Guernsey has an area of rather over 24 square miles – that is under two-thirds of that of a square – yet there are over 900 marked for it in the *Atlas* and that total is incomplete. The precise number of wild plants credited to the island depends on personal assessments of how far back one goes for records, what unsupported claims one believes to be accurate and what casuals and ex-garden plants one includes. But in this book are set out some 1340 species, subspecies and hybrids, plus over 130 clones of Bramble, Rose, Dandelion, Daffodil and Bamboo, making over 1470 plus, again, varieties and forms. Another 330 or so species etc. recorded on the other islands of the Archipelago and not in Guernsey are accounted for, which would make the CI list nearly 1800.

What are the glories of Guernsey's wild flowers? Most visitors are attracted by sheer colour and they will never see better than on Guernsey's south cliffs in April and May. Here are the golds of the massed clumps of Gorse and, locally, Broom, the pink or white carpets of Thrift, Sea Campion and Ox-eye Daisy, the red or blue drifts of Red Campion, Bluebells and Sheepsbit, the pink, grey and white of English Stonecrop added to the fresh greens of the grasses, the browns of the soils, the russets of the rocks and the whites and blues of the sea. In the south-west there are mats of Prostrate Broom, glowing golden sheets above silvery young leaves; and in many other areas too the Gorse is almost overpowering in its sumptuous flower and fragrance. In March and April millions of naturalised Narcissi bedeck fields, hedges and cliffs. Demurer are the Primroses and Violets and Ferns, which luxuriate in the lanes more plentifully than in any of the other islands.

The discerning visitor and resident will find delight of a less obvious nature on the cliffs and in the tapestry of the short turf of the north and north-west, a rewarding pleasure for those who go on hands and knees, or sit, or lie, and stare and drink it all in. The closer they look, the more they will see, fresh minute beauties, and some of these it would be hard to find elsewhere, certainly in plenty.

It is not only in the flush of spring and early summer that there is beauty to be seen: there is interest at all seasons. This comes partly from the mild climate, which allows plants to overwinter which could never survive in most parts of England. But in winter there are two special quarries. One is Greater Lords and Ladies, which can be told with certainty from the Common one by the fact that its leaves appear well before Christmas, an agreeable object for a dander in October or November. The other is Dwarf Adder's Tongue, which may have vanished by the time the spring flowers are at their best. I hope its extreme rarity nowadays is more apparent than real, because few go to look for it at the right time or in other than its standard areas.

Guernsey must have proportionately as many rare plants as any part of the British Isles. They have been a lure to visitors for nearly a century and a half. It has more rare Ferns than anywhere. Nowhere else in the world has its own hybrid between Black and Lanceolate Spleenworts yet been found. Nowhere else in the world is the hybrid to be seen between Hart's Tongue and Lanceolate Spleenwort. That between Hart's Tongue and Black Spleenwort has similarly been found practically only in Guernsey and is overdue to be rediscovered; it has been much searched for. In addition, there is much more Sand Quillwort than in all the rest of the British Isles combined. And there are other rare and special Ferns, two of them foreigners, naturalised here as nowhere else. Four of these specialities appear on postage stamps of 1975, the first set ever devoted solely to Ferns.

Perhaps the scarcest Guernsey speciality is generally only 1″ high and rarely exceeds 3″ in any direction – usually wider than tall. It is the so-called Guernsey Centaury, and indeed resembles a Centaury, for in Guernsey its flowers are always pink: on the Continent they may be pale yellow. Probably equally scarce, and also known nowhere else in the British Isles, also small and inconspicuous in the turf, is Dwarf Millet. Details of these (and of all the plants mentioned here) are of course in the main text, and most are illustrated there too. In general an illustrated plant will have some special Guernsey interest. But all seventy-six will not be referred to here, and indeed it might be argued that many more than that were of special interest.

Largely because of the climate, it has been possible for several plants to get established which either do not, or at best just, reach Great Britain and Ireland. The most widespread and abundant of these, decking roadsides and too much else in spring and disappearing in early summer, is obloquated nowadays as Stinking Onions – it is also called plain Garlic and, erroneously, White Bluebells. It is Mediterranean in origin, but it was in Guernsey that it was first noted in the British Isles, in the 1840s, and even then was said to be abundant. Recently another attractive Mediterranean Onion has started to spread, the one known and sometimes grown locally as Star of Bethlehem, although that name really belongs to another species. The true owner of the English name is in Latin *Ornithogalum umbellatum* (and that may occasionally be seen too), that of the pretty usurper *Allium neapolitanum*. Yet a third similar spreader, of which there is probably most in Guernsey, is Honey Bells, which is put in a different genus from the Onions, *Allium*, precisely because it lacks the garlic smell and in fact its flowers smell quite deliciously of honey. All these wayside bulbous plants seem positively to gain from the regrettable use of weedkiller, because this does not apparently penetrate the polished coats of their bulbs, and they are released from the competition of their susceptible neighbours.

A pretty plant first recorded wild from Guernsey in the middle of the last century is St Peter Port Daisy, which originated in Mexico and was doubtless imported to ornament gardens, which it well does. Now it is to be seen on countless walls and is also in other warmer parts of the British Isles. Yet another special and attractive wall plant is Throatwort, from the Mediterranean, which has also been known naturalised in Guernsey for about a century and has only lately been found in Jersey. It is very like Red Valerian, another Mediterranean plant of walls, but its flowers are purple and lack the spur at the bottom end.

A weed which is bad enough to blind people to the beauty for which it was no doubt originally introduced is the Oxalis. In truth there are three species with pink flowers, but only two have the terrible small bulbils round their tap roots, which make them hard to eradicate. Undoubtedly lovely however is the yellow one called Bermuda Buttercup, although it comes from South Africa. In many parts of the world it is a bad weed because of its bulbils, but in Guernsey it keeps its place and gives great delight. It was on one of the first wild flower stamps issued by the Guernsey Post Office.

Guernsey has other special weeds, plants of waste and cultivated ground. Three are grasses. Lesser Quaking Grass, possibly the most ornamental of all its genus, has been known in the island for over 200 years, and who is to say if it has not 'always' been there? Its congener, the Greater Quaking Grass, has made itself at home in hot dry places and is rightly grown for its decorative qualities – to which it might owe its arrival in the island. The third is the Guernsey Canary-grass, usually taller and stouter than the Common one and with a cylindrical spike and differences in the shape of its attractive bi-coloured florets. Also called after the island is Guernsey Fleabane, which has recently become well established. It is South American.

Most people know the annual garden Marigold with yellow or orange flowers some 2″ across. In an increasing number of arable fields may now be seen its taller counterpart, which also comes from the Mediterranean, with more and smaller, always orange, flowerheads, gay when the sun is out and they are open; and yet it is a plant hardly known elsewhere in the British Isles. From the Cape (of Good Hope) came Cape Cudweed, reaching Guernsey towards the end of the last century and now very common, but unknown in Britain outside the Channel Islands. It is frequently mistaken for the so-called Jersey Cudweed.

Plants now to be found wild in Guernsey have originated in many different areas of the world. Several more than those referred to come from the Mediterranean, plants such as Pot Purslane, Small-flowered Melilot, Mind-your-own-business, Adria Bellflower, Lesser Star Thistle, Tassel Hyacinth and Rosy Garlic. The Cape and Southern Africa have also produced most of the Mesembryanthemums, Curly Water Thyme, African Lily, Red-hot Poker, Onion Grass, and Arum Lily, as well as the Guernsey Lily. From South America too have come Gunneras and Tall Nightshade, more specifically from the Argentine, Pink and Pink Bulbous Oxalis, Cocks Eggs, Green Cyperus and Rescue Grass. Primarily from Chile are Alderney Geranium, Fragrant Evening Primrose, Fuchsia, Escallonia and Spring Star Flower.

Many other parts of America are represented. The Gallant Soldiers and Guernsey Fleabane are from Peru as well as, predictably, Apple of Peru and Marvel of Peru. Similarly Mexican Oxalis is Central American, and Greater Stonecrop is Mexican too. Originally North American, chiefly Californian, are Water Fern, Monterey Pine (and Monterey Cypress), Californian Poppy, Button-hole Plant and Pink Purslane (which is also native in Siberia), Lupins, Fringe-cups, Lesser Evening Primrose, Sunflowers, Ragweed, Canadian and Early Golden-rods, Beach Aster, Canadian Fleabane, Pineapple Weed, Slender Rush and Honey Bells.

Donkey's Rhubarb, Japanese Privet, House Holly Fern and most of the Bamboos are Japanese. A few come from China, as do Fishbone Cotoneaster and Buddleia. Himalayan Balsam betrays its origin: so does Khasia Berry from the north of India, whence came also Wallspray, Tree Cotoneaster and the Anceps Bamboo.

Sea Fig is Eastern Australian, so is Tongue Fern, which also grows in New Zealand, as do the small Willow-herb, Wire plant, Kangaroo Apple, Hedge Veronica, New Zealand Holly and other Olearias and Cabbage Palm.

Common Field Speedwell is Near-Eastern and Slender Speedwell, two Stone-crops and the Common Rhododendron come from the Caucasus, although the original introduction of this last was from the south of Spain, where it is surprisingly also native. The towering Giant Echium is from the Canaries and Greater Herb Robert from Madeira. Some weeds are pantropic now, such as Cocklebur and the Amaranths. Finally there is Montbretia, which did not exist anywhere a hundred years ago, for it is the result of a cross made in France about 1877 between two South African species.

A brief word on two other aspects of Guernsey's flowers. One is the persistence of some over the ages, an evocative link with the past. One example is the delightful, unweedy, Sea Bindweed. Its pollen is in the peat at Vazon, so it will have been thereabouts when the dolmens were still in use; Gosselin the pioneer of the Guernsey flora, collected it there nearly 200 years ago, and there it still is, surviving drastic land changes and uses and now, just, erosion by trippers. Other plants, such as Dittander have been on the west coast at least since Gosselin collected them there, while Dwarf Elder is still at Paradis, where Carré told Babington it was in the 1830s. Many others survive similarly too.

Very different are the plants which Guernsey has apparently never had at all, and yet might have been expected to grow there on our present knowledge of their needs and history. Some are unknown wild in any of the Channel Islands – Marsh Marigold, Common Valerian or Harebell for example. Some are in one island and not another in seemingly irrational fashion. Why are Nottingham Catchfly and Carline Thistle easy to see in small nearby Herm, but not or hardly in Guernsey? Why are Wood Anemone, Wood Sorrel, Greater Stitchwort, Angelica, Dog's Mercury, Cross-leaved Heath, Bilberry, White Dead-nettle and Golden-rod in Jersey only? – and Guernsey has plants which Jersey has not. The oddities of distribution and frequency can be seen in the summary at the end of the account of each species, and are matched by several animals too.

We are of course dealing with small areas, but the fact is that plants only grow or do best, in certain conditions, and only after they have managed to get a foothold; and we are woefully ignorant just what most plants do like. But the general conditions are often indicated by the associated plants, distinctive ones tending to be found growing together, indicating that they like similar, but rarely if ever identical, habitats. One of the advantages Guernsey has is a good variety of habitats, although some, such as bogs and thick woods have gone.

One sort of soil, rock indeed, which Guernsey has never had is chalk and limestone. Consequently it never has had typical chalk and limestone plants. It does however have some which get enough calcium, that is the basic stuff of chalk and limestone, from ground-down sea shells close to shore and in the maritime turf. Indeed the dunes and the sandy turf probably contain more of Guernsey's special plants than any other habitat. They still are widespread in the north and north-west, but their area is sadly diminished from their earlier extent down the west coast. The Guet for example was a well-known locality for short-turf specialities and such places reached as far as Rocquaine. On them grazing, and on the golf-course mechanical mowers, assist the naturally well-drained conditions to keep the vegetation short, which warms small plants and prevents them being smothered by ranker ones. Here grow numerous clovers, annual and perennial, many of them scarce or rare, and related species such as Bird's-foots and Bird's-foot Trefoils, and Rupturewort which with its deeper roots keeps green when the surrounding sward is brown and parched, crackling underfoot. Here too are Dwarf Millet and Small Hare's-ear and, still, Bee Orchids. Here too grew the Small Restharrow – is it really gone? and it is in such coastal turf that Field Eryngo recently settled down in the sort of place one would have expected to see the similar Sea Holly, which is still surviving locally. It is one of the best areas to see Autumn Squill and Sand Crocus, the latter so rare elsewhere in the British Isles, which also brighten dry cliff tops in the sunshine. And it is one of the two places where French Oat has made itself at home and Deptford Pink.

The hollows among the dunes, the slacks, with water just below ground level in summer, are where Sand Quillwort, Guernsey Centaury and Yellow Cicendia grow with Chaffweed and Flax-seed, posies for a doll's house and usually invisible to anyone not on hands and knees. The rougher slacks are where the great tufts of the excessively well-pointed Sharp Rush are. The fragrant Great Sea Stock likes the looser sand, a plant now ever rarer in the British Isles, and in Guernsey too, where it is very seriously diminished (the ordinary Stock now decorates some quarry-sides). Also here are the interesting Dwarf Spurrey and the ever-attractive Hare's-tail Grass of intriguing provenance. Other rare grasses have been on and by dunes, such as Rush-leaved Fescue, Bulbous and Early Meadow-grasses. The last is to be seen in other sorts of places, indeed it will grow much fatter where it is better fed, but like the Dwarf Spurrey, and unlike their weedy relations, Annual Meadow-grass and Common Spurrey, vanishes before summer. In the more open sand near the sea grow the species, hybrids and clones so difficult to tell apart of Couch-grasses, including the well-known garden and arable weed. Bermuda-grass, widespread in the tropics, has long been known on firmer dunes at Vazon and is elsewhere on that coast too.

Vazon was the place where botanists went to see, and usually to pick, Marquand's Sage in its only station (jargon for a place where a plant grows), where it is now extremely scarce. Generations have found it excessively hard to be sure they really had got it, and now it is considered to be no more than a form of the common Clary. Vazon too had Rough Star Thistle for at least two hundred years, but that is now very much reduced and indeed was not seen at all for a few years recently. Two foreigners have decoratively colonised some of these sandy areas, Fragrant Evening Primrose and Tree Lupin, the latter so successfully that it has been locally kept in check. Two other introduced plants have settled down here too and form thick patches, whereas elsewhere in Britain they are usually found only as scattered plants – Alsike Clover and Small-flowered Melilot. The Mediterranean garden annual Sweet Alison is established in masses on some of the sandy ground.

The north part of Guernsey was separated from the rest of the island until the first decade of the last century by an arm of the sea called the Braye du Valle, which was bounded by salt marshes of varying breadth. There is a good article on it in the *Transactions* of the Société Guernesiaise for 1935. For about 70 years thereafter typical salt marsh plants grew there (and by the Château des Marais), the most notable being Shrubby Seablite, Common and Long-leaved Scurvy-grasses, and Common and Perennial Beard-grasses. Now the only part which survives is the Vale Pond, just south of the Vale church, where Bulbous Foxtail has been added, which no doubt must have been in those parts all along undetected. There is a small salt marsh at Pulias, the remains of one in the ditches at Claire and Rousse Mares, and waves breaking over the road to the south have produced, or maintained, the same sort of effect near Rocque Poisson. Here one can still see Common Seablite, Hard-grass and even fleshy Glasswort.

Guernsey now has few shingle banks, but the fine one at L'Erée grows Yellow Horned Poppy well with its fantastically long seed pods, and there is good Sea Kale there, the origin of a too rare vegetable (but wild ones are much too tough to use!). This striking plant is to be seen in various other places round the coast. The shore line is where two very rare plants used to be found, Purple Spurge and Sea Knot-grass. Both still occur on other islands of the Archipelago and it is a matter for conjecture why neither has been seen in effect since the last century. Even Ray's Knot-grass, which has often been mistaken for the latter, has not been noticed for the last dozen years.

Guernsey's many wet places are now much reduced by drainage, or are even practically gone. With these have gone some of Guernsey's special flowers, most notably the Summer Lady's Tresses Orchid and the Wintergreen of the Grande Mare, and the Water Germander of Grandes Rocques. The Grande Mare does still have a small area of Sphagnum moss which could hold the orchid, but perhaps it is now too small and overgrown by sallows. Yet the good area in 1891 was little more than an acre in extent. Many of the wet areas in the west and north of the island however still have the striking so-called Jersey Orchid, of which there always has been much more in Guernsey than in Jersey – it just was first found in Jersey – and which is known nowhere else in the British Isles. Cotton-grass survives in the inner part of the Grande Mare and Bog-rush can also be seen. The fields there have a very rare Marsh Dandelion. Other wet places are where such Guernsey rarities grow as Tubular Water Dropwort, Purple Loosestrife, Skull-cap, Water Speedwell and Bur-reed. Here too are, locally, Dittander and, more commonly, Galingale. Indeed it is often a weed, but in days not so long gone by was used to make ropes and other articles. Damp fields can be glorious in July and August with Yellow Bartsia.

Stream-sides once had the delicate Ivy-leaved Bell-flower. Also apparently rarer is the Creeping Water Forget-me-not and the unobvious Cornish Moneywort, always a pleasure to detect, and never more surprisingly than when it was recently found matting a wet lawn. Wet meadows are the sort of place in Guernsey where the elegant Smooth Sedge grows rather than in woods; and the stools of Tussock Sedge like wet places too.

There is more open water since the Reservoir was filled in the late 1940's. Shortly afterwards, interesting plants appeared in and by it, notably two or three Water Buttercups and the Green Cyperus. The water Buttercups have been known elsewhere, but lead a chequered existence as their pools get overgrown, dried or filled in. So too the Pondweeds, which reach flooded quarries, probably with water fowl; and Water Lilies, which are put there nowadays by humans. Humans who keep aquaria are probably responsible for the two Hornworts, Curly Water Thyme and, sometimes at least, Water Milfoils, which can clutter up garden and other ponds. Water Fern also gets introduced to such places for decorative reasons. Least Water Starwort is an elusive stream or pond rarity anywhere. Rivers there is hardly room for in Guernsey, and what streams there are are made no easier to find by their being quite unmarked on the standard

3″ map. But their courses may be traced with the help of Warren's paper in the *Transactions* for 1948.

All the present woodlands were originally planted by man, although now various trees sow themselves. Marquand firmly wrote first in 1891, 'there are no woods or copses in the island.' Consequently aboriginal woodland plants are lacking, at any rate as woodland plants. The Hairy Woodrush has never been known, and the similar Narrow-leaved Woodrush is only a-top one artificial lane bank – where however it has persisted for well over a century. Three plants typical of woodland in Britain grow in Guernsey chiefly or only on cliffs. One of these is Great Wood-rush, which is very locally dominant on a few stretches of the south-west cliffs, and nowhere else. Another is Wood Spurge, which is also to be seen, but only very scarcely, inland: and the third is Butcher's Broom. The cliffs of St Martin's south of Fort George are remarkable for the plants which grow nowhere, or practically nowhere else, plants such as Bush Vetch, Black Mustard, Black Bryony and the Woodrush, or are commoner there, such as Prickly Shield-fern. Here too for a century was the only place where the large Wild Leek could be, or was, seen. In the last few years however it has been recorded increasingly in other parts of the island.

Hedges often harbour woodland plants, and in hedge banks grow Guernsey's three rarest ferns, two of them hybrids unknown outside the island, the third the annual Jersey Fern, a speciality of Guernsey and Jersey. The Sour Cherry was once much used for hedging, but is now rare, and it is in hedges that odd trees of Medlars may be found. Many hedges nowadays are made of alien plants, not hardy much farther north or inland, such as Euonymus, Escallonia, Myrsine and Olearia and, nearer the sea, Tree Purslane and Tamarisk, with Holm Oak and Monterey Cypress as trees equally resistant to salt spray and wind. That puzzling speciality of the Channel Islands, the Alderney Geranium, seems always to need the support and shelter of banks or hedges, which are also a frequent habitat for Balm-leaved Figwort, the commonest species of that genus in the islands.

I have mentioned the glory of the cliffs in spring, but this lingers on in transmuted form throughout the year, being perhaps brightest when the Bell Heather is out, for most of it is of a particularly rich purple. It is in the trade as 'Guernsey Plum', along with three or four other good variants from the Bailiwick. The only place in Guernsey where one can now see Lady's Fingers, usually a chalk-loving plant, is low on the south cliffs. Indeed there are several good plants low on these cliffs, well protected by their inaccessibility. One of these is Sea Spleenwort, another Sea Purslane. Normally this is a plant of the oozy edges of salt marsh creeks, but in Guernsey it grows up the cliffs, to 150 feet or more. Another special plant here is Dwarf Asparagus, which also grows on one part of L'Ancresse.

A diminutive pleasure early in the year is the Dwarf Pansy. Most books say this grows in sand dunes, and it has been seen in them in the north-west. But it is at its best on the barer places of the cliff tops in the south-west. Dwarf Chickweed, Dwarf Rush and Early Sand-grass are other small plants to be seen in both sorts of places. The rush was new to the British Isles when it was collected in Guernsey about 1780, and taken to be a sort of Sedge. Atlantic Clover received its Latin name of *Trifolium occidentale* only in 1961, after astute work by David Coombe. It proves to be all round the coast, but always apparently within a short distance of the cliff top or the seaward edge of the vegetation. Quite the earliest known specimens of this from anywere were collected in Guernsey in the 18th century.

Drier cliffs and banks facing south – which can get very hot – are the places where puzzling St John's-worts grow, which approach, but nowadays rarely fully match, Flax-leaved St John's-wort. Lesser Bird's-foot is in such places too and, more rarely, the Least one. Least Soft Brome and Glaucous Fescue are both on the south cliffs, the latter scarce and easily confounded by the less expert with the plentiful glaucous-leaved forms of Red Fescue.

Nearly all round the coast can be found abundantly the coarse Sea Radish. Golden Samphire, less weedy, is in several coastal areas too. Especially on the lower coasts, Kaffir Figs are freely planted. They may take a knock in severe winters, but portions at least survive, which is enough. In addition to this large coarse yellow or pink-flowered species, there is a daintier one always pink, and two or three smaller Mesembryanthemums, to which genus all the species were attached before it grew so unwieldy that it got divided.

Of all the erstwhile cultivated plants which may survive, or spread, after their cultivation has ceased, the daffodils are pre-eminent. Many survive and flourish after being thrown out to make room for newer varieties, or as unhealthy (which they rapidly cease to be), or have been left when fields were put down to grass. Those who name them will find countless old varieties still persisting showing uniquely just what these were like in days gone by, living history. A very different crop plant which can propagate itself by seed annually is – the tomato. It does this locally where water seeps. or flows. on to a sandy shore; but it appears most often on waste ground and rubbish tips. A very different plant again which can, and does, sow itself and settle down, is the striking Gunnera, often mis-called Giant Rhubarb. Striking in another way is the 8–10 feet Giant Echium, which sows itself easily in gardens and its seedlings may manage outside too, even on wall tops. Some old-fashioned garden roses manage outside by a different method, by suckering, and have thrived in natural associations thus for many decades.

At what stage a garden plant becomes wild is always a matter of opinion and *quot homines tot sententiae*. But any plant which can sow itself on a wall and flourish must be impressive – those who have tried to sow plants there themselves will know. Ivy-leaved Toadflax has spread all over the British Isles by this ability, for it is practically never in any natural habitat. Curiously, Yellow Corydalis, which has done this plentifully over most of England, has always been rare in Guernsey. St Peter Port Daisy, Red Valerian and Throatwort have already been mentioned. Buddleias are appearing on walls too, aided by their winged seeds which get blown into the chinks. Cotoneasters and other berried shrubs may be here, their seeds softened in the gut of the birds that eat them and then deposited with their own manure. Most Ferns can be found on walls, including Guernsey's non-native ones. Maidenhair Fern might well be expected to grow in crannies near the sea, but apparently does not and is known only in masonry inland. Flattened Meadow-grass is only on a wall.

The foot of walls is often a good place for southern warmth-loving plants – where too the water runs down from the face, and roots can be cool. There may also be calcium from the mortar. This is the typical place for Honey Bells and later the attractive annual Fingered Grass. Water Bent seems most at home here, although it is now to be seen in various other places, and so does Fern Grass, which has its largest and most open panicles of flowers by walls. Such a site will suit the often tropical Amaranths, so lacking in the beauty one might expect from their classical name, but curiously few have been seen in Guernsey. The Perennial Amaranth however has resisted attrition by the Vale Power Station. Here too may be seen the rare Greek Sand Spurrey, which needs a practised eye to be sure of, but is in fact in several warm gravelly places.

Two particularly remarkable plants have been found naturalised in waste places. One is the Tall Nightshade, which was in Sark, but is otherwise known only from Guernsey. Here it has managed to persist near the large quarry at St Sampsons, despite such handicaps as mounds of road metal dumped on top of it. How it got here, and hardly anywhere else in the British Isles, is anybody's guess. The other is the fine Greater Herb Robert which makes a 3 feet wide and tall plant of great delicacy. When a sprig of this was brought me in 1968, I jokingly suggested it was a large, polyploid Herb Robert – and so it proved to be! But it was more than that, it was different enough to be just being described as a species new to science, and up to then known only from Madeira itself. I might here refer to Onion Grass, which seems to be nowhere else in the northern hemisphere, and yet is thoroughly at home in a hot bare area in Guernsey.

An untidy sprawling plant of waste places that is always attracting notice is Cocks-Eggs, another one cannot imagine anyone wishing to introduce. Much prettier is Rosy Garlic, which beautifies the dunes near Rousse, opposite one of the places for Cocks-Eggs, and has appeared elsewhere. It was on waste ground too that Purple Broomrape, so long lost, was refound. Cornish Mallow is usually in waste places where it can grow very tall, and has much increased in recent years. So has Hoary Mustard.

All this only touches on some of the special plants Guernsey has or had, and leaves out many which might have been mentioned, and has not started on garden plants. But it should show that wherever one goes, at whatever time of the year and to whatever habitat, there is something to see.

The Discoverers of Guernsey Plants

ALTHOUGH Guernsey was never glaciated, its climate and countryside will have been tundra-like during the Ice Ages. But no fossils of any sort have ever been found in the island, and until the 1960's there was very little knowledge of what its plants were before the Middle Ages, and very little more of what they were before the end of the 18th century.

In a general way, we know that at one time there were woods, possibly dense, for buried stumps have for long been revealed close together by storms and low tides, especially on the west coast. It is said the woods lasted longest on the higher ground in the south, evidenced in part by the names of the parishes of the Forest and St Peter in the Wood. These woods probably survived well into the megalithic period, when the numerous passage graves and standing stones were erected, relatively few of which survive. This may have begun about 3000 BC and lasted for a millenium or more.

The woods will have followed the tundra, as the climate ameliorated. They were in their turn overwhelmed as the northern ice melted and the sea rose and largely fresh-water lagoons were formed behind the shingle banks pushed up by the sea at the mouth of the valleys. Eventually peat developed in them and under the advancing shingle. Now peat has remarkable powers of preservation, and not the least remarkable thing it preserves is pollen. The outer coat of the microscopic pollen grains of all the main groups of plants, sometimes down to the individual species, has a different pattern of sculpturing, which, incredibly, can last intact indefinitely. Peat is still revealed at times on the west coast, and may still be used for fuel. It is known locally as gorban. In addition to preserving the pollen grains, it may also preserve larger so-called macroscopic remains (but small enough in all conscience), usually bits of fruits or leaves, which can be named by the expert. These are more reliable indicators of what grew locally because pollen can get blown considerable distances, although it may be taken that the great bulk of the pollen in the Guernsey peat will have originated in the island.

It was Peter Girard who took the initiative in the early 1960's to send peat samples for analysis with the kind co-operation of Sir Harry Godwin; and as a result we have a list of 80 or more different groups of plants which were growing in Guernsey approximately 3,500 years ago, or perhaps rather less: 30 feet down the peat is some 7,000 years old – it is in more than one layer (compare *Transactions* for 1949), and in any event there is much more work to do in interpreting the findings. But it is a fascinating start, naming indeed some 40 actual species. The relevant facts are given under the appropriate plants in the main text, but for those who want them, the details so far are in the Société's *Transactions* for 1964 and 1966; see also 1972, p. 179.

Between those days and the late Middle Ages, is another sea of ignorance; and our knowledge of what the Guernsey scenery looked like even 300–400 years ago is scanty. We can learn or conjecture a certain amount by inference from documents and geology. Wet ground was still widespread – the Grande Mare was a mile in circumference and reached to the coast at Vazon, the slimy area, with no road between, until it was trenched and drained in the late 18th century; and numerous other mares and marais on the map were also more extensive, and held more water. One which has wholly disappeared is the Taye Marquand, a favourite hunting ground for Joshua Gosselin, which seems to have been where the Bouet, the muddy area, now is. There was more waste, rough ground, and salt marshes along the Braye du Valle, until this was eliminated by Sir J. Doyle early in the last century, when the northern part of the island ceased to be itself an island. There were probably no woods of any size for many years until the present century, and even now Guernsey has few wooded areas. Changes of course continue, nature acting on its own, or reacting to Man – for example the dunes at Rocquaine Bay seem to have turned to shingle when the sea wall was built in the last century, thus eliminating from there such plants as the Great Sea Stock.

The earliest record in print of any Guernsey plant – there has been no exhaustive search – seems to be in Henry Lyte's *Niewe Herball* which appeared in 1578, only 30 years after the first herbal printed in England. On pages 152–3 are references to 'Garnesee, or Garnesie, Violets' – his spelling, like Shakespeare's, wavered. It seems that he meant by this a stock, but possibly the one, or the origin of the one, we still delight to grow in our gardens. He added the name in translating his *Herbal* from the Flemish and French originals – whence? It appears also in the 1619 edition on pages 108–9 as Stocke-Gillofers or Garnsie Violets.

Nineteen years later appeared John Gerard's famous *Herball* – his spelling wavered too for he is 'Gerarde' on the title page. On page 373 he uses Garnsey Violets, which is repeated in the 'Emaculate' editions by Thomas Johnson of 1633 and 1636. On page 343 Gerard reports that *Holosteum salmanticum* the 'Flowring Sea Plantaine' and *H. parvum* the 'Small Sea Plantaine' 'have been founde . . . in the Iles of Garnsey and Iarsey.' These were probably forms of Ribwort Plantain. Two pages later he has *Coronopus* 'Sea Buckehorne' and *C. sive Serpentina* 'Small Sea Buckehorne', which he had 'heard say . . . grew upon the rocks in . . . Garnsey' – these were no doubt Buckshorn Plantains. These remarks are reprinted in Johnson's editions on pages 424 and 426, with a slight variation in spelling – e.g. Gernsey.

To carry these records further, there appeared 74 years later, in 1710, Dr William Salmon's *English Herbal* or *Botanologia*. On pages 878-9 the same wood blocks are used, the plants now being called 'Greater and Lesser Spanish Sea Plantains, still *Holosteum salamanticum* but now *H. minus*' (they suffered from name changes even in those days), and said to grow 'in the Isles of Jersy and Gernsey.' The third plant is now *H. angustifolium majus*, The Greater Grass-leav'd Sea Plantain and *H. angustifolium minus*, the Lesser. The locality is more definite 'upon the rocks in . . . Garnsey.'

One wonders who sent this long-repeated record in to Gerard. A guessed answer is Thomas Andros (later, as Seigneur of the fief of Saumarez, Thomas de Saumarez). He wrote, in French, a manuscript with a number of medical remedies, cosmetic suggestions and gardening hints, mentioning a number of plants, which presumably grew in the island at that time. It is dated 1589, but some of the gardening part may date from nearly a century later, added by a later hand, possibly his son Charles. It was published in 1972 in the *Channel Islands Annual Anthology*, ably translated and edited by Miss D. Cook. Its records are incorporated in the main text here. But he does not mention any plantain. Lord Zouche, the ardent horticulturist, spent nine months as Deputy Governor in Guernsey in 1600, but there is no record of any plant he grew or saw.

Between 1680 and 1699 appeared *History of Plants* by the difficult Scot Dr Robert Morison, who was never in the island. In it was told for the first time the story of the bulbs of the Guernsey Lily being cast from a wrecked ship *inter Sparta marina*, which was Parkinson's name for Marram. But this record can be rejected as little more than suitable embroidery for this largely fanciful tale about the Lily itself. The huge scale of its culture in Guernsey, and Guernsey alone – 20,000 to 30,000 roots in just one garden – only 60 years after its first mention, in 1664, as the Garnzy Lily, suggested remarkable success in propagating it. So Thomas Knowlton, a celebrated gardener, was sent specially to the island in May and June 1726 to find out why it did not succeed in England. He had also a knowledge of wild plants and in his spare moments did some botanising, recording the results in his diary, now among the Hunterian manuscripts at Glasgow. Here we find about a dozen first records, two of them, of Ivy Broomrape and Sand Crocus, the first for Britain.

The collection of Sir Hans Sloane formed the basis of the British Museum after he died in 1753. In his herbarium there is a small twig sent by C. Parey from Guernsey in 1734 as 'the leaves of the Tree of the Balsam of Peru growing in that island.' His high-sounding specimen is not of the medicinal plant of that name, but of a Balsam Poplar from North America, of which this is a very early record; and this the oldest known specimen of any Guernsey plant. Knowlton had in fact seen this in 1726 and named it correctly.

T. Yalden was a student of Physic at Edinburgh, 'a most sagacious and unwearied naturalist' as Rev. J. Lightfoot wrote in his *Flora Scotica* which first came out in 1778, with which Yalden helped. Little else is known about him, except that he is once described as 'of Winchester' and that he 'died at Venice and is buried in the sands there.' His plants were bequeathed to Lightfoot, in whose herbarium at Kew they now are. Lightfoot's annotated copy of Ray's *Synopsis* now at Oxford records plants Yalden found in Guernsey dated 1774. They were Tree Mallow, Sea Stork's-bill, Galingale and Lesser Quaking Grass, but a specimen of only the last has survived. This is probably the oldest definitely wild example of a Guernsey plant and the oldest for this species in the British Isles.

James Dickson, an able nurseryman, distributed between 1785 and 1802 *Fascicles of British Plants*. In those for 1794 and 1802 are Hare's-tail Grass and Greater Sand Crocus, both from Guernsey. The latter is of special interest, for reasons discussed in the main text.

Capt. John Finlay is noted in the same books as Yalden as recording some of the special plants of Guernsey in 1787, but all will have been seen at least five, and possibly eight, years earlier. He was a bright young Scottish army officer whose regiment was stationed in the Channel Islands from 1778 to 1782. He was later on the staff of the Duke of Richmond, Master-General of the Ordnance and died, an FRS, in 1802 aged only 42. He it was in fact who first found Dwarf Rush, which he described minutely in Latin as *Schoenus minimus*, together with Sand Crocus and Early Sand Grass, in a letter to Sir J. Banks in February 1787. The name and record got into print eleven years later, with no mention of Finlay's name at all. This was thought by Marquand to be the earliest mention of any Guernsey plant in print, and he guessed wrong who might have made it. Finlay wrote a Catalogue of Guernsey plants, of which, alas, no more is known. There is a long account of his life in the *Review of the Guernsey Society* for Winter 1972.

The illustrious contemporary, already mentioned more than once, of at least Finlay, Dickson and Banks (all of whom seem to have known, or known of, each other) was Guernsey's own Joshua Gosselin. Marquand's knowledge of him was meagre, but he was certainly right in saying that he was an acute and painstaking observer. His earliest list is of garden flowers and shrubs in bloom at various times in 1767, which is supplemented by further lists of them with notes, especially on propagation. He was 28 at the time, and working quite on his own with, at first anyway, only a very ancient book to help him name his plants, Parkinson's *Theatre* of 1640. Later he acquired Hudson's *Flora Anglica*, which would not always have been of use in naming Channel Island plants, then almost totally unknown.

In 1789 he met in London that Mycaenas of the sciences, Sir Joseph Banks. On 29 November 1790 he was writing to him 'As I am but a sorry botanist, with more relish than science, but not having the advantage of any body here to give me the least instruction or assistance, it compels me to confine myself to the making of a collection of the indigenous plants in this island. Now as I am collecting the best specimens I possibly can of every one of our plants, and sticking them on paper in the manner you was so kind to direct me, I would wish to have the right names of them, and the only means I can devise to come at it, is to take the liberty to send you a specimen of each in order to request that you will please Sir to have the goodness to get the Latin and English names wrote on the sides of them.' By 1792 he had nearly completed his 'Herbal', waiting only for the return of the parcel he was then (16 January) sending, to finish it. It may be safely said that all Gosselin's trouble was richly justified. We now have specimens for nearly all his records, i.e. well over 400, which show that a few are wrong. But most, thanks no doubt in measure to Banks, or his librarian Dryander, are right. His plants are preserved in three ways. Some are loose in, usually named, folders, perhaps awaiting mounting, some, relatively small, – those he sent to Banks? – are in two bound scrapbooks; and the rest are stuck on sheets. These are nearly all magnificent specimens beautifully mounted, in superb condition and a delight to the eye, quite apart from their great historical and botanical value. In addition, his copper-plate handwriting is a joy to read. I know no finer collection of any age, and we are indeed fortunate it has survived not a few vicissitudes. It has been gone through, with rewarding results, unknown to Marquand who, surprisingly, never looked at it himself, relying on a report for his *Flora*, and, wrongly, stigmatising it as very incomplete. As a result, in order to give credit where credit is due, Gosselin's name constantly occurs in the pages which follow.

Marquand dated Gosselin's specimens as 1788. We know that some at least were not collected until three years later, but there is no knowing just when any were, for the one thing lacking from his sheets is a date. The '1788' comes from the heading to the printed version of his *Flora Sarniensis*, or *Genera of Guernsey Plants*, arranged alphabetically . . . by the late Joshua Gosselin, Esq., . . . 1788. This appeared as the Appendix to Berry's *History of Guernsey* in 1815. But two drafts for this survive, which add appreciably to its value, notably by giving localities for the plants, which were omitted from the printed version. The date on both these drafts is 'begun', or 'began' as he spelled it, 'in 1788'. There is no indication when he finished it, but there are reasons for believing that it was before 1793. Gosselin's life has been written up at some length for eventual publication. But here it may be added that even if plants were an absorbing interest, at any rate for most of his life, he also did pioneering work in other sciences. Another of his manuscript notebooks, *Conchologia Sarniensis*, dated 1810, gives a full, annotated list of the shells, marine and non-marine, of the island, and in it he says he had been collecting them ever since his younger days. Then in a letter dated 9 November 1811 to Sir J. Banks, which was published in 1814, he gives the first account of the remarkable megaliths of the island, illustrated by six of his sketches and plans. He was a very competent artist and well over 100 other water-colours of his survive, most of them in the possession of his descendant Geoffrey Gosselin. It seems he also collected coins and medals, and was interested in geology.

But these activities were all hobbies. Gosselin held the important post of Greffier from 1767 for a quarter of a century, resigning perhaps because of his other duties as Colonel of the Militia of the North, just as revolutionary France was becoming threatening. Such a post was extremely responsible, and when he retired aged 62, he was publicly thanked by the British Commander-in-Chief. His tenure of office as Greffier was made much more difficult by the then Bailiff, but Gosselin had his attitude upheld by the Privy Council in London. He was a member of one of the island's leading families, and at the same time in touch with personalities in England, notably, from our point of view, Banks, Dickson and Sir J. E. Smith, Founder of the Linnean Society. His unostentatious work gave Guernsey a firm documented basis for recording its wild flowers such as no other area I know of has been fortunate enough to have.

There was little recorded in the half century between Gosselin's *Flora Sarniensis* and Babington's *Primitiae Florae Sarnicae*, which added about 138 species to Gosselin's list, although the gap in the printed record was much shorter. There was so much to discover in Guernsey, that useful additions were quite easily made. About nine visitors are now known in this period, the most notable being Sir W. C. Trevelyan, J. Woods, the author of the *Tourists Flora*, and J. Gay, first of the too few French visitors, who was in the island for only 48 hours. Woods was there for only one day! But all these made first records unknown to Marquand.

In addition, Dr J. MacCulloch, FRS, a prolific author born in Guernsey, uncle of the Bailiff-folklorist, who qualified and worked largely in Scotland, mostly on geology, produced about 1812 a *List of the Flowers of Jersey and Guernsey*. It was published in 1815 as an Appendix to a *General View of the Agriculture of the Islands* by Thomas Quayle, drawn up for the English Board of Agriculture. It noted some 600 flowering plants and ferns plus another 100 or so lichens and seaweeds 'such plants as I was able to discover during the residence of a few months' as he wrote. The *List* has features in common with Gosselin's (who seems to have known him), but many of the new records are almost certainly erroneous. Furthermore since there are no means of checking their accuracy or even of knowing on which island any plant occurred, it seemed best, with regret, to ignore this list in the text here. I do this despite Quayle's comment 'In saying that the Insular Flora comes from the pen of Dr MacCulloch, enough is said to impress the reader with a perfect reliance on its accuracy.' He also wrote a paper in the Quarterly Journal of Science in 1826 *On the Naturalisation of Plants with Remarks on the Horticulture of Guernsey*, but its relevance is small, and another in 1829.

Babington, Professor C. C. Babington as he was for 34 years, had two companions on his visits in 1837/8 and local helpers as well. The two chief of these were H. O. Carré, later a Lieut-Bailiff and F. C. Lukis, who had learnt archaeology from Gosselin. He in turn shared his enthusiasm with the young Babington, so much so that Babington on several days of his all too short time in Guernsey investigated 'Druidical remains'. Carré was later an enthusiastic member of the short-lived but vigorous Guernsey branch of the Acclimatisation Society, an organisation which seems to have left no mark on the flora of the island, nor indeed on its fauna. Babington himself became perhaps the dominating figure of British Botany in Victorian times, but he was under 30 when he visited the Channel Islands. The miracle is how much he managed to see and record and describe and collect (for his *Herbarium Sarniense* now at Cambridge) in the seven main islands of the Archipelago, down to Crevichon, in a total of only 18 weeks. He was in Guernsey altogether for only seven weeks in the two years; neither visit was earlier than 22 June and the intervening winter was very severe, killing many plants. He sadly misjudged Gosselin's List as 'very imperfect' and does not refer to it thereafter, so the bulk of the entries are Babington's alone, aided by Carré and others. But one wonders how much of their knowledge would have come to light if Babington had not opened the door.

There are a few unproven entries or probable errors in his *Flora*, but this is, alas, far from unique: only those who have tried know how subtly errors creep in. It has been suggested some of his slips were due to confusion of local names, for he wrote and produced it remarkably quickly. He left the Islands on 8 August 1838, and was immediately actively botanising as far north as Northumberland, and writing his *Manual of Botany* at the same time. Yet his *Primitiae Florae Sarnicae* was published on 12 June of the following year, a noteworthy achievement. This able and energetic young man produced a neat, clear and permanently useful 'outline' as a result of his two visits. During both he stayed with a Mr Poulsford at 18 Havilland Street in, no doubt, the present house there.

Babington's *Flora* opened the eyes of botanists to the riches and possibilities of the Channel Islands, and many of the ablest visited Guernsey as a result, all finding new plants. First of these was Babington's friend, Rev. W. W. Newbould, then only 22, who returned twice. Rev. T. Salwey, primarily a lichenologist, who also came twice and, shortly before his death, W. A. Bromfield, author of the *Flora Vectensis* (Isle of Wight for those who have not the Latin), were among those who came in the next ten years. 1850 saw two special visitors, F. Townsend, author of the *Flora of Hampshire* and commemorated in the hybrid Cord-grass, and H. C. Watson, author and pioneer plant geographer, commemorated in the Journal of the Botanical Society, who came four times in fifteen years. Marquand overlooked the considerable contributions of all these people, with the solitary exception of Salwey's connection with Stinking Onions, and even that he did not trace back to its source. Dr J. B. Syme arrived in 1852 and returned the next year. He it was who wrote the text for the third edition of *English Botany*. At about the same time came Prof. H. Henslow of Cambridge, father-in-law of Sir J. D. Hooker, and in 1859 for only four, stormy but productive, days, A. G. More, co-author of the *Cybele Hibernica*, the original work on the distribution of Irish plants.

A longer-staying visitor was Captain, later Major, H. Smith of the Royal Marines, indeed Ansted says he was a former resident. He was in HMS *Bellerophon* in 1815 and there witnessed the surrender of Bonaparte, and was twice in HMS *Victory*, as well as seeing service in South Africa and the West Indies. He finished as a recruiting officer after some bouts of ill health, which caused his retirement in 1848. It is then he seems to have been in Guernsey, contributing to Ansted's *Channel Islands*, which first came out in 1862, by which time he had apparently left. Marquand saw a copy of Babington's *Flora* annotated by him, which seems now lost; but did not know of another document, also now lost and even more grievously. In 1928 Iolo Williams, who had visited Guernsey that year, bought and presented to the British Museum an undated alphabetical list of 687 British plants in the island of Guernsey, with fairly detailed localities, made by Major

Smith. It is listed in the Museum catalogue, but has proved untraceable. However a very short extract from it in presumably his handwriting was found in a copy of Marquand's *Flora* bought in Edinburgh in 1937 by Miss Isobel Hutchinson, from which it has been possible to quote. But it is a minuscule substitute for the real thing.

Guernseymen, and women too, were adding to our knowledge of the island plants at this time. Miss Mary Le Lievre, sister of Peter, the artist, contributed to Ansted's account, and specialised in seaweeds. Ansted does not refer to Miss Mary Elizabeth Guille, daughter of the Rector of St Andrew's. She was collecting from 1844 to 1856 (plus one record in 1883) very usefully, making several first records, and obviously in touch with local discoveries. Yet she and her work managed to remain unknown until after she died in 1903, and this although she had been a member of the Guernsey Society of Natural Science (as it then was) from the date of its first membership list in the 1880's. During this time Marquand was very actively collecting material for his *Flora* and was for two years President of this Society. But so it was, and one wonders what he might not have learnt from her personally if only he had had the clue. Her herbarium has not been seen for many years.

Capt. Joshua Carteret Gosselin, RN, a grandson of the previous Joshua, serendipitiously found the Guernsey Centaury in 1850 – it was just one in a bag of plants he sent Townsend to name, new to the British flora, and still unknown outside Guernsey. Miss Guille collected it the same year. George Wolsey, also of St Andrew's, was at one time thought to have been the first finder of this plant, which he collected for other people from 1858. He was 'an exceedingly intelligent nurseryman' and the expert to whom visiting botanists turned. Guernsey owes much to him, particularly for his first finding, new to the British flora, the retiring Sand Quillwort, and first recognising Small Rest Harrow; and he seems to have been an agreeable personality too.

The mid-1850s saw the Victorian Fern craze well started and Guernsey had its addicts, active around 1860, notably C. Jackson, who also lived near Barnstaple, and John James of Vauvert Road. And that is about all we know about these two, apart from the references in contemporary books of ferns telling which varieties they found and grew. Jackson achieved fame by his discovery of the hybrid between Hart's-tongue Fern and Black Spleenwort, then new to science and later called *Jacksonii* after him. But the year before, 1855, Miss Isabella Wilkinson had found another hybrid new to science, although it too was not formally recognised as such until 1940. This was between Hart's-tongue and Lanceolate Spleenwort, which she must have shown to Jackson the same year and to Miss Guille the next. It is said she was maid to Dr and Mrs S. E. Hoskins – he was a notable GP, FRS and Secretary of the Acclimatisation Society, who gave his herbarium of local plants to the Guernsey Society, since when it too has vanished. Miss Wilkinson collected other plants as well and has her niche in Guernsey history alongside her employer. In 1850 Dr Thomas Bellamy published a treatise in Latin *Noctes Sarniae*, which includes a few quoted details.

In 1862 appeared the first edition of Prof. D. T. Ansted of Cambridge's excellent book on the *Channel Islands*, which he wrote after four years' residence in the island. Carré contributed to it, thus happily linking the *Flora Sarnica* with the next full list of Guernsey plants. This was in the chapter on plants, which is identical in the second edition of 1865, but was shortened for the third of 1893, which adds nothing. Thirteen of the records Marquand rejected, but most justify a place in the island list. Narrow-leaved Wood-rush, for example, he stigmatised as 'certainly an error' and yet the record had been in print elsewhere for over half a century, backed by specimens, and the plant still grows in the same place. It is much the same with Perennial Beard-grass and others. Each of these is discussed in the main text. Marquand seemed unaware of the calibre, or even of the existence, of some of the visitors, or even residents, who made records and kept vouchers; and perhaps underrated the acumen of people such as Smith and Wolsey, both of whom seem to have been reliable, and had a hand in the compilation of Ansted's lists. True, he repeated records of Babington's which have never been proved, but there was no certainty relatively shortly after his *Flora* that so august an authority had nodded. All in all, this is a generally reliable record of knowledge a quarter of a century after Babington's visits.

In the next quarter of a century even more botanists came, aided no doubt by improved communications. Dr H. Trimen, co-author of the *Flora of Middlesex* when he was only 26, came twice; so did Sir W. Thistleton-Dyer, the other co-author also aged 26, and later Director of Kew; and C. Bailey, the voracious collector, thrice. G. Bentham, of 'Bentham and Hooker' and much else, holidayed in July and August 1864 but his diary mentions no plant at all. Other active collectors included Rev. H. E. Fox, W. H. Beeby, J. C. Melville twice – it is remarkable how many made return visits, T. B. Blow over in his thirties in 1876, who died 65 years later, F. A. Hanbury of Cambridge, who visited thrice in the 1860s, F. J. Hanbury, co-author of the *Flora of Kent*, Prof. W. Hillhouse and W. W. Reeves each twice and Rev. A. Ley, author of the *Flora of Herefordshire*. In 1877 Dr G. C. Druce, then a younger visitor than Babington, made the first of four visits, meeting Marquand on the last three, all resulting in copious records. He was the author of several county *Floras*.

In the autumn of 1888 E. D. Marquand arrived. He had been born in Guernsey, but returned there only when he was 40, after living in New York, London, the New Forest, Penzance, Devon and on the Continent; and seven years later, when he married, he was away again, to Richmond in Surrey, and then in 1899 to Alderney. He was in Guernsey again from 1903 to 1910 and lived in five other places before he died during the First World War. His only child, a botanist at Kew, died in a boating accident in the second war. Marquand himself was at Kew from 1896–99 'on special cryptogamic work' as he put it, but apparently never looked at any of the numerous Guernsey specimens of flowering plants there, and even now this vast collection has only been chancily searched. The defect of the invaluable *Flora* he published in 1901 is that he seems to have seen no dried plants outside Guernsey, not even Babington's at Cambridge, and to have overlooked much of the written evidence there was – he cites only 40 visitors during a time when there were at least 120. This has meant that very many of his first records have been antedated – which is usually the reason for mentioning what I normally consider a relatively useless item of information, some rejected records reinstated and a considerable number added which he had overlooked. The odd identification of his has proved to have been incorrect. But, having said that, there can be nothing but praise for his readably written and scholarly achievement. His *Flora* covers the whole Bailiwick and the whole range of plant life, down to the diatoms, in a way no other *Flora* has done; and some of the groups have not been tackled at all since. Nor was the breadth of his ability confined to plants. He was secretary for some years of the ornithological section of the Société, and an expert on geology, mammals, shells, insects, spiders and Guernsey-French as well, a President of the Société and one of its first Honorary Members. Druce wrote of him that he was a delightful companion. His bright cheery face, his trick of humming tunes as he walked, his eyes ever on the alert, his happy home life, all marked him out from the crowd. A delightful reminiscence of him was given in a letter in 1969 from T. A. Jackson to Miss R. de Sausmarez. 'I have a clear and very happy picture in my mind of Mr Marquand. I think he was not very tall, but fairly broad with a very quiet manner, and a very kind face. He was always willing to talk to a small boy and answer questions about everything, from the plants growing between the stones of the high wall of the Manse garden (on Alderney) and the sea birds of Burhou and the Ortac, to the Hanging Rock . . . a man who seemed to understand and talk naturally to a small boy, never in a hurry, or too busy, or too important as many grown-ups were, a very kindly and indeed a lovable man.' His widow and her stamp collection are still remembered at Kew, where she went to live with her son.

But I have anticipated. In 1888 there had been a lull, empty gap rather, in Guernsey botany for nearly 20 years, and even the recently founded Society was at a low ebb. True, Edgar Dupuy, a dispensing chemist in St Peter Port (Stonelake's now, who acquired his business) had made a useful collection of plants in 1864/5, which still survives. (At the turn of the century he owned Gosselin's herbarium which his daughter gave to Miss Evelyn Marquand who presented it to the Société.) But, curiously, he contributed nothing except in those years. In 1860 however had come to Guernsey from Bristol G. T. Derrick to be Headmaster of the British Boys' School, the building for which is still to be seen in New Place. He liked pottering for flowers and continued to find them until shortly before his death, but had then no one to guide him or accompany him. In 1877 he lit on the Jersey Fern in the only, small, area it has ever been known from in the island; and in 1882 he produced an excellent account of the Ferns of Guernsey, and in 1888 a List of its flowers for the Society, which included some finds of his own. He was also interested in birds, history, archaeology and so on, a good Victorian naturalist, and a worthy President of the Society.

From 1888 however, Marquand took over and fostered local keenness. Shortly before his return, Miss Margaret Dawber started collecting and soon became the great source of Guernsey specimens for English collectors, accompanying in the field at least some of the visitors. She was a member of the Watson Botanical Exchange Club, to which she contributed no less than 512 sheets in 1886 and 587 in 1887. About 1897 she became Mrs Lewis and disappeared from the scene. Nevertheless in these ten or twelve years she had made a valuable contribution. I wish I knew more about her, and others of Marquand's collaborators.

C. R. P. Andrews was a brief but glorious visitor from 1898 to 1900. His connection with Guernsey was through Miss B. A. Agnew, who lived there, and in these same years also made valuable records, whom he married in 1900. His great discovery was of the small grass Dwarf Millet in 1899. The difficulties this subsequently caused are related in the notes on that plant, which were finally cleared up only six months before he died. Yet, like Miss Guille, no one was aware that he was then still alive, and in Kent, whence he had returned after spending most of his life in Australia, ending as Pro-Chancellor of the University of Western Australia. He did good work also in recognising the Guernsey Canary-grass and in various other ways.

Other useful visitors in the decade before Marquand's *Flora* were I. H. Burkhill, who happened to collect what later proved to be the first specimens of Early Meadow-grass when he was 21, 75 years before he died, Rev. J. D. Gray, who came over four times in the 1890's, W. F. Millar, J. G. Groves, the younger of the two brothers who named Townsend's Cord-grass, Dr D. T. Playfair, J. W. White, author of the *Bristol Flora* and Rev. W. Moyle Rogers, the chief authority at the time on the brambles. He is still the only such specialist who has worked on them in the island, for Babington had not begun to study them in the 1830s.

Marquand wrote his *Flora* in Alderney, with the attendant disadvantages of not being on the spot. It was said by his contemporaries to be so exhaustive as to leave little room for further discoveries, and even fifteen years later scarcely to need review – but already in 1890 the Society had looked on Marquand's interim list of 1891 as exhaustive, and the herbarium for practical purposes as complete – which it still is not. Nevertheless the euphoria had the effect of inhibiting local work, and no new Guernsey botanist appeared on the scene until after the first war, except for R. Metman, who was briefly Secretary of the Botanical Section before he joined up, and no more is heard of him. Visitors did come over, but their visits were unknown to local botanists, as has been so often true, and still is. Some were well-known people, such as J. A. Wheldon, C. E. Salmon, author of the *Flora of Surrey*, Dr C. T. Vachell and his daughter, Miss E. Vachell, Lady Davy, who returned twice after the war, E. W. Hunnybun, W. C. Barton, T. J. Foggitt who was back in 1926 with Miss Gertrude Bacon, whom he married three years later, and H. W. Pugsley, the specialist on Fumitories, Hawkweeds, Eyebrights and much else. All left their mark.

The rousing from local slumber was initially due to Mrs Julia Hichens at the end of the war, although she soon handed over the Secretaryship of the Botanical Section, which she had resuscitated, to Mrs McCrea – Patty. Mrs McCrea immediately set about preparing a Supplement to the *Flora*, painstakingly listing all the plants that had come to the notice of the Société, which was by no means all that had been found during that time. She had little help with this and only occasional contact with visitors, but we would be the poorer without her devoted service for over 20 years. I have happy memories of meeting her twice just after the war and H. A. Harvey, who had worked at Kew.

Among other visitors she did meet were Ted Lousley, author of the *Flora of the Isles of Scilly*, who has been to Guernsey at least six times, Iolo Williams, A. J. Wilmott, Deputy Keeper of Botany at the British Museum and Dr Dick Burges. Others she may not have met, or did not, were Douglas Simpson, author of the *Bibliographical Index*, Francis Druce, Col. R. Meinertzhagen, Prof. Irene Manton, the pioneer fern cytologist, H. S. Redgrove, T. A. Stephenson, the orchidologist, and a party from France in 1933 led by Auguste Chevalier. But this was in general a quiet period in the story.

Restrictions made work difficult during the second war, when of course there were no visiting botanists, well, English botanists. For unknown to those in Guernsey, one of the German officers of the garrison, E. Ewald, was an arboriculturist and a competent botanist. He wrote the section on flowers in the book the Germans produced on Alderney, and sent seeds of Evening Primroses of great interest to Berlin from Guernsey. All my efforts to trace him have failed: even the one-time German Commander, Baron von Aufsess, could not help.

After the war all was different. Mrs McCrea's day passed and she was succeeded as Secretary of the Botanical Section by Peter Girard, Headmaster of the Câtel school, who later became President of the Société. The volumes of its *Transactions* show the variety of his interests, but no one in the history of Guernsey botany has found so many remarkable plants, and this in a now apparently well-worked island. His first was the hybrid fern Miss Wilkinson discovered 110 years before and had long been lost. Not only did he refind it, and from horse-back, but he later found over a dozen further plants in different places. Despite close search only four other people have managed to find a plant. Shortly after, in the course of a year or so, he brought to light Tongue Fern, the remarkable Onion

Grass, not apparently otherwise known in the northern hemisphere, Greater Herb Robert, not otherwise known outside Madeira and at that moment not yet even given a Latin name, and he found new to the island both the Spring and Autumn Cyclamens and Lesser Periwinkle.

Shortly after, Nigel Jee came to Guernsey to join the staff of Elizabeth College, of which he became senior Biology Master and is, as I write, President of the Société and Chairman of the National Trust. He too is a polymath, able not only with plants, but with other branches of natural history and archaeology, is the authority on the history of Guernsey cattle, runs his own dairy farm and has numerous sidelines as well. He is the author of the admirable *Natural History of Guernsey*, first edition 1967, second 1972. Evidence of his influence on Guernsey botany is the contributions his pupils have made, from Dr R. Arnold to Miss B. Elliott. But there are other useful people on the island, some of whom are mentioned at the end of the Introduction, and others I refer to in the text.

Visitors continued to come after the war. Prof. Tom Tutin, the key author of the *Flora of the British Isles* and of *Flora Europaea*, was over in 1949 with John Raven, author of two good botanical books, and made two important discoveries. Dr Charles Hubbard, the great authority on the grasses, made invaluable collections of them in 1953. Bob Ross, now Keeper of Botany at the British Museum, spent a profitable family holiday on L'Ancresse in 1954. Dr Humphrey Bowen, author of the *Flora of Berkshire* and several other books, has been over three times and done a mass of useful work; Dr Cyril West, the expert on Hawkweeds, has been twice; Dr David Coombe, detector of the Atlantic Clover, four times, and Dr Cecil Prime, author of the fascinating monograph *Lords and Ladies*, has searched on several occasions for them with his constant companion Oliver Buckle. Other specialists have included Dr R. H. Richens, who has expertly supported the views on Elms of Nigel Jee, Dr Donald Young, the unraveller of *Oxalis* and Dr John Richards, the author of the *Taraxacum Flora*. Richard Fitter has been twice, author of numerous books on Natural History, and so has Ken Beckett, a very able all-round plantsman and Dr Roger Butcher, author of the *New Illustrated British Flora*. Dr A. Melderis, then Deputy Keeper of Botany at the British Museum, in 1968 and Edgar Milne-Redhead, then Deputy Keeper of the Herbarium at Kew, in 1970 made welcome collections, when Dr Bruce Campbell, another author of excellent books, was over briefly but usefully.

Three field meetings of the Botanical Society and the Wild Flower Society were held in 1969–71 in conjunction with the Société. These attracted over a hundred people, many of them able, and resulted in a surge of knowledge. Among this group it is almost more invidious to know whom to mention. But Lady Anne Brewis was tireless on all three, and later, visits, and much is owed too to her uncle Hon. Lewis Palmer, who came to live in Guernsey in 1969. Lever Howitt and his wife Brenda, co-authors of the *Flora of Nottinghamshire* and knowledgeable on willows, Alan Newton, author of the *Flora of Cheshire* and our main adviser on the brambles of Guernsey and Dr John Dony, author of the *Flora of Bedfordshire* and *Flora of Hertfordshire*, and his wife Chris came, and among the useful and promising young were Alan Leslie and Alan Silverside. The British Pteridological Society held a field meeting in 1971 on which Dr Anne Sleep made her most skilful discovery of a fern hybrid new to science, which she called formally after Guernsey *Asplenium* × *sarniense*. Clive Jermy, who is in charge of the cryptogams at the British Museum, was over shortly after and has a special interest in certain of the island's ferns. Most visitors come just to see the island's standard rarities in the same standard places. So these visitors, searching all over the island, reaped long-hidden rewards.

The tally of the island's plants stood at about 684 when Babington wrote in 1839. In the 62 years up to Marquand's *Flora* 273 were added, to make 957. In the 73 years since, some 383 more have been found, 156 in the past seven years, making about 1,340 in all. (The extra in this book comprise all the hybrids and clones, which were hardly considered in the earlier *Flora.*) It is not to be doubted the number will increase, for several reasons. One is that the old records are clung on to in case the plants reappear, as Beard-grass did recently: it is rarely safe to call a plant extinct. To these get added the new plants which arrive from commerce, horticulture, agriculture and so on. Regrettable though apparent, or real, losses are, these are everywhere outweighed in numbers by new arrivals. Another reason is that nobody will ever find all the plants in an area, even as small as Guernsey, so no list can ever be complete. And finally there is the tendency now sometimes being reversed, to 'split' species, deciding that two forms hitherto grouped under the same name are sufficiently distinct to be treated as two species. Thus Guernsey now has two Parsley-pierts, whereas only one was recognised until recent years. The increase of over 40% in the total since Marquand's days is no reflection on Marquand's achievement. I do not think he missed much that was actually to be seen in the island at that time. I hope the same may be true of this account, thanks to all the numerous helpers it has had over the ages.

A Note on Conservation

THIS book shows what a wealth of plants Guernsey has, or has had. This heritage needs care, great care in the face of the pressures of the expanding world. Once their habitats are altered or gone – and some plants are very particular – they are lost for ever; and Guernsey is the poorer. It has already lost four very special natives from the wet areas of the west, two of them orchids, two other orchids from elsewhere during this century, and other plants in the previous one. Some of those that remain have the most tenuous hold. Their only hope is public awareness, buttressed by full consultation with those who are knowledgeable in the island's Natural History, the Société and the Trust, before any change is agreed, or even such matters undertaken as planting, mowing or hedge cutting, where timing can make all the difference. Nor are only the plants at risk: it is the associations in which they grow, including the insects and other animals which depend on them, for plants are at the base of every food chain. No plants, no animals. Hence the enduring need for sensitive and sensible conservation, taking the long and thorough view before risking irrevocable loss. It is very important that everyone in Guernsey should realise this is their responsibility, and be very wary, and proud of their riches.

The Flowers

FERNS AND FERN ALLIES

Pteridophyta

CLUBMOSSES AND QUILLWORTS Lycopsida

Clubmoss Family Lycopodiaceae

Stag's-horn Clubmoss *Lycopodium clavatum* L.
This is in one of Gosselin's early lists, from the Grande Mare, where it could never have grown. There is no other record. J –. A –. S –. H –.

Mossy Clubmoss Family Selaginellaceae

Mossy Clubmoss *Selaginella Kraussiana* (Kuntze) A. Braun
Found under some trees at Le Vallon by J. Gallienne in 1947, where it could not be seen in 1971; and by Rhododendrons at Sausmarez Manor in 1967, where too it seems no longer to be. But a good patch was found in damp grass in the Fermain Valley in 1971, and it has been reported as a garden weed elsewhere. This is a plant of South Africa and the Azores, which sometimes forms carpets under the staging of greenhouses, and can persist and spread outside. J rare. A –. S –. H –.

Quillwort Family Isoetaceae

Sand Quillwort *Isoetes histrix* Bory
A speciality of Guernsey added to the British flora in 1860 by G. Wolsey, and illustrated from L'Ancresse on Plate 1828 of the Third Edition of *English*

Sand Quillwort $\times\frac{2}{3}$

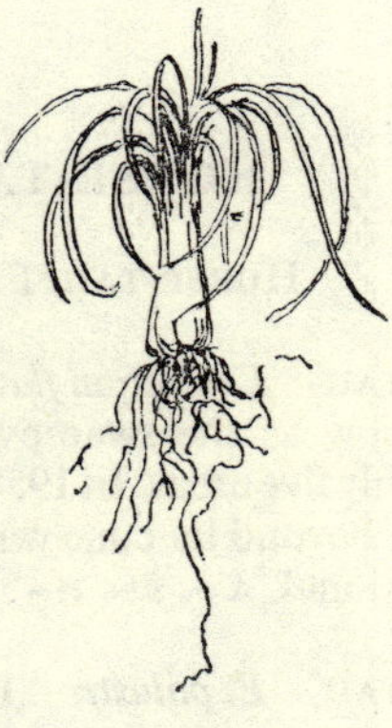

Botany. (In the text to this, Guernsey is, not for the only time, confused with Jersey.) The discovery was announced in a letter dated 19 December read to the Linnean Society the next day, and in the *Phytologist*. There may well be more of this plant in Guernsey than in both its other known localities in the British Isles, Alderney and cliffs on the Lizard peninsula in Cornwall. It was found at a time when the existence of a terrestrial Quillwort was hardly suspected – it is one of the two species adapted to life on land in a genus the rest of whose members usually grow under water. How it gets fertilised, and its spores widely distributed when they are underground in fixed turf is a mystery, but worms have been proposed for a related South African species. Do springtails, or springtail- or worm-seeking birds, come into it? Or is it capable of self-fertilisation, or of producing fertile spores without fertilisation? It is to be found in turf wet or flooded in winter and still damp in summer. Its leaves usually wither by late June (the month when it was first found), but they have been seen still green in a wet August. Knowledgeable eyes are needed to spot it, so it is likely to be less local than its records suggest. Its stronghold is apparently L'Ancresse, where it can still be turned up in at least five places from Fort Doyle to the La Varde area. It was collected at Cobo in 1910–13; towards La Rochelle in 1928; and in 1957 detected on Hommet Paradis and Hommet Benest, and on Lihou, where at least two patches are known. Albecq was added in 1969. But it has not been re-seen, indeed hardly looked for, at the Guet or near Petit Port, nor in its most inland station, a marshy field between Vale School and L'Ancresse, whence it was collected in 1906. There are useful references to this plant by Marquand in the *Transactions* in 1889, by Dr D. H. Scott (to whom Derrick sent specimens from L'Ancresse in 1899) and T. G. Hill in the Annals of Botany in 1900, pp. 413–54, and by Prof. I. Manton in her book *Problems ... in the Pteridophyta* 1950, pp. 155–9. It is depicted on one of the 1975 postage stamps. Recently C. Jermy examined the spores of some specimens from Guernsey to see if some might not be of *I. Durieui* Bory. This more southerly species has a reticulate pattern on its male megaspores, *I. histrix* having its rather more prominent tubercules separate. He found some plants from L'Ancresse (and all those from Alderney) to be good *histrix*, but others from L'Ancresse and those from Cobo seemed to be conspecific with *I. Chaeturetii* Mendes from west Portugal, which has an intermediate pattern on its spores. But *I. Delalandei* Lloyd also needs taking into account. Further investigations are in hand. So the wheel turns, for in 1885 it was reported that 'there seems great doubt as to whether the Guernsey plant is *I. histrix*'. J error. A rare. S –. H –.

HORSE-TAILS **Sphenopsida**

HORSE-TAIL FAMILY Equisetaceae

WATER HORSE-TAIL *Equisetum fluviatile* L. (*E. limosum*)
Very restricted now as the swampy places it likes become ever scarcer, and recently seen in only five areas. In 1958 a very unusual form with the stem growing through and well beyond its cone was collected in the Grande Mare. Its cause is unknown. J occasional. A –. S –. H –.

MARSH HORSE-TAIL *E. palustre* L.
Local now, for the same reason as the last species, but this can stand competition

better, so is less scarce. The spores of this or some other species of Horse-tail have been found in the peat deposits at Vazon. The f. *polystachion* Weigel, with cones on the side branches as well, may still be seen in the Grande Mare. J occasional. A local. S last record 1896. H claimed 1837 and 1962.

WOOD HORSE-TAIL *E. sylvaticum* L.
Listed by Gosselin, but the specimens, loose, in his scrapbook by this entry are of Common Horse-tail, which he also collected and named correctly. J –. A –. S error. H –.

COMMON HORSE-TAIL *E. arvense* L. Coue d'Rat
Never the pest it can be, but noted from nearly every square, except on the south cliffs. J common. A occasional. S local. H rare.

GREAT HORSE-TAIL *E. telmateia* Ehrhart (*E.* '*maximum*')
Said, by Major Smith, about 1850, to grow near St Peter Port, but definitely found only in 1957, in a garden at St Jacques, where it is well entrenched: the plant has on occasion been offered to gardeners. In 1969 it was discovered in some quantity on the site of dismantled greenhouses at Richmond, growing with the last species. J –. A rare. S –. H –.

FERNS Pteropsida

ROYAL FERN FAMILY Osmundaceae

ROYAL FERN *Osmunda regalis* L.
An ancient inhabitant of Guernsey, its spores recognised in the peat at Vazon and Catioroc, and indeed the much more widespread fens and marshes would have suited it. But drainage followed by human rapacity during the Fern craze of the mid and late nineteenth century ensuring that any root dug up could be sold (and it was) drastically changed this. Derrick, a particular fern enthusiast, in 1888 knew of only six places where it occurred wild. He was given three roots by Mr Smith of the Caledonia nursery, which he planted out in two places. Yet by 1900 it was doubtful if a single wild plant could be found, even in St Saviour's valley, where ten years earlier there had still been four or five. But it was in St Saviour's in 1968 that the plant was next seen, by P. Burgess, in the artificial habitat of the embankment of the relatively new reservoir, where it is under water when the level is high. The two plants are still there, but the puzzle of their origin and status is unsolved. J local. A planted. S very rare. H planted.

FILMY FERN FAMILY Hymenophyllaceae

TUNBRIDGE FILMY FERN *Hymenophyllum tunbrigense* (L.) Smith
Two roots of this were planted out by Derrick in the early 1880's, but it is hardly surprising that no more was heard of them. Hooker's *Student's Flora*, from 1870 right down to 1934, recorded it from the Channel Islands, perhaps a reference to the Jersey specimen. J 1865. A –. S –. H –.

BRACKEN FAMILY Dennstaedtiaceae

BRACKEN *Pteridium aquilinum* (L.) Kuhn (*Pteris aquilina*) Fouaille
This grows all over the island, wherever it gets the chance, a feugré being brackeny land. Its spores are found in the Vazon peat, but no subsequent clear reference to

it has been traced until Gosselin's time. He wrote, cryptically, on 8 April 1791 to Sir J. Banks 'Pteris, I have no other specimen of but that which I sent, but shall endeavour to find it out, tho' very scarce. You'll see another Pteris . . . which is the only one I also ever found but if scarce with you, I shall look for it.' The specimen in his scrapbook named *Pteris* is clearly this species, so is the next named *Pteris aquilina*. Derrick called it the Fish Fern and said it was extensively used as bedding for cattle, as indeed it still was until recent times. It is now however known to contain a chemical which can cause a variety of cancers in animals, and a toxin can be passed on in cows' milk. Bracken was one of the plants used in Guernsey's Green Beds, called Lits de Fouaille. For an account of these and the history of the Guernsey-French names, see the article by J. H. Lenfesty and P. J. Girard in the *Channel Islands Anthology* 1972/3. Two or three crested and other forms have been recorded from Guernsey. J common. A common. S common. H common.

JERSEY FERN FAMILY Gymnogrammaceae

JERSEY FERN *Anogramma leptophylla* (L.) Link (*Gymnogramma leptophylla*) A charming speciality of the Channel Islands and our only annual fern. It was discovered on 200 yards of a hedgebank in St Saviour's in 1877 by Derrick, just a quarter of a century after it was first found in Jersey, whence unproven rumour said the plants came. His discovery was put in print and, he wrote, 'Forthwith I was waited upon by half a dozen individuals all anxious to commence the work

Jersey Fern $\times\frac{2}{3}$

of extermination: a carriage was at my service.' But the locality was kept secret, so much so that many books on ferns, even two recent and authoritative ones, credit this species to Jersey alone. Derrick could never find it anywhere else and made attempts, in vain, to spread it. Eventually Warry proved to be the only person who knew its whereabouts. Just in time, on Easter Day 1957 (the year before he died), he took a party to the spot, where he had not been since before the war. The lane banks proved to have been rebuilt and lacked even a hedge, and the fern was not there. But he was so sure of the precise spot that he would allow nobody to search farther afield. Nevertheless one member, Mrs Russell, did and, 300–400 yards to the north, in the next parish of Câtel, found it. It is still there, usually in some plenty in a position vulnerable to traffic and chemicals, but watched. In the Channel Islands at any rate it seems always to grow in the company of the Liverwort *Lunularia cruciata* (L.) Dumortier. It is on a 3p stamp of Jersey of 1972. J local. A—. S—. H—.

MAIDENHAIR FERN FAMILY Adiantaceae

MAIDENHAIR FERN *Adiantum Capillus-veneris* L.
Formerly a notable absentee from Guernsey, and still unknown in a natural habitat. It was reported by Ansted in 1862, but first definitely recorded only in 1957 by and above General Grant's and Thomas Hart Davies' tombs in Candie cemetery, where it was well established. Here it just survives the onslaughts of weedkiller, despite promises to spare it. In 1969 it proved also to have grown for many years high on a garden wall at Clifton, St Peter Port, where it had doubtless originated from spores from cultivated plants. Moore's form 'Incisum' was recorded in 1880 as 'found in Guernsey by J. James'. But was the plant wild? J rare. A errors? S –. H 1923.

HARD FERN FAMILY Blechnaceae

HARD FERN *Blechnum spicant* (L.) Roth ssp *spicant* (*B. boreale*)
Gosselin collected this along the douit of the Vauquiédor. Derrick called it common and often very luxuriant (and collected it with forked fronds), but 20 years later Marquand said it was not common and seldom in any quantity. Certainly it is now scarce and never in plenty and only in the southern half. J frequent. A last record 1937. S rare. H –.

(Sensitive Fern, *Onoclea sensibilis* L., is naturalised in Jersey.)

SPLEENWORT FAMILY Aspleniaceae

HART'S-TONGUE FERN *Phyllitis Scolopendrium* (L.) Newman
(*Asplenium Scolopendrium. Scolopendrium vulgare*) Langue d'boeuf
Very common especially on walls, where it perforce can be very small. But in moist shady valleys it can grow lushly and fronds reach 3 feet. In 1862 a visitor recorded that he could have collected hundreds of 2′ lengths. Derrick wrote that the fame of their beauty drew troops of excursionists every summer. Gosselin regarded it as a Plante Médécinale; one of his specimens shows a forked tip to the frond – so do Derrick's. In all no less than 49 named forms have been found in Guernsey, several being first recorded from there, and some never seen elsewhere, indicating the natural variation that was observed in Guernsey during the years of the Victorian Fern craze. The finders were Jackson, James and Allchin. In a book in 1972 it was said to be known as Christ's Hair from the single black vascular strand in the stalk. It received the AGM in 1973. J frequent. A frequent. S common. H local.

BLACK SPLEENWORT *Asplenium Adiantum-nigrum* L. Petit Capillaire
Very common, especially on walls and hedgebanks, its fronds at their best in late summer. One of Gosselin's specimens has forked fronds: five other forms have been recorded. J common. A common. S common. H occasional.

(The Mediterranean *A. Onopteris* L. was reported from Jersey in 1845.)

LANCEOLATE SPLEENWORT *A. Billotii* F. W. Schultz (*A. 'lanceolatum'*)
Locally common and often very fine, its fronds at their best in spring. One named form has been recorded. J frequent. A rare. S occasional. H occasional.

GUERNSEY SPLEENWORT *A.* × *sarniense* Sleep (*A. Adiantum-nigrum* × *A. Billotii*)
This hybrid, naturally or artificially created, was unknown to science until 1971, when Dr Anne Sleep first postulated it and the next day, 22 April, discovered it near the Reservoir. Since then rather over a score of other plants have been found, two in the Câtel, all the others in the three south-west parishes, where there are more suitable habitats. One plant grew low on an old ivy-covered wall, but all the rest were on well-clothed hedgebanks, usually intermingled with the

Guernsey Spleenwort ×⅓

parents. Because this hybrid is sterile, each example of it is a separate creation, and no two will be identical. Some are neatly intermediate, but many resemble Black Spleenwort so closely that only microscopic proof that the spores are infertile will clinch their identity. Details of this most interesting plant, known nowhere else in the world – search has failed in Jersey – are in the British Pteridological Society's *Newsletter* No. 9 and their *British Fern Gazette* in 1971, in *Watsonia* for July 1972 and in the Société's *Transactions* for 1972. A frond is depicted on one of the 1975 postage stamps. J –. A –. S –. H –.

(There is a specimen of Rock Spleenwort, *A. fontanum* (L.) Bernhardi, from Jersey in 1837, status unstated.)

SEA SPLEENWORT *A. marinum* L.
Gosselin collected this from caves near the sea at Petit Bot (which was, erroneously, said in 1862 to be its only locality) where it still is, and in St Martin's and it is still on most parts of the coast, but not in quantity, and fronds are no longer seen 3′ in length. Its most surprising station is on the east wall of the Câtel church in the centre of the island. Five forms have been noted, one of which was catalogued in 1888 for sale at 21/–. J locally frequent. A locally frequent. S common. H frequent.

MAIDENHAIR SPLEENWORT *A. Trichomanes* L. ssp *quadrivalens* D. E. Meyer
Rather scarce, always on walls – perhaps there is most in the northern parts of St Peter Port and none on the south coast. Where it does grow, it tends to be the only fern locally. Gosselin's specimen retains the jeweller's label round it with 'grows on the Câtel Church', as it still does today, nearly two centuries later. J frequent. A occasional. S rare. H rare.

WALL-RUE *A. Ruta-muraria* L.
Rather scarce, also always on walls and also tending not to grow with other species – Gosselin collected it from church walls. Marquand called it rather frequent in 1890, but ten years later, rather rare. J common. A rare. S rare. H rare.

FORKED SPLEENWORT *A. septentrionale* (L.) Hoffmann
Planted in 1941 on a wall in the Couture Lane, but not heard of since. J –. A –. S –. H –.

JACKSON'S FERN × *Asplenophyllitis Jacksonii* Alston (*Asplenium Adiantum-nigrum* × *Phyllitis Scolopendrium*)
This is an extremely rare, sterile, hybrid between Black Spleenwort and Hart's-tongue. Its first record anywhere in the world was in Guernsey, by Jackson, an ardent pteridologist, in June 1856. It was then called a variety of Sea Spleenwort, but this was soon altered to a variety, *scolopendrioides* or *microdon*, of Black Spleenwort. Specimens also exist dated 1857–8–9 and 60, almost certainly from

Jackson's Fern ×½

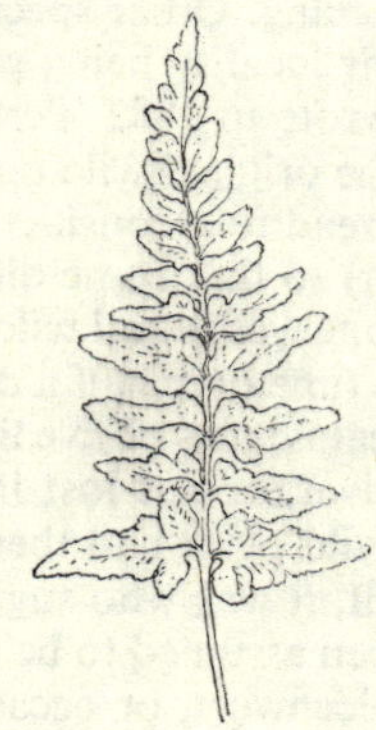

cultivation, for it is probable that it was dug up – there is no mention of more than one wild plant. It was propagated and listed by at least four fern nurseries between 1865 and 1928, but has not been seen in the wild since Jackson's days – he reported it also from Devonshire. Stansfield still had it in 1936. Its parentage was suggested in 1920 by him, its name given it in 1940 and its parentage proved experimentally in 1969 (cf *British Fern Gazette*, pp. 63–7). It differs from the next hybrid in its markedly triangular shape and in the more centrally placed sori. J 1863. A –. S –. H –.

THE GUERNSEY FERN × *A. microdon* (T. Moore) Alston (*Asplenium Billotii* × *Phyllitis Scolopendrium*)
This equally interesting inter-generic triploid fern has never been proved to grow anywhere other than in Guernsey, except for one miserable specimen from a ruinous building near Penzance in 1856. Miss I. Wilkinson was the first person to find it, on a bank of rough masonry without mortar in St Peters in 1855, and Jackson collected it the same year. Mrs Hoskins, wife of Dr Hoskins, who seems to have been Miss Wilkinson's employer, is also, once, credited with being the original finder. There is another specimen dated 1856 from Miss Guille, but very likely Miss Wilkinson showed it to all these people. It was said to have been collected later from other places by Miss Mansell of Le Chêne and by Jackson,

The Guernsey Fern ×⅓

but details are lacking. Other specimens are dated, 1856, 1857, 1860, 1863 and 1874 without their locality being given. Very likely these came from cultivated plants. Derrick wrote in 1882 'Perhaps the only ones now to be had are those cultivated from the original wild ones', though this 'had obtained so firm a footing as to have spread to a considerable extent (as I learn from one of the ladies who discovered it) so that some diligent searcher may yet be able to bring wild specimens,' and one was found wild on a wall in St Peter's two years later. In the fern books of the time over half a dozen people are mentioned as growing it and it is listed in the catalogues of five firms from as early as 1859 down to 1902. The last plant in cultivation was lost in the winter of 1916/17, when no other plant was known; no wild plant had then been heard of for 32 years. Stansfield, who had this last plant, it was who suggested, in 1920, the hybrid origin for it too – hitherto it had been assumed to be a variety, first *apiculatum*, but soon *microdon*, of Lanceolate Spleenwort, or occasionally of Sea Spleenwort. Its present name was given it in 1940, when the hybrid genus was published in the *Proceedings of the Linnean Society*. In 1969 Drs Lovis and Vida proved this plant to be this sterile hybrid – see their paper in the *British Fern Gazette*.

But this is anticipating. 81 years after the last plant was found in the wild, P. Girard saw an unusual fern on a shady bank at Les Effards in the Câtel – there is a photo opposite page 167 of the 1967 *Transactions*, which, with the *British Fern Gazette* for 1968, contains full details. His find was confirmed as this long-lost and long-sought hybrid. In the subsequent seven years, some 18 more have been discovered in ten squares, all in the south-west, always with Lanceolate Spleenwort and Hart's-tongue close by. The great majority were spotted by Girard. All were on inland banks, except for one on a shady wall and one on the bank of a cliff path above Portelet Bay, west of Petit Bot. As with Guernsey Spleenwort, no two plants are quite the same, but all are clearly intermediate between the parents. It tends to be hidden by vegetation after April. It appears on a postage stamp of 1975. Its recent history is to be found in the *Proceedings of the Linnean Society* for 1940, pp. 132–44; in the Société's *Transactions* for 1967, pp. 167–72; in the *Proceedings of the BSBI* for 1968, pp. 387–9; and in the *British Fern Gazette* for 1968/9, pp. 1–8 and 53–67. J –. A –. S –. H –.

RUSTY-BACK *Ceterach officinarum* DC (*Asplenium Ceterach*)

Very scarce and apparently always has been. Gosselin collected it from old walls and, interestingly, clefts of moist rocks. Derrick planted out a great many roots, but apparently without success. For many years after the last war it was either not known at all or known only from one wall. But since 1968 it has been seen in at least five other localities in the north, and in 1973 in St Peters. J occasional. A occasional. S –. H 1957.

LADY FERN FAMILY Athyriaceae

LADY FERN *Athyrium Filix-femina* (L.) Roth Fouâle d'Orvé
Common and often very fine, but little noted recently in the north. Gosselin collected it, once as *Polypodium cristatum*, from the lane of Havelet and beyond the rivulet of the Vauquiédor. Derrick wrote that it was the most abundant of the large ferns, which it probably still is, bracken of course excepted. Eight forms are on record, found by Jackson, James and Derrick, one of his with a forked frond survives. J frequent. A occasional. S frequent. H rare.

BLADDER FERN *Cystopteris fragilis* (L). Bernhardi
This is another fern planted out by Derrick in the 1880's, but he never saw a plant in the third season, although it grew like a weed in his greenhouse. J four records. A –. S –. H –.

MALE FERN FAMILY Aspidiaceae

MALE FERN *Dryopteris Filix-mas* (L.) Schott (*Lastrea Filix-mas*)
Quite frequent, even on walls. About half a dozen forms have been recorded, two very recently. J common. A frequent. S frequent. H occasional.

GOLDEN-SCALED MALE FERN *D. pseudomas* (Wollaston) Holub & Pouzar (*D. Borreri*)
Much less frequent, but not always typical, and some forms approaching the last species are being studied. Its fronds often persist green throughout the winter. Two hortal forms are recorded. It received the AGM in 1973. J occasional. A rare. S ? frequent. H occasional.

COMMON BUCKLER FERN *D. austriaca* (Jacquin) Woynar (*L. dilatata*)
Quite widespread, but chiefly in the centre and south, the fronds sometimes being magnificent; and it may also grow epiphytically. A small taxon with triangular fronds and concolorous scales is not rare and is being studied. Two garden forms are noted. Gosselin's plants antedate Derrick's by a century. J frequent. A frequent. S occasional. H rare.

HAY-SCENTED BUCKLER FERN *D. aemula* (Aiton) Kuntze (*L. aemula*)
Said by various mid-Victorian authors to have been found in Guernsey by James, who ought to have known. But there is no specimen and no other record: Derrick and numerous successors have searched in vain. It could have been mistaken for the triangular form of the last species. Yet it is an unexpected absentee. J error. A –. S –. H –.

SOFT SHIELD FERN *Polystichum setiferum* (Forskål) Woynar (*P. angulare*)
Local and usually only a few clumps together, least scarce in the south-east and

not in the north. Nevertheless Jackson and James recorded six varieties. Derrick described it in 1882 as being 'barbarously exterminated' – he was not its first discoverer, but Newbould, in 1841/2. J frequent. A rare. S rare. H local.

HARD SHIELD FERN *P. aculeatum* (L.) Roth (*P. lobatum*)
Thrice recorded, once by Carré, once by Jackson, who ought to have known, once backed by a specimen which was at Oxford, said to be confirmed by Stansfield. J error. A –. S –. H –.

HOUSE HOLLY FERN *Cyrtomium falcatum* (L.f.) C Presl
A plant from the Far East, which seeds itself on or by walls. It was first seen by Mr and Mrs Howitt by the Royal Hotel in 1969 (who were the first people to spot it in the British Isles, in Scilly), then in the next two years in Candie gardens, at

House Holly Fern ×½

Tongue Fern (p. 47) ×⅓

Les Fontenelles, St Briocq, Perelle and at the foot of a heather plant in Mount Durand. In at least two places the seedlings have seeded themselves. J –. A –. S –. H –.

MARSH FERN FAMILY Thelypteridaceae

LEMON-SCENTED FERN *Oreopteris limbosperma* (Allioni) Holub
(*Lastrea montana*)
Derrick in 1882 wrote of 'the golden tinted Mountain Fern high up the (Petit Bot) valley', doubtless a slip of the pen for one of the Male Ferns. J 1896 and 1924. A –. S –. H –.

OAK FERN *Gymnocarpium Dryopteris* (L.) Newman
The pollen of this was detected in the peat beds at Vazon. J –. A –. S –. H –.

POLYPODY FAMILY Polypodiaceae

POLYPODY *Polypodium vulgare* L. ssp *prionodes* (Ascherson) Rothmaler
(*P. interjectum*) Grand Capillaire Gugeu du Djable
Common on walls, banks, and tree boles in many sizes and several shapes,

known from its spores in the peat at Vazon, and collected by Gosselin. Three named forms only are on record, but others occur – Derrick collected it with a forked frond. Despite much special search and many collected specimens, nothing has been found to match ssp *vulgare*, ssp *serrulatum* Arcangeli (*P. australe*) or the hybrid *vulgare* × *prionodes*. J common. A frequent. S frequent. H occasional.

TONGUE FERN *Microsorium diversifolium* (Willdenow) Copeland
An Australian epiphyte first found well established on a wall at the Caledonia Nursery in 1969 by P. Girard. It is not in the Nursery, but is to be seen forming ground cover in and near a few gardens elsewhere. J –. A –. S –. H –.

MARSILEA FAMILY Marsileaceae

(Pillwort, *Pilularia globulifera* L., has been long extinct in its only locality in Jersey.)

WATER-FERN FAMILY Azollaceae

WATER-FERN *Azolla filiculoides* Lamarck
A native of America, which comes and goes. It was first noted in the Channel Islands in 1952 by Miss W. Frost in a pool in the hotel grounds above Petit Bot, where it was doubtless introduced, then the next year in a stream at Kings Mills, in 1957 in a garden pond near the Vale Road and in the lake at Saumarez Park. It is now to be seen in none of these places. However in 1968 it was noticed again at Kings Mills, carpeting thickly two of the tanks of the pumping station, which it continues to do in fluctuating quantity. It may also appear more or less briefly in the odd ornamental pond, or stretch of water. J last seen 1967. A 1972. S 1965. H –.

ADDER'S-TONGUE FAMILY Ophioglossaceae

MOONWORT *Botrychium Lunaria* (L.) Swartz
Known for certain in the Channel Islands only from Wolsey in 1864, who collected it in 'Guernsey', called it rare and did not give its precise locality. J –. A –. S –. H –.

COMMON ADDER'S-TONGUE *Ophioglossum vulgatum* L. ssp *vulgatum*
Not recorded between 1938 and 1957, but said by Marquand to have been plentiful here and there in typical Adder's-tongue fashion. Derrick, who was shown a specimen before he found it himself, said it was to be seen abundantly all along the strip of damp meadows inside our north-western barrier, the pebble ridge which carries the coast road from the Vale Church to Pleinmont. But at present it has been re-seen only near Grandes Rocques and in 1974 at the Reservoir. Major Smith was the first person to record it, about 1850, but its spores are in the Vazon peat. J local. A rare. S Brecqou. H –.

SMALL ADDER'S-TONGUE *O. vulgatum* L. ssp *ambiguum* (Cosson & Germain) E. F. Warburg
First recorded in print in 1881, before the last species was, from L'Ancresse, where it was collected for over half a century. All attempts to refind it have failed. J –. A –. S 1961. H –.

Least Adder's-tongue *O lusitanicum* L.
One of the famous rarities of Guernsey, illustrated from there on Plate 1836 of the Third Edition of *English Botany*. It is the only place it has ever been known from in the British Isles, except, since 1950, St Agnes in Scilly. The first record is a specimen collected by Miss Guille in November 1853, but it was seen two months later, on 17 January in full fruit, by Wolsey, who wrote an account of it in the *Phytologist* for March 1854, saying it grew in some abundance, but making no mention of his neighbour, Miss Guille. In 1855, the very next year, it was

Least Adder's-tongue ×1

reported that the greediness of collectors had almost exhausted it in the original locality, but that it was fortunately to be met with in others not yet published. Wolsey, Jackson and others and, later, Derrick, found it abundantly and dug it up to grow, and die. In 1882 it was said there were two distinct districts for it with more than a mile of cliff between destitute of a root, although there were many favourable sites. There was not much fear of its being exterminated, for three of the patches where it occurred were about sixteen feet square, but it was still much sought after by collectors. Ten years later Marquand noted it as plentiful in 17 stations from Petit Port to Les Sommeilleuses, and shortly after as so widely distributed and abundant as to dispel all fear of possible extirpation. Yet within living memory it had been known only in three or four minute patches in one very small area east of Petit Bot. Old prints show how the cliffs in the last century, and early in this one, were much more open with cotils, the gorse constantly cut for fuel, and sheep and goats helped. Wolsey wrote that 'on this elevated down are a few scattered and stunted furze bushes and around these . . . the Adder's-tongue is not quite so minute as on the level turf.' But the furze bushes are nowadays far from scattered or stunted and many a prickly expedition had been made through them and their accompanying brambles to get to the few apparently suitable still open spots, but in vain. Marquand wrote in 1890 that there was nothing to indicate why it grows in one spot more than another. Rabbits find the fronds succulent winter feeding, and wire cages have been used to try to keep them off. Then in 1973 a patch about a yard square with at least 200 fronds was refound at Les Sommeilleuses with two smaller areas close by, and another at Icart Point, the result of much searching by Mrs Burridge, Miss de Sausmarez and Mrs Ryan. It seems to have been changed agricultural practices and not so much collectors which have drastically reduced the stocks of the fern. The plant usually surfaces after the autumn rains, often not before November, and normally shrivels by April. But it has twice been seen exceptionally at the end of August. Prof. Manton in her *Problems . . . in the Pteridophyta* of 1950 discusses this plant and, remarking that it has about 252 chromosomes (actually, 240) in each cell, comments 'quite enough for such a tiny plant'. It is shown on a 1975 postage stamp. J unsuccessful introductions. A error. S error? H –.

SEED-BEARING PLANTS

Spermatophyta

CONIFERS Gymnospermae

Pine Family Pinaceae

Scots Pine *Pinus sylvestris* L.
Occasionally to be seen, but no seedling seems to be on record. The pollen of some pine has been found in the peat from Rousse, Vazon and Catioroc, and this species seems the most likely source. J planted. A –. S –. H –.

Maritime Pine *P. Pinaster* Aiton
A rugged Mediterranean species, which can be quite at home and survive well near the coast. But there is no evidence of its perpetuating itself. J rarely planted. A –. S –. H –.

Corsican Pine *P. nigra* Arnold
Another planted Mediterranean pine, which grows well enough but of which no seedlings have been reported. It is the pine of the main, lower, part of the Pine Forest. J –. A –. S –. H –.

Black Pine *P. Thunbergii* Parlatore
This important Japanese timber tree has been planted at the Guet. It can be a good doer on exposed sites, but is not producing seedlings. J –. A –. S –. H –.

Monterey Pine *P. radiata* D. Don (*P. insignis*) Sapin
The supreme pine of present-day Guernsey, the pine of the upper part of the Pine Forest, doing very well all over the island, often in the face of the fullest exposure, where however its needles may brown. As a native tree it is to be found only in a very restricted area on the cliffs of southern California, an example of a plant infinitely more plentiful elsewhere than in its homeland. Its cones have the habit of staying on the branches, and even the main trunk, for many years getting ever more firmly annealed. The theory is that they open only in forest fires, when there will be bare ground for their seed to germinate. Less heat will in fact open them (commercial seed is obtained thus), and cones do eventually gape on the trunks and branches. But either the seed is then too old to germinate, or it does not, or its seedlings have never been noticed naturally. But, this apart, it could hardly come nearer to being a naturalised Guernsey plant. J frequently planted. A planted. S planted. H planted.

European Larch *Larix decidua* Miller
A deciduous conifer, which may well be seeding itself unobserved. It is the only conifer marked for Guernsey in the *Atlas*. J occasional. A –. S –. H –.

Cypress Family Cupressaceae

Monterey Cypress *Cupressus macrocarpa* Hartweg
Another not quite naturalised conifer on Guernsey, seedlings of which appear in gardens, but do not seem to survive outside. But the tree itself does superbly well. It too is native of the same area of California, in fact a strip two miles long and 200 yards wide only. J frequent and seeds. A –. S –. H –.

(Lawson's Cypress, *Chamaecyparis Lawsoniana* (A. Murray) Parlatore is used for hedging in Jersey and persists thereafter.)

Yew Family Taxaceae

Yew *Taxus baccata* L. If
No yew is recorded as sowing itself in Guernsey, but its pollen was in the peat at the Catioroc. J rarely seeds. A –. S –. H –.

FLOWERING PLANTS

Angiospermae

DICOTYLEDONS Dicotyledones

BUTTERCUP FAMILY Ranunculaceae

(Marsh Marigold, *Caltha palustris* L., was recorded in 1845 in Jersey and has also been planted out there and in Herm, and there is an unconfirmed record for Alderney. But it is unknown as a native in the Islands.)

(Monkshood, *Aconitum Napellus* L. was collected in Jersey in 1925 and 1968.)

LARKSPUR *Consolida orientalis* (Gay) Schrödinger (*Delphinium orientale*)
This is probably the species nearest to most garden Larkspurs, which appear outside as brief waifs. Gosselin grew them in the mid-18th century. In the absence of specimens it is not possible to determine precisely to which species all the old records belonged. The usual name used was *D. Ajacis* or *D. Consolida* (see below): some were just 'Larkspurs', doubtless escaped from gardens. Examples are records of 1844, 1889, 1891, 1893 (one of this date is of this species) and 1925. Two gatherings in 1958 and one in 1971 seem to belong here. J last record 1926. A –. S 1953. H –.

BRANCHING LARKSPUR *C. regalis* Gray ssp *regalis* (*D. Consolida*)
Claimed in 1864, but see the comments under the previous and the next species. J 1926. A –. S –. H –.

WILD LARKSPUR *C. ambigua* (L.) Ball & Heywood (*D.* '*Ajacis*')
The only definite records are from Miss Dawber from Bordeaux and Gray from Grande Rocque in 1894, Portinfer in 1958 and St John's in 1971. But Dupuy's specimen of 1864 may also be this. Precision is however not easy with these outcasts. J last collected 1926. A –. S –. H –.

WOOD ANEMONE *Anemone nemorosa* L. Animône
This has been naturalised under trees at Le Vallon, and 'Vestal', with double white flowers which received the AGM in 1973, grows similarly at Sausmarez Manor and Courtil Rozel. J rare. A –. S –. H –.

BLUE ANEMONE *A. apennina* L.
A survivor in a long neglected small garden at Petit Bot. The species was awarded the AGM in 1934. J –. A –. S –. H –.

JAPANESE ANEMONE *A.* × *elegans* Decaisne (*A. hupehensis Lemoine* × *A. vitifolia*) B. Hamilton
This garden plant is a good persister and has done just this on some waste ground off Hauteville in St Peter Port. J –. A –. S –. H –.

LENTEN ROSE *Helleborus × hybridus* Hort.
There are seedlings of this on a wall at Caledonia. J –. A –. S –. H –.

(Seedlings of *H. lividus* Aiton ssp *corsicus* (Willdenow) Tutin were seen flowering on a wall in Jersey in 1973.)

TRAVELLER'S JOY *Clematis Vitalba* L.
Not common, usually on walls whence no doubt it obtains the lime it likes. It is unmentioned by the earlier writers and with little doubt will always have been originally planted, as elsewhere in the Channel Islands. The Traveller's Joy was an inn at the top of the Ville au Roi, destroyed in the 1930s. J occasional. A rare. S –. H –.

WINTER CLEMATIS *C. cirrhosa* L.
In its form which is often given specific status as *C. balearica* Richard, several plants grow, self sown, in the walls of the Fosse André by the Caledonia Nursery, whence it doubtless originated. It grows also on a garden wall at the La Porte Hotel. It starts to flower in January, and was named by Lord Talbot de Malahide during the visit of the International Dendrology Society in 1969. J –. A –. S –. H –.

MEADOW BUTTERCUP *Ranunculus acris* L. ssp *acris*. Pid d' Llaön à rachaenes. Boutaön d'or. Piépot.
Common in meadows and damp grassland, first collected by Gosselin. In the past, forms of this species in Guernsey were given such names as *Boreanus*, *Stevenii* and *tomiophyllus*, but these were almost certainly misapplied. From the shape of its leaves it is called Crowfoot in English, but Lion's foot in Guernsey-French. J common. A frequent. S frequent. H rare.

CREEPING BUTTERCUP *R. repens* L. Pid d' Llaön lattaï
Common in rather wetter places and as a garden weed. Gosselin collected it first. A form with double flowers was collected at Côte des Vardes in 1973. J common. A frequent. S occasional. H frequent.

BULBOUS BUTTERCUP *R. bulbosus* L. ssp *bulbosus*. Pid d' Llaön a nouaïe
'Grows in dry ground,' wrote Gosselin (who considered it a poisonous plant) on his specimen, and so it does. It is possibly not so common as the last two, but it vanishes from sight much sooner, so has tended to be under-recorded. Marquand found an apetalous form in 1889, and Trimen in 1873 an oddity which proved to be fungus-infected, as oddities often are. There is comment on the 'bulb' of this species in the *Transactions* for 1964, p. 562 and in *Watsonia* for January 1973. J locally plentiful. A common. S frequent. H frequent.

(Jersey Buttercup, *R. paludosus* Poiret first recorded on 13 May 1872, is now known to be not as rare as was thought in Jersey. It likes places thoroughly wet in winter (hence its specific epithet) but dried out in summer, when it soon shrivels. It might be in others of the Channel Islands.)

CORN BUTTERCUP *R. arvensis* L.
First recorded by Gosselin from a cornfield opposite La Masse in the Câtel, but the impression left in his scrapbook by his lost specimen suggests a misidentification. Seed-testing however came in only in 1869, and the only three occurrences in Guernsey since then, 1898, 1923 and 1929, have all been in gardens,

where it was very likely to have been an impurity in chicken or other bird food. J rare. A –. S –. H –.

HAIRY BUTTERCUP *R. sardous* Crantz (*R. hirsutus*)
Either rarer than in 1859 or 1901 (when it was called common, and frequent), or overlooked – Gosselin put a specimen in his scrapbook unaware what it was. It is usually in grassland not far from the sea. J occasional. A –. S rare. H local.

SMALL-FLOWERED BUTTERCUP *R. parviflorus* L.
Very scarce. Recorded only four times since 1900, always in the north-west, either in sandy ground or as a weed of cultivation, but still persisting. J rare. A occasional. S rare. H locally plentiful.

WOOD GOLDILOCKS *R. auricomus* L.
This is in Gosselin's list from clover fields, an unlikely location, and his scrapbook proves his plant to have been Meadow Buttercup. J collected 1890 and 1925. A –. S –. H –.

GREATER SPEARWORT *R. Lingua* L.
The only records are by Babington in 1837/8 and Hillhouse in 1879, both later Professors. It could well have been an indigenous plant, but is now only to be seen planted by garden ponds. J last record 1924. A last noted 1906. S –. H –.

LESSER SPEARWORT *R. Flammula* L. ssp *Flammula* Far de Lance
A variable species, Guernsey forms having received such names as var *angustifolius*, *serratus* and *pseudoreptans*. Gosselin collecting it noted it as a poisonous plant and that it grew in all the marshy places. As they get scarcer, so does this plant. But it is still widespread. Half of a fruit very like this species was detected in the Vazon peat. J common. A occasional. S local. H local.

(Snake-tongue Crowfoot, *R. ophioglossifolius* Villars, was well-known in Jersey from Babington's day until St Peter's marsh was drained. The last specimens are dated 1884, and 1928.)

CELERY-LEAVED CROWFOOT *R. sceleratus* L. ssp *sceleratus*
Always very scarce and only in one place at all far from the sea. Another 'Plante Vénéneuse' to Gosselin. J rare. A –. S –. H –.

IVY-LEAVED CROWFOOT *R. hederaceus* L.
Collected first by Gosselin, from the same horse-pond as Ivy-leaved Duckweed. It is another plant of the wet edges of ponds, streams etc. that is now doubtless rarer than it was. There are only two or three recent records. J rare. A rare. S rare. H rare.

WESTERN IVY-LEAVED CROWFOOT *R. omiophyllus* Tenore
Recorded, as a variety of the last species, by Marquand from the Château des Marais, but there are no specimens in support, nor has it been seen since. J –. A –. S –. H –.

(*R. tripartitus* DC was collected in Jersey in 1925.)

HAIR-LEAVED WATER CROWFOOT *R. trichophyllus* Chaix ssp *trichophyllus* (incl. *R. Drouetii*)

Water Crowfoot fruits are abundant in the Vazon peat, not surprisingly, and nowadays this is probably Guernsey's least scarce species. It was known only in the north until Hon. L. Palmer found it in the reservoir in 1968. J rare. A rare. S unconfirmed. H rare.

COMMON WATER CROWFOOT *R. aquatilis* L. (incl. *R. heterophyllus* and *R. triphyllos*)

Only in the extreme north-west. In a letter dated 24 December 1873 to H. Groves, Babington said he had 'the true *triphyllos* from Guernsey (Braye du Valle),' and in his *Manual* for 1881 onwards gives it for Guernsey only. J errors. A –. S –. H –.

LARGE-FLOWERED WATER CROWFOOT *R. peltatus* Schrank (incl. *R. floribundus*)

Also in the north-west only until found in the reservoir in 1968. J gone. A –. S unconfirmed. H –.

SEASIDE WATER CROWFOOT *R. Baudotii* Godron

Prof. C. D. Cook, who has seen all the specimens of Guernsey Water Crowfoots, detected one of Gosselin's specimens as this species; but no other record was known until the 1890's, when it was collected near the Château des Marais. It has not been seen there since; instead it has been found on L'Ancresse, in 1958, and is the third species to appear in the Reservoir, in 1970. De Baudot, the plant's discoverer, in 1837 was a lawyer at Sarrebourg. J gone. A –. S one pond. H –.

HYBRID WATER CROWFOOT *R.* × *Segretii* A. Félix (*R. Baudotii* × *R. trichophyllus*)

Recorded in 1958 from the pond by the bus-stop on L'Ancresse. The specimen seems now lost, the pond is now filled in and anyway the plant is a sterile annual. J 1956–58. A –. S –. H –.

LESSER CELANDINE *R. Ficaria* L. ssp *Ficaria* Pissenllet

Abundant, and glorious, in March and April. It varies in the number of its 'petals' and how broad they are. Tall diploid forms, which Dr B. M. G. Jones agrees resemble f. *luxurians* of Moss in the *Cambridge British Flora* of 1920 (Plate 128), have been collected in Caledonia and St Saviour's. They are probably states due to shade, tall vegetation or good feeding; and not ssp *ficariiformis* Rouy & Foucauld as once thought. The earliest specimen of this species is in Gosselin's scrapbook. J abundant. A common. S common. H frequent.

PHEASANT'S EYE *Adonis annua* L. Goutte de Sang

Thrice recorded, in 1865, 1917 and 1923. The first and last at least are correct. J last collected 1929. A –. S –. H –.

MOUSETAIL *Myosurus minimus* L.

Listed by Gosselin, recorded in the 1830's, but not seen again until 1957, by Dr H. Bowen on the coast by Hougue Patris, where repeated search has failed to refind it. J last collected 1930. A –. S –. H –.

COLUMBINE *Aquilegia vulgaris* L. Herbe d'Llaön
Seven records in rather more than a century, all doubtless of plants originating in gardens, once with white flowers, and never persisting. Gosselin was growing it in 1767. J casual. A –. S 1953. H 1957.

(Love-in-a-mist, *Nigella damascena* L., was collected in Jersey in 1926.)

BARBERRY FAMILY Berberidaceae

DARWIN'S BARBERRY *Berberis Darwinii* Hooker
A showy garden shrub discovered in Chile by Charles Darwin on the voyage of the *Beagle* in 1835, which can persist and may appear bird-sown. It was reported thus in two places in 1969. J –. A –. S –. H –.

COMMON BARBERRY *B. vulgaris* L.
Listed as naturalised by Ansted in the mid-19th century. J collected 1926. A –. S –. H –.

OREGON GRAPE *Mahonia aquifolium* (Pursh) Nuttall
Recorded from the Calais area in 1971. It is planted for ornament and cover and may seed itself. It comes from western North America. J –. A –. S –. H –.

MAGNOLIA FAMILY Magnoliaceae

[Guernsey has for long had a special reputation for its Magnolias of many different species. The North American *M. grandiflora* L. is to be seen, nearly always as free-standing trees, in many gardens. The original plant of its clone 'Goliath' is magnificent in the Caledonia Nursery, where several other species have been for many years and are very fine. Perhaps best of all are the trees of the Himalayan *M. Campbellii* Hooker f. & Thomson with their great dark pink goblets of flowers on bare branches against the blue of a March sky. Those at Caledonia are probably the oldest in the British Isles.]

DRIMYS FAMILY Winteraceae

[Winter's Bark, *Drimys Winteri* J. R. & G. Forster also does exceptionally well in Guernsey gardens. Capt. W. Winter was in one of Drake's ships in 1578 when he brought this back from Tierra del Fuego for its bitter tonic bark.]

LAUREL FAMILY Lauraceae

BAY TREE *Laurus nobilis* L.
A seedling of this Mediterranean shrub, the true Laurel, was reported from the Fort George cliffs in 1969. J occasional. A –. S –. H –.

WATER LILY FAMILY Nymphaeaceae

WHITE WATER LILY *Nymphaea alba* L.
On the evidence of its pollen in the peat at the Catioroc and Vazon, a prehistoric

inhabitant of Guernsey. But there is no other record until the last fifteen years, and then from such places as the pond at Saumarez Park, where it will certainly have been planted, or from quarries whither it presumably arrived from a laudable desire to beautify the water there, in some of the places betraying its horticultural origin by its pink or yellow flowers. Nevertheless these colonies may be called naturalised, in so far as they survive the development of their sites. J planted. A –. S –. H –.

HORNWORT FAMILY Ceratophyllaceae

RIGID HORNWORT *Ceratophyllum demersum* L.
Marquand was unaware of the basis for the record for this species by Ansted. This was doubtless Watson in 1852, but Babington later altered the name in his copy of *Flora Sarnica* to the next species. And so it has been with any other claims for which evidence is available, except that from Miss Elliott in 1971 from a quarry pool north of Bordeaux which no longer exists. But the two unvouched records might have been right. J collected 1926. A –. S –. H –.

SPINELESS HORNWORT *C. submersum* L.
Specimens exist of this species from four localities in Guernsey – Watson's was from Vazon Bay. This was presumably native, but all the others are from artificial habitats, quarries or goldfish pools – it persisted in a quarry on L'Ancresse from at least 1925 to 1946. Both this and the last species are used as oxygenators by aquarists. J 1838/9. A –. S –. H –.

POPPY FAMILY Papaveraceae

CORN POPPY *Papaver Rhoeas* L. Coque. Pavot Sauvage.
A richly gay annual still to be seen quite frequently over most of the island, despite the rarity of corn. It is variable, and the source of the garden Shirley Poppies. In 1971 Shirley-type plants were seen in a potato field at St John's, some with no black blotch, some with pink petals. They were probably garden escapes, but might have been similar mutants to those from Shirley in Surrey in 1880. Two purely botanical varieties have been reported on other occasions. J frequent. A frequent. S rare. H scarce.

LONG-HEADED POPPY *P. dubium* L.
Said to be common in 1901 and 1931. Nowadays it is widespread but surprisingly scarce with usually only isolated plants. J frequent. A frequent. S last record 1907. H rare.

BABINGTON'S POPPY *P. Lecoqii* Lamotte
Recorded by More on his visit in 1859, a species about which he had for some time been in correspondence with Babington and Newbould. But no specimen of his from Guernsey has been located. J –. A –. S –. H –.

BRISTLY POPPY *P. hybridum* L.
Babington listed this from L'Ancresse in 1837/8, but since then there have been only six records, all of odd plants and all between 1879 and 1894. J rare. A occasional. S –. H –.

PALE POPPY *P. Argemone* L.
Also listed by Babington from L'Ancresse, but never seen again, except for one likely but sadly unconfirmed record 130 years later. J rare. A –. S –. H rare.

OPIUM POPPY *P. somniferum* L.
Another variable species, the source of opium to those who know how to tap it, and consequently much grown in certain warmer countries. In Guernsey it is grown as a garden annual and now appears occasionally outside them; but in the long past it was also in cornfields, and indeed was seen in arable at Les Granges in 1969. Its seeds are not narcotic and are used in confectionery and for birds, as Blue Maw – whence it also appears in waste places. Its first record was by Haslam in 1839 from behind the Vale Church, its next by Miss Dawber from L'Ancresse in 1887. J frequent. A occasional. S rare. H rare.

WELSH POPPY *Meconopsis cambrica* (L.) Viguier
Welcome as a mild weed in moister gardens, and as such to be seen in the grounds of La Favorita in St Martins. J rare. A –. S –. H –.

(The Violet Horned Poppy, *Roemeria hybrida* (L.) DC, appeared in Alderney in 1956.)

YELLOW HORNED POPPY *Glaucium flavum* Crantz (*G. luteum*)
Nowadays much scarcer, because of the pressure of visitors on the beaches. Indeed, away from the shingle banks at L'Erée and Hougue Patris, it is hardly more than occasional, even round L'Ancresse, where Gosselin collected it. J local. A frequent. S –. H rare.

SCARLET HORNED POPPY *G. corniculatum* (L.) Rudolph
Found by M. Torode in 1936 at Rocque Poisson where it persisted for at least five years, an unusual event. J last collected 1926 and 1965. A 1903. S –. H –.

GREATER CELANDINE *Chelidonium majus* L.
Still 'rather rare and usually in small quantity in each locality', as Marquand wrote, and not on the south, west or north coasts. Gosselin collected it, noting it grew wild in his garden and in walls; and said it was poisonous. J occasional. A –. S 1852. H –.

CALIFORNIAN POPPY *Eschscholzia californica* Chamisso
A gay garden plant (the State emblem of its native California), which not only appears in waste places and on rubbish tips, but persists, by overwintering (it is by nature often perennial) or by seed, on dry dunes or cliffs. Three of its records are from walls, where it had sown itself. J casual. A occasional. S –. H 1958.

YELLOW CORYDALIS *Corydalis lutea* (L.) DC
Strangely rare, ever since it was first noted, only in 1898. In all there seem to have been only eight records, but it does still grow in small quantity on two or three walls. J occasional. A –. S –. H –.

(Climbing Corydalis, *C. claviculata* (L.) DC, occurs rarely in Jersey. *C. solida* (L.) Swartz was collected there in 1899.)

RAMPING FUMITORY *Fumaria capreolata* L. ssp *Babingtonii* (Pugsley) P. D. Sell (*F. pallidiflora*)
Generally distributed, but never common. Its variations were discussed by Pugsley in the *Journal of Botany* in 1912 and 1914. Comment on var *speciosa* Jordan is under Martin's Fumitory. J occasional. A rare. S rare. H –.

PURPLE FUMITORY *F. purpurea* Pugsley
A species endemic to the British Isles, two clumps of which were seen on dumped soil north of Vale Castle in 1970, but which were buried in 1971. All that remains now is the vouching specimens. J –. A –. S –. H –.

BASTARD'S FUMITORY *F. Bastardii* Boreau (*F. confusa*)
Apparently scarce and elusive, not always easy to tell from Boreau's Fumitory, so it is probably often unrecognised, and could prove commoner than it seems. Pugsley discusses it in the *Journal of Botany* for 1912. Mons. T. Bastard lived from 1784 to 1846. J rare. A last record 1938. S last record 1906. H 1894.

HYBRID FUMITORY *F. Bastardii* × *F. muralis* ssp *Boraei*
One, sterile, plant was found by Pugsley at Cobo in June 1914. J –. A –. S –. H –.

MARTIN'S FUMITORY *F. Martinii* Clavaud
Collected on two occasions by very experienced botanists, first by Pugsley himself

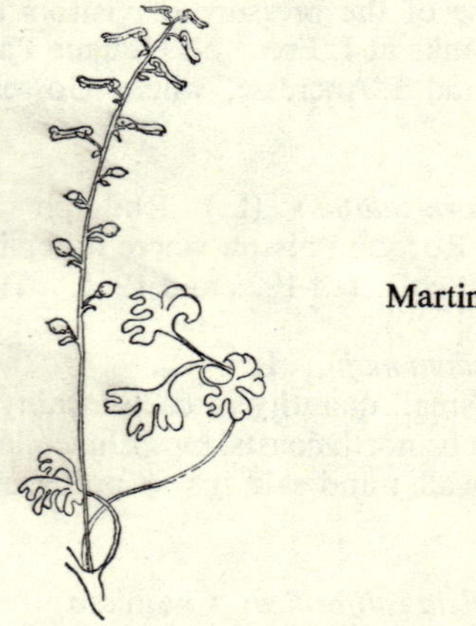

Martin's Fumitory ×1

in 1914 and then, still in the Petit Bot area, by Wilmott in 1928. That area seems no longer suitable, but the plant tends to come and go and could be easily overlooked by those who have never seen this rare species. Pugsley thought Andrew's '*F. capreolata* var *speciosa*' might have been this – cf *Journal of Botany* for 1914, p. 328. Mons. Martin was an ornithologist who collected his Fumitory in the Loir et Cher before 1886. J –. A –. S –. H –.

WALL FUMITORY *F. muralis* Sonder ex Koch ssp *muralis*
One record in 1876, one in 1879, one in 1900, of none of which Pugsley in 1912 said he had seen specimens from the Channel Islands. The records were queried by Wilmott and are ignored in the *Critical Supplement to the Atlas*, no doubt reasonably, for this is a very variable species. Pugsley thought these records were probably of his var *britannica* and subvar *sarniensis* of the next subspecies. J error? A –. S –. H –.

Boreau's Fumitory *F. muralis* Sonder ex Koch ssp *Boraei* (Jordan) Pugsley. Feumeterre
This is by far the commonest Fumitory in Guernsey. Wilmott after his visit in 1928 wrote that there were lots of forms; and indeed many have been given names. The usual one is rather miserable, pale and thin, but early forms can be fine and have been taken for Martin's Fumitory, which has a much longer inflorescence. Those interested will consult the writings of Pugsley in the *Journal of Botany* in 1912 and 1914 and in the *Journal of the Linnean Society* in 1919. His subvar *sarniensis* with almost globose fruits and a suberect much-branched habit is based on a plant Andrews collected at Graie in 1900 and was seen subsequently at Vazon. It is apparently confined to Guernsey. Gosselin called Fumitory a medicinal plant. Bellamy wrote of it: '*excellentissime Fumarium herba.*' Mons. A. Boreau (1803–75) was a distinguished French botanist. J common. A common. S common. H frequent.

Painter's Fumitory *F.* × *Painteri* Pugsley (*F. muralis* ssp *Boraei* × *F. officinalis*)
A rare, sterile, hybrid, collected by Andrews in 1900. J –. A –. S –. H –.

Common Fumitory *F. officinalis* L. ssp *officinalis*
By no means the common Fumitory of Guernsey, and currently unrecorded in the south. J occasional. A occasional. S rare. H rare.

(*F. officinalis* L. ssp *Wirtgenii* (Koch) Arcangeli was recorded from Jersey about 1880.)

Crucifer Family Cruciferae

Wild Cabbage *Brassica oleracea* L. ssp *oleracea* Caboche
This native of the south coasts of Britain was said, by Gosselin, to have been sent by him to Sir J. Banks on 8 April 1791, and seed of it later to Sir J. E. Smith. Banks' specimens do not survive, but those of Gosselin's so labelled are all Stinkweed. Knowlton's record of 'Sea Cabidge' from Fermain in 1726, an 'old acquaintance', and Haslam's in the 1830's from the same area, rocks by Clarence Bay, have never been substantiated. Indeed there is no confirmation of its occurrence in such native places in the Channel Islands. But it is a polymorphic species, the origin of numerous garden vegetables such as Broccoli (grown locally as a crop – brocôlus), Brussels Sprouts and the various Kales (choux), notably the Giant Cabbage of the Channel Islands (on which a booklet was written by S. Parker and G. S. Cox in 1970), the Choux Cavaliers, the stalks of which have reached 16 feet. It was recorded in 1862 that nearly all the cultivated cabbages were 'Drumhead'; and in 1851 that a soup – 'Guernsey Soup' – in very general use in the upper ranks and the almost universal food of the peasantry was based on cabbage (cf p. 165). Seeds from these vegetables get to rubbish tips and occur in bird seed mixtures freely, so it is surprising that this plant was not even reported from there until 1969. This is partly a reflection on the scarcity of tips in the island, and partly an example of how people think such a plant not worth noting, or so common as not to need it. J casual. A –. S –. H –.

Rape *B. Napus* L. ssp *Napus* Rabette
A plant with none of the excitement its English name might hint at. It is now usually grown as green manure and some survives, or it appears in bird seed. The English name is in fact merely a corruption of, confusingly, the Latin name of the

next species, with which it is often muddled, which meant a turnip in classical times. So did *Napus*! It occurs only rarely. Swedes, the second year form of this species, have been little grown. J occasional. A scarce. S rare. H 1958.

BARGEMAN'S CABBAGE *B. Rapa* L. (*B. campestris*) Navet
This is another variable species, much selected for agricultural purposes, and long used to develop in the second year into Turnips. In 1859 'Purple Top' and 'Tankard' were grown agriculturally, the latter yielding 20–30 tons per acre. It is also grown as green manure or for fodder. No one has determined to which subspecies any Guernsey plant has belonged and, because of its present fugitive and unnatural nature, such a fact is of small importance. It is uncommon. J casual. A recorded. S –. H –.

BLACK MUSTARD *B. nigra* (L.) Koch (*Sinapis nigra*)
As in earlier times, this is definitely known only from the cliffs of the Fort George area, where it can be plentiful, and from north and south of St Sampson's Harbour. J casual. A 1969. S 1908. H 1837.

(Chinese Mustard, *B. juncea* (L.) Czernajew, was collected in Jersey in 1924. *Erucastrum gallicum* (Willdenow) O. E. Schultz occurred there in 1973.)

ISLE OF MAN CABBAGE *Rhynchosinapis monensis* (L.) Dandy
'In the Island of Guernsey, Mr Finlay,' runs a manuscript entry in Lightfoot's copy of Ray's *Synopsis* at Oxford. Was this Stinkweed? Finlay will then have been about 20. J –. A –. S –. H –.

WALLFLOWER CABBAGE *R. Cheiranthos* (Villars) Dandy ssp *Cheiranthos* (*Brassica Cheiranthos*)
This persisted in the Vale Castle area for some twenty years from 1889. J locally frequent. A error? S error? H –.

CHARLOCK *Sinapis arvensis* L. Berzac. Beurze. Poinfeis
Quite frequent as an arable weed, the variety *orientalis* (L.) Koch & Ziz (*villosa*) with hairy pods not noted for some time. Gosselin's specimen is the oldest. 'Mustard seed brused' was an ingredient in an 18th century cure for dropsy. J occasional. A common. S rare. H very rare.

WHITE MUSTARD *S. alba* L. Moutarde
A scarce casual only, apparently never persisting. The name by Gosselin's specimen was altered by him to the last species. J frequent. A rare. S 1908 & 1957. H rare.

HOARY MUSTARD *Hirschfeldia incana* (L.) Lagrèze-Fossat (*Sinapis incana*)
Locally frequent in dry sandy and waste places in the north and west. It has increased very considerably in frequency since its first record in 1891. J locally frequent. A locally common. S –. H –.

STINKWEED *Diplotaxis muralis* (L.) DC
Not common now, and chiefly in the north and west, occasionally in the stouter var *caulescens* Kittel (*Babingtonii*). J frequent. A occasional. S –. H Jethou.

VINEYARD STINKWEED *D. viminea* (L.) DC
An annual recorded in waste places at St Peter Port by the young Newbould in

1841, and later plants from there are said to have been given this name. But the only specimens which seem to survive so labelled, from Fox in August 1867, are ordinary Stinkweed. Brébisson in his *Flora of Normandy* of 1859 wrote 'a dwarf state (of Stinkweed) has often been taken for *D. viminea*'. The true Mediterranean plant is one of the ancestral parents (the other is Wall Rocket) of Stinkweed. J –. A –. S –. H –.

WALL ROCKET *D. tenuifolia* (L.) DC
Locally quite plentiful near the coast also chiefly in the north and west. J locally frequent. A locally abundant. S –. H –.

WILD RADISH *Raphanus Raphanistrum* L. ssp *Raphanistrum*
Quite frequent with yellow, f. *concolor* Beck, pink, f. *carneus* Thellung or white, f. *arvensis* Beck, petals, which may also be veined. Gosselin collected it twice, but once it was Charlock, which has spreading sepals. J occasional. A rare. S frequent. H 1958.

SEA RADISH *R. maritimus* Smith
Very common round most of the coast, less so inland. Gosselin collected it unawares, and both Gay and Woods recorded it before Babington. The flowers are sometimes white, and Wilmott based his subvar *albiflorus* on specimens from the Channel Islands, which had in fact been first noted by Gay. This plant is often thickly enclustered with snails. The States of Guernsey attempted to reduce the numbers of this coarse weed by chemical means. At first they succeeded, depriving the snails of their main food, who therefore migrated wholesale to neighbouring cabbages and tomatoes, the result being much worse. In any event the plants very soon recovered. J common. A locally common. S unconfirmed. H frequent.

GARDEN RADISH *R. sativus* L. Radishe
May persist for a short while after being grown for a crop, or appear on rubbish tips. J casual. A 1962. S –. H 1958.

SEA KALE *Crambe maritima* L.
Now to be found in many more places than have been recorded before – Marquand called it very rare. Such beach plants have mostly diminished or succumbed from human competition. This one moreover often forms striking sumptuous mounds on the shingle or sand, and to those who know has other interests too. Yet it has happily not only held its ground, but seems to have spread, although not in great quantity in any one place. It is probably best on the shingle bank at L'Erée, but is still on Lihou, where it was first noticed in the 1830s, and is now not only in two other places on the west coast, but also on the east, at Bordeaux, and in the south at Pezeries and La Bette Bay. Gosselin collected it on the Banque des Grandes Maisons and at the Vazon. Victor Hugo cultivated it at Hauteville in 1875 and said it tasted like asparagus. J increasing. A rare. S –. H 1939.

BASTARD CABBAGE *Rapistrum rugosum* (L.) Allioni
First noted by G. Morgan on L'Ancresse in 1951 and near Les Vauxbelets, about two dozen plants in each place; then, persisting, in greater quantity near the Newlyn Vinery in 1970; and on the St Sampson's tip in 1971, a form with very bristly fruits. It originated in the Mediterranean. J 1928, 1957, 1958. A –. S –. H –.

SEA ROCKET *Cakile maritima* Scopoli ssp *maritima*
A seaside plant which has diminished and is now not much seen, and then often only in singletons. J local. A locally frequent. S 1838 and 1879. H rare.

(*Conringia orientalis* (L.) Dumortier has been in Jersey.)

GARDEN CRESS *Lepidium sativum* L.
Very occasionally appears from (Mustard and) Cress seed, but never lasts. It is a native of the Near East. J occurs similarly. A 1903. S –. H –.

COMMON PEPPERWORT *L. campestre* (L.) R. Brown
A single plant in 1892. Otherwise only misclaimed for the next species. J –. A –. S –. H –.

SMITH'S CRESS *L. heterophyllum* Bentham (*L. Smithii*)
Local now with only one record from the north. Gosselin sent seed of it to Sir J. E. Smith, after whom Sir W. J. Hooker later named it. J common. A rare. S common. H 1904.

NARROW-LEAVED PEPPERWORT *L. ruderale* L.
Always very rare, and not noted during the present century, except for the entry in the *Atlas*, the basis for which has been forgotten. Indeed the only vouched records have been between 1889 and 1899. J rare. A last record 1900. S Brechou 1902. H –.

DITTANDER *L. latifolium* L.
Still to be seen growing thickly in a few places on and near the west coast from Rocquaine Bay to Port Soif and until recently Pulias. It has very persistent underground parts and has certainly been in the Grandes Mielles area for nearly two centuries, and was at Cobo in 1832. The English name is a corruption of *Dictamnus*, a quite different European plant, which became attached to it in the Middle Ages. Lyte in 1578 wrote: 'It is fondly and unlearnedly named in Englishe Dittany. It were better in following the Douchemen to call it Pepperwort' – for it was much cultivated as a condiment until the introduced Horse-radish supplanted it – and it is decorative too. Nevertheless it may be native in its Guernsey localities, for it likes to be beside the seaside. J collected 1926. A –. S –. H –.

(*L. perfoliatum* L. and *L. virginicum* L. were collected in Jersey in 1925 and 1926.)

COMMON WART-CRESS *Coronopus squamatus* (Forskål) Ascherson
(*Senebeira Coronopus*) Cône de Cherf. Kersounette
Rather scarce; collected by Gosselin near the College and Longstore. J scarce. A locally frequent. S occasional. H –.

SLENDER WART-CRESS *C. didymus* (L.) Smith (*Senebeira didyma*)
Still 'generally distributed and much more plentiful than the last species', indeed common. It is said to have originated in South America, but has now spread over most of the world, and over the southern half of the British Isles since Gosselin's time. J common. A frequent. S frequent. H frequent.

HOARY CRESS *Cardaria Draba* (L.) Desvaux ssp *Draba* (*Lepidium Draba*)
Usually untidy and dusty, but not the nuisance weed it can be elsewhere. It has now been recorded in all the parishes, and is probably less rare than at the beginning of the century. Its original discovery in Guernsey, on 28 July 1838 on the Rohais road, constituted its sixth British record, but it is no longer there. It is supposed to have reached Britain from southern Europe early in the last century. J scarce. A occasional. S 1907. H –.

(Annual garden Candytufts, *Iberis amara* L. and *I. umbellata* L., have appeared as casuals in Jersey.)

COMMON PENNY-CRESS *Thlaspi arvense* L. Moutardier
No longer rare – it was said to be extending its territory in 1931 – but still not really common. Gosselin collected it from his kitchen garden and the Vale. J rare. A –. S rare. H common.

SHEPHERD'S CRESS *Teesdalia nudicaulis* (L.) R. Brown
Still quite frequent on the south cliffs, but also known since 1947 on west and east L'Ancresse. It has not been noted inland since the *Flora*. Gosselin collected it between the Taye Marquand and the sea shore and noted it from Les Vardes in Town, in neither of which localities it has been seen since. J frequent. A locally common. S common. H –.

SHEPHERD'S PURSE *Capsella Bursa-pastoris* (L.) Medicus Pid' Mouisson
A polymorphic species, collected by Gosselin, then and now common. Its forms have not yet been satisfactorily split into species or even tenable varieties. Names exist for apparently distinctive leaf and fruit shapes, but none have met with lasting acceptance – which leaves a challenge. None have been applied to Guernsey gatherings. The species is inbreeding, like many other annuals and especially crucifers, which favours the perpetuation of special forms. J common. A frequent. S common. H frequent.

HUTCHINSIA *Hornungia petraea* (L.) Reichenbach
The sole evidence for the occurrence of this in Guernsey is 'L'Ancresse' written by a specimen, all the rest of which on that sheet come from Jersey, dated April 1907 by Druce. He makes no mention of this discovery in print, and all efforts to see it on L'Ancresse have failed. J local. A –. S –. H –.

COMMON SCURVY-GRASS *Cochlearia officinalis* L.
Collected by Newbould in 1841 and reported by Watson in 1852, records Marquand seems to have been unaware of. J collected 1926. A locally frequent. S –. H –.

EARLY SCURVY-GRASS *C. danica* L. Escorvie
Often plentiful on the coast, starring the early spring turf; much less common inland, where it may also grow on roofs – as Gosselin noted when he collected it, as *C. groenlandica*. Its leaves were used in Guernsey, as elsewhere, as an anti-dote to scurvy. J common. A common. S common. H common.

ENGLISH SCURVY-GRASS *C. anglica* L.
There are specimens of this in Gosselin's herbarium and in his scrapbook, without localities. But he seems always to have noted if a plant was collected in any other island of the Bailiwick: indeed only three were. J error. A –. S –. H –.

WARTY CABBAGE *Bunias orientalis* L.
Three clumps in meadows near Ozanne's Tower in 1899. J –. A –. S –. H –.

(*B. Erucago* L. was in Jersey in 1900.)

HONESTY *Lunaria annua* L. ssp *annua*
Grown by Gosselin in the mid-18th century, and cultivated as a crop for export until fairly recent times for the shining central partition of its fruits, and still a favourite plant in gardens. It ceased to be grown commercially because it 'ran out', being a host plant for Club root of Brassicas. Outside gardens it never lasts for more than a year or so. J casual. A 1957. S –. H –.

SWEET ALISON *Lobularia maritima* (L.) Desvaux (*Alyssum maritimum*)
Very common on some of the roadsides of the west and north coasts, and to be seen occasionally elsewhere but hardly in the south, except on the hot south-facing cliffs of Les Terres Point where it looks completely natural. It is much bedded out in gardens which was no doubt how it started on its way in Guernsey, where it was first collected by Dupuy in 1865. It is a Mediterranean annual. J locally common. A occasional. S rare. H rare.

HOARY ALISON *Berteroa incana* (L.) DC (*Alyssum incanum*)
Single plants in 1889 and 1899. J last collected 1924. A –. S –. H –.

WALL WHITLOW-GRASS *Draba muralis* L.
Credited to Guernsey in the *Armorican Flora* of 1971 by erroneously copying the entry under *Diplotaxis* for '*D. muralis*' on page 175 of Lester-Garland's *Flora of Jersey*. J similar error. A similar error. S –. H –.

COMMON WHITLOW-GRASS *Erophila verna* (L.) Chevallier ssp *verna* (*Draba verna*)
Another self-pollinating annual, which appears in many forms. It is not plentiful and has dried up before most visitors arrive; few have been collected and fewer named. '*Verna*' was the name generally used for all specimens, but Dupuy's from Portinfer seem to belong here, so do some from L'Ancresse in 1963 from Miss V. Leather. J frequent? A frequent? S –. H last record 1893.

BROAD WHITLOW-GRASS *E. verna* (L.) Chevallier ssp *spathulata* (A. F. Láng) S. M. Walters (incl. *E.* '*praecox*')
Plants collected by Gosselin have been attributed to this species, but no others were until 1907 and 1962. It could be the right name for many of the Guernsey plants – see the *Critical Supplement to the Atlas*, p. 8.
J frequent. A 1962. S 1930. H –.

EARLY WHITLOW-GRASS *E. praecox* (Steven) DC
Plants from L'Ancresse were named thus by Druce in 1907, but the true species is probably unknown in the British Isles, and his gathering belongs with the last species. J error. A –. S –. H –.

HORSE-RADISH *Armoracia rusticana* Gaertner, Meyer & Scherbius
Widespread and very persistent with its deep roots. It may be a native of Russia, but has been grown for the sauce from its ground roots since the Middle Ages, eventually superseding Dittander for this purpose. It is on record as an 18th-century cure for dropsy; and during the last war was cultivated for use in making a food paté. J occasional. A occasional. S –. H –.

Lady's Smock *Cardamine pratensis* L. ssp *pratensis*
A polymorphic species from which the next may be separable, but the forms have not been looked at properly. Consequently the relative frequency of them cannot be given, but those grouped under this one seem scarce. *C. fragilis* Lloyd, named from the Grande Mare by D. E. Allen, is probably only a form. Double-flowered forms have been recorded. J aggregate common. A –. S rare. H –.

Large-flowered Lady's Smock *C. pratensis* L. ssp *palustris* (Wimmer & Grabowski) Janchen
This group of plants with the higher chromosome numbers may prove to be the common, or even sole normal, Lady's Smocks of Guernsey. But proof is needed. See *Watsonia* for January 1974. J aggregate common. A –. S –. H ?

Wavy Bitter-cress *C. flexuosa* Withering
There are fine specimens of this collected by Gosselin, ante-dating Marquand's by a century. It seems not to be all that common, or in the drier north. J frequent. A last record 1900. S occasional. H –.

Hairy Bitter-cress *C. hirsuta* L.
Common to those who recognise it. Babington called it also *C. parviflora*. J common. A common. S common. H common.

Common Winter-cress *Barbarea vulgaris* R. Brown
Only four or five records, some of single plants, the last in 1928, not all vouched. J rare. A –. S 1902. H –.

(*B. stricta* Andrzasovszky is recorded from the Channel Islands in the *Flora of the British Isles*.)

Early Winter-cress *B. intermedia* Boreau
The Winter-cresses have been confused, often understandably, so unsupported records have to be taken at their face value. The first good one for this species proved to be by Miss Dawber in 1893 from Vale Castle, which had been called *B. verna*. Six others are down as this, and may well have been. It is said to have been introduced from Central Europe. J occasional. A rare. S occasional. H –.

American Land-cress *B. verna* (Miller) Ascherson (*B. praecox*)
Not particularly early – as its Latin names imply (the last species is the earliest), nor is it American as the English name implies, nor English as the French name Cresson anglais implies, but south-western European. Land-cress is used to distinguish it from Watercress. It is a plant usually but still too little grown for its fresh green leaves for winter salads – for which in fact the other species will serve too. There are seven records of it during and before the last century, but the only one since is of about 50 plants at Rousse in 1957, of which no sign was seen subsequently. J rare. A rare. S 1906. H –.

Hairy Rock-cress *Arabis hirsuta* (L.) Scopoli
Very local in the sandy turf of the north-west. Newbould reported it from St Martin's in 1841/2, and one plant was seen south of the Coudré Mill in 1968. J last collected 1924. A frequent. S –. H –.

(Garden Arabis, *A. caucasica* Willdenow, was recorded on Brechou in 1957.)

AUBRETIA *Aubretia deltoidea* (L.) DC
A familiar garden rockery plant from the Mediterranean which may sow itself on walls, and does so freely and colourfully in at least three places in Guernsey. J rare. A –. S –. H –.

WATERCRESS *Nasturtium officinale* R. Brown Kerson
Probably the commonest watercress in Guernsey, and apparently the one collected by Gosselin, but too few people have discriminated their records; moreover good fruits are needed for certainty, which prevents young plants from being properly sorted. The telling character is that the seeds of this one have about 25 pits on their surface, which are visible under a hand lens. It was used herbally in the 18th century, for scurvy. J aggregate frequent. A scarce. S locally frequent. H local.

BROWN-LEAVED WATERCRESS *N. microphyllum* (Boenninghausen) Reichenbach
Four times recorded, from Saumarez Park and western L'Ancresse in 1968, and in 1971 from the remains of the pond in the centre there and from the Château des Marais. It differs from the last in having, so it is said, about 100 pits on the seeds, which are therefore so minute that they cannot be made out with a hand lens. J recorded. A –. S –. H –.

HYBRID WATERCRESS *N.* × *sterilis* (Airy-Shaw) Oefelein (*N. microphyllum* × *N. officinale*)
Collected from the ditches by the Château des Marais in 1958. J 1960. A rare. S –. H –.

CREEPING YELLOW CRESS *Rorippa sylvestris* (L.) Besser (*Nasturtium sylvestre*)
Half a field yellow with it south-west of the Château des Marais, but no other certain record since the war. Before that, there had been nine in various parts, none specifically said to have been as a garden weed, which it can successfully be, spread by nurseries which have the misfortune to be infested. J occasional. A –. S rare. H –.

MARSH YELLOW CRESS *R. palustris* (L.) Besser (*R.* '*islandica*')
Two records, both in the last twenty years, both likely, both needing confirmation. J last collected 1928. A –. S error. H –.

SEA STOCK *Matthiola incana* (L.) R. Brown Violette. Giroufflaie
Lyte's *Herball* of 1578 first refers to Garnsee Violets, apparently meaning this species (T. Britten and R. Holland in their *Dictionary of English Plant Names* of 1878–1886 and G. van Wijk in his great *Dictionary of Plants* of 1911 specifically say it does), but with no indication if they grew wild. The name appears in print for the next 58 years. No subsequent mention of this plant in Guernsey has been traced until the entry in Babington's *Journal* for 12 August 1837, when he 'crossed to Long Port and saw *Matthiola incana*'. No doubt however this was a slip of the pen, for in his *Flora* he gives only the next species and that from Grand Cobo, where Long Port is. Marquand does not allude to this species at all, nor is there any further record until 1934, and then no other until the mid-1950's, when it was gaily and fragrantly decking the sides of some quarries in the north-west, sometimes with white flowers. It may appear as an escape from cultivation elsewhere too, where it is grown for pleasure and for profit. Gosselin was growing double stocks in 1767. J occasional. A locally common. S –. H –.

GREAT SEA STOCK *M. sinuata* (L.) R. Brown (*Cheiranthus sinuatus*)
Survives now only at Rousse, precariously, and at Portinfer much more precariously. Formerly it was known right down the west coast from L'Ancresse to Rocquaine Bay, and was indeed called very common in 1872. The decline is due to human impact on its habitats. Gosselin sent a specimen to Sir J. Banks on 8 April 1791 and seed on 16 January 1792. J now rare. A –. S –. H –.

VIRGINIAN STOCK *Malcolmia maritima* (L.) R. Brown
Occasionally seen as a waif from some garden. The species, genus indeed, is Mediterranean, not American at all. J casual. A casual. S –. H –.

(Dame's Violet, *Hesperis matronalis* L., was grown by Gosselin in 1767, and has been reported wild from Jersey, Alderney and Brechou. *H. laciniata* Allioni was collected in Jersey in 1926.)

TREACLE MUSTARD *Erysimum cheiranthoides* L.
Miss Guille knew this as a weed at St George in 1883, where Marquand saw it in 1894, but where it seems to be no longer, and it was at Fermain House in 1892/3. But no more was heard of it until 1958, when one large plant was recorded from Portelet, and 1968 when it appeared in a new sown ley in the Câtel. J 1925. A –. S –. H –.

SMALL MAUVE WALLFLOWER *E. scoparium* (Willdenow) Wettstein (*Cheiranthus scoparius*)
A Canary Islands plant recorded in 1941 by Warry. There is no specimen, but he is likely to have known it from his Kew days. J –. A –. S –. H –.

(*E. hieracifolium* L. (*E. strictum*) has been claimed in Jersey.)

WALLFLOWER *Cheiranthus Cheiri* L. Violette d'Châté.
Not as frequent as one would wish, but still to be met with, yellow or brown-flowered, on several walls and quarry sides, where it mingles its fragrance with that of the stocks. Gosselin grew it in his garden, and collected it wild. J frequent. A occasional. S occasional. H 1957.

GARLIC MUSTARD *Alliaria petiolata* (Bieberstein) Cavare & Grande (*A. officinalis*)
Not common. Gosselin collected it close to the gate of his house at L'Hyvreuse, and considered it a medicinal plant. J occasional. A locally frequent. S occasional. H –.

HEDGE MUSTARD *Sisymbrium officinale* (L.) Scopoli
Quite common – there is a good specimen in Gosselin's herbarium marked Plante Médécinale. The distinctive var *leiocarpum* DC with paler foliage and hairless pods occurs here and there, locally exclusively. J common. A frequent. S occasional. H occasional.

LONDON ROCKET *S. Irio* L.
Recorded in 1941 sans specimen. J recorded. A –. S –. H –.

EASTERN ROCKET *S. orientale* L.
First recorded in 1923, and then not until 1947. It is still rare, and shows no sign of spreading from St Sampson's, and the north. J local. A rare. S Brechou. H –.

TUMBLING MUSTARD *S. altissimum* L.
Recorded in 1945, again with no supporting specimen. J last collected in 1926. A –. S –. H –.

THALE CRESS *Arabidopsis Thaliana* (L.) Heynhold (*Sisymbrium Thalianum*)
Common. Gosselin collected it as a garden weed. J common. A rare. S common. H frequent.

GOLD OF PLEASURE *Camelina sativa* (L.) Crantz
1904. But it is a frequent ingredient in bird seed and must surely have occurred unnoticed, before being again seen on a dump at Mont Cuet in 1970. J last record 1896. A –. S –. H –.

(Flixweed, *Descurainia Sophia* (L.) Webb ex Prantl, was last collected in Jersey in 1926.)

MIGNONETTE FAMILY Resedaceae

WELD *Reseda Luteola* L. Herbe à toindre
Gosselin said it grew 'partout' and his herbarium sheet lists several localities for it. Nowadays it is locally not uncommon, but never in much quantity, and very rare in the south-west. It is one of the most ancient dye plants, 'weld' having the same origin as 'woad', although weld dyed yellow and woad blue; it is also called Dyer's Rocket. J frequent. A occasional. S locally frequent. H rare.

WILD MIGNONETTE *R. lutea* L.
The Secretary of the Botanical Section of the Société in his report for 1929 referred to this plant as quite common on L'Ancresse. This must have been a slip for the last species, for in fact this one is, curiously, a great rarity in the island. There are only three records – a single plant on ballast in 1894, another on L'Ancresse in 1930, and in 1954 it was collected near the Hermitage by R. Ross, unaware how exciting his find was. Maybe it has been similarly unappreciated by other visitors. J rare. A rare. S –. H 1950 & 1958.

WHITE MIGNONETTE *R. alba* L. (*R. suffruticulosa*)
Five records, 1893, 1926, 1934, 1946 and 1973, with the implication it was a garden outcast. J casual. A –. S –. H –.

(Garden Mignonette, *R. odorata* L., has occurred as a casual in Jersey.)

VIOLET FAMILY Violaceae

SWEET VIOLET *Viola odorata* L.
Babington recorded this from several parts of Guernsey, adding 'near houses and not native'. Marquand scoffed at this. But Sweet Violets have been a prime favourite for so long there is no doubt they were growing in Guernsey in the 1830s: Gosselin had them in flower in February 1767. From our point of view the only question is, how wild they were. The various patches in the island today are all near, or on the sites of abandoned, gardens. There, however, they can spread contentedly, at ease with neighbouring vegetation, i.e. they are naturalised.

All these patches have violet or white flowers, except one in the grounds of Côte des Vardes, long known to the de Jerseys there, which is the pink 'Coeur d'Alsace'. J frequent. A –. S 1961. H –.

COMMON DOG VIOLET *V. Riviniana* Reichenbach (*V.* '*canina*') Coucou. The common dog violet indeed, and most decoratively abundant all over the island. There is a specimen in Gosselin's herbarium, and he sent another Violet to Sir J. Banks on 8 April 1791. Robust plants from Petit Bot have been referred to var *intermedia* Le Grand by Mrs Gregory, rather than to the f. *nemorosa* Neumann. *Riviniana* commemorates A. Q. Bachmann (1652–1723) of Leipzig, who Latinised his name, as *Rivinus*. Bach is German and *Rivus* Latin for a stream. J common. A common. S common. H common.

WOOD DOG VIOLET *V. Reichenbachiana* Jordan ex Boreau (*V. sylvatica*) Marquand's 1891 plant was a form of the last species. Watson's *V. sylvatica* refers also to the last species. Both may have been based on some dark-spurred plants which occur in St. Martin's, notably by Fort George. J –. A –. S –. H –.

HEATH DOG VIOLET *V. canina* L. ssp *canina* (*V. flavicornis*) Watson reported this, from L'Ancresse in 1852, and Druce the var *ericetorum* Reichenbach from Petit Bot in 1907, but specimens of neither seem to have survived. Mrs MacAlister Hall recorded it from L'Ancresse in 1935, but before the record ever appeared in print, her specimen had been annotated by P. M. Hall 'No sign of *canina* here. Small *V. Riviniana*.' The nearest to this species is a violet in the turf near Pezeries and in a lane bank in St Peter's, which Dr Walters thinks might be a hybrid of this with the Common species. J rare. A –. S –. H –.

PALE HEATH VIOLET *V. lactea* Smith There is a fine specimen of this species in Gosselin's herbarium without a locality. But all his in effect came from Guernsey. It is also recorded by Dizerbo in the *Bulletin of the Breton Scientific Society* for 1970, but he writes that this is an error for Jersey, where the record is also an error. J error. A –. S –. H –.

HEARTSEASE *V. tricolor* L. ssp *tricolor* 'Very rare' wrote Marquand, and so at best it still is, with only one recent claim even. Gosselin's specimens are not of this, but the next species. Nor has there even been a claim which has proved to be just of degenerate garden pansies, Pensées (hybrids, with more blotched and overlapping petals, grouped as *V.* × *Wittrockiana* Gams), which are often misrecorded for this species, which is probably one of its parents. It could well be that the true plant has never occurred in the island. J –. A –. S rare. H rare.

FIELD PANSY *V. arvensis* Murray An exceedingly variable species, which not so long ago was split into several 'species'. These however are now realised to be no more than forms, or hybrids with the last species – such have been named from Sark. The odd plant may be found which has upper petals purple and nearly long enough to approach the last species. This species is not rare, but certainly not common, as it was said to be in the *Flora* and even in 1931. J occasional. A occasional. S common. H frequent.

(Examples of *V. arvensis* × *V. tricolor*, some labelled *V. obtusifolia*, have been collected in Sark.)

DWARF PANSY *V. Kitaibeliana* Schultes (*V. nana*)
One of the special plants of Guernsey, first noted for the British Isles by Trimen on his visit to the Channel Islands in 1871, a reward for the early visitor endowed with keen sight and an appreciation of the miniature. For it is just a wee Field Pansy enshrouded shyly in the hood of its sepals, since the flower does not open

Dwarf Pansy ×1

wide. Books say it can be 4 inches high, in long grass presumably, but it is often under one inch on the bare cliffs of the south. Its other, and more usual habitat generally, is in open sandy turf, on Lihou and from Rousse to L'Ancresse, where it is elusive. Normally it is over by early summer, but it was still in flower on 5 July 1902. Druce grew it in 1908 from seed from L'Ancresse and found it came true. Drabble has a note on it in the *Journal of Botany* for 1928, p. 129. J local. A –. S –. H rare.

MILKWORT FAMILY Polygalaceae

COMMON MILKWORT *Polygala vulgaris* L. Squinancie. Coucou de Jaonnière. Herbe d' Paralysie
Marquand called this frequent, but it now seems very scarce and only in small quantity. Forms occur which in the past would have been referred to *P. oxyptera* Reichenbach (*P. dubia*), but it has been realised for some time that this merges indistinguishably into the main species. Gosselin's specimens came from his family territory, the Terres Gosselin. J local. A rare. S common. H frequent.

HEATH MILKWORT *P. serpyllifolia* Hose (*P. depressa*)
Not always easy to tell from the last species, but probably rather less scarce. Close to the sea at Fontenelle Bay and nearby grows a form with rich Hyacinth blue flowers (HCC 40). What may have been a similar colour form was noted by Mrs McCrea above the Vinaire Nurseries in 1922. Gosselin collected this species with the last, calling both *P. vulgaris*, as was often done until relatively recent times. J locally common. A occasional. S occasional. H –.

ST JOHN'S-WORT FAMILY Guttiferae

TUTSAN *Hypericum Androsaemum* L.
Usually single plants here and there, possibly native in likely woods and banks. It occurs also on wall-sides and self-sown in gardens. Gosselin grew it in 1767, commenting it may be planted under trees. J locally frequent. A –. S occasional. H scarce.

TALL TUTSAN *H. inodorum* Miller (*H. elatum*)
This is much confused with the last and the next, its presumed parents. It has been seen once or twice as a relic. J –. A –. S –. H 1957.

GOAT-SCENTED TUTSAN *H. hircinum* L.
This is sometimes grown as a hedge, and can continue to do so after the owner has ceased to care for it, but neither this or the last are impressive as wild plants of Guernsey, although this one especially gets noticed with its fine flowers. Its leaves do not always smell of goat, when it can be told from the last by its deciduous sepals to the fruits. It comes from Central and Southern Europe. J ? A –. S –. H –.

ROSE OF SHARON *H. calycinum* L.
Dupuy pressed a specimen of this from Bonair in 1864, but Marquand said it grew only in places where it had been intentionally planted. It seems to be little grown in Guernsey even for ground cover, and the only other record of it is on dumped soil north of Vale Castle in 1970. The species was introduced from W. Turkey probably about 1676, and rarely if ever fruits in our climes, but can spread well vegetatively. The English name, which it shares with other plants, dates back no more than about a century – the species is not found in Palestine at all. It was Sir George Wheeler's Tutsan to Fairchild in 1722. J rare. A –. S –. H –.

COMMON ST JOHN'S-WORT *H. perforatum* L. Herbe à mille pertus
Now apparently rather scarce. Who is to say which species was – or were – known to Andros under this name in Tudor times? But Gosselin's specimens are clearly this one. J frequent. A –. S 1879. H –.

SQUARE-STALKED ST JOHN'S-WORT *H. tetrapterum* Fries
Occasional in wetter places. Gosselin's specimens came from his orchard at Glateny, where no marsh is now! J frequent. A frequent. S locally frequent. H rare.

TRAILING ST JOHN'S-WORT *H. humifusum* L.
To be seen in most parts of the island, but never in plenty and chiefly in the south. The var *decumbens* Petermann with glandular-ciliate sepals predominates and may indeed be the only one present: Gosselin's specimens from the Douit de l'Aumône are of this variety. Since such glands are often made the key character for separating this species from the next, it may be understood that much confusion has resulted. The var *ambiguum* Gillot is recorded from Petit Bot and may be another source for records of the next species. The name was intended to cover intermediates between the two. J frequent. A not infrequent. S occasional. H frequent.

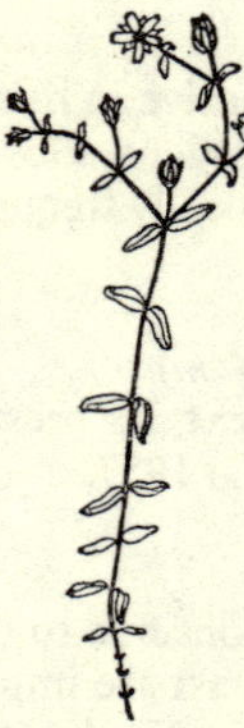

St John's-wort ×½

FLAX-LEAVED ST JOHN'S-WORT *H. linarifolium* Vahl
This has been claimed from the island on several occasions since 1845. But only three gatherings, by Miss Palmer in 1889 and Gray in 1894, both from Moulin Huet, and by Mrs Burridge from Les Sommeilleuses in 1973, seem to Dr Robson to match the true plant, with equal sepals and no pellucid glands in the leaves. But in 1971 Mrs Garrett collected specimens from a roadside bank south of Kings Mills, and in 1972 Mrs Burridge and Mrs Ryan some from near Corbière, which approach this very closely. Marquand's specimen from the south cliffs is just a narrow-leaved example of Common St John's-wort. Small erect plants still grow, but now very sparingly, on these warm cliffs, which might pardonably be taken by the wishful for this species. They are however intermediate to the last species, and are presumably the remains of an introgressed or hybrid swarm, and seem to have been more plentiful in the last century – in 1847 they were said to be all over the cliffs of the south coast. They were called *H.* × *caesariense* by Druce, but this name has never been properly published – see the note on it in *Hybridization and the Flora of the British Isles*, and Pugsley's comments in the *Journal of Botany* for 1914, p. 329, and 1915, pp. 162–70. Another name which has been used in this connection is var *approximatum* Rouy, but possibly var *ambiguum* of the last species is the most suitable. Flax-leaved is an erroneous (or clipped?) translation of the Latin epithet, which means Toadflax-leaved, but is now the established English nhme. J local. A rare. S claimed 1901. H –.

ELEGANT ST JOHN'S-WORT *H. pulchrum* L.
Beautiful, elegant indeed, a pleasure perhaps not always appreciated, but apparently not common now, and un-noted in the north. Gosselin collected it at La Contrée du Varclin. J frequent. A rare. S frequent. H 1838.

PALE ST JOHN'S-WORT *H. montanum* L.
Claimed by a Professorial botanist in 1879 from Icart, but with no corroboration. J collected 1926. A –. S –. H –.

MARSH ST JOHN'S-WORT *H. Elodes* L.
Now much diminished as suitable wet places diminish. J rare. A last record 1900. S –. H –.

PITTOSPORUM FAMILY Pittosporaceae

(A seedling of *Pittosporum tenuifolium* Gaertner, from New Zealand, was noticed on Herm in 1958; and of *P. crassifolium* Solander ex Putterl in Jersey in 1960.)

CAMELLIA FAMILY Theaceae

[Camellias (*Camellia japonica* L.) have been known since the early years of the last century to grow exceptionally well in Guernsey. Very old bushes with thick trunks can be seen in many a garden, their flowers a notable sight in the spring. Several varieties originated in the island. The Large Silver Medal was awarded to J. Priaulx by the Horticultural Society in London on 6 April 1841 for 'Marchioness of Exeter'. Other varieties came from the Caledonia Nursery, notably 'Lady de Saumarez', a sport of 'Tricolor' found by Jane Anne, Lady de Saumarez. Some came as seedlings in the 1870's from Belgium from L. van Houtte (1810–1876) but were named and distributed by this famous nursery. The International Camellia Conference visited Guernsey in 1973.]

ROCK-ROSE FAMILY Cistaceae

COMMON ROCK-ROSE *Helianthemum nummularium* (L.) Miller (*H. vulgare*).
Mr Field saw this in the middle of the last century near a house on Pleinmont. There have been two other claims since, but never a specimen. J –. A –. S –. H –,

(Annual Rock-rose, *Tuberaria guttata* (L.) Fourreau, is locally plentiful in Jersey and a small patch still exists in Alderney.)

TAMARISK FAMILY Tamaricaceae

TAMARISK *Tamarix* cf *gallica* L. Cypre. Tamariske.
Collected by Gosselin and much planted as a boundary shrub on the sandier soils, successfully persisting there and growing thick trunks. In 1862 it was remarked that it did not grow in the south-east, which is still largely true. It was also once used to make the bottoms of crab pots. But there is no sign of natural regeneration. These shrubs have a traditional place in the British flora, but hardly deserve it. The species are difficult to tell apart. J frequent. A occasional S rare. H occasional.

SEA-HEATH FAMILY Frankeniaceae

SEA-HEATH *Frankenia laevis* L.
This grew in the salt marshes bordering the Braye du Valle, and lingered on there

for half a century after it was drained – the last specimen is dated 1865 from Watson. A curious still unnamed tuft was collected as this in 1893 by Miss Dawber at Grandes Rocques, but it wasn't. It was presumably the plant growing in two sandy fields, shown by Derrick there to Marquand, who named it, although not in flower. Another erroneous claim was made in 1924. J rare. A rare. S –. H –.

WATER-WORT FAMILY Elatinaceae

WATER-WORT *Elatine hexandra* (Lapierre) DC
Noted for Guernsey in Ansted's list 1862, with no confirmation. J rare. A –. S –. H –.

PINK FAMILY Caryophyllaceae

BLADDER CAMPION *Silene vulgaris* (Moench) Garcke ssp *vulgaris* (*S. inflata*)
No record has been traced between Gosselin collecting it and Derrick reporting it a century later from ballast heaps, a long-extinct habitat. It is still very scarce indeed. J rare. A locally frequent. S Brechou. H –.

SEA CAMPION *S. maritima* Withering Eillet d'côti.
Collected by Gosselin 'le long des Banques', and still plentiful in many places round the coast, but local inland. On the cliffs of the south it is one of the glories of early summer. The smut *Ustilago violacea* Persoon sometimes infects it. Channel Island plants are discussed in *The Bladder Campions* by Marsden-Jones and Turrill, 1951. J common. A common. S common. H common.

MEDITERRANEAN SAND CATCHFLY *S. conoidea* L.
Gosselin sent seeds under this name to Sir J. Banks in 1792, but the specimens so labelled in his herbarium are of the next species, a similar error to that so long perpetuated in Jersey and Normandy. J 1923 only. A –. S –. H –.

SAND CATCHFLY *S. conica* L. ssp *conica*
Common no longer, but rather locally scattered in the sandy turf of the north. It was first found by Finlay about 1780 and first collected by Gosselin soon after. J locally plentiful. A locally frequent. S –. H –.

(Forked Catchfly, *S. dichotoma* Ehrhardt ssp *dichotoma*, was collected in Jersey in 1926 and recorded from Sark in 1902.)

SMALL-FLOWERED CATCHFLY *S. gallica* L. (incl. *S. anglica* and *S. quinquevulnera*)
A widespread but not very common plant occurring in three colour forms. The most frequent, also the dingiest, regrettably connected by Linnaeus with England, has been called var *anglica* (L.) Clapham. Next best is the var *gallica* with pink petals. These are usually pale and, being small, make small impact. In 1970 however two colonies were seen on L'Ancresse with Rose Madder petals (HCC 23/2), which were good enough for a garden border. But the best variety, also called a species by Linnaeus, but also probably really no more than a form, is var *quinquevulnera* (L.) Koch. For the increasing majority who know no Latin,

Variegated Catchfly ×½

it may be explained this means five wounds. The relevance is that at the base of each of the five petals, otherwise white, is a blotch of crimson, rich in the best forms, paler in others. The effect is unfailingly appealing. It is rather scarce – perhaps not in the south – but has been known since Gosselin's time. He called it Variegated Catchfly and collected it from a field near Albecq. J frequent. A frequent. S common. H occasional.

(*S. Armeria* L., *S. annulata* Thore, *S. Csereii* Baumgartner, *S. muscipula* L. and *S. pendula* L. have all been reported from Jersey.)

NOTTINGHAM CATCHFLY *S. nutans* L. ssp *nutans*
This is included in Gosselin's List, but his herbarium specimen clearly marks it as collected in Erm – as he always spelled it. Newbould claimed it from St Martin's in 1841/2, but there is no corroboration. There are specimens dated 1905 labelled Guernsey, but not by the collector. Herm and Guernsey plants have been confused before. But it is a strange absentee. J locally frequent. A rare. S 1902. H frequent.

NIGHT-SCENTED CATCHFLY *S. noctiflora* L.
This was listed by Ansted in 1862, but the record was stigmatised by Marquand as an error. Certain it is however that a few very fine plants of it appeared in a ley in the Câtel in 1968; almost certain is it too that it was seen in the Vale in 1966. J collected 1926. A –. S –. H –.

RED CAMPION *S. dioica* (L.) Clairville (*Lychnis diurna*. *Melandrium rubrum*) Violette d'Fossaï. Violette sauvage. Violette à Vée
Happily still generally common, its pink a part of the early summer glory of the southern cliffs. Occasional plants have pale pink flowers and paler foliage, or white flowers. In 1945 a plant was reported from Les Hubits with very small flowers; and one in 1946 with white flowers on one branch and red on the other, all staminate. Its local English name is Soldiers' Fleas, from the black spots this plant sometimes shows as a result of anther smut in its flowers. J common. A rare. S common. H common.

WHITE CAMPION *S. alba* (Miller) E. H. L. Krause (*Lychnis vespertina*)
Very rare to Marquand, and still very rare, although it was reported to be becoming frequent in 1894/5 and getting more common in 1923. There have been only three records since. J occasional. A occasional. S occasional. H occasional.

HYBRID CAMPION *S.* × *intermedia* (Schur) Druce (*S. alba* × *S. dioica*)
It is not easy to be sure of this hybrid, when Red Campion can vary, especially in flower colour. Druce recorded it in 1906, and likely examples were collected in 1970 and 1971, without the white parent being observed; and it has been claimed in between. J rare. A common. S occasional. H rare.

RAGGED ROBIN *Lychnis Flos-cuculi* L. Violette au Vaër
Not as plentiful as it used to be, but still fairly frequent. It was first collected by Gosselin. Plants have been seen with white flowers. Vaër in Guernsey-French means worm – perhaps in allusion to the narrow pink petals. J common. A occasional. S –. H –.

ROSE CAMPION *L. Coronaria* (L.) Desrousseaux
This Southern-European garden perennial was seen as an outcast at Bordeaux in 1973. J casual. A –. S –. H –.

(*L. pyrenaica* Bergeret has also been recorded as a casual in Jersey.)

CORN COCKLE *Agrostemma Githago* L. (*Lychnis Githago*) Rose d'Tchen
Gosselin's specimens and first list indicate this was not uncommon in his day, but by Marquand's it was rare, although it was said to be abundant in 1902 in a heavy crop of vetches in Mount Durand, and on L'Ancresse in 1931. All the same, the final record was only three years later. J casual. A last record 1932. S last record 1902. H –.

(Berry Catchfly, *Cucubalus baccifer* L., was collected in 1930 in Jersey.)

DEPTFORD PINK *Dianthus Armeria* L. ssp *Armeria*
This was collected by Newbould near St Peter Port in 1841, perhaps from the same area where M. English found four plants in 1957, 37 in 1958 – the cliff north of Fermain Bay. It is also on L'Ancresse near the Doyle Rock, a semi-prostrate ecotype according to E. A. Ellis who first found it here. J rare. A last record 1900. S rare. H –.

CLOVE PINK *D. Caryophyllus* L. Eillet
Carnations are grown as a greenhouse crop, and discarded plants or slips may survive outside. There have been three such records recently, but the plants never get naturalised, as they have across the water on Mont St Michel. J last seen in 1950's. A –. S –. H –.

MAIDEN PINK *D. deltoides* L.
Found by H. Nicolle in 1968 established by the cliff path near Icart. The source was, unknown to its new owner, the adjoining garden, where it had also settled into the lawn. It has in addition been reported from the cliffs at Torteval. J last seen in 1960's. A –. S 1953. H –.

(Jersey Pink, *D. gallicus* Persoon, has been known in St Ouen's Bay, Jersey, since 1897. *D. plumarius* L. has been recorded: *D. Carthusianorum* L. is an error there.)

(Childling Pink, *Petrorhagia Nanteulii* (Burnat) Ball & Heywood (*Dianthus prolifer*), is plentiful in St Ouen's Bay, Jersey.)

COW BASIL *Vaccaria hispanica* (Miller) Räuschel (*Saponaria Vaccaria*)
Found in 1900, possibly from grain, in which it is likely to have occurred since

unobserved before 1971, when Lady Anne Brewis saw it at St Sampson's tip. But it is also grown as an annual in gardens. J casual. A –. S –. H –.

SOAPWORT *Saponaria officinalis* L.
Marquand knew the double form of this (Bouncing Bet) by 1891 over-running a low hedge near Cobo, but later wrote that it had no title to a place in the Guernsey list. Yet this is just how it so often appears, and is in fact firmly established, for its roots run deep and far. Unknown to him, it had been recorded earlier by Newbould from the then new Doyle Column. It has been seen since in four or five other places, usually with single flowers. Gosselin grew it over two hundred years ago, noting that it would flower under trees. J occasional. A rare. S rare. H rare.

DUSTY MILLER *Cerastium tomentosum* L.
To be seen occasionally established on dry banks, but all its records need clarifying with the next species, which seems less variable. J aggregate local. A –. S recorded. H –.

SNOW-IN-SUMMER *C. Biebersteinii* DC
Also recorded, but before the days when the two species could be told apart with any certainty. This one tends to be robuster and erecter. Its leaves are larger, more white-felted, and blunter at the tip, the petals less deeply notched and the seeds larger – 2mm instead of 1.6mm, for those who can measure this. It is often said this has the teeth of the capsule erect, while the last species has them curled back, but this cannot be relied on. Most established plants seem to fall between these two sets of characters, and only a chromosome count can settle to which they belong, or if they are fertile hybrids, for all plants seem to produce seed. This species has $2n = 36$, while the last is tetraploid, $2n = 72$. J probably occurs. A recorded. S –. H –.

(There is a specimen of Field Mouse-ear, *C. arvense* L. ssp *arvense*, from Jersey dated 1932, but the collector was not always reliable in his labels.)

COMMON MOUSE-EAR *C. holosteoides* Fries (*C. triviale*)
Common indeed. The annual var *pentandrum* Syme was noted from Petit Bot in 1907. J common. A common. S common. H common.

STICKY MOUSE-EAR *C. glomeratum* Thuillier
Also common. Its petals can look whiter and make the plant relatively showy. This is another self-fertilised species. J common. A frequent. S common. H frequent.

DARK MOUSE-EAR *C. diffusum* Persoon ssp *diffusum* (*C. tetrandrum*)
Quite common – nearly always near the coast. J locally common. A common. S rare. H common.

LITTLE MOUSE-EAR *C. semidecandrum* L. ssp *semidecandrum*
Probably quite plentiful on the sandhills of the north and west, and has been noted from the south cliffs. But it dries up quickly and eludes most observers, many of whom anyway do not know how to tell it. J locally frequent. A frequent. S misclaimed. H frequent.

(Water Chickweed, *Myosoton aquaticum* (L.) Moench, has been in Jersey since 1965.)

COMMON CHICKWEED *Stellaria media* (L.) Villars ssp *media* Moudräon
Common. Gosselin was the first to list and collect this. J common. A common. S common. H common.

(Wood Chickweed, *S. nemorum* L. ssp. *nemorum*, has been recorded from Jersey.)

LESSER CHICKWEED *S. pallida* (Dumortier) Piré (*S. Boraeana*. *S. apetala*)
Occasionally luxuriant in sheltered sandy places; probably locally plentiful, but no doubt under-recorded, as it is an early plant which may soon shrivel. J frequent. A rare. S rare. H occasional.

(Greater Chickweed, *S. neglecta* Weihe, has been claimed, probably erroneously, from Jersey. Greater Stitchwort, *S. holostea* L., common in England, Normandy and Jersey, is unrecorded elsewhere in the Archipelago. Marsh Stitchwort, *S. palustris* Retzius, was collected in 1926 in Jersey.)

LESSER STITCHWORT *S. graminea* L.
Very rare. Gosselin listed it, but his specimens are of Bog Stitchwort and Dwarf Chickweed, so did Carré without a specimen. Nothing more was known for 53 years, when Miss Dawber found it near Ozanne's Mill. The area there is still suitable for it, indeed it seems wrong it is missing from such a collection of typical associates, but so it is. However it did turn up in 1970 nearly 1½ miles to the west in the Rue des Buttes St Andrew's, found by A. Silverside, a small patch atop the east bank. J frequent. A rare. S last record, Brechou 1902. H –.

BOG STITCHWORT *S. Alsine* Grimm (*S. uliginosa*)
Like most other plants of wet places, less common and indeed now rather local. But it seems often not to be noticed, so may be under-recorded. Gosselin collected it in the Vauquiédor. J frequent. A –. S rare. H rare.

(*Holosteum umbellatum* L. was collected in 1924 in Jersey.)

DWARF CHICKWEED *Moenchia erecta* (L.) Gaertner, Meyer & Scherbius ssp *erecta*
Locally common round much of the coast, but another plant needing practised eyes to spot, and so missed by many who would appreciate its special charm. There is no record of it inland this century. Gosselin was the first to collect it. J common. A rare. S locally common. H local.

FRINGED PEARLWORT *Sagina apetala* Arduino ssp *apetala* (*S. ciliata*)
The nomenclature of these weedy annuals has gone topsy-turvy in recent years. That the number of them treated as species should be reduced was fair enough, and indeed that the two main groups should be lumped under one major species probably represents the facts better, for the two are self-fertilising (which helps perpetuate variation) and have been on occasions hard to tell apart. But unfortunately the Latin names have been reversed, so care is needed in using them. This subspecies is the one which usually has the sepals appressed to the ripe fruit and seems about as common as the next. The earliest record, by Newbould, antedates Marquand's by a half century. J probably uncommon. A frequent. S occasional. H occasional.

ANNUAL PEARLWORT *S. apetala* Arduino ssp *erecta* (Hornemann) Hermann (*S.* '*apetala*')
This is the one with the sepals usually spreading away from the ripe fruit. It seems about as common in Guernsey. J probably common. A frequent. S occasional. H common.

SEA PEARLWORT *S. maritima* G. Don
Quite frequent round the coast, with a neat firm often glossy character all its own, often enhanced by purple stalks. J locally frequent. A occasional. S occasional. H frequent.

MOSSY PEARLWORT *S. procumbens* L. ssp *procumbens*
Common, and even in Guernsey in some lawns. J common. A frequent. S frequent. H common.

HEATH PEARLWORT *S. subulata* (Swartz) C. Presl
Seems scarce, but no doubt overlooked, especially when growing ¼ inch high in tight tufts on the cliffs, its fine flowers not open. J local. A occasional. S occasional. H local.

KNOTTED PEARLWORT *S. nodosa* (L.) Fenzl
Little recorded since the *Flora*, and no longer 'generally plentiful where it occurs'. Babington's own copy of his *Flora* adds Petit Bot Bay etc, and Jerbourg on the authority of Newbould. J collected 1925. A occasional. S recorded. H –.

(Fine-leaved Sandwort, *Minuartia hybrida* (Villars) Schischkin, occurs rarely in Jersey.)

SEA SANDWORT *Honkenya peploides* (L.) Ehrhardt
Inevitably scarcer as the beaches get ever more used, but still to be seen in many places on the sandy coasts. Gosselin got it at Vazon. J locally plentiful. A frequent. S last record 1872. H last record 1899.

(Three-veined Sandwort, *Moehringia trinervia* (L.) Clairvaux, is frequent in Jersey.)

THYME-LEAVED SANDWORT *Arenaria serpyllifolia* L.
Quite frequent but apparently not in the south. Gosselin's specimens are of the next species. Dwarf forms from L'Ancresse with stalked glands were thought to be near var *viscidula* Roth by N. D. Simpson. He also collected the var *macrocarpa* Lloyd (*A. Lloydii*) from Vazon and the Doyle Rock in 1923 and 1949, but even he has failed to refind it. It has flower stalks shorter than the sepals and, as the name says, large fruits. J frequent. A common. A 1879. H common.

SLENDER THYME-LEAVED SANDWORT *A. leptoclados* (Reichenbach) Gussone
Possibly very uncommon, certainly very little noted – Marquand knew it was in Alderney – but this is another plant not discriminated by many. Gosselin collected it unawares. J probably frequent. A occasional. S –. H 1950.

(Mossy Sandwort, *A. balearica* L., has been recorded in Jersey.)

SPURREY *Spergula arvensis* L. Genouollère
A common weed in light soils, its pollen detected in the Vazon peat. In Guernsey and Jersey the var *nana* E. F. Linton (cf *Journal of Botany* 1907, p. 380) is fre-

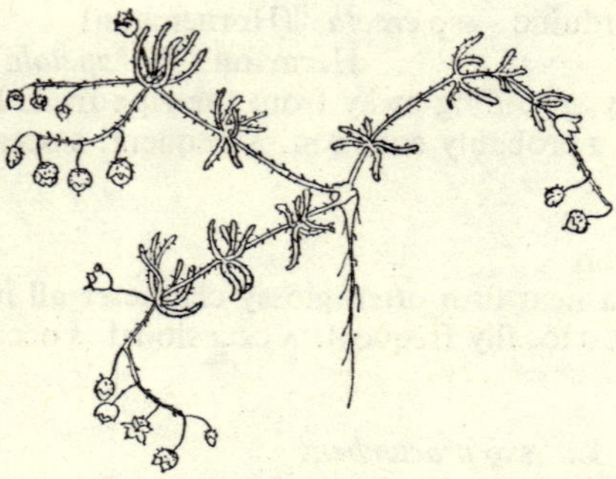

Dwarf Spurrey ×1

quent. Typically this is dwarf, as its name implies, spreading sideways and never erect, it flowers earlier and soon withers (while the common weedy form lasts the summer through), and it grows in such native habitats as the turf of the sandy commons (where it can bespangle the turf like the Milky Way, and has a sweet scent as well) and the southern cliffs. It suggests an ancestral strain from which the widespread weed developed. In its extreme form, it is quite distinct, and comes true from seed, but from hybridisation or other causes, it will be found merging into the common form with no clear dividing line of habit or habitat. It is figured on Plate 15 of Vol. III of the *Cambridge British Flora* of 1920. Gosselin collected it too, and noted its distinctness as 'var β'. J common. A occasional. S common. H frequent.

SAND SPURREY *Spergularia rubra* (L.) J. & C. Presl (*Lepigonum rubrum*)
Fairly frequent in drier sandy or gravelly places. J frequent. A occasional. S occasional. H 1957.

GREEK SAND SPURREY *S. Bocconii* (Scheele) Ascherson & Graebner (*S. atheniensis*)
Apparently always in ruderal localities, i.e. track sides and waste places, and consequently likely to be an introduction from south-west Europe, where its headquarters are. Furthermore it seems to have been unnoticed and uncollected

Greek Sand Spurrey ×1

until 13 August, 1912 (by Barton), and then not again until 1953. Nevertheless those who recognise its smaller, shorter-stalked flowers than the last species and often much longer, curving, fruiting spikes will find it in several parts of the island. The name of the Sicilian Dr P. Boccone (1633–1703) is spelt differently in this plant and in his clover. J rarely recorded. A –. S –. H –.

CLIFF SPURREY *S. rupicola* Lebel ex Le Jolis (*Lepigonum rupestre*)
The first published record of this plant for the British Isles was made by Syme from Guernsey in 1857, when it was soon realised to be the commonest species there. In fact however Gosselin had collected specimens of it, mixing them with others of Sand and Sea Spurrey; and Babington had it in his herbarium too, the second time under the name of '*S. marina/rubra*' and it was also collected in 1846. It may sometimes be seen inland. J common. A common. S common. H common.

SEA SPURREY *S. marina* (L.) Grisebach (*S. neglecta*. *Lepigonum salinum*)
Scarce, and its scarcity intensified by the reduction in suitable brackish or saline ground. Nevertheless it has been seen recently in at least six different places in the north and west, if never in much quantity. J very locally plentiful. A –. S error. H claimed 1879.

(Greater Sea Spurrey, *S. media* (L.) C. Presl (*S. marginata*), was collected in 1926 in Jersey; and two hybrids have been recorded, *S. Bocconii* × *S. marina*, and *S. media* × *S. marina*, which, Dr Ratter says, will have been winged-seeded *marina* or wingless *media*: the latter hybrid has never been successfully made.)

GUERNSEY CHICKWEED *Polycarpon tetraphyllum* (L.) L.
The apt English name was coined by Lady Anne Brewis in 1969 and is much to be preferred to Four-leaved All-seed, the direct translation of the Graeco-Latin name, which has been used hitherto. It is very rare in Britain, but here very common in all sorts of places, varying in mien with its habitat and its nourishment. Indeed the exuberant weeds of cultivated ground seem to have little in common with the compact or thin plants of close dry turf, except of course that their floral characters are identical. *Flora Europaea* says this species has its leaves not purple-tinged and inflorescence lax, spreading with many conspicuous

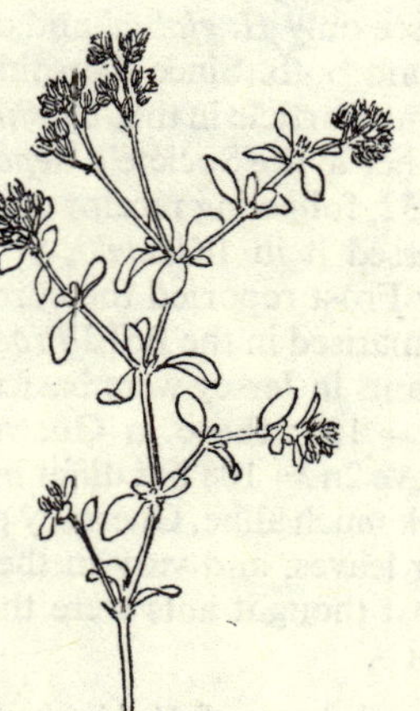

Guernsey Chickweed ×1

branches. It contrasts this with *P. diphyllum*, which has stems usually simple, leaves paired, rarely whorled and often purplish tinged, and inflorescence condensed, few-flowered without conspicuous branches. There is a specimen at Kew collected by Gray in 1894 labelled *P. diphyllum* (and another from Jersey), but there is in fact every intermediate between these sets of characters. N. D. Simpson, who knew *P. diphyllum* in Egypt, pounced in 1968 on the colony on the hot bank just south of the Vale church as this, but soon saw that it was no more than starved forms of *P. tetraphyllum*. If *P. diphyllum* is a good taxon elsewhere, it is not recognisable as such in Guernsey – compare Pugsley's note on p. 329 of the *Journal of Botany* for 1914. The first record is a manuscript note by Lightfoot in his copy of Hudson's *Flora Anglica* at Oxford; 'In the Island of Guernsey under the walls at the Foot of the Breast Works near the Town, just by the Sea side'. J common. A frequent. S common. H common.

TWO-LEAVED ALL-SEED *P. diphyllum* Cavanilles
The only firm record for this is, as stated above, Gray's specimen of 1894. But there seems little doubt that all the plants in Guernsey are forms of the last species. J claimed. A –. S –. H –.

CORAL NECKLACE FAMILY Illecebraceae

(Strapwort, *Corrigiola littoralis* L., has been recorded from Jersey.)

SMOOTH RUPTUREWORT *Herniaria glabra* L.
As explained below, the species were misunderstood in the past and all the numerous records for this one, however augustly made, are misidentifications of the next one. J similar error. A –. S –. H –.

FRINGED RUPTUREWORT *H. ciliolata* Melderis ssp *ciliolata* (*H. ciliata*)
Its green mats are still to be seen in the sandy turf of the north and west, but rarely in much plenty – Marquand described it in 1905 as carpeting the ground in places at Vazon, where hardly any survives at all. Specimens exist collected in 1951 and labelled from Fermain and St Sampson's. All the plants from Guernsey belong to this species, which was not separated from *H. glabra* until 1836. Yet Babington only a year or two later recorded both species, Watson wrote that he could 'see only *H. glabra*' and even Marquand managed to convince himself he had found both. Since then this species has been much examined. Pugsley came first in an article in the *Journal of Botany* in 1914, pp. 330–2. Then Dovaston wrote another in the Société's *Report* for 1939, and Dr K. B. Blackburn more in that for 1952, following receipt of specimens from P. Girard. Dr A. Melderis in 1957 discussed it in *Watsonia*, pp. 42–3, and showed it needed a new name. Finally Dr Frost reported the chromosome numbers in 1964, and in 1966 in a paper summarised in the BSBI *Proceedings* for that year, pp. 368–9. This showed that the plants in Jersey were basically different from those elsewhere in Britain, having $2n = 108$: those in Guernsey and Alderney have $2n = 72$. Those in Brittany have $2n = 108$ but differ in being self-fertilising. The two in the Channel Islands look much alike, Guernsey plants having thicker stems and broader sometimes paler leaves, and vary in the degree and distribution of the hairs on the leaves. Frost thought ants were the main pollinating agents. J rare. A last seen 1956. S –. H –.

(There is a specimen of *H. hirsuta* L. from Jersey collected in 1876.)

KNAWEL *Scleranthus annuus* L.
Four records only in nearly 200 years – Gosselin, Babington, Hillhouse 1881 and Derrick 1904. Such apparent extreme rarity is hard to understand, when there seems suitable ground – it has been collected in cornfields and on the south cliffs. It is in all the other main islands and is common in Brittany. J occasional. A rare. S common. H local.

(Coral Necklace, *Illecebrum verticillatum* L., is shown for all the Channel Islands on the map on page 762 of Vol. III (2) of Hegi's *Flora von Mittel-Europa* 1961, maybe in reference to the specimen collected in 1926 in Jersey.)

PURSLANE FAMILY Portulacaceae

BLINKS *Montia fontana* L.
The most satisfactory way to group the forms of this variable species was settled, so far as the British Isles were concerned, only in 1953 when Dr S. M. Walters published his paper *Montia fontana* in *Watsonia* 3 (1), pp. 1–6. This showed that the only character that remained constant was the nature of the seed coat, to which he gives a whole page of illustrations. Because of previous bewilderment, only records interpreted by this paper can be relied on. The plants in the Channel Islands, many of which have been seen by Dr Walters, group themselves into three. One is ssp *amporitana* Sennen (*intermedia*) with seeds finely tuberculate at the edge and rather shiny. This had been collected by Gosselin and, much later, at Mont Cuet and east of Petit Bot. The next is ssp *chondrosperma* (Fenzl) S. M. Walters which has, as its specific epithet implies, its seeds covered with gritty tubercles, and dull. This was at Pleinmont in 1885 and L'Ancrosse in 1949. Last is the prevailing one quite frequent in Guernsey, in which the seeds are intermediate between the other two – there is no name for this group. Both the other sub-species, *fontana* and *variabilis* S. M. Walters (*rivularis*) have been claimed, but the claims lack proof, and indeed these two are not so likely to occur. J common. A occasional. S frequent. H occasional.

BUTTON-HOLE PLANT *Montia perfoliata* (Donn ex Willdenow) Howell (*Claytonia perfoliata*)
This seems the neatest English name, but elsewhere it is called, as in Western North America, whence it hails, Spring Beauty or, more originally Miner's Lettuce, for it was eaten by the gold diggers. Its first record was in 1929. It came from Miss Walker, whose family lived at La Favorita, now a hotel, at Fermain. No specimen survives. Visit her garden now, and the plant to be seen there is the next species, which also has a pair of perfoliate leaves, which suggests an error. But in 1970 undoubted plants of this species were seen in no less than four places elsewhere and in a fifth in 1971. That one of these was on dumped soil (where it was plentiful in 1973), suggests a source as yet untraced. Since another was, just, in the Caledonia nursery, this suggests it may get to other gardens. J locally plentiful. A –. S –. H Jethou 1956.

PINK PURSLANE *M. sibirica* (L.) Howell
Miss D. Mauger brought this North American, and Siberian, plant from St Martin's in 1969, from the Fort Road. The place proved to be near La Favorita, where it may have been thirty years before – compare the last species. Later Miss N. Hichens found it as a weed in another nearby garden. It has been planted recently in several others and may be expected to spread. J rare. A –. S –. H –.

POT PURSLANE *Portulaca oleracea* L. ssp *oleracea*
This has been known in a garden at L'Islet for many years where it is regularly weeded, and survives. It appeared also in two others at Four Cabot in 1969/70 source unknown. It comes from farther south in Europe, where it may be grown as a vegetable – hence its specific epithet. J frequent. A –. S –. H –.

Pot Purslane $\times \frac{2}{3}$

Sea Fig $\times \frac{1}{3}$

(Red Maids, *Calindrinia ciliata* (Ruiz & Pavon) DC, a Californian annual, was in an arable field in Sark in 1957 and a garden weed in Jersey in 1970.)

MESEMBRYANTHEMUM FAMILY Aizoaceae

KAFFIR FIG *Carpobrotus edulis* (L.) N. E. Brown
This is likely to grow into thick heavy mats wherever it is planted (which it still frequently is), especially near the sea. Fruit is produced, which has been eaten locally, but it is not known if it is fertile: no seedlings have been noted. It must however be regarded as naturalised for it flows over cliffs and sandy stretches submerging lesser vegetation in its path. Native plants get their chance after hard winters, when this South African species may be largely killed by frost. So far most clumps have retained life in at least a few shoots, and these have proved enough for it to regain its lost ground quite quickly. Its flowers are perhaps more often yellow than pink, which was the colour chosen for its depiction on the 7½p postage stamp of 1972. MacCulloch wrote in 1826 that Mesembryanthemums were fully hardy, but did not specify which; nor did Carré in 1862 when he remarked that many species were grown and some of them were very hardy. Marquand does not mention this family in his *Flora*, and even in 1913 implied none existed. Yet he had told in print an inquiring visitor in 1886 that it was known in a semi-wild state. Another visitor, Green, had recorded it in print in 1893. J locally frequent. A killed out 1962/3? S –. H –.

SEA FIG *C. glaucescens* (Haworth) Schwantes
This was first noticed in Guernsey by Miss Elliott at Fontenelle Bay in 1970 and was named by Dr S. T. Blake of the Queensland Herbarium. It differs in its smaller, always pink, flowers with smaller leaves. It has been planted elsewhere where it will very likely persist, for example at Jerbourg. It comes from Eastern Australia, but the species are difficult to discriminate and the name is not absolutely certain. J rare. A occasional. S –. H local.

LAMPRANTHUS *Lampranthus roseus* (Willdenow) Schwantes
A bushy South African plant, of a group hard to name. This one was collected from the cliffs by the Bec du Nez by Hon. R. Palmer in 1971, where it is difficult of access; and from the cliffs by Le Gouffre by J. Bichard in 1972. They were named by Dr J. Rourke at Kirstenbosch. Similar plants were by Fort Pezeries for several years until 1973. J –. A –. S –. H –.

APTENIA *Aptenia cordifolia* (L.f) N. E. Brown
This South African is presumably what Mrs McCrea called '*Mesembryanthemum* var *cordifolia*' which she found at the crossroads near the Vale church in 1928. No specimen survives. But one does from Richmond in 1973, collected by Mrs Ryan. Here it proved to have sown itself in the walls and in the vegetable patch for a very long time. J lost 1962. A –. S –. H –.

DROSANTHEMUM *Drosanthemum floribundum* (Haworth) Schwantes
This grows happily on an old gun emplacement in Belle Grève Bay, first noticed in 1970 by Cdr Annett. J rare. A –. S –. H –.

(*Disphyma crassifolium* (L.) L. Bolus grows in Jersey.)

NEW ZEALAND SPINACH *Tetragonia tetragonoides* (Pallas) Kuntze
Reported in 1913. This too rarely grown vegetable from the Antipodes can sow itself in light soils. J casual. A –. S –. H –.

Lampranthus × ½

Marvel of Peru × ⅓

MIRABILIS FAMILY Nyctaginaceae

MARVEL OF PERU *Mirabilis Jalapa* L.
Happily a long-tolerated weed in the garden of Adm. and Mrs de Jersey at Côte des Vardes. It has also been collected on rubbish heaps elsewhere, for it is sown and grown in other gardens. Gosselin grew it in his in 1767. J rare. A –. S –. H –.

PIGWEED FAMILY Amaranthaceae

COMMON PIGWEED *Amaranthus retroflexus* L.
Surprisingly the only records are from Vazon in 1952 by Dr Bowen and from St Peter's in 1971 – but Pigweeds are unexpectedly rare in Guernsey. This is a universal weed which probably originated in North America. J frequent. A 1957. S 1898. H 1958.

WHITE PIGWEED *A. albus* L.
One plant collected at Les Hubits in 1958, a native of Central North America, first seen in Europe about 1880. J collected 1927. A –. S –. H –.

PERENNIAL PIGWEED *A. deflexus* L.
Quite well established round the Vale Power Station at St Sampson's first noticed in 1970 by Mrs S. C. Holland. It is another pan-tropic weed, spreading in Brittany. J local. A –. S –. H –.

Perennial Pigweed ×½

GREY PIGWEED *A. lividus* L.
Yet another pan-tropical weed, this one found persisting in a greenhouse in Barras Lane in 1970 by Miss Elliott. All CI Pigweeds have been seen by Mr Brenan. J –. A –. S –. H –.

(The following have been collected only from Jersey – *A. acutilobus* Uline & Bray, in 1928, its only British record; *A. caudatus* L.; *A. graecizans* L. ssp *sylvestris* (Villars) Brenan; *A. hybridus* L. ssp *hybridus* and ssp *incurvatus* (Timeroy, ex Grenier & Godron) Brenan and *A. spinosus* L.)

(Cockscomb, *Celosia cristata* L., was collected in Jersey in 1931.)

GOOSEFOOT FAMILY Chenopodiaceae

GOOD KING HENRY *Chenopodium Bonus-henricus* L.
This appears in Gosselin's first manuscript list from Belle Grève Bay, but his specimen so labelled from there is an Orache. J last record 1932. A –. S –. H –.

MANY-SEEDED GOOSEFOOT *C. polyspermum* L.
Frequent. Collected by Gosselin as a garden weed. J frequent. A rare. S occasional. H occasional.

STINKING GOOSEFOOT *C. Vulvaria* L. Bllanche S'nile.
Recorded by Gosselin, Babington, Newbould and Blow before Marquand's *Flora* said it was not uncommon, sometimes occurring in plenty from Cobo to L'Ancresse – it had also been seen at St Peter Port, L'Erée, Rocquaine and Bordeaux. Yet since 1906 there have been only four records for this plant, unobvious to the unknowing until it is touched – the cloying odour is said to come from trimethylamine – and only one place is currently known for it. Gosselin's plant came from Vazon. J rare. A errors? S –. H last record 1899.

FAT HEN *C. album* L. ssp *album* Snile. Nère S'nile.
A notoriously variable plant, originally collected by Gosselin, as 'an Arrach', common wherever it gets a chance. J common. A common. S frequent. H frequent.

GREEN GOOSEFOOT *C. suecicum* J. Murr (*C. viride*)
Perhaps this is what Marquand intended by his variety *viride* of the last species. There is no specimen. J claimed. A –. S –. H –.

GREY GOOSEFOOT *C. opulifolium* Schrader ex Koch & Ziz.
A casual with records only in 1906 and 1953. J last collected 1928. A 1906. S –. H –.

FIG-LEAVED GOOSEFOOT *C. ficifolium* Smith
Quite common, but by no means always recognised. J rare. A rare. S –. H –.

NETTLE-LEAVED GOOSEFOOT *C. murale* L.
Nearly as common as Fat Hen, and also collected by Gosselin. It not infrequently overwinters and can be found in flower at any time. J common. A frequent. S occasional. H occasional.

SOWBANE *C. hybridum* L.
Listed by Gosselin, but his specimen is of Halberd-leaved Orache; and claimed in 1971, without a specimen. J last record 1924. A –. S –. H –.

RED GOOSEFOOT *C. rubrum* L.
Usually uncommon, but locally plentiful in some years. The fruits of either this species or the next were very abundant in the Vazon peat. J rare. A –. S 1874. H –.

SMALL RED GOOSEFOOT *C. botryodes* Smith
Still very rare, but still on Lihou with the last species. It needs much skill to tell the two apart, but the smaller less toothed leaves of this one are a starting clue. J last record 1920. A –. S –. H –.

OAK-LEAVED GOOSEFOOT *C. glaucum* L.
Not recorded since 1906. Indeed the only previous record, from Watson in 1865, is of an unusual form with long almost entire leaves and an interrupted flower spike. J last collected 1928. A –. S –. H –.

(There are records from Jersey of *C. ambrosioides* L. (1929); *C. Botrys* L. (1902); *C. foliosum* Ascherson (1927); *C. Probstii* Aellen (1930); *C. Schraderanum* Schultes (1929) and, almost certainly erroneously, *C. urbicum* L.)

SEA BEET *Beta vulgaris L.* ssp *maritima* (L.) Arcangeli Bette d'Banque
'Grows by the sea shore all round the island', as Gosselin wrote on the back of his herbarium sheet of this, some 60 years after Knowlton had reported 'Sea-beats' from Fermain. Plants inland may be relics of Mangold or vegetable growing and so of the ssp *vulgaris.* At one time seed for this was specially grown on from selected plants. In 1859 Mangolds, then a principal and heavily manured crop, were expected to yield 40–50 tons per acre. J common. A frequent. S common. H frequent.

GRASS-LEAVED ORACHE *Atriplex littoralis* L. (incl. *A. marina*)
Apparently very local now, and mostly by Rocquaine Bay. J 1926. A rare. S –. H –.

COMMON ORACHE *A. patula* L.
Common and variable. Collected by Gosselin. J occasional. A occasional. S frequent. H frequent.

HALBERD-LEAVED ORACHE *A. triangularis* Willdenow (*A. deltoidea. A. 'hastata'*) Platte S'nile
Also common, also variable, also collected by Gosselin – as Sowbane. J common. A frequent. S occasional. H frequent.

BABINGTON'S ORACHE *A. glabriuscula* Edmondston (*A. Babingtonii. A. 'rosea'*)
Babington wrote in his diary on 22 August 1837: 'gathered an *Atriplex* probably undescribed, which I have named *stricta*, in a potato field (near) Fort George'. This, and what he called *A. rosea* and had collected on Herm the day before, both belong to this species. It can have a jizz all on its own; but it can also be almost impossible to separate from the last one. Indeed it is doubtful if it should be treated as more than a form of it, or at best a subspecies. It is rather local. J local. A occasional. S rare. H scarce.

FROSTED ORACHE *A. laciniata* L. (*A. farinosa*)
That near contradiction in terms, a pretty Orache – for such this can be with its rich pink stems setting off its silvery leaves – is to be seen locally on the sandy coasts. Gosselin collected it before Babington, whom Marquand credits with the first record, was born. J local. A frequent. S last record 1892. H last record 1893.

GARDEN ORACHE *A. hortensis* L.
Twice recorded in 1970, having presumably come from a garden or garden seed – one was a seedling; and there were a score of plants on the shingle bank at L'Erée in 1971. All these have been of the beetroot-red var *rubra* (L.) Roth, cultivated since Tudor times. J rare casual. A –. S –. H –.

TREE PURSLANE *A. Halimus* L.
Although this S. European shrub has been recorded since only 1926, it hardly justifies a place in the Island's wild flora, for it is never better than an occasional hedging shrub which may outlast its original purpose. Gosselin knew it in 1767 and propagated it by cuttings. J frequent and fine. A –. S –. H –.

SEA PURSLANE *Halimione portulacoides* (L.) Aellen (*Obione portulacoides*)
Gosselin does not say where he knew this plant, of which no specimen of his

survives – very likely the Braye du Valle – but all the localised records – and there were none until 1889 – were from the south cliffs, except one from L'Erée and one from the Château de Rocquaine. These steep, warm, well-drained slopes are a very different habitat from the normal sloshy sea mud, and it remains to be seen if these thriving colonies differ in other ways too. They are to be seen thus at intervals from Pleinmont to Jerbourg and may even reach to near the top, 175 feet above the sea, e.g. at Mont Hérault. In 1972 it appeared in a more usual habitat, by the pond at Pulias. Was this what Knowlton recorded in 1726 from the saltpans as *Kali cymosum*? J local. A rare. S –. H –.

COMMON SEABLITE *Suaeda maritima* (L.) Dumortier
Not at all common and rarely in much quantity, but recently seen in over half a dozen places in the north. Gosselin collected it at the Braye du Valle. It could have been what Knowlton in 1726 there called *Kali caule purpureo*. J local. A –. S –. H –.

SHRUBBY SEABLITE *S. vera* J. F. Gmelin (*S. "fruticosa"*)
The only definite record is by Druce in 1877 'growing sparingly by the side of St Sampson's saltpans'. There is a specimen in support. But Carré had reported it to a disbelieving Babington in the 1830s. J last collected 1928. A –. S –. H –.

SALTWORT *Salsola Kali* L. ssp *Kali*
Gosselin collected this and knew it at Vazon, L'Ancresse and on sandy sea shores, which implies it was not infrequent. Marquand called it rare, but now it is thoroughly rare. Indeed there have been only two unequivocal records for it since 1939, one at L'Ancresse in 1966, and a dozen plants in Rocquaine Bay in 1972. J local. A occasional. S 1838. H rare.

(There is a specimen of *S. Kali* L. ssp *ruthenica* (Iljin) Soó collected in 1928 from Jersey.)

COMMON GLASSWORT *Salicornia europaea* L. (*S. herbacea*)
This name covered all, or most of, the records of Glassworts until not long ago; and even now there is no unanimity how to classify them. Furthermore they are difficult to dry recognisably. Gosselin collected this one from the Braye du Valle, but Marquand's records may all belong to the next or another species. The only good current one for this was made by Hon. L. Palmer in 1969 from the Claire Mare, confirmed by Prof. T. G. Tutin. J rare. A –. S –. H –.

PROSTRATE GLASSWORT *S. ramosissima* Woods
It may well be that the plants Marquand noted as var *procumbens* and var *patula* belong here. It has been seen in recent years, and named by Prof. Tutin, only by the Vale Pond, by the pond at Pulias, on Lihou and by the Rousse Mare, but never in plenty – the extent of suitable habitat limits it. J last claim 1925. A –. S –. H –.

(Poke-weed, *Phytolacca americana* L., – Phytolaccaceae – grows in Jersey.)

LIME-TREE FAMILY Tiliaceae

SMALL-LEAVED LIME *Tilia cordata* Miller
The pollen of this has been recorded from Catioroc, and of an unnamed Lime from Vazon. But it seems nowadays not even to be planted. J –. A –. S –. H –.

COMMON LIME *T. vulgaris* Hayne
Planted, but not noticed to produce seedlings, as it can do. J planted. A planted. S planted. H –.

MALLOW FAMILY Malvaceae

MUSK MALLOW *Malva moschata* L.
Rare, and likely to have come out of gardens, recently at any rate. It was first recorded half a century before Marquand, by Newbould at St Peter's. J rare. A last record 1932. S rare. H –.

COMMON MALLOW *M. sylvestris* L. Mauve
By Gosselin's specimen is written that it grows almost everywhere. It is still undoubtedly common, but undoubtedly also now confused with Cornish Mallow. Gosselin marked it as a Plante Médécinale. In 1905 it was said still to be highly valued for gatherings, when made into a poultice, boiled and mixed with bread. J common. A common. S frequent. H occasional.

(*M. nicaeensis* Allioni was collected in Jersey in 1928.)

DWARF MALLOW *M. neglecta* Wallroth (*M. 'rotundifolia'*)
Rather local and never in plenty – rather than the 'frequent' of Marquand's day, let alone 'common' as another observer wrote in 1931. Gosselin collected it, as a Plante Médécinale, and noted three places for it. A plant with white flowers was seen in 1958. J frequent. A rare. S occasional. H occasional.

LEAST MALLOW *M. parviflora* L. (*M. 'borealis'*)
Marquand's single 1892 plant was of this species. The only other record, of 1922 not in print, proved to be the last species. These small mallows were much muddled and still need care. They come from farther south. J claimed. A –. S –. H –.

(*M. crispa* (L.) L., a form of *M. verticillata* L., was collected in 1926 in Jersey, and *M. pusilla* Smith in 1960.)

TREE MALLOW *Lavatera arborea* L. Grande Mauve
Tree-like, or at any rate bush-like, but only a biennial, its pale dead stems surviving picturesquely into the next season before breaking up. The first record is a note by Lightfoot 'At the end of the Town in the Island of Guernsey, Mr Yalden', by 1774, which is probably earlier than Gosselin collected his specimen. On the cover of his specimens he wrote 'grows in my garden at Glateny', and it was noted as cultivated in 1832. It still is occasionally. But most plants at least will be native, very likely taken into gardens rather than escaping out of them. It is nearly all round the coast, but can no longer be said to be locally common. J frequent. A occasional. S occasional. H rare.

CORNISH MALLOW *L. cretica* L. (*L. sylvestris*)
The beginning of June is a good time of the year to learn how locally plentiful this little-recognised plant is. Its smaller, pale puce, more cup-shaped flowers are then well out, ahead of the darker, redder ones of Common Mallow. The set of the two plants usually differs too. This one is commonly erecter with open growth and can be very tall – 10 feet has been measured and it is often over

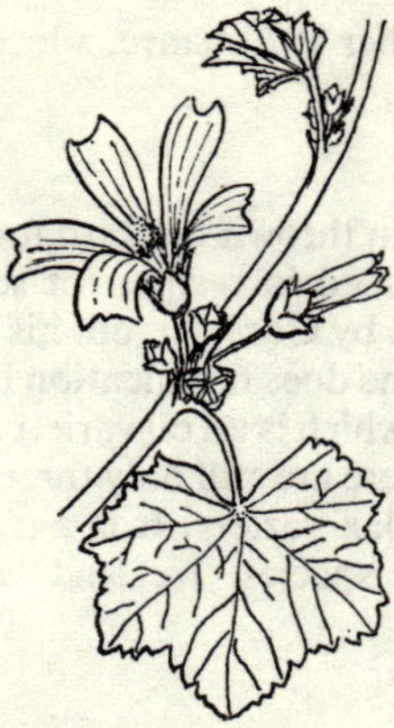

Cornish Mallow ×⅔

6 feet. The common one has a thicker darker look. The leaves of this one are paler, greyer-green, softer, rounder and less lobed, and there is the technical character which separates, or tries to, *Malva* from *Lavatera* i.e. that the outer pair of calyx lobes of the former are not joined at the base into a small cup. But this is not always clear. This one has hairs which are usually branched. In 1877 Trimen said it had not reached the Channel Islands. In 1897 White found it in Jersey and wrote that it was a new addition to the flora of the C.I. But it was not. Reeves collected it in Guernsey before 1886, and seed of it was gathered from Ruettes Brayes in 1888 by Griffith (who grew it in his garden in England). Miss Dawber, who lived there, collected it in 1891 and 1893, in which year it was shown to Green (by her?) as 'extremely rare'. Marquand knew it round St Sampson's in the early 1890's. Druce said in 1907 it was a casual only; but the year before it was reported to be spreading. It seems to have done so greatly in the last few years, and is now locally plentiful, except in the extreme south. It is Mediterranean J rare. A –. S –. H –.

FRENCH MALLOW *L. olbia* L.
Twice collected outside gardens in 1971. '*Olbia*' indicates it to be native in the Iles d'Hyères. J –. A –. S –. H –.

HOLLYHOCK *Alcea rosea* L. Passerose
A garden plant, originating in the Near East and familiar to everybody, which may for a short while be seen outside. It is known nowhere as a wild native plant. J casual. A –. S –. H –.

MARSH MALLOW *Althaea officinalis* L.
Another loss to Guernsey, presumably resulting from the loss of the Braye du Valle. Gosselin's specimen, marked Plante Médécinale, shows it was there about 200 years ago. J last collected 1926. A –. S –. H –.

(*A. hirsuta* L. was last collected in 1929 in Jersey.)

(Velvet Leaf, *Abutilon Theophrasti* Medicus, was collected in 1928 from Jersey.)

FLAX FAMILY Linaceae

PALE FLAX *Linum bienne* Miller (*L. angustifolium*)
Local now, growing most perhaps in the Bordeaux/St Sampson's area, where it

was measured 2 feet 9 inches high in November 1970. J rare. A locally common. S frequent. H 1838.

LINSEED *L. usitatissimum* L. Liss. Len
Nowadays this appears almost exclusively from thrown-out bird food or imports by edible oil merchants – its seeds were included in recipes for scrofula and a cough in the 18th century. The first record was by Gosselin, but his plant was the last species; the next by Babington (although he does not mention it in his *Flora*) of the var *humile* (Miller) Persoon (*crepitans*), which is an oil variety. It was a crop recommended to farmers in 1852. Yet in all there are still only three records of it, 1837, 1906 and 1970, none apparently of a Flax variety. It is a plant unknown wild, assumed to be derived from the last species. J casual. A last record 1902. S 1953. H –.

FAIRY FLAX *L. catharticum* L.
Possibly more frequent than it seems, for it is easily overlooked, despite its grace and charm. Gosselin collected it from dry pastures. J very locally frequent. A occasional. S –. H common.

FLAX-SEED *Radiola linoides* Roth (*R. millegrana*)
Still quite frequent by the coasts and still an unfailing miniature pleasure to light on. It was first collected by Gosselin. J local. A rare. S locally frequent. H –.

CRANE'S-BILL FAMILY Geraniaceae

MEADOW CRANE'S-BILL *Geranium pratense* L.
Twice recorded outside gardens. J –. A rare. S 1944. H –.

(French Crane's-bill, *G. Endressii* Gay, was collected in 1924 in Jersey.)

PENCILLED CRANE'S-BILL *G. versicolor* L. (*G. striatum*)
Still on the roadside bank east of St Andrew's church, where Miss Dawber collected it in 1889, as new to Guernsey. It may well have been at Sausmarez Manor even longer, for it was said to have been known for fifty years when it was noted there in 1924, where it still is, in more than one place – the patch outside the gates cheering that road with its delicate flowers during the summer months. None of Marquand's other localities have been refound, but the Moulin de Haut at Kings Mills and two places in St Saviour's have been added, and it was behind Cobo Rectory in 1940. It is native in the E. Mediterranean. J rare. A 1881. S rare. H –.

BLOODY CRANE'S-BILL *G. sanguineum* L.
This is reported as long known on a bank near Le Gouffre, and is also on one in Cobo, where however it is no more than practically in a garden. J rare. A very rare. S –. H –.

PYRENEAN CRANE'S-BILL *G. pyrenaicum* Burman f.
This was recorded, and a specimen preserved, by Mrs McCrea in 1931 from an arable field at Le Varclin, St Martin's. Close search there one morning in 1970 failed to refind it, but that afternoon it was found at the opposite end of the island just north of the Amarreurs Road on L'Ancresse. J rare. A –. S –. H –.

LONG-STALKED CRANE'S-BILL *G. columbinum* L.
Gosselin listed this from Les Maingys at L'Epine, which is in the same general area as Ronceval and Portinfer, where Marquand knew it and it was refound by Miss V. Gordon in 1956, and still is. It has not been refound near Footes Lane. J last record 1929. A last record 1900. S –. H –.

CUT-LEAVED CRANE'S-BILL *G. dissectum* L.
Frequent and all over the island. Gosselin collected it as a field and garden weed. J common. A frequent. S occasional. H occasional.

ALDERNEY GERANIUM *G.* cf *submolle* Steudel
This was collected by T. J. Foggitt from a laneside at Paradis or Fort Doyle or near Hermitage in July 1926, and named as *G. Core-Core* Steudel, with some doubt, by Dr Thellung for Lady Davy and others, but the plant has eluded later searchers there. In 1968 it was collected at the other side of the common, north of the Amarreurs Road, close to where Pyrenean Crane's-bill was refound in 1970 (but not this one); in 1970 it was seen by Dr and Mrs Dony ¾ mile to the north in a hedge north of the Golf Club house, where it still is. The precise identity of this plant is not settled, various other names having been suggested

Alderney Geranium ×½

such as *G. microphyllum* Hooker f. which is wrong, and *G. retrorsum* L'Héritier ex DC which probably is. It is one of two or three similar South American species, and seems to be unrecorded in the northern hemisphere outside the Channel Islands. Foggitt's specimens are the first, after which no more was heard until it was collected unawares in 1938 in Alderney and independently there in 1957. A summary is in *Watsonia* 8 (1) 1970, p. 47. It differs from the last species by being a taller perennial scrambling up hedges etc., with appressed hairs and larger eglandular flowers with less notched petals on longer stalks. J gone? A local. S –. H –.

ROUND-LEAVED CRANE'S-BILL *G. rotundifolium* L.
Rather rare. It is still in the Chouet and St Sampson's areas, and fairly reliably to be seen on the waste ground inland from Grandes Rocques, and occasionally elsewhere. J frequent. A locally frequent. S 1930. H –.

DOVE'S-FOOT CRANE'S-BILL *G. molle* L.
Common and variable in colour and size, partly because it is self-pollinated. It is to be told from the next by its hairless fruits. It is known also with white flowers. J common. A common. S common. H frequent.

SMALL-FLOWERED CRANE'S-BILL *G. pusillum* L.
Confidently and not improbably recorded from the Fort Road in 1968, but with, alas, no vouching specimen. Had it downy fruits? J rare. A rare. S 1958. H rare.

(Shining Crane's-bill, *G. lucidum* L., is rare in Jersey.)

HERB ROBERT *G. Robertianum* L. ssp *Robertianum* Rouâge Gambe. Epiles

Widespread and quite frequent, often very fine and stout. Gosselin's specimens from St Jacques have a slip with them marked 'Colonel Gosling', which is a variant of the family name. He called it a Plante Médécinale. J common. A frequent. S rare. H –.

SEA-SHORE HERB ROBERT *G. Robertianum* L. ssp *maritimum* (Babington) H. G. Baker
A single small specimen now at Kew was collected in 1939 by Dovaston at La Rochelle. It was identified as this subspecies by Prof. Baker in *Watsonia* for February 1956, p. 274. The specimen looks like Little Robin and all attempts to find the subspecies have failed – Little Robin in varying shapes is frequent in that area. Baker has consequently written that field observations are worth far more, and he is sure this subspecies should disappear from the list of Guernsey plants. It is not taken up in *Flora Europaea*. J –. A –. S –. H –.

GREATER HERB ROBERT *G. rubescens* Yeo
A fine colourful Madeiran endemic, found in 1968 by P. Girard at La Charroterie. This was the year before this plant was formally named – see the *Journal of the Royal Horticultural Society* for September 1970, p. 411 – there is a colour photo of it on Plate 205. How it got to Guernsey is anybody's guess. Unfortunately alterations to its site in 1970 exterminated it there, but it still grows nearby and flourishes in several gardens from seed. It is a polyploid Herb Robert, 2n = 64, with Phlox Purple (HCC 632) petals twice the size – 3cm. J –. A –. S –. H –.

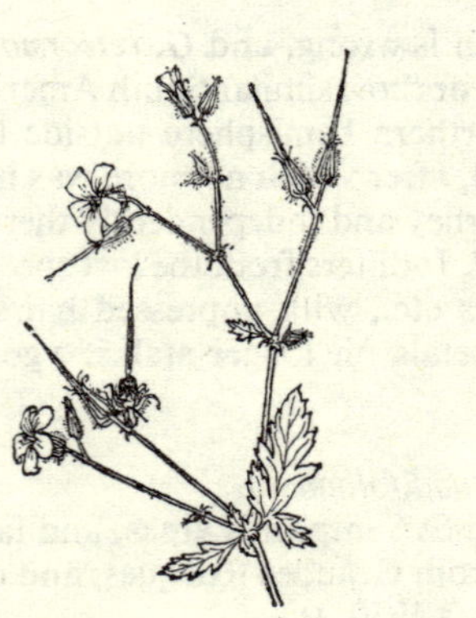

Greater Herb Robert ×½

LITTLE ROBIN *G. purpureum* Villars ssp *purpureum* (*G. modestum*)
Locally quite plentiful, its headquarters perhaps on the north-east coast. The earliest date for the plant in Guernsey is 1839, from Haslam from the Bouet, its first record in Britain. The English name was invented by Miss C. M. Rob and seems now to be accepted. J locally plentiful. A rare. S –. H –.

SEASIDE LITTLE ROBIN *G. purpureum* Villars ssp *Forsteri* (Wilmott) H. G. Baker
A British endemic recorded by Baker in *Watsonia* for February 1955, p. 166, from four places on the north-east coast since 1876. Here plants are still to be seen, notably on Banque Imbert, under the feet of the trippers, which tally with the prescription for this subspecies. But plants may also be found there which show every intermediacy to the last subspecies, the habit following closely the habitat, prostrate on the shingle, erect off it in the lusher vegetation. The notes on *G. purpureum* × *G. Robertianum* in *Hybridization and the Flora of the British Isles* are relevant; and this taxon is ignored in *Flora Europaea*. J –. A –. S –. H –.

SEA STORK'S-BILL *Erodium maritimum* (L.) L'Héritier
Unexpectedly rare, both in Marquand's time and now. Yet it was clearly recorded by Knowlton towards Fermain in 1726. Yalden had it 'about the old Castle' by 1774. It was collected by Gosselin and implied by Babington not to be rare. But there was then no other record until 1889. Since Marquand's day it has been seen on L'Ancresse and Icart, and, interestingly, on a parapet by the bus station at St Peter Port. Now this is almost exactly where Gosselin will have collected it, 'on the parapet of south pier'. There is also a record of it from Fort Hommet. The 27-year-old Druce reported it in 1877 from the Grande Havre with white flowers to the exclusion of the ordinary colour. But how often are its petals to be seen at all? J scarce. A occasional. S frequent. H common.

MUSK STORK'S-BILL *E. moschatum* (L.) L'Héritier Bec de Grue. Epiles ès Bergiers. Musque sauvage.
Quite frequent and well distributed, a plant which has been spreading in Brittany during the past hundred years. It seems almost incredible that this dull and coarse weed was for centuries cultivated for the aroma of its leaves (which can be barely detectable, nowadays anyway), and as a pot and medicinal herb. Parkinson commented in 1640 on the 'sent which some resemble to Muske, but the sent of true and good Muske is much differing from it'. The var *cicutarioides* Delile ex Godron with the leaves dissected as in the next species was found on Mont Cuet in 1958. Gosselin collected his specimens 'near the great gate of the Truchot'. J common. A occasional. S occasional. H frequent.

COMMON STORK'S-BILL *E. cicutarium* (L.) L'Héritier ssp *cicutarium*
Common indeed, mostly near the coast. Small early plants on the cliffs with rich pink flowers can rival any alpine beauty. Gosselin labelled his specimens *Geranium scutarium* (the genus *Erodium* had not been then created), but spelt it correctly in his lists. J common. A common. S common. H common.

DUNE STORK'S-BILL *E. cicutarium* (L.) L'Héritier ssp *dunense* Andreas
This was collected by Gosselin, but then not until 1912 by Barton on Lihou. It is to be found in the sandy turf of the north and west, but small dune forms of the last species are frequent and it is doubtful if this deserves rank as a subspecies – it is not given in *Flora Europaea*. Tell it by its having at most 3-4 smaller flowers

on each common stalk, and fruits on stalks less than 13mm with only a small furrow at the base of the beak which is not over 1 inch long. J –. A rare. S –. H –.

STICKY STORK'S-BILL *E. cicutarium* (L.) L'Héritier ssp *bipinnatum* (Cavanilles) Tourlet (*E. glutinosum*)
Often claimed from Guernsey and not unlikely to occur, but no valid specimen exists. Its characters are set out by P. M. Benoit in BSBI *Proceedings* for May 1967, p. 336. J rare. A –. S claimed. H –.

WOOD SORREL FAMILY Oxalidaceae

WOOD SORREL *Oxalis Acetosella* L.
Gosselin's specimens labelled this are of the next species and of a rare variety of Upright Oxalis. Pale Oxalis is also mistaken for it. There is no indication that this has ever been a Guernsey plant. J local. A –. S error. H –.

YELLOW SORREL *O. corniculata* L.
The ordinary yellow Oxalis of Guernsey, varying much in its habit, taller, often very tall, plants being mistaken for Upright Oxalis, which however lacks stipules. It may be found in cultivated ground almost anywhere, including in greenhouses, but is still not very common. It was freely recorded in the mid-19th century e.g. as very common in 1858 and 1867, especially in the north. Yet it was rare to Marquand. The rich purple-leaved variety *atropurpurea* van Houtte ex Planchon also occurs; while a pale purple-leaved variety was collected at Sausmarez Manor in 1970. The smaller var *repens* (Zuccarini) Thunberg has been noted. J frequent. A –. S occasional. H local.

LEAST YELLOW SORREL *O. exilis* A. Cunningham
This is the small very neat-leaved plant, a native of New Zealand, called for some time var *microphylla* of the last species. It can be told by its leaflets being never more than 6 mm in any direction and its blunter capsules never over 7 mm, the lowest length for the last species being 12 mm, with 3–4 seeds as opposed to 6 or more, and its always 1-flowered inflorescence. Once its jizz is known, it is unmistakable. It seems rather scarce in Guernsey, but occurs among paving stones and in greenhouses. J occasional. A –. S –. H occasional.

(The American *O. stricta* L. has been known for certain only from two places in the British Isles, one of which is Sark.)

UPRIGHT OXALIS *O. europaea* Jordan
Endlessly misclaimed, but only twice proved. It was in greenhouses at Moulin Huet in 1957, named by Dr D. P. Young, who on being later sent one of Gosselin's specimens labelled *O. Acetosella*, pronounced it to be the extremely rare var *Bushii* (Small) Wiegand of this species, the earliest record for this – the leaves are covered with appressed hairs. Gosselin wrote that it grew in gardens near the town as a weed, but he presumably was really referring to the common yellow one. How to tell this species from the others is set out in *Watsonia* for February 1958, pp. 57–8. Despite its epithet, it is probably also American in origin, but now a ubiquitous weed. J 1928. A –. S –. H 1958.

PINK OXALIS *O. articulata* Savigny (*O. floribunda*)
First noted in 1953, but to be seen outside gardens all over the island, perhaps

most typically on dunes or hedgebanks, although there are never many plants in any one place. It has been seen with white and pale pink as well as dark pink flowers. Unlike the next species, its knobbly fibrous rootstock with no detaching bulbils enables it to grow in thick tufts. Its leaves have prominent orange dots beneath. It is a native of the Argentine. Like many species of Oxalis (including all the bulbous ones), this is trimorphic, i.e. its anthers and stigma will be in one of three positions. Plants which have the filaments and style of the same length cannot cross to produce good fruit. All three variations have been noted on this species; so where two grow in proximity, good seed is produced. R. P. Libbey has noticed some plants with glandular hairs on the flowers and stalks. J frequent. A locally frequent. S occasional. H occasional.

PINK BULBOUS OXALIS *O. corymbosa* DC
The hardier of the two South American pink Oxalis which are such a pest of cultivated ground, but the first record was only in 1937. Care is needed in distinguishing it from the next species. This one has hairier leaflets broadest about the middle, with tiny reddish dots on the edges of the underside. There are good drawings of it in Mrs Le Sueur's *Oxalis in Jersey* in the *Bulletin of the Société Jersiaise* for 1969, p. 50. This seems to be all of one clone, but spreads readily vegetatively by its bulbils. J too frequent. A 1959. S rare. H –.

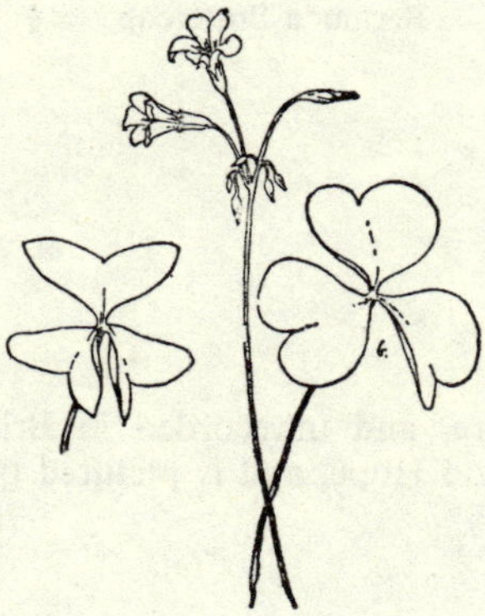

Pink Bulbous Oxalis ×½

MEXICAN OXALIS *O. latifolia* Kunth
Probably the commoner of the two nearly ineradicable pink Oxalis, but the more susceptible to frost – it comes more from Central America. It was very considerably reduced in the winter of 1962/3, but soon recovered. It may have begun to spread after the First World War. Its leaflets are hairless, typically ('Continental type') with a pronounced fish-tail shape. Some frequent clones in Guernsey have them more rounded ('Cornish type') and can mimic the last species, but lack also the dots on the undersurface, and are still broadest near the top – cf the drawing in Dr Young's paper in *Watsonia* for February 1958, p. 61. It is not certain that both these are of the same species. For one thing the Continental type may get heavily infected with the rust *Puccinia oxalidis*, while the Cornish type ones in the same bed remain free. This was first detected in the British Isles from the Channel Is in 1973, cf. RHS *Journal* May 1974 pp. 187-8. Dr Young named three short-styled clones from Les Eturs, Câtel in 1969 as 'Cornish-type, with pinkish-white and quite white flowers (a somatic mutation?)

and Continental-type with deep red flowers'. They are still there with the usual pink Continental type plants. J too widespread. A occasional. S rare. H rare.

(Four-leaved Oxalis, *O. tetraphylla* Cavanilles, has been known, now locally abundantly, in Jersey since during the First World War.)

DEPPE'S OXALIS *O. Deppei* Loddiges ex Sweet
This was said by Chevalier to be a weed common in some gardens in Jersey and Guernsey in 1933, but there is no confirmation, or specimen to check if it were not perhaps the last, also four-leaved species, with which he combined it in 1940. Dr Dizerbo considers his plant was *O. tetraphylla.* J garden escape. A –. S –. H –.

BERMUDA BUTTERCUP *O. pes-caprae* L. (*O. cernua*)
Known currently, usually in small colonies, on banks or walls by gardens in widely scattered parts of the island, always a bright pleasure and never the pest

Bermuda Buttercup ×½

it is in Scilly – or Bermuda – or elsewhere, and unrecorded in Brittany or Normandy. It came from the Cape of Good Hope, and is pictured on the 2p stamp of 1972. J rare. A –. S –. H rare.

PALE OXALIS *O. incarnata* L.
Locally very fine indeed, for example on the shady banks of some of the upper paths above Fermain Bay, but not all that common and unknown in nearby France. It is still mistaken for the missing Wood Sorrel, but is a South African. Different style lengths have been found. J occasional. A occasional. S occasional. H occasional.

NASTURTIUM FAMILY Tropaeolaceae

NASTURTIUM *Tropaeolum majus* L. Capuchäon
A South American annual, familiar in gardens, which is occasionally to be seen for a short while outside them. It usually has orange flowers, but was seen at Perelle in 1971 with yellow ones. J casual. A occasional. S –. H –.

Balsam Family Balsaminaceae

Touch-me-not *Impatiens noli-tangere* L.
One plant was recorded in 1924. The specimen was discovered in 1970 and proved to be the first record for the next species, which was not given in the Floras then available. J –. A –. S –. H –.

Himalayan Balsam *I. glandulifera* Royle
First seen by Mrs Hichens in the Saints Bay Road in 1924, escaped from a garden, whence maybe came the colony lower down first noted in 1958, since when it has multiplied prodigiously. It was also, in 1947, by Les Grands Courtils, where it seems not to have persisted, and has been reported from the Fauxquets Valley and in St Saviour's. It is indeed Himalayan. J 1929. A –. S –. H –.

Tree of Heaven Family Simaroubaceae

(The Tree of Heaven, *Ailanthus altissima* (Miller) Swingle, seeds itself in Jersey.)

Maple Family Aceraceae

Sycamore *Acer Pseudoplatanus* L.
A frequent tree, self-sowing itself readily. It is hard to realise it was unknown in Britain before the Middle Ages – it is a native of Central Europe. Its English name is a misnomer, for it has no connection with the true Sycamore up which Zacchaeus climbed. Various explanations are given of how this mistake arose. Gosselin spelt it Sycomore in his notes. The f. *purpureum* (Loudon) Rehder first recorded anywhere in Jersey about 1828, is liable to appear in any batch of seedlings and does so in Guernsey. J common. A common. S frequent. H occasional.

Norway Maple *A. platanoides* L.
There are several trees in the Moulin Huet Valley. J planted. A –. S –. H –.

Field Maple *A. campestre* L.
Two records, both by Professors of Botany well before they became Professors of Botany, by Babington in 1839 and by his protégé Hillhouse 40 years later. Neither collected a specimen. Marquand knew it planted, for example at La Ramée in 1891, but it is not so known today. And yet, there is *Acer* pollen in the Vazon peat. J rare. A –. S –. H –.

Horse Chestnut Family Hippocastanaceae

Horse Chestnut *Aesculus Hippocastanum* L.
This tree, of Balkan origin, was listed by Anstead as naturalised, but there is no evidence it successfully regenerates. Its dried leaves were used for tobacco during the occupation. J occurs. A rare. S rare. H –.

Holly Family Aquifoliaceae

Holly *Ilex Aquifolium* L. Housse
Holly pollen was in the peat at Catioroc, but present-day Holly is no certain native. It is quite widespread, but many plants seem no more than bird sown from gardens. Its generic name is confusing, belonging classically to the Holm Oak, whose leaves are said to resemble Holly's. Its specific epithet is the name used for Holly by Pliny 1900 years ago, and means needle-leaved – nothing to do with *aqua*, water. J frequent. A –. S occasional. H planted.

Spindle Family Celastraceae

Spindle *Euonymus europaeus* L.
According to de Putron in 1934, formerly grown as an ornamental shrub or in hedges, and thrice recorded from them. J rare. A –. S –. H –.

Euonymus *E. japonicus* L.
Much used for hedges and shelter near the sea. It survives magnificently and is said to produce seed. It does indeed come from Japan. The cultivar 'Ovatus Aureus' with rich buttercup yellow leaves is quite often to be seen. J planted. A –. S planted. H –.

Box Tree Family Buxaceae

Box *Buxus sempervirens* L. Buisse
Another plant whose pollen is in the peat at Catioroc, but nowadays at best to be seen as a survivor capable of long life. J planted. A –. S –. H –.

Grape-vine Family Vitaceae

Grape-vine *Vitis vinifera* L. Grappe
Grape pips thrown out may germinate. Seedlings have been reported from St Peter's and a wall above Fermain beach; and any plant which can sow itself in a bare wall is on the way to naturalisation. In any event its pollen is reported from the peat at Catioroc. Grapes used to be cultivated in vineries in a large way, the trade dwindling rapidly before and after the Second World War. At one time, 3,400 tons were exported in one year. Its leaves were smoked during the occupation. J occasional. A –. S –. H –.

Virginian Creeper *Parthenocissus quinquefolia* (L.) Planchon. Vaënne.
All three species of this genus which are commonly grown on the sides of houses etc can survive long after their support has gone. This one stayed on, on the site of a deserted garden at Pleinmont. Its generic name comes from its country of origin, which was named after the Virgin Queen, Elizabeth I. Parthenos is Greek for a virgin – and cissus for a vine. J occasional. A –. S rare. H –.

TREE LUPIN *Lupinus arboreus* Sims
Although unrecorded until 1958 this has been well, decoratively and fragrantly naturalised for much longer, especially south and west of the Grande Havre, with flowers of white and many shades of yellow. But there are good colonies elsewhere, for example on east L'Ancresse, Belle Grève Bay, Vazon and Rocquaine. It may do too well, and has been sprayed near the Hermitage and otherwise discouraged. It is North American. J locally common. A occasional. S occasional. H rare.

GARDEN LUPIN *L. polyphyllus* Lindley
A familiar plant originally from Western North America, which can get established. But the only record for Guernsey is from a rubbish heap. J rare. A –. S –. H –.

(*L. angustifolius* L. was collected in 1925 in Jersey. *L. luteus* L. seeds itself there.)

COMMON LABURNUM *Laburnum anagyroides* Medicus
Although basically a Mediterranean tree, this is always liable to sow itself, and was so reported from near the Reservoir in 1970. J collected in 1926. A –. S –. H –.

(Dyer's Greenweed, *Genista tinctoria* L., is rare in Jersey.)

GORSE *Ulex europaeus* L. ssp *europaeus* Jaon
Widespread and common. Gosselin – and others – called it Furze. The trunk of one bush on the south cliffs was measured at 13½ inches' circumference, and others in the prickly thickets looked larger. It was frequently sown and grown in the not so distant past for fuel for heating ovens (cut every third or fourth year), for fodder, hedges and shelter, and was much used during the last war. Sir G. Head wrote in 1837: 'A high mound of earth surrounded by a strong furze hedge is the usual fence in the country. Therefore the premises of a Guernsey farmer are as impregnably fortified and secured as if he were owner of an estate and farm surrounded by a high stone wall.' P. Girard has written: 'Whole bushes were placed on staddle-stones to make a base for a corn-rick, or on the ground for a hay-stack, or between the joists as a floor in the stable loft.' But it is doubtless also a native of the island, and place names such as Le Jaonnet Bay are connected with it. That it is usually showing some flower has proverbial osculatory advantages, but for this it may need the assistance of the next species. J common. A common. S common. H common.

HYBRID GORSE *U. europaeus* × *U. Gallii*
Specimens sent to Dr Proctor in 1973 were said by him to look like this hybrid. Others from Pleinmont also suggested a bit of *Gallii* influence on a *europaeus* bush. J –. A –. S –. H –.

WESTERN GORSE *U. Gallii* Planchon
This has a different jizz readily noticeable to the discerning, who do not need to use technical characters to tell it from the last species. Its most obvious trait is that it is in full flower in late summer and autumn, when the other has rarely started. The common species has its buds ready in late summer and can itself

be an autumn flowerer, except that the weather usually holds it up for the heady burst in springtime. This species seems scarce and never in much quantity but is scattered over the island. The darker squatter bushes with deeper yellow flowers often grow among colonies of the common one. J locally frequent. A locally common. S locally frequent. H –.

LESSER GORSE *U. minor* Roth (*U. nanus*)
It needs skill and the use of a combination of characters to tell this species from the last, and records of the last were for long put under '*U. nanus*'. But the geographical distributions of the two are remarkably and neatly mutually exclusive (see *Watsonia* for October 1965, pp. 177–87). This one grows east of a line roughly from Dorchester to all except the north-west tip of the Cotentin peninsula and Dinard, and Western Gorse to the west. Consequently this species would not be expected to occur in the Channel Islands, and any records for it need checking. Nevertheless the single specimen from Guernsey, from the Rue des Salines near St Sampson's in 1892, has been confirmed by Dr Proctor. It has never been seen since. The *Armorican Flora* records it for all the Channel Islands, 'sauf peut-être Guernesey'! J ? 1859. A ? S –. H –.

COMMON BROOM *Cytisus scoparius* (L.) Link ssp *scoparius* (*Sarothamnus scoparius*) Genêt. Bringe.
Still rather local, apparently now not on the west coast, and not often plentiful. There is an old saying 'A quand les sorchiers väont au Catioroc l'passent par dessus bringe bissäone', and yet Sir E. MacCulloch wrote that green sprigs were believed to be efficacious in averting the evil influence of spells. 11 spoonfuls of Broom ashes dried and burnt in an oven were used against the dropsy in the 18th century. J locally plentiful. A occasional. S common. H occasional.

PROSTRATE BROOM *C. scoparius* (L.) Link ssp *maritimus* (Rouy) Heywood (*Sarothamnus scoparius* var *prostratus*)
Locally plentiful and indeed superb on the south-west cliffs, superb not only with its sheets of yellow flowers, but also in the soft silvery grey mats of its silky young foliage. This comes true from seed, but cannot stand much frost. J locally plentiful. A locally plentiful. S claimed 1969. H –.

PURPLE BROOM *Chamaecytisus purpureus* (Scopoli) Link (*Cytisus purpureus*)
De Putron identified as this a broom Sir H. de Sausmarez discovered near the Watch House at Pleinmont in 1930, which he had long known growing wild in that vicinity. It has not been seen since. It is South European. J –. A –. S –. H –.

MONTPELLIER BROOM *Teline monspessulana* (L.) C. Koch (*Cytisus monspessulanus*)
About ten bushes were reported by Dr Bowen in 1957, from an old sand pit at Grandes Rocques, but not seen subsequently. It derives from the Montpellier region. J –. A –. S –. H –.

REST-HARROW *Ononis repens* L. (*O.* '*arvensis*') Reglisse. Arrête-boeu.
Common in the sandy turf of the north-west, occasional elsewhere, chiefly on the coast. Very occasionally it may have white flowers, or spines. Reglisse means liquorice, which the chewed roots are said to resemble. J locally common. A frequent. S frequent. H common.

(Spiny Rest-harrow, *O. spinosa* L. ssp *spinosa,* is claimed for Jersey and has been erroneously recorded for Sark.)

SMALL REST-HARROW *O. reclinata* L. ssp *reclinata*
First found by Wolsey on 8 June 1862 near the Hermitage on L'Ancresse, in which month he showed it to Naylor and F. A. Hanbury. There was very little the next year, and it has usually been reported to grow sparingly, but it was still there until at least 1930. The ground remains apparently suitable, but no one has managed to refind it. Miss Dawber collected it from Portinfer on 28 June

Small Rest-harrow ×½

1884, where it was still to be seen in 1934, but not since. Its third locality was just north of the big car park west of Pembroke Bay, where it grew in 1947 on the then open bank to the north. In 1953 it was noted as 'about to be overwhelmed' but was still there in 1956, and very fine. But the bank is now rankly overgrown, and quite unsuitable for this annual rarity. It flowers in May and early June, before the common perennial, for which it is so often hopefully claimed. It is said to be the var *Linnaei* Webb & Berthelot. J collected 1871 and 1924. A rare. S –. H –.

SICKLE MEDICK *Medicago falcata* L.
Four records stretching from 1894 to 1954. J 1878. A –. S –. H –.

HYBRID LUCERNE *M.* × *varia* Martyn
Four records since 1950. It could be that some of those for the next species belong here, for there is extensive hybridisation between it and the last species to produce agricultural forms suitable to varying requirements. Indeed it may be hard to decide how to name some roadside waifs. Like the next species, its deep roots enable it to persist and remain green in dry conditions. J occurs. A –. S –. H –.

LUCERNE *M. sativa* L. Luzerne
Like the last two, always an introduction. Its cultivation in the islands commenced about 1750 with seed from Cette, which it was then customary to sow broadcast. Hillhouse was the first to collect it wild, in 1879, and it has been noted locally since, never in quantity, and unable to establish itself against competition. Alfalfa derives from its Arabic name, for it was brought to Spain by the Moors, and thence across the Atlantic, whence the American use of this ancient name. J frequent. A frequent. S occasional. H –.

Black Medick *M. lupulina* L.
Common. Gosselin collected four specimens, three of them curiously small-flowered and leaved. J common. A common. S rare. H occasional.

Bur Medick *M. minima* (L.) Bartalini
Possibly overlooked, but doubtless also very rare. It has been collected only three times, in 1898 by Kitching, in 1928 by Wilmott and 1953, always on L'Ancresse. J locally frequent. A –. S –. H –.

Toothed Medick *M. polymorpha* L. (*M. denticulata*)
Not very common. The var *microdon* (Ehrenburg) Urban (*brevispina, apiculata*) has been recorded by several observers from Babington onwards. J frequent. A rare. S error. H 1957.

Spotted Medick *M. arabica* (L.) Hudson (*M. maculata*)
Locally common all over the island, varying in luxuriance widely with the excellence of its feeding. Gosselin's specimens are labelled Heart Medick, Trefoil or Claver, following his identifying Flora, Hudson's *Flora Anglica*. This name derives from Gerard's *Trifolium cordatum*. J common. A frequent. S rare. H occasional.

(*M. orbicularis* (L.) Bartalini is on record from Jersey.)

Golden Melilot *Melilotus altissima* Thuillier (*M.* '*officinalis*')
This is the species with the darker yellow flowers and hairy almost black pods. Records for *M.* '*officinalis*' need care, for both the usual species have borne this name. This is less common in the British Isles and has been noticed, if the records have been sorted right, only once in Guernsey, in 1890. But it has been claimed at other times. J last collected 1924. A rare. S –. H –.

Common Melilot *M. officinalis* (L.) Pallas (*M. arvensis*)
Uncommon – no longer 'very rare', and fairly well established in one or two places. J occasional. A locally frequent. S –. H –.

White Melilot *M. alba* Medicus
The agricultural Bokhara Clover – where it is native – with eight records since Marquand first noted it in 1890. J casual. A 1906. S –. H 1876.

Small-flowered Melilot *M. indica* (L.) Allioni (*M. parviflora*)
Now the commonest Melilot in Guernsey, being locally plentifully established in long grassy sandy turf, for example on west L'Ancresse, where it was first noted in 1947 and down to Vazon. It is also on the east side, north and south of St Sampson's and occasionally elsewhere. Its native area does include India, but nowhere else in Britain is it known other than as a casual. The source of these vigorous colonies can hardly be just the single specimen recorded by Marquand in 1894 near the Doyle Monument. The only other record before the last war was at Vale Castle in 1928. J locally well established. A locally frequent. S Brechou 1902. H –.

Sicilian Melilot *M. messanensis* (L.) Allioni (*M. sicula*)
One large plant in 1894. It does belong to Messina, Sicily. J –. A –. S –. H –.

(*M. sulcata* Desfontaines was collected in 1927 in Jersey.)

(*Trigonella hamosa* L. was collected in Jersey in 1876.)

FENUGREEK *Trifolium ornithopodioides* L. (*Trigonella ornithopodioides. Falcatula ornithopodioides*)
Easily overlooked, and so all the greater pleasure suddenly to spot in coastal and cliff turf. But it does not seem frequent. Druce in 1877 and F. J. Hanbury in 1884 were its first collectors. J frequent. A occasional. S occasional. H frequent.

RED CLOVER *T. pratense* L. Grand Träeffle
Common, rarely with white flowers. The plants in natural turf, long-lived perennials with solid stems, are the typical variety. Those of road and field sides, short-lived and with hollow stems, are likely to be one or other of the numerous forms of var *sativum* Schreber used in leys etc. Clover was at one time grown as a crop for its seed. Gosselin collected it and in his list follows Parkinson, his other work of reference, in calling it Field Honeysuckle, in allusion to the drop of honey at the base of the tube children, and others, like to suck out. It was Honeysuckle Trefoil to Hudson. J common. A common. S common. H occasional.

A HYBRID CLOVER *T. incarnatum* × *T. pratense*
No specimen has been traced of Miss Agnew's 1898 find which Marquand suggested was possibly of this parentage, a cross recorded nowhere else before or since – see *Hybridization and the Flora of the British Isles.* J –. A –. S –. H –.

(There is a doubtful record of Sulphur Clover, *T. ochroleucon* Hudson, from Jersey.)

ZIG-ZAG CLOVER *T. medium* L. ssp *medium*
Twice recorded, in 1899 and 1939. No vouchers known. J –. A 1953. S –. H –.

SEA CLOVER *T. squamosum* L. (*T. maritimum*)
Still rare, but no longer in profusion where it occurs. Nevertheless it has been seen in a considerable number of places – in addition to those noted in the *Flora* it was known thenabouts at the Vale and Château des Marais. Between the wars it was recorded from Cobo, L'Erée and L'Ancresse; since the war, by the Maison de Bas, in the Grande Mare, by the Mare de Carteret and at Portinfer. J last record 1929. A –. S –. H –.

(Starry Clover, *T. stellatum* L., was collected on Alderney in 1933, but was not to be seen the following year.)

CRIMSON CLOVER *T. incarnatum* L. ssp *incarnatum* Incarnate
Rarely if ever cultivated in Guernsey, so its opportunities of straying to roadsides etc. have been limited. Its reported occurrences are four, between 1894 and 1963, the last in a new ley. J casual. A last record 1937. S rare. H 1904.

(*T. incarnatum* L. ssp *Molinerii* (Balbis ex Hornemann) Syme is a well-known speciality in Jersey; it is credited, on erroneous evidence, to Herm in the *Armorican Flora.*)

HARE'S-FOOT CLOVER *T. arvense* L.
A softly charming annual, patches of which can be seen quite frequently in sandy turf or on the cliffs, usually near the coast. Its flowers can not only look white, but be white. Gosselin's specimens came from Les Terres Point, where it still fits the scene perfectly. J frequent. A locally frequent. S occasional. H occasional.

SOFT CLOVER *T. striatum* L.
Quite widespread, also usually near the coast and also collected by Gosselin, but never in much quantity. It was gathered 2 feet 1 inch high in St Peter's in 1972. J locally plentiful. A occasional. S last record 1896. H –.

ROUGH CLOVER *T. scabrum* L.
Commoner than the last, as in Marquand's time, and often with it, nearly always on the coast. J locally plentiful. A frequent. S very rare. H –.

(*T. Bocconei* Savi was discovered in Jersey in 1934.)

BURROWING CLOVER *T. subterraneum* L.
Fairly common, to be seen inland too. This is a real curiosity, with the weird way the teeth of the fruiting calyx develop into claws which burrow the fruits into the ground. It was seen with pink flowers at L'Ancresse in 1957. Gosselin followed Hudson in calling it Dwarf Trefoil, yet two of his specimens are far from dwarf! J common. A frequent. S occasional. H. occasional.

UPRIGHT CLOVER *T. strictum* L.
A neat rarity, to the existence of which in Guernsey only very few books – not even Marquand's *Flora* – make reference. Recent efforts to refind it have not succeeded, but there is no doubt it was a Guernsey plant. Its first record is from Watson 'on a stony knowle (sic) on L'Ancresse not far from the Vale Church' in

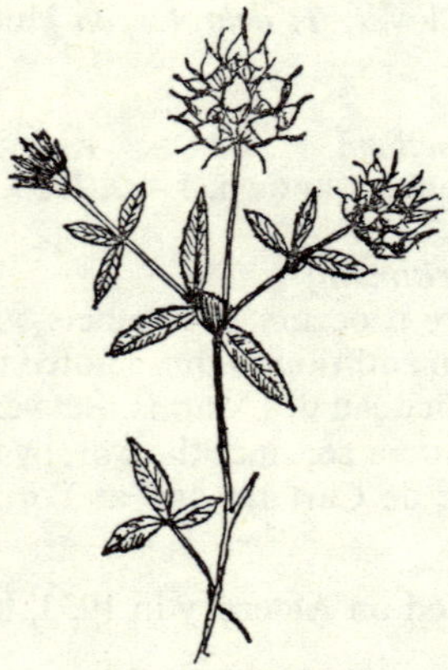

Upright Clover (in fruit) ×1

August 1852. N. D. Simpson collected it on Hommet Benest in 1923; and finally Miss M. Cobbe found it in an old quarry on L'Ancresse where it lasted from 1925 until at least 1933. Another collector described the locality as a quarter of a mile from the Great Cromlech. Does it still linger somewhere? It could be overlooked. J rare. A –. S –. H –.

CLUSTERED CLOVER *T. glomeratum* L.
Hardly frequent nowadays, but rather scarce. Druce saw some specimens over a yard across in an old quarry. Gosselin collected it from dry path sides. J locally plentiful. A occasional. S rare. H occasional.

SUFFOCATED CLOVER *T. suffocatum* L.
This flowers very much earlier than most books say: it can be in March. Well before many holiday-makers arrive, it has dried up and its brown remains soon

crumple to dust. Marquand wrote that so inconspicuous a plant was very easily overlooked, but not by those who have their eye in for it and its whitish-green clusters of flowers. He called it very rare, but that it certainly is not now, and very likely was not then. He and his contemporaries recorded it only thrice. But his was far from the first record. Haslam had had it from the Grande Havre over half a century earlier in 1839, Watson got it in 1852, Fox in 1867 and Druce in 1877. It is to be seen not only in dune turf, but also on the south cliffs. J local. A occasional. S occasional. H occasional.

ALSIKE *T. hybridum* L. ssp *hybridum*
Usually an agricultural waif, which persists for only a short while on verges and the like. So possibly was it in Marquand's time, for there were only three records of it before 1947, the last in 1926. But since the war its status has changed dramatically, and it is now to be seen well established in the sandy turf of west L'Ancresse, Grandes Rocques and Albecq, in a way not reported anywhere else; and there are only rare reports of it as a waif. J frequent. A rare. S rare. H –.

(*T. hybridum* L. ssp *elegans* (Savi) Ascherson & Graebner, with smaller flower-heads and nearly solid stems has been seen in Jersey.)

WHITE CLOVER *T. repens* L. ssp *repens* Bllanc Träeffle
Common, both wild and from agricultural use in leys etc. In over half a dozen places plants have been seen with varying shades of Magnolia Purple flowers (HCC 030/1–3), matching plants called var *Townsendii* Beeby from the Scillies. N. E. Brown wrote in 1899 that 'comparison with an authentic specimen conclusively proves this (*Townsendii*) to be the variety *rubescens* of Seringe' (published 50 years earlier). But var *carneum* S. F. Gray is four years earlier still – 1821 – and could well be the right name for this variety, or probably better, colour form. Var *proliferum* S. F. Gray (*phyllanthes*), with leafy flower-heads, was first collected by Newbould in 1841. Pollen from some clover(s) was in the peat from Vazon. J common. A common. S common. H common.

ATLANTIC CLOVER *T. occidentale* D. E. Coombe
In 1957 Dr D. E. Coombe of Cambridge became aware that among the forms of White Clover on the cliffs of the Lizard, in Cornwall, there was a quite distinct one. In 1959 he visited the Channel Islands and discovered identical plants. Among those he took to study in detail were two from Grandes Rocques and Port Soif – for comparison he took also a plant of ordinary White Clover from Cobo. Two years later he formally named them – see his paper in *Watsonia* for

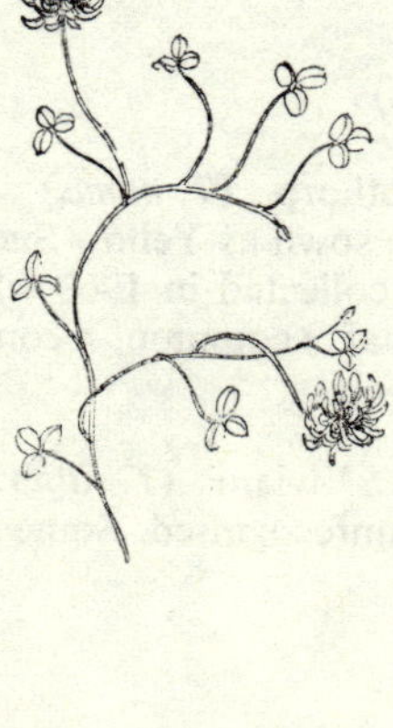

Atlantic Clover ×⅓

December 1961, pp. 68–87 (and also for June 1967, pp. 271–5). It was an astute piece of taxonomic detection, for this has proved to be quite distinct from White Clover, not even hybridising with it – the flowers are self-compatible, unlike White Clover's. It can be told by its thicker, always small dark green leaflets with non-translucent veins. The flowering stems are prostrate with a stocky appearance of their own. The flowers, which are never fragrant, appear in early May, at least three weeks before those of White Clover. When this species was described, one character was that the leaflets never had any of the light or dark markings that White Clover often has. But there is a tiny patch at Port Soif which has dark markings on its leaflets, the only one known. That this patch is true *occidentale* has been proved by a count of its chromosomes, 2n = 16, whereas White Clover has at least twice as many. This new species has proved to be widespread round the coast, nearly always within a few yards of the cliff or turf edge. It is known elsewhere only from the Atlantic coast of Cornwall, Normandy and Brittany. There are specimens of both this and of White Clover in Gosselin's herbarium; those of this are by far the oldest known. J local. A locally frequent. S occurs. H occasional.

STRAWBERRY CLOVER *T. fragiferum* L.
In the second volume of *Flora Europaea*, Dr Coombe treated *T. Bonannii* as a subspecies of Linnaeus's species. But he now finds enormous variation within this species, and is not happy about the distinctions. Several gatherings from Guernsey have been examined by him. Some approach one subspecies, some the other, while most are intermediate, e.g. with calyces 6–7 mm. In Guernsey at any rate it seems best not to attempt to split this species. It is rather local in the north and west, down to Rocquaine, but not rare. J rare. A rare. S –. H –.

SOUTHERN STRAWBERRY CLOVER *T. Bonannii* C. Presl
There is a specimen at the British Museum from L'Ancresse in 1950 determined as this species by J. Holub. But in view of the comments under the last species, the determination seems at best to cover only a form of it. J 1850. A 1932. S –. H –.

REVERSED CLOVER *T. resupinatum* L.
This lasted for three years by the Vale Castle in the 1890s, and was seen in 1897 'in a rabbit warren' and in St Saviour's in 1944. It gets its name from the flower stalk being twisted so that the standard petal of the flower is below and the keel above. It is also called Persian Clover from its area of origin. J last collected 1926. A –. S –. H –.

HOP TREFOIL *T. campestre* Schreber (*T. procumbens*)
Quite frequent, chiefly near the sea. Gosselin was the first to collect it. J frequent. A frequent. S occasional. H occasional.

(*T. aureum* Pollich has been claimed for Sark.)

COMMON YELLOW TREFOIL *T. dubium* Sibthorp (*T. minus*) Sain Träeffle
Common, and collected by Gosselin, but also sown as Yellow Suckling. At the Claire Mare and Grande Mare plants were collected in 1968 which are very floriferous and may be the var *umbellatum* Knaf. J common. A common. S common. H occasional.

SLENDER YELLOW TREFOIL *T. micranthum* Viviani (*T. filiforme*)
Seems scarce, but is likely to be passed by unrecognised. Some of Gosselin's

specimens, from the roadside near Saints Bay, where it still is, are magnificent. J frequent. A occasional. S rare. H rare.

KIDNEY VETCH *Anthyllis Vulneraria* L. ssp *Vulneraria*
The typical variety, var *Vulneraria*, was collected by Tennant in 1905 and named by Dr Cullen, who has seen all the Guernsey specimens. J (var *Langei*) local. A locally common. S –. H –.

BALTIC KIDNEY VETCH *A. Vulneraria* L. ssp *maritima* (Schweigger) Corbière
Recorded by the *Armorican Flora*, also for J recorded. A recorded. S recorded. H –.

CORBIÈRE'S KIDNEY VETCH *A. Vulneraria* L. ssp *Corbierei* (Salmon & Travis) Cullen
Always very rare – Marquand knew no Kidney Vetch in the island in 1890 – and now to be seen only at La Bette Bay, where it was found by M. English in 1957 adjoining Le Jaonnet Bay. *Flora Europaea* specifically records it for Sark only of the Channel Islands. The species has been recorded also from Fort George and Vale Castle, but in the absence of specimens it is not possible to say to which subspecies they belonged. J –. A –. S rare. H –.

HUNGARIAN KIDNEY VETCH *A. Vulneraria* L. ssp *carpatica* (Pantocsek) Nyman
The variant *pseudo-vulneraria* Sagorski was found plentifully at the Mare de Carteret in 1895, very possibly introduced agriculturally. J –. A –. S –. H –.

COMMON BIRD'S-FOOT TREFOIL *Lotus corniculatus* L.
Common, and gay. Gosselin sent a specimen to Sir J. Banks on 8 April 1791 adding 'Is it not what Curtis calls *Trifolium procumbens*?', but this specimen does not seem to have survived. J common. A common. S common. H common.

NARROW-LEAVED BIRD'S-FOOT TREFOIL *L. tenuis* Waldstein & Kitaibel ex Willdenow
Still at Albecq, where it was found in 1900, but there is very little of it. J 1958. A –. S –. H –.

GREATER BIRD'S-FOOT TREFOIL *L. uliginosus* Schkuhr (*L.* '*major*') Träeffle d'iaou
First collected by Gosselin as a variant of the Common species, and still quite frequent, sometimes as the hairless var *glaber* Brébisson. The pollen of a *Lotus* species, very likely this one, is in the Vazon peat. J common. A occasional. S occasional. H occasional.

LESSER BIRD'S-FOOT TREFOIL *L. subbiflorus* Lagasca ssp *subbiflorus* (*L. hispidus*)
A recently changed name for a plant, which had had the same name ever since it was first added to the British List in 1828. In fact Gosselin had collected it much earlier, without being able to recognise it – he clearly was puzzled by the variation he noticed in the Bird's-foot Trefoils and noted three 'varieties', this being one. Woods was the first to record it as this species from Guernsey on 28 July 1836, followed by Babington just 55 weeks later. It is quite frequent. It was

collected 31 inches high in the Claire Mare in 1968. J frequent. A occasional. S occasional. H frequent.

LEAST BIRD'S-FOOT TREFOIL *L. angustissimus* L. (*L. diffusus*)
Very much scarcer than the last and often misclaimed for it. It too was collected by Gosselin as another variety of the Common one, but was first knowingly collected by Babington on 24 July 1838. Its flowers are paler orange and the plant is less shaggy and its pods far longer – one inch. J rare. A rare. S rare. H rare.

FALSE ACACIA *Robinia Pseudacacia* L.
A distinctive and decorative North American tree, which can spread by suckers on sandier soils, or by seed. Both have been reported in Guernsey. J rare. A –. S –. H –.

COMMON BIRD'S-FOOT *Ornithopus perpusillus* L.
Quite common. There are fine specimens in Gosselin's herbarium. Var *glaber* Corbière has been collected. J common. A frequent. S common. H frequent.

ORANGE BIRD'S-FOOT *O. pinnatus* (Miller) Druce (*Artrolobium ebracteatum*)
First found in the British Isles at the Vale on 14 August 1837 by the 28-year-old Babington. Plate 2844 of the *Supplement to English Botany* was drawn from plants from Guernsey seed. Marquand knew only one place for it in 1890, but ten years later had realised it occurred in many parts of L'Ancresse from the

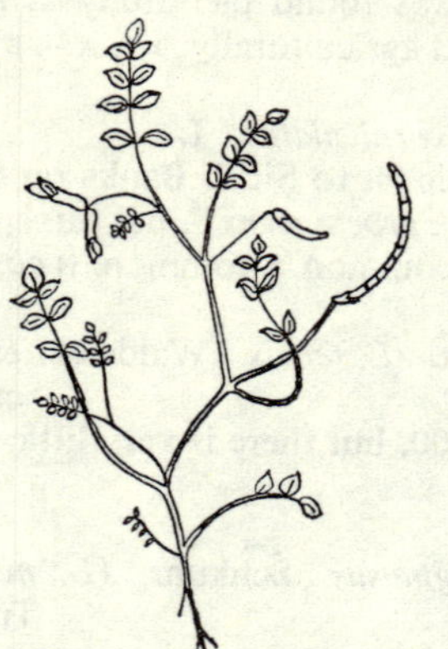

Orange Bird's-foot

west to Fort Doyle. It still is there and also on Hommet and Hommet Benest off Bordeaux Harbour, but has not been refound at Cobo where Marquand got it in 1905. The rosettes of its hairless, clearly stalked leaves are distinctive even before it comes into flower. It is one of the specialities of Guernsey, being now known outside the Archipelago only in the Isles of Scilly. J last collected 1928. A locally frequent. S rare. H 1899 and 1904.

(*O. compressus* L. has recently grown in Jersey and *O. sativus* Brotero ssp *sativus* (*O. roseus*) was collected there in 1926.)

(Horse-shoe Vetch, *Hippocrepis comosa* L., has long been known as a native Jersey plant.)

SAINFOIN *Onobrychis viciifolia* Scopoli (*O. sativa*)
This was grown in Guernsey in the 18th century, and was noted by Gosselin in his first draft 'dans les Prairies'. But there has been no subsequent mention of this S. European agricultural fodder plant. J casual. A –. S –. H –.

PEA *Pisum sativum* L. Peis
Garden and agricultural peas (they were at one time a major item of diet) are liable to get to waste places and sprout and grow, but never, apparently, maintain themselves. There are five such records, all in recent years. In earlier times such obvious intruders were ignored by botanists, and often still are. Pea haulms were one of the coverings used on Guernsey Green Beds. An old saying is 'S'nou lli daönne aën peis, i'prend enne faire'. If he is given an inch, he'll take a foot. J casual. A –. S –. H –.

HAIRY TARE *Vicia hirsuta* (L.) Gray
Quite frequent. The first collector was Gosselin. J frequent. A frequent. S common. H 1957.

SMOOTH TARE *V. tetrasperma* (L.) Schreber
Gosselin collected this too – above the deep road of the Rohais. It seems it is not so frequent. J rare. A rare. S frequent. H –.

(*V. Ervilia* (L.) Willdenow was collected in Jersey in 1926.)

TUFTED VETCH *V. cracca* L. Hazette
Quite frequent, not recently recorded from the southern squares, but rarely as showy as it can be and Gosselin's specimens indicate. The pollen of a vetch-like plant was in the Vazon peat. J frequent. A rare. S occasional. H –.

(*V. tenuifolia* Roth was collected in 1924 in Jersey.)

WINTER VETCH *V. villosa* Roth ssp *varia* (Host) Corbière (*V.* '*dasycarpa*')
A glorious patch found on the west side of the St Sampson's quarry in 1971 by Lady Anne Brewis. This is a variable species sometimes grown for fodder. J gone. A 1902, 1932. S –. H –.

BUSH VETCH *V. sepium* L.
Definitely seen during this century only by the coast south from Havelet and the Val des Terres, and there scarce. But earlier it was known also from St Sampson's, and the Rue des Bergers and the Moulin de Haut in the Câtel. J rare. A –. S Brechou. H –.

YELLOW VETCH *V. lutea* L. ssp *lutea*
This has been known from the L'Erée/Perelle area since Babington's day, and there was a single plant by the Vale Castle in 1894. In 1902 it was seen by Fort Richmond, by 1919 at Vazon, in 1957 on Lihou and in 1970 in further stations as widespread as Fort Doyle, Rousse, Fort Hommet and, inland, by the Dôs d'Ane on a roadside bank. It can hardly have been overlooked in all these places, so presumably has either spread or been introduced, or both. J rare. A –. S –. H –.

(*V. pannonica* Crantz was collected in Jersey in 1930.)

COMMON VETCH *V. sativa* L. ssp *sativa* Vaëche
Collected by Gosselin and in his time much used as a crop agriculturally. As a result stray plants have occurred by roadsides and so on, but it is not easy to demarcate from the next subspecies. J common. A frequent. S occasional. H occasional.

NARROW-LEAVED VETCH *V. sativa* L. ssp *nigra* (L.) Ehrhart (*V. angustifolia*)
This is basically the probable original wild source of the last species, but many plants seem to come between the two in characters, thus making records uncertain. It is possible that most should be referred to this subspecies, in which event it is quite common. Gosselin and Newbould were its first collectors, 100 and 50 years before Marquand. J common. A common. S common. H occasional.

SPRING VETCH *V. lathyroides L.*
Known to Marquand chiefly from the north-west of the island from L'Ancresse to Vazon. In recent years it has also been seen down to L'Erée and Pezeries, and on the east coast at Hommet Benest. In some of these southerly localities the plants are very hairy and look different, but the seeds are typically tuberculate. Gosselin was its first collector. J locally frequent. A 1952. S Brechou. H occasional.

BITHYNIAN VETCH *V. bithynica* (L.) L.
Bithynia, for the benefit of others uncertain in their geography, is the part of Asia Minor opposite Istanbul, where this plant is native, as it may not be in Guernsey, 2,000 miles away. Marquand knew it from waste ground near the Vale Castle in 1890, where it had very narrow leaflets and grew with the also near-eastern Reversed Clover, and persisted until at least 1894. It has been collected since from the Château des Marais, Vazon and Fort Hommet, and is well-established near the Lihou causeway. The earliest note of it there seems to be only in 1957, but it must have been there much longer, and has hardly altered in quantity since. In 1970 it was found on the same bank in the Dôs d'Ane as Yellow Vetch, and in 1971 at L'Islet. J 1928. A rare. S –. H –.

BROAD BEAN *V. faba* L. Faive. Mousette
Like a pea, a patent interloper, ignored by all but recent recorders. The source of the odd plants which are seen can be either garden Broad Beans or agricultural Horse or Tick Beans. J casual. A casual. S –. H –.

YELLOW VETCHLING *Lathyrus Aphaca* L.
Two plants in 1894, found by Collens. J last collected 1900. A 1970. S –. H –.

HAIRY PEA *L. hirsutus* L.
Checked by Druce from the Rousse Tower in 1923, but the specimen seems lost. J 1960. A –. S 1930. H –.

MEADOW PEA *L. pratensis* L.
Apparently less rare than it was, but still scarce. None of its three old stations have been refound; but it has been seen at Fort George in 1903 and 1958, near Rocquaine Bay in 1928 and 1958, in the Vale and Bordeaux in 1970, at Candie cemetery in 1970/1 and at Les Villets, in the Forest, in 1971. J locally frequent. A occasional. S 1971. H –.

GARDEN EVERLASTING PEA *L. latifolius* L.
Known for many years in an unusual place, a marshy spot remote from houses by the Grande Mare. That it should have persisted will be no surprise to those who have tried to dig up its deep tap root, but it has not been seen there for a long time. In late years it has been recorded from St Sampson's, Mont Crevelt, Les Pelleys and in the grounds of Sausmarez Manor, as well as in neglected and other gardens. It was grown by Gosselin in the mid-18th century. It was awarded the AGM in 1973. J occasional. A 1969. S –. H 1904.

(*L. Cicera* L. was collected in Jersey in 1935, *L. niger* (L.) Bernhardi ssp *niger* in 1962/3 and *L. Ochrus* (L.) DC noted in 1965.)

ROSE FAMILY Rosaceae

SPIRAEA *Spiraea japonica* L.f.
The cultivar 'Anthony Waterer' was carted to a dump north of the Vale Castle, where it seemed to be settling down in 1970, but was overwhelmed with fresh dumpings in 1971. The species is Japanese. J –. A –. S –. H –.

(*S. salicifolia* L. has been recorded from Jersey.)

MEADOW SWEET *Filipendula Ulmaria* (L.) Maximowicz
Surprisingly rare in the Channel Islands. It was not included in Marquand's *Flora* at all, although Derrick had found it growing naturalised in St Peter's in 1886. The place was near a farmhouse, and when he next found it, in 1902 at another spot in St Peter's, it was in the meadow next to the Rectory. Both finds were ignored by Marquand when he summarised recent records six years later. Yet Marquand himself had recorded the plant from a neglected enclosure below St Saviour's church in 1891. We now know that in fact the first record was by Miss Guille from near St Andrew's Rectory in 1856. The last time it was seen, '10 feet of it', was by Mrs McCrea in 1928 in a damp ditch near the Claire Mare, where she thought it must be an escape from some grower. It has been refound in none of these places. It was grown by Gosselin as the Queen of the Meadows; but unknown to all these pillars of Guernsey botany, pollen of this species was lying in the peat below Catioroc, close by the Claire Mare and also at Vazon. So it seems that once upon a time it grew in Guernsey away from anyone's house. J rare. A –. S –. H –.

RED MEADOW SWEET *F. purpurea* Maximowicz
A garden plant from Japan long surviving in wet grass in the Fermain valley. J –. A –. S –. H –.

(Dropwort, *F. vulgaris* Moench, was collected in 1924 in Jersey.)

(*Aruncus dioicus* (Walter) Fernald was collected in Jersey in 1948.)

RASPBERRY *Rubus Idaeus* L. Franbouiaise
A native plant in many parts of the British Isles, reinforced by bird-sown seedlings from gardens. Such seedlings have, rarely, been reported, once on steps close by the Town church. But the only place where there is even a small fruiting colony seems to be by a path from Le Bordage to Petit Bot. In 1862 those in the market, at 4d. per lb, were said to be particularly luscious. J occurs. A last record 1900. S –. H –.

DEWBERRY *R. caesius* L.
Needs care in naming, but plants like this occur in scraggier sandier places. J occurs? A frequent? S –. H –.

LOGANBERRY *R. loganobaccus* L. H. Bailey Grosse Franbouiaise
This has been collected on two or three occasions, usually near derelict habitations, no doubt tip-rooted thence. The original plant was found by Judge Logan of Santa Cruz, California in 1881. J rare. A –. S –. H –.

BLACKBERRY *R. fruticosus* L. Ronche. Maeure (the fruit)
About 400 'microspecies' of blackberry have been described from the British Isles, and nobody doubts that there are more still to be added. The cause of this plethora is that most reproduce asexually, which means that aberrations are perpetuated. Few, very few, people have specialised in this genus, and those that have by no means always agree. This account is the result of consultation with A. Newton, and the arrangement is based on his recommendations and namings, help which is much appreciated. The 1968, and some earlier, gatherings were determined by Miles who also saw a sheet gathered by Watson in 1852, which is a distinct species he could not name. Several other gatherings, including at least three different species, remain unnamed.
Babington was a pioneer specialist, but the three species he recorded cannot all be interpreted until his specimens are located. Thirty years after he was in the island he added another species in his *The British Rubi*. But the only at all thorough look at Guernsey brambles was based on a nine-day visit in 1897 by Rev. W. Moyle Rogers, the leading 'batologist' of his day. His list is repeated in Marquand's *Flora*, and is included with one or two amendments in his *Handbook of the British Rubi* in 1900. He also saw Druce's gatherings in 1906. Since then there have been barely a dozen successful collections made – the lack of success being at least partly due to several of the island's brambles differing from those in the rest of the British Isles. Rogers's specimens it has not yet proved possible to disinter, and until they are, it is unwise, impossible, to equate most of his, or other, names with current ones or even with those in W. C. R. Watson's *Handbook of the Rubi of Great Britain* of 1958.
In the circumstances the safest course seems to be to list definite records as such and to put others in brackets with the names they were given at the time. Gosselin's specimens belong to the Section *Triviales*. Our information is too scanty to indicate frequencies. Their seeds have been found in the Vazon peat. Until quite recently their stems were used for tying bundles; and a cure for boils was to pass under a tip-rooted stem nine times on nine successive mornings. Blackberries were valued during the occupation, not only the fruits for eating, but the leaves as a substitute for tea.

SECTION *Suberecti* P. J. Mueller
(*R. affinis* var *Briggsianus* 1897.)

SECTION *Triviales* P. J. Mueller
(*R. corylifolius*, and its var *cyclophyllus* 1897. Miles thought this might prove to be *R. conjungens* (Babington) W. Watson.)
R. cf *sublustris* R. Lees. Hougue des Doreys 1970.
R. scabrosus P. J. Mueller (*R. dumetorum* var *ferox*) Rogers 1897.

SECTION *Sylvatici* P. J. Mueller
R. laciniatus Willdenow 1897, 1957, 1969, 1970. This blackberry was depicted as long ago as 1691, but is still unknown outside gardens, unless bird-sown.

R. Boulayi (Sudre) W. Watson Fermain 1973 'very close to this'.
(*R. macrophyllus* var *macrophylloides* 1897.)
R. prolongatus Boulay & Letendre. St Andrew and Lower Rohais 1968. A plant near this was collected at the Dôs d'Ane in 1970 by Lady Anne Brewis.
(*R. rhombifolius* 1897.)
R. polyanthemus Lindeberg (*R. pulcherrimus*) 1897. Les Tielles 1971.
R. rubritinctus W. Watson. Given for Guernsey in Watson's *Handbook* and thence in the *Critical Supplement to the Atlas of the British Flora*.
(*R. robustus* 1907.)
R. cardiopyllus Mueller & Lefèvre (*R.* cf *rhamnifolius*) 1839. 1897.
(*R. dumnoniensis* Babington 1897, and its var *cordatifolius* Rogers ex Riddelsdell. Described as new from Petit Bot 7 July 1897 (*Journal of Botany* 1920, p. 102).)
R. Riddelsdellii Rilstone. Château des Marais 1968.
R. herefordensis Sudre. St Andrews. (Watson's *Handbook*, p. 92.)

SECTION *Discolores* P. J. Mueller
R. ulmifolius Schott (*R. discolor*. *R. rusticanus*). The commonest bramble.
R. argentatus sensu Rogers 1898. (*R. Godroni* sensu Rogers 1900. *R. propinquus* sensu W. Watson, non P. J. Mueller. ? *R. crassifolius* Genevier) 1897. Petit Bot 1971.
(*R. thyrsoideus*. Above St Peter Port. Bailey 1863/7.)

SECTION *Sprengeliani* (Focke) W. Watson
R. Sprengelii Weihe. 1897, thence in the *Critical Supplement*.

SECTION *Appendiculati* Genevier
R. leucostachys sensu Rogers 1897 Babington 21 July 1838. ('Not *R. vestitus* Weihe & Nees'.) Vazon 1906. Icart 1971.
(*R. lasioclados* var *angustifolius* 1897. 1906.)
(*R. Boraeanus*. 1897.)
(*R. conspersus*. Noted in Watson's *Handbook* for Guernsey.)
R. radula Weihe ex Boenninghausen. Mount Durand 1968. (For Rogers's record see *R. Leightonii*.)
(*R. rudis* Weihe & Nees 1897.)
R. Bloxamii E. Lees. Fort George 23 July 1838 (record repeated 1869, both under *R. Lejeunei*). Les Pelleys 1968. Guet. St Andrew's 1971.
R. Leightonii Lees ex Leighton (*R. radula* var *anglicanus*) 1897.
(*R. Lejeunei* var *ericetorum* 1897. See also under *R. Bloxamii*.)
R. vectensis W. Watson (*R. Borreri*. ? *R. retrodentatus*). 1897 and Watson's *Handbook*, p. 170.

SECTION *Glandulosi* P. J. Mueller
(*R. Koehleri* 1849.)
J about 20 records. A about 4. S about 7. H about 3.

MARSH CINQUEFOIL *Potentilla palustris* (L.) Scopoli (*Comarum palustre*). Still only in the Grande Mare and nowhere else in the Channel Islands. J –. A – S –. H –.

BARREN STRAWBERRY *P. sterilis* (L.) Garcke (*P. fragariastrum*)
Frequent perhaps rather than common but unrecorded recently in the north; a welcome sign of returning spring frequently mistaken for the later Wild Strawberry, qv. Its first collector was Gosselin. J frequent. A occasional. S rare. H –.

SILVERWEED *P. Anserina* L. ssp *Anserina* Foûale à macré
Widespread but not all that common. The varieties have been noted with leaves silvery beneath, var *Anserina*, and on both sides, var *concolor* Wallroth – such are Gosselin's specimens, who called it a medicinal plant. Var *nuda* Gaudichaud, with leaves all green, could occur. J common. A frequent. S rare. H local.

(There are Jersey records of *P. argentea* L. (a native), *P. norvegica* L. (collected 1926, *P. Tabernaemontani* Ascherson (collected 1923) and *P. recta* L. (a regular escape), and of the last also from Sark.)

TORMENTIL *P. erecta* (L.) Räuschel (*P. Tormentilla*) Esquinancée. Herbe d'Paralysie.
Generally a common plant, but unrecorded for many squares. Once used herbally against quinsy and paralysis. J common. A frequent. S common. H frequent.

TRAILING TORMENTIL *P. anglica* Laicharding
Only one single plant has ever definitely been found in Guernsey – from a roadside between Mouilpied and Les Vauxbelets collected by A. J. Silverside in 1970, and confirmed by Dr Matfield. She commented it was unusually hairy and probably octoploid. Most plants thought to be this prove to be one of the hybrids. Its earliest, unvouched, record is by Newbould in 1841. J ? A –. S unconfirmed. H –.

FALSE TORMENTIL *P.* × *suberecta* Zimmeter (*P. anglica* × *P. erecta*)
This is the fairly fertile hybrid between Tormentil and Trailing Tormentil which may backcross to either parent. It usually most resembles Tormentil, but has larger flowers with sometimes five petals and the lower stem leaves shortly stalked. It has particularly been noticed in the north-eastern parts of L'Ancresse. Gosselin collected it unawares near the Château des Marais. J ? A –. S –. H –.

FALSE CREEPING CINQUEFOIL *P.* × *mixta* Nolte ex Reichenbach (*P. anglica* × *P. reptans*)
This is the sterile cross between Trailing Tormentil and Creeping Cinquefoil. It looks more like a small version of the latter, but with fewer leaflets and sometimes four petals. Syme a century ago said it was sometimes confounded with the former, and so it still is. It tends to be in drier places than true Creeping Cinquefoil, and may be not uncommon. J ? A frequent. S 1953. H –.

CREEPING CINQUEFOIL *P. reptans* L.
Collected by Gosselin and quite frequent in moister places, perhaps chiefly in the north and west. Locally it is very fine with seven or more lush leaflets. The double-flowered form may crop up and is sometimes taken to gardens. It was reported from a garden path in 1935. J frequent. A common. S occasional. H occasional.

(*Duchesnea indica* (Andrews) Focke was recorded from Jersey in 1945.)

WILD STRAWBERRY *Fragaria vesca* L.
Andros recommended strawberry juice as a sovereign remedy. Gosselin in 1767 wrote for April, 'Plant strawberries'. John Wesley wrote in his Journal for Thursday 16 August 1787 'Mr De Jersey's gardens and orchards (at Mont Plaisir, St Peter Port, which Gosselin knew) are of vast extent . . . from one sort

only this summer he gathered fifty pounds of strawberries daily for six weeks together.' Miss D. Cook, who first told me of this entry, adds that they were cheap – 2d. per lb in the early 19th century, and recipes for strawberry brandy used them lavishly. But what sort of strawberries were they? The Tudor Dr W. Butler is the author of the well-known saying 'Doubtless God could have made a better berry, but doubtless God never did.' But in his days all our strawberries were wild ones of this species taken to gardens and often cultivated there en masse. Such could be the source of the few Guernsey records for this species. Early in the 17th century the continental Hautbois *F. moschata* Duchesne was introduced from Central Europe, and shortly after *F. virginiana* Duchesne from North America. A century later came the larger-fruited *F. chiloensis* from the island of Chiloe in South America. These last two hybridised in the mid-18th century in France and produced *F.* × *Ananassa* which was the starting point for all our modern varieties. J. Duncan's *History of Guernsey* of 1841 (p. 554) records 'Strawberries, raspberries and other small fruits are excellent in this island and are brought to market in large quantities. It is remarkable that the best of all strawberries, the 'Carolina' or 'Old Pine' (a late variety), which in England is seldom grown . . . should here . . . have been found superior to every other in fruitfulness, as it is also in flavour. This variety is consequently the only one cultivated for market . . . It is frequently planted in orchards . . . even under the shade of apple trees. Others have been tried . . . but only for the sake of variety.' This was still true 21 years later, and they then cost only 1½d. per lb.
What is certain is that nowadays any strawberry is extremely rare outside gardens. Babington recorded this one in St Andrew's, where it was collected at the Rectory, in 1850. Derrick knew it just to the north-east of the parish boundary, in the Câtel, and a specimen has been seen from the Câtel dated about 1840. Marquand seemed also unaware that Royle had collected it at St George in 1895. It was behind St Saviour's church in 1912; reported at Four Cabot until the 1930s; a record unsupported, but probably reliable, was made in 1958 and in 1968 it was seen in what might have been Derrick's place, on the north hedgebank of the Les Pelleys lane. Finally in 1973 P. Girard found it atop a wall in Montville Drive. It has been claimed elsewhere, but never proved. And yet there seem plenty of suitable places where this species could not only survive and prosper, but also be native. J locally frequent. A –. S –. H –.

GARDEN STRAWBERRY *F.* × *Ananassa* Duchesne Frase
This is the only other strawberry recorded from Guernsey and is also very rare – just twice listed, in 1958 (on a wall) and 1968. J escape. A occasional. S 1934. H –.

(*F. chiloensis* (L.) Duchesne has been known on a bank in Sark since 1933.)

HERB BENNET *Geum urbanum* L.
Occasional and never in plenty. Yet it is marked as common in Gosselin's list. His specimens came from Candie. J common. A occasional. S occasional. H –.

AGRIMONY *Agrimonia Eupatoria* L. ssp *Eupatoria*
Listed, almost certainly for the next species, with which it was often lumped, by the youthful Newbould from St Martin's and in the Câtel in 1841 and by Major Smith shortly after near the Château des Marais and in a lane near Kings Mills. Of none of these have any specimens been traced, and Marquand records the next species from the Câtel, twice. A specimen from 1930 expertly said to have been of this species has proved to be of the next, and so almost certainly is another of 1923. J rare. A rare. S 1892. H –.

FRAGRANT AGRIMONY *A. procera* Wallroth (A. *odorata*)
Rare in Marquand's time, and even rarer since. Three collections antedate his first record, Gosselin from Moulin Huet (who called it a medicinal plant), Dupuy from Jerbourg Point in 1864 and Miss Dawber from Saints Bay in 1888. There are only two later ones, Colborne Hill 1923 and near Fermain Bay 1930, and no note of it since. J last collected 1929. A –. S 1958. H frequent.

LADY'S MANTLE *Alchemilla vulgaris* L.
Gosselin listed this from a field in the Câtel in his first draft. J 1928 (*A. filicaulis* ssp *vestita*). A –. S –. H –.

PARSLEY-PIERT *Aphanes arvensis* L.
Until 1949 all records for Parsley-piert were given under this specific name. In that year Dr S. M. Walters showed that there were in fact two species in the British Isles. This one is apomictic, which is relatively unusual in an annual and in a weed. It has been collected only twice in Guernsey, first in 1970 from the Caledonia nursery, where it was growing exuberantly in one small area, no doubt introduced, the next in 1971 in a cultivated field near Kings Mills. Its grey colour and leafier look first betray it, but the fruiting capsule and calyx must be examined for confirmation. J rare. A rare. S occasional. H ?

LESSER PARSLEY-PIERT *A. microcarpa* (Boissier & Reuter) Rothmaler
Gosselin's specimens are of this species, which is common in the island and particularly typical of sandy turf and cliff tops. J common. A common. S common. H common.

SALAD BURNET *Sanguisorba minor* Scopoli ssp *minor* (*Poterium Sanguisorba*)
Known to Marquand, and indeed others, only from the area near where the Golf Clubhouse now is, on north-west L'Ancresse – Gosselin collected it on 'L'Ancresse Plain'. It now however extends much farther east, to the Doyle Rock. In 1970 it was also found growing tall and lush (which it can do on L'Ancresse) right by the path on Pleinmont Point in the south-west. There seemed reason to suspect this of being the fodder subspecies *muricata*, but its fruits denied it. J unconfirmed. A very rare. S –. H local.

(Fodder Burnet, *S. minor* Scopoli ssp *muricata* Briquet, has been recorded from Jersey and Sark.)

GREAT BURNET *S. officinalis* L.
The pollen of this species was detected in the peat at Catioroc. J last collected 1928. A –. S –. H –.

AMERICAN PILLAR *Rosa setigera* Michaux × ?
A single rambler dating from 1902, which can maintain itself in scrub, outdoing the brambles and all, and does this, for example on L'Ancresse and at Petit Bot. J –. A –. S –. H –.

CEMETERY ROSE *R. Wichuraiana* Crépin
Naturalised in fragrant abundance and exuberance on the north-west edge of the Fort Saumarez promontory in full face of the sea and triumphing over all opposition. It was planted here about 1925 by Mrs H. Walters, according to Miss R. de Sausmarez. It received the AGM in 1973. J –. A –. S –. H –.

DOROTHY PERKINS *R. Wichuraiana* Crépin × a Hybrid Perpetual
This well-known American rambler dating from 1901 survives vigorously in hedges and scrub, for example near Fort Saumarez and on L'Ancresse. J –. A –. S –. H –.

JEAN GUICHARD *R. Wichuraiana* Crépin × a Tea Rose
Another successful survivor on the cliff edge, this time below the Guet at Cobo. Miss M. E. de Putron named this rose and several others. J –. A –. S –. H –.

MAY QUEEN *R. Borboniana* Desportes × *R. Wichuraiana* Crépin
Raised in the USA at the end of the last century and surviving well after nearly half a century beyond Fort Saumarez. J –. A –. S –. H –.

MAIDEN'S BLUSH *R.* × *alba* L.
An 18th century cultivar of uncertain origin (cf *Flora Europaea*, Vol. II, p. 26), which is also to be seen at the cliff edge beyond Fort Saumarez, planted there in the 1920s. J–. A–. S–. H–.

RED ROSE OF PROVINS *R. gallica* L. 'Officinalis'
This is the ancient and magnificent Apothecary's Rose, another to have found its niche in the wild on the Fort Saumarez peninsula. It was first named by G. S. Thomas, who helped with others of these old shrub roses. J –. A –. S –. H –.

SEVEN SISTERS *R. multiflora* Thunberg 'Platyphylla'
Grows with 'Jean Guichard' at Cobo. J –. A –. S –. H –.

CRIMSON CONQUEST *R. multiflora* Thunberg × ?
Has persisted for many years in scrub. J –. A –. S –. H –.

(Odd garden roses are to be seen rarely in the wild in Jersey, and are on record from Alderney, while *R. multiflora* × *R. rubiginosa* L. grows out on the Common on Herm.)

BURNET ROSE *R. pimpinellifolia* L. (*R. spinosissima*)
Still on the sandy ground in the north. It was collected in 1879 on Jerbourg Point, but there is no other record outside L'Ancresse. J locally plentiful. A scarce. S locally common. H common.

(One bush of *R.* × *involuta* Smith is recorded from Alderney.)

RAMANAS ROSE *R. rugosa* Thunberg
Forms of this Far Eastern species are part of the scrub by the cliff paths west of Jerbourg. J rare. A recorded. S –. H –.

(*R. stylosa* Desvaux has been collected in Jersey and listed from Alderney and Sark.)

DOG ROSE *R. canina* L. Rose sauvage.
Dog Roses are the only other native Roses seen in Guernsey since Marquand's *Flora*. But even Dog Roses are uncommon, usually only single bushes, and even then often without flower or fruit. This makes precise identification of this difficult group extra difficult – the basic cause of the difficulty is their unique and

highly remarkable chromosomal behaviour, which Dr R. Melville explained in the *Bulletin* of the Belgian National Botanic Garden in 1967. Various varieties are on record, but specimens have not been traced: the only recent one, in 1968, came from a good colony on a part of the cliffs south of Fermain Bay accessible only by boat, which Dr Melville named f. *eriostyla* (Ripart) Wolley-Dod. Marquand wrote that the roses of the island had not been properly studied (which group of plants has?) and other varieties were certain to be found. This is still true. In days gone by, a sacred briar called Pied-du-chat was worn as a waist belt as an infallible (but surely uncomfortable) talisman against witchcraft. When a man was afflicted with boils, he had to pass, fasting and in silence, for many consecutive mornings under an arch of this same briar. J occasional. A occasional. S occasional. H rare.

A DOG ROSE *R. dumalis* Bechstein
Said by Marquand to be the prevailing form, and possibly this is so. J –. A –. S –. H –.

A DOG ROSE *R. obtusifolia* Desvaux (*R. tomentella*)
Only record 1900 from near Fort Doyle. The *Armorican Flora* says it is common in the Channel Islands. J last record 1928. A –. S –. H –.

(*R. tomentosa* Smith was recorded from Alderney in the *Flora*.)

SWEET BRIAR *R. rubiginosa* L.
Three, scattered bushes recorded in the *Flora*. J last record 1965. A occasional. S rare. H local.

A SWEET BRIAR *R. micrantha* Borrer ex Smith
One bush in 1892, above Fermain Bay. J rare. A only record 1900. S last record 1896. H 1879 and 1968.

BLACKTHORN *Prunus spinosa* L. Nère Epäenne. Mais d'Avril
Hard to delimit from the next species. Indeed Lloyd in his *Flora of the West of France* of 1876 wrote that these were less distinct plants than groupings of forms which it was very difficult to separate. But if criteria for this one include stiff blackish stems close set with stiff branches often at right angles, stout thorns and relatively late flowers usually before the leaves appear, this is not all that common. One of the blurring taxa is the var *macrocarpa* Wallroth, often called var *fruticans* Weihe, which has the leaves appearing at the same time as the flowers. Marquand noticed it. The fruits, sloes, are prunelles or blôches in Guernsey-French. J frequent. A recorded. S frequent. H last record 1904.

WILD PLUM *P. domestica* ssp *domestica* Prunier
If criteria for this species include pliable brown often thornless erect branches, flowers not quite so late as the last and with the leaves and the whole plant tending to be more of a small tree than a bush, this too occurs – there is a fine example on the left of the path climbing up to the cliffs east of Petit Bot (but no fruit has been noted for colour or shape). It was said to be not uncommon in 1922. Plums in several varieties used to be grown for market in the days not all that long past when Guernsey could be very much more self-supporting in its food supplies. J rare. A common. S frequent. S common.

WILD BULLACE *P. domestica* L. ssp *insititia* (L.) C. K. Schneider
Bushes occur with characters between those of the last two taxa, and so presumably belong here, where indeed the cliff scrub may fit best. Damsons share the same Latin name, and were grown in the past – stones of a damson or large plum were found in peat at Vazon after a storm in 1847. J rare. A ? S ? H ?

CHERRY PLUM *P. cerasifera* Ehrhardt
Used for hedging in two or three areas in the south, and first spotted thus by Lady Anne Brewis only in 1969. This has greenish very pliable stems and the earliest flowers of all, with the leaves. J –. A –. S –. H –.

WILD CHERRY *P. avium* (L.) L.
Planted at Fermain, and much noticed and recorded from there, but only since 1968. There seems no other clear record, and yet cherries were grown in the past. Cherry trees are mentioned in proceedings before the Greffier on 26 June 1736. Gosselin lists this species from a hedge between the Rohais and the Câtel church, but this will doubtless have been the next one, with which it was at one time combined. J planted. A –. S planted. H planted.

MORELLO CHERRY *P. Cerasus* L. Ch'lise Bayot
This has long been planted in hedges, where it stays, suckering and sometimes producing good fruit. It has been recently noted in five places, in St Peter's, the Câtel, St Andrew's, St Martin's and St Sampson's, but is easily passed by. Metivier wrote of 'Les Chlisiers, provenus d' la Normandie, bllàncs coum la née.' J occasional. A –. S 1953. H –.

(Cherry Laurel, *P. Laurocerasus* L., is occasional in Jersey, and Bird Cherry' *P. Padus* L., planted.)

KHASIA BERRY *Cotoneaster Simonsii* Baker
Has been recorded self-sown. It comes from N.E. India. J –. A rare. S –. H –.

FISH-BONE COTONEASTER *C. horizontalis* Decaisne
A native of China to be seen bird-sown atop walls, a reward for looking up. It has been noted thus in four places, all in the south. J –. A –. S –. H –.

TREE COTONEASTER *C. frigidus* Wallich
A spray from a plant of this Himalayan species was collected by the cliff path south of Fermain Bay in 1958. J –. A –. S –. H –.

WALLSPRAY *C. microphyllus* Wallich ex Lindley
Similarly liable to appear on walls. It is to be seen in several places; in one of these, at Les Gigands, H. Nicolle reports he has known it for fifty years. It originated in the Himalayas. J rare. A –. S –. H –.

HAWTHORN *Crataegus monogyna* Jacquin ssp *nordica* Franco. (*C. oxyacantha*) Bllanche Epäenne. Mais d'mai
Known to Andros in the 16th century and still planted, above all for quick hedges (heismies), or as boundary marks. Bushes were put near houses to keep the devil away, for it was considered sacred. Since it fruits freely, birds can spread it far and wide and it is recorded from every square. The fruits, haws, are hagues in Guernsey-French – tou plloin d'hague, fre hivaer is the island version

of the erroneous old saying. J common. A locally common. S common. H occasional.

MIDLAND HAWTHORN *C. laevigata* (Poiret) DC
Recorded by the *Armorican Flora* for all the Channel Islands, largely through a misinterpretation of Linnaeus's *C. oxyacantha.* J recorded. A recorded. S error. H recorded.

HYBRID HAWTHORN *G × media* Bechstein (*C. laevigata* × *C. monogyna*)
Some hedges seem to contain bushes with leaves of this hybrid. It occurs readily where the parents grow within crossing distance and is fertile, and always liable to appear in planting material. J –. A –. S –. H –.

MEDLAR *Mespilus germanica* L. Meslier
Single scattered small trees, usually with spiny branches, are currently known in five places, all in the south. A tree at Four Cabot is said to be at least 50 years old. Andros knew it in Tudor times, and Knowlton 137 years later found them in plenty near Saltpans. He added later that it grew 'in all the hedgerows and rocky mountains' and that the fruit was smaller than in gardens. At about the same time a recipe used ripe medlars 'for restoring smoaky wine'. But Ansted in 1862 wrote that it ripened fruit badly and hardly repaid cultivation. A bush on the cliff path west of Le Gouffre has flowers with up to twice the normal number of flowering parts. J local. A –. S 1960. H –.

(*Amelanchier Lamarckii* F.-G. Schroeder is established in Jersey.)

ROWAN *Sorbus aucuparia* L. (*Pyrus aucuparia*)
Seen in Fermain in 1969 by E. A. Ellis, presumably through birds giving a helping hand to a non-native plant – for it is normally to be seen only in gardens in the Channel Islands, although Ansted called it naturalised. J rare. A –. S 1970. H –.

(White Beam, *S. aria* L., is planted in Jersey.)

PEAR *Pyrus communis* L. Pairier
Recorded from Fermain incorrectly in 1924 (it was an Apple) and correctly in 1957, but no doubt as planted as the Cherry there. A record from La Moye was also in fact not this but an Apple. Dwarf pears were noted by Knowland in 1726. Pears used to be grown for market, and the 'Chaumontel' variety was famous. One in 1859 weighed 38 oz.; in 1862 it was said 8–10,000 were exported each year, weighing between 9 and 18 oz. each, plus 2–300 bushels of smaller ones; and the *Gardeners Chronicle* for 28 April 1877 reported that Prince Bismarck after eating some wrote that he had always heard that Guernsey was famous for its pears. Metivier indeed wrote 'Et l'cieu de nos periers d'Chaumontel. Il est rinoummai dans la grande terre'. J rare. A rare. S rare. H planted.

(Wild Pear, *P. Pyraster* Burgsdorf, or something like it, has been known from Jersey for some time.)

WILD CRAB *Malus sylvestris* L. Miller (*Pyrus Malus*)
Claimed, but so far without good evidence. J –. A –. S –. H –.

APPLE *M. domestica* Borkhausen Poummier (*Pyrus Malus* var *mitis*)
Apples were specially commented on in gardens by Knowlton in 1726. In 1751

it was remarked that there had been 'of late years a great Increase of Cyder and the Inclination of the People to that Liquor preferably to Beer.' The Duke of Richmond's map of 1787 shows the great extent of orchards at that time, and the *Encyclopedia Britannica* of 1792 said the island was so full of gardens and orchards whence cyder was so plentiful that the common people used it instead of small beer. In 1830 7,587 bushels of apples were exported and in 1833 no less than 116,832 gallons of cider. 60 varieties were exhibited by one man at the 1837 horticultural exhibition, 'each without a speck'. In 1859 the beverage was still, at all times, cider. 54 varieties were known and grown in the island in 1862, in which year a visitor remarked that some trees must have outlived nearly a century. Metivier refers to 'd'cidre fort et doux, comme i n'y en a guerre'. La Pomare in St Peter's was once the centre of a cider-growing district, and the Hougue du Pommier gets its name from an apple tree. Yet the tree is now rare outside gardens – did none of these vast orchards leave any descendants? There is an article on cider-making in the *Transactions* for 1953, and another in the book on the *Guernsey Farmhouse*. The punishment in 1611 for stealing apples was 'mis en collyere', a collar round the delinquent's neck. J scarce. A rare. S rare. H 1922.

STONECROP FAMILY Crassulaceae

CAUCASIAN STONECROP *Sedum spurium* Bieberstein
A frequent easy rock garden plant from the Caucasus, which may find life easy outside too. It has been recorded thus from waste ground in the Garenne d'Ancresse in 1968. J rare. A 1963. S –. H –.

SLENDER CAUCASIAN STONECROP *S. stoloniferum* S. G. Gmelin
A scarce plant much confused with the last and also Russian, but quite distinct to those who know it. It differs in its smaller entirely hairless stalked leaves and spreading fruits on tall slenderer stems. A fine patch was found by Lady Anne Brewis in 1968 where it still flourishes, under bramble bushes not far from the Reservoir. J –. A – .S –. H –.

(Marquand found a single plant of Orpine, *S. Telephium*, in Alderney in 1900, doubtless out of a garden.)

(*S. dasyphyllum* L. was recorded from Jersey in 1926.)

ENGLISH STONECROP *S. anglicum* Hudson Pain d'Souari
Very common round the coast, not so common inland. First collected by Gosselin. J common. A common. S common. H common.

WHITE STONECROP *S. album* L. ssp *album*
Marquand knew only two places for this. Nowadays, thanks no doubt to gardeners, it has been noted in very many more. But its status is not good. J frequent. A occasional. S rare. H local.

WALL-PEPPER *S. acre* L.
Hardly any longer 'rather common generally', but still to be seen not unplentifully locally, chiefly in sandier ground. Gosselin collected it from the Longstore to St Sampson's. J locally common. A common. S 1897. H occasional.

ROCK STONECROP *S. Forsteranum* Smith
There is only one record of this since the *Flora*, and this will surely have never been more than a garden plant temporarily outside. J recorded. A –. S –. H –.

LARGE YELLOW STONECROP *S. reflexum* L. Groumil
Another rockery and herbal plant which can be tenacious of life outside. The earliest record is from Newbould from St Martin's in 1841/2. There are a few recent ones, but it is not known if the plants survive. It was used in bygone days as a tisane with Thyme, being said to be useful in diabetic disorders. J occasional. A –. S –. H –.

GREATER STONECROP *S. praealtum* A. DC
A quite frequent garden plant, which can form mounds up to 3 feet high and across. It is not always clear which can be said to be outside gardens, but one or two at least, for example north of Bordeaux, certainly are. It comes from Mexico as does the similar *S. dendroideum* Moçiño & Sessé, for which it has been taken. J since 1922. A –. S –. H –.

Greater Stonecrop × 1/6

HOUSELEEK *Sempervivum tectorum* L. Jaune Barbe
Gosselin noted it from housetops, but 'I doubt its being indigenous'. 'The houseleek covers the roofs of thatched cottages,' wrote Ansted in 1862. 'Formerly common on the roofs of farm buildings, but now very rare and almost extinct,' wrote Marquand in 1901. Delete from 'very to almost' and that is the subsequent position. Indeed was it ever other than planted and surviving? Did it ever warrant its hallowed place in the British flora? Its flowers are red, not yellow, and the Guernsey-French name is a corruption of Joubarbe, itself derived from *Jovis Barba*, Jupiter's Beard. He was God of Thunder, and this herb was deemed a protection against it, wherefore it was planted on roofs. J collected 1924. A –. S –. H –.

MOSSY STONECROP *Crassula Tillaea* Lester-Garland (*Tillaea muscosa*)
Quite frequent in suitable places, i.e. bare dry ground, mostly on the coasts, but obvious even to the knowing only for a few weeks in April and May, when its fascinating tiny threadlike stems go bright scarlet. Soon after, it has seeded and vanished until the following spring. Its current Latin name was given it in 1903 by the author of the *Flora of Jersey*. It could not become *Crassula muscosa* because this had already been used by Linnaeus for an African plant. J locally frequent. A –. S common. H occasional.
(Another *Crassula* species grows in Jersey.)

WALL PENNYWORT *Umbilicus rupestris* (Salisbury) Dandy (*Cotyledon Umbilicus*) Etriqueur
Very common all over the place. In lusher shadier habitats it can have very large leaves – and has been measured 2 feet 6 inches high – while on walls it can be diminutive. It was first collected by Gosselin. J common. A frequent. S common. H occasional.

SAXIFRAGE FAMILY Saxifragaceae

RUE-LEAVED SAXIFRAGE *Saxifraga tridactylites* L.
One of the delightful small May ephemerals, a few plants always liable to crop up in the more open parts of sandy ground or on walls, but only in the north-west as far south as Vazon. Gosselin collected his 'on the Grand-miles'. J locally common. A frequent. S –. H frequent.

(Meadow Saxifrage, *S. granulata* L., grows in Jersey with double flowers.)

(London Pride, probably *S.* × *urbium* D. A. Webb, was recorded from Alderney in 1963 and in Jersey.)

PERSIAN SAXIFRAGE *S. Cymbalaria* L.
A gay garden annual which can sow itself freely and may do so outside them. It was spreading to the Rue à l'Or in St Saviour's in 1972. J –. A –. S –. H –.

(The Californian Umbrella Plant, *Peltiphyllum peltatum* (Torrey ex Bentham) Engler, has survived where it was planted for Sir C. Mackenzie on Herm in the 1920s.)

BERGENIA *Bergenia* × *Schmidtii* (Regel) S-Tarouca (*B. ciliata* (Haworth) Sternberg × *B. crassifolia* (L.) Fritsch.)
The Asiatic Bergenias with their stout rootstocks and leathery leaves can outlast other plants in derelict gardens. One was recorded in St Martin's in 1969, another on the Vale dump in 1973 which H. C. Pugsley and Dr Yeo named as above. J recorded. A –. S –. H –.

FRINGE CUPS *Tellima grandiflora* (Pursh) Douglas ex Lindley
A western American plant which can naturalise from seed in shadier places. It does so in two uncultivated parts of the Caledonia Nursery. J –. A –. S –. H –.

GOLDEN SAXIFRAGE *Chrysosplenium oppositifolium* L.
Said by Marquand to be common in the middle and south. But the most northerly places at present known are the Fauxquets Valley and Oberlands. Gosselin collected it also near St Andrew's. J locally frequent. A –. S –. H –.

(*C. alternifolium* L. was collected in 1925 in Jersey.)

HYDRANGEA FAMILY Hydrangeaceae

HYDRANGEA *Hydrangea macrophylla* (Thunberg) Seringe ssp *macrophylla*
This familiar late summer bush with nearly all sterile flowers derives from an ancient Japanese form 'Ajisai' of a plant wild in Honshu. It has been popular

since the end of the 18th century and can, does, persist magnificently. But it does, can, do no more and should hardly be included among our wild plants. Nevertheless it is an important feature of the island and few plants flourish better, especially near the sea. MacCulloch in 1826 wrote that 'there were cut in one case from one plant at the same time 1054 flowers [presumably he means inflorescences] and each of them of very large size'. A book on Guernsey of 1834 refers to them as Hydrungeers. Botany Bay is still a widespread local name for them, origin unknown. J planted. A planted. S planted. H planted.

ESCALLONIA FAMILY Escalloniaceae

ESCALLONIA *Escallonia macrantha* Hooker & Arnott
Another shrub superbly suited to Guernsey conditions, also especially near the sea, although it suffers in cold winters. It has been grown since at least 1860. It makes a familiar and decorative hedge, which can long survive, partly by suckering. Seed seems to be produced as well. It comes from South America, as do all Escallonias. J planted. A planted. S planted. H planted.

GOOSEBERRY FAMILY Grossulariaceae

RED OR WHITE CURRANT *Ribes rubrum* L. Gradille
Noted two or three times outside gardens, usually as seedlings, once with white fruits. J scarce. A –. S rare. H –.

BLACK CURRANT *R. nigrum* L. Nère Gradille
Noted similarly about three times outside gardens, once on a wall. J scarce. A –. S –. H –.

FLOWERING CURRANT *R. sanguineum* Pursh
An American shrub grown for its early pink flowers and for hedging. Its dusty blue fruits are less noticed, but the birds take them and so it appears in the wild. Indeed it has been noticed thus, first in 1958, more than other currants. It too has been seen on top of a wall. J collected 1926. A –. S –. H –.

GOOSEBERRY *R. Uva-crispa* L. Guerouaisier
So far noted only twice, both in recent years in hedges. J rare. A rare. S rare. H rare.

SUNDEW FAMILY Droseraceae

COMMON SUNDEW *Drosera rotundifolia* L.
'Mr Butler found it in the Grande Mare in 1812.' So he may have, but no more is known, not even who Mr Butler was. J rare. A –. S –. H –.

LOOSESTRIFE FAMILY Lythraceae

PURPLE LOOSESTRIFE *Lythrum Salicaria* L.
Still rare, indeed perhaps rarer, and yet one might have expected it to have been

plentiful in the wetter Guernsey of the past and to have held on in many places. So it has in very small patches in Footes Lane and in the Marais to the north of the Château des Marais, where Gosselin collected it. It was noted also from L'Aumône crossroads in 1939, and might still be in the Vale. J locally frequent. A –. S –. H –.

GRASS POLY *L. Hyssopifolia* L.
A rare plant which comes and goes and reappears, often years later. But there is no record of its reappearing after any of its occurrences in Guernsey in 1862 (F. A. Hanbury), 1892 and 1898 (Kitching). J rare. A –. S –. H –.

GREATER GRASS POLY *L. junceum* Banks & Solander
The plant reported as the last species in 1924 from Le Varclin collected by Mrs Hichens proves to be of this larger-flowered Mediterranean species. It is always liable to appear in bird seed. J 1969. A –. S –. H –.

WATER PURSLANE *L. Portula* (L.) D. A. Webb (*Peplis Portula*)
Still very rare and on L'Ancresse only. It was noted near Fort Doyle in the *Flora* and in 1923 and 1934, but seems now to survive only in extremely tenuous quantity by a pool in the south-west. Gosselin however collected it from the Camp-duré and the Forest, but no one else has; and Babington recorded it from the Grande Mare. J rare. A –. S rare. H –.

MYRTLE FAMILY Myrtaceae

[The Chilean Myrtle *Myrtus Luma* Molina (*Eugenia apiculata*) thrives in the Guernsey climate, and very fine bushy trees with lovely reddish trunks are to be seen in many gardens. These not only flower superbly, but fruit freely, and seedlings appear in quantity. But so far none have been noticed outside gardens. The Myrtle whose abundance astonished Knowlton in 1726 will have been the Common one, *M. communis* L.]

DAPHNE FAMILY Thymelaeaceae

SPURGE-LAUREL *Daphne Laureola* L. ssp *Laureola*
Possibly bird-sown and not planted in the Moulin Huet Valley in 1957. It was earlier, in 1921, recorded, surely bird-sown, on top of a wall at Les Vardes, St Peter Port. Ansted called it naturalised in 1862, but it seems barely even that: Marquand ignored it. These are the only records. J rare. A –. S –. H –.

ELEAGNUS FAMILY Eleagnaceae

ELEAGNUS *Eleagnus glabra* Thunberg
This Far Eastern species is frequently and decoratively planted for hedges, and particularly large bushes survive near the Mare de Carteret. It has fragrant flowers in late autumn. J –. A –. S –. H –.

ELEAGNUS *E. umbellata* Thunberg
There is a fine old specimen of this Asiatic bush in a field hedge near Kings Mills, found by A. Leslie. J –. A –. S –. H –.

(Sea Buckthorn, *Hippophae Rhamnoides*, L. has been planted in Jersey.)

WILLOW-HERB FAMILY Onagraceae

(*Ludwigia palustris* (L.) Elliott was last collected in Jersey in 1926.)

ROSE-BAY *Epilobium angustifolium* L. (*Chamaenerion angustifolium*)
At the time the *Flora* was written, Rose-bay was a distinctly rare plant in the British Isles. For reasons still only guessed at, it began to spread in the wild before the First World War in clearings in woods, by railways and on waste ground. Hitler having ensured more waste ground during the Second World War, its spread was thereby accelerated. Guernsey has no clearings in woods and no railways, and Hitler's attentions took on a different form, which may explain its tardy and slow spread in the island, or Guernsey has a different less aggressive genotype. Very likely the plants now in the wild will have come from gardens – Gosselin grew it as French Willow in the mid-18th century. Good colour forms, white included, can be good indeed and two were given the Award of Merit of the RHS just before the last war. But gardeners eventually find its rhizomes too questing and its seeds too prolific, so out it goes, if it hasn't got out already on its own. In Guernsey it was first found in the wild in a peat patch on L'Ancresse in 1935, and then in a furze brake on Mont Varouf in 1937, which is now under the Reservoir. Fourteen years later it was seen at Icart, and seven years after that on the cliffs of Mont Hérault. Ten years later still it was reported elsewhere on the cliffs and inland. It has since been seen in other places, but it is still a scarce plant. J scarce, since 1923. A occasional. S very rare. H –.

GREAT WILLOW-HERB *E. hirsutum* L. Violette d'Praï
Still quite frequent in wet places perhaps chiefly in the northern parts. In Saumarez Park some of the flowers are of a particularly rich pink, and the form with almost white flowers which deepen to apple blossom colour, *albo-rosea* (cf *Proceedings BSBI* December 1968, p. 390), was by the Mare de Carteret in 1968. Gosselin's specimens came from the Mare de Carteret. Miller's *Gardener's Dictionary* 1763 edition, which Gosselin used, says 'The leaves of this plant being rubbed emit a scent like scalded apples, from whence some have given the name of Codlins and Cream to this plant.' But do they? J common. A frequent. S 1874. H rare.

HYBRID WILLOW-HERB *E. × subhirsutum* Gennari (*E. hirsutum × E. parviflorum*)
What was almost certainly this was collected growing with its parents at Saumarez Park, but the specimens have got mislaid. It has also been claimed from near Hougue Patris, and may well have been there. J –. A –. S –. H –.

HOARY WILLOW-HERB *E. parviflorum* Schreber
Quite frequent – chiefly in the north? J local. A occasional. S occasional. H rare.

HYBRID WILLOW-HERB *E. adenocaulon × E. parviflorum*
Detected by Dr T. Pennington among gatherings from Sous l'Eglise in 1971. J –. A –. S –. H –.

HYBRID WILLOW-HERB *E.* × *dacicum* Borbás (*E. obscurum* × *E. parviflorum*)
Named by Ash from Picquerel in 1958. J –. A –. S –. H –.

HYBRID WILLOW-HERB *E.* × *weissenburgense* F. W. Schultz (*E. parviflorum* × *E. tetragonum*)
Named by Dr Pennington from Sous l'Eglise in 1971. J –. A –. S –. H –.

BROAD-LEAVED WILLOW-HERB *E. montanum* L.
Fairly frequent only. Gosselin was its first collector. J frequent. A occasional. S rare. H 1958.

(*E.* × *aggegratum* Celakowsky (*E. montanum* × *E obscurum*) was determined by Ash from Herm in 1958. *E.* × *neogradense* Borbás (*E. lanceolatum* × *E. montanum*) was collected in 1940 in Jersey.)

SPEAR-LEAVED WILLOW-HERB *E. lanceolatum* Sebastiani & Mauri
A distinctive and graceful willow-herb, which occurs occasionally, but never in much quantity. It was collected by Gosselin and recorded by Watson in 1852. J frequent. A occasional. S –. H 1958.

HYBRID WILLOW-HERB *E lanceolatum* × *E tetragonum*
Collected on spoil from a war-time tunnel at Sous l'Eglise in 1971 and named by Dr Pennington. J –. A –. S –. H –.

(*E. roseum* was gathered in Jersey in 1968.)

AMERICAN WILLOW-HERB *E. adenocaulon* Haussknecht
Much sought for and wishfully claimed, but never successfully until 1971 when two gatherings by E. Milne-Redhead, from Sous l'Eglise and St Peter Port, proved to include this spreading American species. J rare. A –. S –. H –.

SQUARE-STALKED WILLOW-HERB *E. tetragonum* L. ssp *tetragonum* (*E. adnatum*)
Fairly frequent? J frequent. A occasional. S rare. H occasional.

SOUTHERN WILLOW-HERB *E. tetragonum* L. ssp *Lamyi* (F. W. Schultz) Nyman
A critical plant claimed by Mrs McCrea in 1928 from the Coudré Mill, but without a voucher. J –. A –. S –. H –.

(*E.* × *thuringiacum* Haussknecht (*E. obscurum* × *E. tetragonum*) was reported from Jersey in 1907.)

SHORT-FRUITED WILLOW-HERB *E. obscurum* Schreber
Collected by Gosselin over a century before Marquand. Druce recorded the var *strictifolium* Haussknecht, which has been mistaken for the last species. Generally common. J frequent. A occasional. S occasional. H occasional.

MARSH WILLOW-HERB *E. palustre* L.
Still in the Grande Mare, in quantity in one place in 1968. A plant with white flowers was seen in 1971. It has been claimed elsewhere, but without evidence. J collected 1925. A –. S –. H –.

NEW ZEALAND WILLOW-HERB *E. brunnescens* (Cockayne) Raven & Englehorn (*E. 'nerterioides'*)
This appeared in 1968 among heathers from England in Hon. L. Palmer's garden in St Saviour's. He took care not to eradicate this interesting Antipodean weed, which had hitherto not reached the Channel Islands, and it persists. J –. A –. S –. H –.

LESSER EVENING PRIMROSE *Oenothera biennis* L.
First definitely recorded in 1941 by Ewald. Earlier claims are uncertain for, following 'Bentham & Hooker', all Evening Primroses tended to be called *O. biennis*, and no vouchers are known, except for the earliest records, which prove them to have been of the Fragrant species. It is now very rare indeed, and may always have been so. It has only two post-war records, both in 1967, both confirmed by Dr K. Rostanski in Poland. Parkinson in 1629, only ten years after its introduction to Europe from America, called it the Tree Primrose of Virginia 'smelling somewhat like a primrose; as the colour is also (which hath caused the name).' J –. A –. S –. H –.

LARGE EVENING PRIMROSE *O. erythrosepala* Borbás (*O. 'Lamarkiana'*)
Because of self-pollination and other causes, individual variations may become perpetuated, and naming of Evening Primroses can be difficult. The first record for this large-flowered species, the commonest generally nowadays, was made in 1942 by Ernst Ewald an officer of the German Occupying Forces, a record taken up in Garcke's *German Flora* of 1972. It was next noted in 1958 and 1961 and on about a dozen occasions since, but rarely seems to be in any quantity. Once there was but a single plant on top of a wall. Its identity has been confirmed by Dr Rostanski. J locally plentiful. A rare. S rare. H rare.

HYBRID EVENING PRIMROSE *O.* × *albivelutina* Renner (*O. biennis* × *O. erythrosepala*)
Appeared from seed from *O. biennis* sent in 1941 from Guernsey by Ewald to Dr O. Renner of Berlin, the specialist in the genus. Some of the seedlings were said to resemble *O.* × *velutirubata* (*O.* × *fallax*) which, Dr Raven writes, suggests an earlier history of hybridisation between these two species. *O* × *albivelutina* is the normal hybrid to be expected when *O. biennis* is the female parent and *O. erythrosepala* the male. But the aberrant seedlings had a constitution which suggested that the male parent should itself have been the hybrid of male *O. erythrosepala* and female *O. biennis*, because it had red veins instead of the white ones of *O.* × *albivelutina*. The original paper is in the *Report of the German Botanical Society* for 1942, p. 457. An up-to-date account of the genus is *Oenothera* by R. E. Cleland 1972. J –. A –. S –. H –.

FRAGRANT EVENING PRIMROSE *O. stricta* Ledebour ex Link (*O. odorata*)
The unblatant unweedy really fragrant Evening Primrose, whose flowers turn a good tangerine colour as they go over. It is a South American plant which takes kindly to sandier places, and has made itself a home locally in such areas, all but one in the north and north-west. It was first collected by Salwey at the Vale on 16 July 1847 and then by Dupuy at Les Godaines in May 1864, both of them calling it *O. biennis*. Miss Dawber named it correctly when she distributed it to the Watson Botanical Exchange Club in 1887 from L'Ancresse. J locally plentiful. A occasional. S –. H rare.

(Evening Primroses under the names of *O. muricata* L. and *O. parviflora* L. have been claimed from Jersey.)

GODETIA *Godetia amoena* (Lehmann) Lilja
A western American, a basis for the gay garden annuals, which was reported as a casual in 1970. J –. A –. S –. H –.

FUCHSIA *Fuchsia magellanica* Lamarck Patoreille
Fuchsias are sometimes planted and may persist after neglect. Ansted recorded in 1862 their attaining a height of fifteen or twenty feet with large woody tree-like trunks. But there is no evidence that they reproduce themselves by seed or sucker. The typical plant of this species is from Southern Chile. Its variety *gracilis* (Lindley) L. H. Bailey persists similarly. The Guernsey-French name means 'Ear-rings'. J planted. A –. S planted. H planted.

ENCHANTER'S NIGHTSHADE *Circaea lutetiana* L.
Not all that common and, as in Marquand's time, chiefly, but not solely, in gardens in the St Peter Port area – there are no records from the north. Gosselin collected it as a weed in his garden then at Glateny and noted it as 'dans les épines' there, and also from Les Maisons de Lac at L'Hyvreuse, which he calls the officers' barracks in his draft list, adding moist hedge bottoms and shady lanes for places where it grew. He noted it as a medicinal plant. So did Bellamy in 1850. J locally frequent. A occasional. S –. H –.

WATER MILFOIL FAMILY *Haloragaceae*

WHORLED WATER MILFOIL *Myriophyllum verticillatum* L.
There are two scraps among Gosselin's specimens which could be of this species. Its pollen and nutlets were detected in the Vazon peat. J –. A –. S –. H –.

SPIKED WATER MILFOIL *M. spicatum* L.
Detected, from pollen and nutlets, in the Vazon peat, but not otherwise definitely correctly recorded since then, except by Gosselin, until found in a goldfish pool at Four Cabot in 1972. J extinct. A rare. S –. H –.

ALTERNATE WATER MILFOIL *M. alterniflorum* DC
Still rare, although collected by Gosselin, and by Babington on Sunday (a day he usually went to church) 26 July 1838, from the Château des Marais. All the records are from the north of the island and the places where it still is to be found are inevitably at the mercy of the developer, who drains their pools. It is currently known in two places in north-west L'Ancresse and at Ville Baudu. Its pollen has been found in the Vazon and the Catioroc peats. J rare. A –. S –. H –.

GIANT RHUBARB *Gunnera tinctoria* (Molina) Mirbel (*G.* '*scabra*')
Gunneras are huge imposing plants quite unrelated to real rhubarbs. Both have large leaves, but Gunneras have truly gigantic, prickly ones, on prickly stalks. This species is naturalised in various parts of Guernsey, all in the south, and has been for well over a century. They were first introduced from Mexico, so it is recorded, in 1851 by Mrs Henry Dobrée of St George, who was ten years later a member of the lively but short-lived branch of the Acclimatisation Society. In 1863 they were said to grow best there; but are not there at all now. If these plants did indeed come from Mexico, it must have been en route from Chile, where this species is native, and whence it had been introduced to Belgium, and to Europe, only two years earlier. Another version indeed relates that they came from Chile

via van Houtte in Belgium – they have been called *G. chilensis*. Plants were also put out at Le Vauon by de V. Carey (who rebuilt that house), later President of the Acclimatisation Society, where they flourished, but are also no longer to be seen. They were said to produce large quantities of seed which germinated spontaneously when thrown carelessly aside on rubbish heaps. The plants at Moulin Huet, where Marquand said it was at its best, were seedlings from Le Vallon close by. He had known it there quite 20 years before 1886, and to be thoroughly naturalised in various other sheltered valleys in 1890. In 1884 there was a luxuriant mass about 200 yards long in the Fermain Valley from which 'many visitors in excursion cars were carrying leaves 5 ft. to 6 ft. across and using them as sunshades'. Here it still grows and seeds, as it does at Havilland Hall and down a cliff north of the Bec du Nez. It has also been reported from Saints Bay, Petit Bot, near Les Sages and the Mare de Carteret and in the grounds of Sausmarez Manor. Yet it is unknown in Brittany. It received the FCC in 1875. J rare. A –. S occurs. H planted 1920–23.

GUNNERA *G. manicata* Linden ex André
This differs from the last not only in being even huger, its leaves often towering well above human height, but in its also huger inflorescence. When this is ripe it has an open, almost ragged look from its thin branches up to 5 inches long; while that of the last species is composed of stubby flask-shaped close-set

Gunnera $\times \frac{1}{24}$

branches 1½–2″ long, making a compact mass rounded at the top. The drawings in the *Garden* for 8 November 1879, p. 413, are helpful, but the leaf distinctions are not always clear, and it could be that some of the colonies in less wet places noted under the last species belong here. But what seems clearly to be this one thrives in the damp thicket in the middle of the Caledonia Nursery, where it was already reported as acclimatised and in great perfection in 1881, only twenty years after its introduction from the Sierra do Mar in southern Brazil to Europe by the Belgian, Joseph Linden (1817–1898). Even in 1909 it was said to be a very scarce plant. J –. A –. S –. H –.

Mare's-tail Family *Hippuridaceae*

Mare's-tail *Hippuris vulgaris* L.
Abundant fruits of this, the true Mare's-tail (as opposed to Horse-tail) with its distinctive single stamen, single style and single ovary, have been found in the Vazon peat. It was, much later, collected by Gosselin, but since then it has been seen no more. J rare. A locally plentiful. S –. H –.

Water-starwort Family Callitrichaceae

Common Water-starwort *Callitriche stagnalis* Scopoli
Quite the commonest species. *Callitriche* remains have been collected from the Vazon peat. J frequent. A rare. S occasional. H –.

Larger Common Water-starwort *C. platycarpa* Kützing (*C.* '*verna*')
A plant collected by Gray in Torteval in June 1894 as the last species was determined as this critical one by Dr J. P. Savidge in 1955. It has in addition been claimed on other occasions and specimens even annotated by him as 'probably this', including Babington's of 26 June 1838. J 1968. A –. S 1896. H –.

Blunt-fruited Water-starwort *C. obtusangula* Le Gall
First collected by Salwey in 1847 (five years before the species was described) and then by Blow in 1876, who claimed it as the first record. It has been found on and off since, but remains elusive if not indeed rare. J occurs. A –. S –. H 1958.

Narrow-leaved Water-starwort *C. hamulata* Kützing ex Koch (*C. intermedia*. *C.* '*pedunculata*')
Collected by Babington at Bordeaux harbour in 1838, by Newbould near Vale Castle, by Tennant at Pont Vaillant in 1905, but recently only in the north-west. J rare. A –. S –. H 1957.

Short-leaved Water-starwort *C. truncata* Gussone ssp *occidentalis* (Rouy) Schotsman
A rare plant anywhere in the British Isles. It used to be abundant from Kings Mills to the Grande Mare and Vazon Bay, and was last reported, without a voucher, from the first in 1956. Close search of this area since has been in vain.

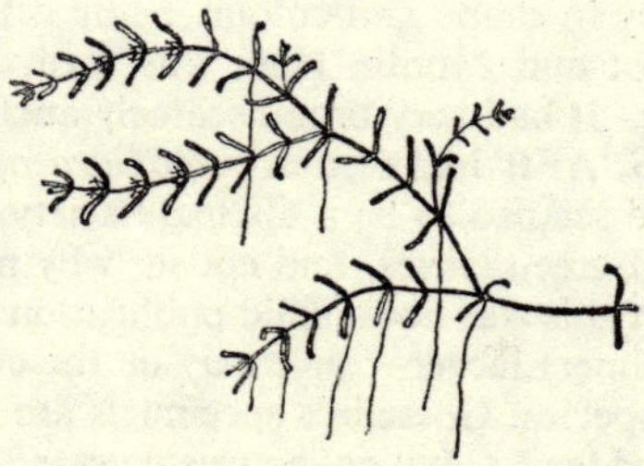

Short-leaved Water-starwort ×1

It was also known from a pool at Fort Doyle, but there is no longer one there. In 1968 it was collected in the pond at Saumarez Park, an unusual habitat for a plant of running water, but in 1970 it was not to be seen there. J –. A –. S –. H –.

MISTLETOE FAMILY Loranthaceae

MISTLETOE *Viscum album* L. ssp. *album*
Mistletoe grows in at least two places in Guernsey. One is in the Caledonia Nursery, where it has been for many years on neighbouring trees of an apple and of *Malus* × *purpurea* (Barbier) Rehder 'Aldenhamensis'. These are berrying females. The other is near Le Vallon, where a male plant arrived on an apple tree in 1967. J rare. A –. S –. H .–

SANDALWOOD FAMILY Santalaceae

(Bastard Toadflax, *Thesium humifusum* DC, is rare in Jersey and Alderney.)

CORNEL FAMILY Cornaceae

RED-OSIER DOGWOOD *Swida alba* (L.) Holub or *S. sericea* (L.) Holub
These two shrubs, which are better known under *Cornus* as *C. alba* and *C. stolonifera*, are a vicarious pair, the former coming from N.E. Siberia, the other from the other side of the Bering Strait, in N. America. They can be difficult to tell apart and indeed ought perhaps to be treated as subspecies, or even as ends of a cline. The good character is the shape of the stone of the fruit, higher than broad, and pointed, in *S. alba*, and vice versa and blunt in *S. sericea*. But so far no good fruits have been collected to apply this test. The colonies, by the Mare de Carteret, form thickets up to ten feet high and compete with all comers. J –. A –. S –. H –.

(Common Dogwood, *S. sanguinea* (L.) Opiz ssp *sanguinea*, was last collected in 1927 from Jersey.)

IVY FAMILY Araliaceae

IVY *Hedera Helix* L. ssp *Helix* Yerre
Still common everywhere, perhaps at its most impressive on cliff rock in full blast of the sea spray. Its leaves vary widely in shape and colour, being often highly decorative. One form from Petit Bot and Moulin Huet was formally described by Druce in 1912 as var *sarniensis*. It had very broad scarcely angled deep green leaves. Earlier, on 23 October 1886, 'AFB' had written in the *Gardeners Chronicle* that the common Ivy of the island seemed to be a distinct variety of compact growth and with beautiful emerald green leaves, and ended 'why not call it the Guernsey Ivy, var *sarniensis*?' But this was not a valid publication of this name. Comment on var *hibernica* (Kirchner) Jaeger – or it may be the cultivar 'Hibernica' – is made under the next species. Gosselin's specimens are all with unusually deeply and unevenly 5–6 lobed leaves. Ivy pollen was detected in peat from Vazon Bay and the Catioroc. Its covering the ruins of the Château des Marais, 'Ivy Castle', was noted as early as 1726 by Knowlton, 'which I suppose

gives it the name'. Its fruits were boiled during the occupation. J common. A frequent. S locally frequent. H frequent.

CANARY IVY *H. Helix* L. ssp *canariensis* (Willdenow) Coutinho
Recorded by Chevalier from Pleinmont Point in 1933, a record taken up in Fournier's *Quatre Flores* down to the present day. It has much starrier hairs – compare Plate I in Vol. 38 of the German Dendrological Society's Proceedings 1927 and the article by F. Tobler generally. Chevalier also said that intermediate forms occurred, possibly hybrids, linking it with ordinary Ivy, and that K. Schneider called these intermediate forms var *hibernica*. But Dr Heine of Paris writes 'that Chevalier mistook *H. Helix* "Hibernica" for *H. canariensis* is very obvious, from his publications as well as from his *determinavit* slips . . . and all the French horticulturists do the very same, right up to this day'. Irish Ivy differs from ordinary Ivy in having both sorts of hairs and twice as many chromosomes as either subspecies. J same error. A –. S same error. H –.

(*Aralia elata* Seeman has been strikingly planted in Jersey.)

UMBELLIFER FAMILY Umbelliferae

MARSH PENNYWORT *Hydrocotyle vulgaris* L. Dôve
Inevitably less common as wet places get scarcer, but still to be seen in several parts of the island nestling in the grass, sometimes very fine indeed, as for example in the small pond south of the Golf Clubhouse. Its pollen was, hardly surprisingly, in the Vazon peat. J frequent. A occasional. S frequent. H local.

SEA HOLLY *Eryngium maritimum* L. Cardaon d'banque
Now very local, as pressures increase on its dunes; and holiday-makers dislike sitting on it. But it may still be seen in places on the sandy coasts in its full charm and delicate colouring. Gosselin collected it, noting it for the sand about the sea coast, especially mentioning Long Port. J local. A locally frequent. S 1838. H local.

FIELD ERYNGO *E. campestre* L.
Two records only. A single plant at Bordeaux in 1892, and a small but growing patch (one plant?) near the sea in the centre of L'Ancresse Bay in 1968 found by Dr Bowen. J error? A –. S –. H –.

ROUGH CHERVIL *Chaerophyllum temulentum* L.
Was Babington's otherwise not improbable record for this an error? Visitors do tend to 'remember' after they have left, 'seeing' plants common at home, not realising they are very rare or unknown in the Channel Islands. He collected no voucher. J occasional. A 1838 too. S –. H –.

BUR CHERVIL *Anthriscus Caucalis* Bieberstein (*A. neglecta. Chaerophyllum Anthriscus*)
A distinctive and delicate plant typical of sandier places, now only to be found locally. Gosselin noted it from the Pirouin Battery, which has long ceased to be a likely place for it. J common. A frequent. S 1944. H common.

COW PARSLEY *A. sylvestris* (L.) Hoffmann (*Chaerophyllum sylvestre*)
A real rarity in Guernsey and of strange distribution in the Archipelago. Derrick

knew it in Sausmarez Manor and as a weed in an unspecified garden in Mount Durand, and in some quantity in Saumarez Park. But despite special search no one has seen it there this century or in his other places. It proved however to have been a weed at St George, just to the south of Saumarez Park, until quite recently, when it was eradicated in ignorance of its importance – and after all it is abundant in England. J rare, plentiful on the Ecrehos. A very locally common. S –. H –.

(Chervil, *A. Cerefolium* (L.) Hoffmann, Cherfiel in Guernsey-French, has been seen wild in Jersey.)

SHEPHERD'S NEEDLE *Scandix Pecten-veneris* L. ssp *Pecten-veneris*
Five recorded occurrences, the only one this century being from the Grande Havre in 1924. J last record late 1960s. A 2 records. S 2 records. H –.

HEDGE PARSLEY *Torilis japonica* (Houttuyn) DC (*T. Anthriscus*)
Marquand said this was rather common, but seldom occurred in any quantity. It is now definitely scarce, both in space and in quantity. Gosselin collected it, appropriately, in hedges. J occasional. A last record 1907. S occasional. H –.

(*T. arvensis* (Hudson) Link was collected in 1926 in Jersey.)

KNOTTED BUR-PARSLEY *T. nodosa* (L.) Gaertner
Still scarce, and mostly found near the sea. Gosselin's specimens came from the pebbles between the fort at Belgrave and the Tonelle aux pendus. J scarce. A frequent. S –. H –.

HEDGEHOG-PARSLEY *Caucalis platycarpos* L. (*C. daucoides*)
1900 only, perhaps in grain. J last collected 1926. A –. S –. H –.

BROAD-LEAVED HEDGEHOG-PARSLEY *Turgenia latifolia* (L.) Hoffmann (*Caucalis latifolia*)
Thrice, 1898, 1900 and 1902. This and the last seem to have been less rare as casuals in those days. Both come from the Mediterranean. J error? A –. S –. H –.

CORIANDER *Coriandrum sativum* L.
A Mediterranean annual flavouring herb reported by Druce as naturalised at St Sampson's in June 1877. J casual. A –. S –. H –.

BIFORA *Bifora testiculata* (L.) Roth
A Mediterranean annual, which arrived in 1900, presumably in grain. J –. A –. S –. H –.

ALEXANDERS *Smyrnium Olusatrum* L. Alisant
Not 'rather common' as Marquand wrote, but nowadays often abundant, being most obvious in early summer, when it seems to engulf many roadside banks. By August it might escape the notice of all but those who recognised its jet black fruits on dead keck stems. It has even increased materially in recent years. N. Jee has observed that horses consider it a delicacy, but cows leave it alone, unless they are exceptionally hungry, preferring Hogweed. Gosselin recorded it vis à vis la Porte de la Maison de la Grange, where it still is. On his specimens he noted it also between Mr Carey's garden at Beauregard and James Robillard's, and near Martel's house at the Pierre Percée. It is an old alternative to celery,

no doubt introduced as such from farther south. J locally plentiful. A occasional. S frequent. H common.

HEMLOCK *Conium maculatum* L. Chue
Not common. Gosselin's exquisite specimens, marked rightly 'Plante Vénéneuse', came from near the house of St Clair. J frequent. A locally frequent. S occasional. H frequent.

THOROW-WAX *Bupleurum rotundifolium* L.
Claimed, without a specimen and at the same time and place as the next, in 1900. J collected 1926. A –. S –. H –.

NARROW-LEAVED THOROW-WAX *B. lancifolium* Hornemann (*B. protractum*)
This and not the last is the almost invariable species occurring where bird seed is able to germinate. Its first record was in 1900, its next in 1908. It was recognised in four different gardens where birds had been fed during the winter from 1963 to 1968. In at least two of these the plants persisted from seed, which rarely if ever happens in England, even in places where the last species does so regularly. It was seen also elsewhere in 1970 and 1971. It was illustrated by Mrs Burridge in the Société's *Transactions* for 1967. All the specimens seen have been of the species in its strict sense, and not of the similar, larger, *B. intermedium* Poiret. J casual. A –. S –. H –.

SMALL HARE'S-EAR *B. baldense* Turra ssp *baldense* (*B. 'aristatum'*)
This is one of the rewards for kneeling on the sandy turf of the north-west, down to Vazon. Here it is usually about 1 inch high, and at most 2 inches, but it has been collected in fruit at 3 inches; while the books say the species can reach

Small Hare's-ear ×1

over 4 feet! It varies much however according to habitat – it was named from Monte Baldo in N. Italy, and our plant may well come under the form *minus* (Facchini) Thellung (*nanum*). Babington was the first to note it, on 27 June 1838. Marquand in his *Flora* called it rare, but four years later wrote that it grew plentifully in nearly all the sandhills near the sea, which is nearer the truth today. But it does need searching for, and is invisible to anyone standing up. J locally frequent. A locally frequent. S –. H local.

SLENDER HARE'S-EAR *B. tenuissimum* L. ssp *tenuissimum*
Claimed for Guernsey in Ansted's *Channel Islands*, and it could well have occurred in the salt marshes of the north. But no one else seems to have mentioned it. J –. A –. S –. H –.

WILD CELERY *Apium graveolens* L.
Babington thought this common, Marquand rather common, but it is now scarce, with at most six recent records. Gosselin collected his specimens from Mr Lefebure's Saltpans. J rare. A rare. S –. H –.

FOOL'S WATERCRESS *A. nodiflorum* (L.) Lagasca Bêle
Still frequent, indeed common, in wet places. Small plants may come under the form *minus* (Koch) Godron (*repens*), which has often been misclaimed for the true *A. repens*. The form *ochreatum* (DC) O. Kuntze is also on record. J common. A frequent. S frequent. H local.

CREEPING MARSHWORT *A. repens* (Jacquin) Lagasca
Claimed in 1881 from the Château des Marais, but it was only a small form of the last species, qv. J unconfirmed. A –. S –. H –.

MARSHWORT *A. inundatum* (L.) Reichenbach f.
Known near Fort Doyle until at least 1923 and perhaps 1949. Recorded about 1898 near Grande Havre, at the opposite end of L'Ancresse, and found near Mont Cuet in 1958, and 1 km to the south in 1970, but in very small quantity. The unsupported Les Douvres locality of 1951 was most likely a misidentification. J rare. A –. S 1838. H –.

PARSLEY *Petroselinum crispum* (Miller) A. W. Hill (*P. sativum*) Persi
Only rather locally to be seen now, but it is all down the west coast. The typical wild plant, perhaps native on the coast, has ordinary leaves. The usual garden form with crisped leaves, var *foliosum* (Alefeld) Thellung f. *crispum* (Miller) Fiori & Paoletti, may be seen self-sown. Parsley, Mrs de Garis records, worn under the armpits by men, or drunk as tea in copious quantities by a married couple, ensured fertility. Such tea drunk in early spring cleared the skin. Root of Parsley was recommended for dropsy. J local. A occasional. S rare. H –.

(Corn Parsley, *P. segetum* (L.) Koch, grows rarely in Jersey.)

(Cowbane, *Cicuta virosa* L., was collected in 1924 in Jersey.)

STONE PARSLEY *Sison Amomum* L.
Listed by Gosselin from a field to the south and adjoining the Câtel churchyard and from cornfields. There is a small voucher in his scrapbook, but no other record. J last collected 1925. A –. S –. H –.

BULLWORT *Ammi majus* L.
Miss Dawber 1888. Mrs Burridge 1968, the latter occurrence definitely ex bird seed, and sowing itself until 1971. J –. A –. S –. H –.

LONGLEAF *Falcaria vulgaris* Bernhardi
Three good records. First by Miss Cobbe in 1925 from L'Ancresse Bay, next in 1947–9 on the bank north of the large car park west of Pembroke Bay – the same place? But it was no longer to be seen there six years later. The 1951 record from Grandes Rocques is unvouched. J rare. A rare. S –. H –.

CARAWAY *Carum Carvi* L.
'Three or four plants on a rubbish heap close to the Rabbit Warren in 1904.' But Marquand never wrote where the Rabbit Warren was, nor has any specimen been traced of this sometimes misclaimed plant. J casual. A –. S –. H –.

(*C. verticillatum* (L.) Koch is a rare and interesting native of Jersey.)

PIGNUT *Conopodium majus* (Gouan) Loret (*Carum flexuosum*)
Scarce, perhaps, rather than rare, and not recorded recently in the Vale, St Peter's or Torteval parishes, although there are apparently suitable places for it. J occasional. A –. S –. H –.

BURNET-SAXIFRAGE *Pimpinella Saxifraga* L.
Twice reported, without supporting evidence, in the 1830's and in 1956. J only collection 1925. A –. S –. H –.

(Aniseed, *P. Anisum* L., was collected in Jersey in 1927, a plant known to Gosselin as a cordial and carminative.)

GOUTWEED *Aegopodium Podagraria* L.
A dozen localities – none in the north – noted in a dozen recent years, and never apparently the execrated pest it can be. It has long been used herbally. J common. A 1972. S rare. H rare.

(Greater Water Parsnip, *Sium latifolium* L., has been known in Jersey since 1967.)

LESSER WATER PARSNIP *Berula erecta* (Hudson) Coville (*Sium angustifolium*)
Claimed by Babington in 1839, but there is no specimen in his herbarium from any of the Channel Islands. J 1839. A 1839. S –. H –.

ROCK SAMPHIRE *Crithmum maritimum* L. Perchepierre. Casse-pierre.
Quite frequent round the coasts. It was noted by Knowlton from Fermain in 1726, and used as a pickle at a dinner on 17 May 1748 on the day of the execution of Catherine des Landes. J common. A common. S locally abundant. H common.

TUBULAR WATER DROPWORT *Oenanthe fistulosa* L.
Still managing to survive in the Grandes Mielles area where Gosselin collected it nearly two centuries ago. Still managing to survive too in Les Mielles at the Vale, where Dupuy collected it over a century ago. There have been no other records. J local. A –. S –. H –.

(*O. pimpinelloides* L. ss has been claimed, probably in error, from Jersey.)

PARSLEY WATER DROPWORT *O. Lachenalii* C. C. Gmelin (*O. 'pimpinelloides'*)
Now very local, but only three records in the last 42 years must understate its frequency. J rare. A –. S –. H –.

HEMLOCK WATER DROPWORT *O. crocata* L. Pain-faie
Still common and often extremely exuberant and lush in wet places. It is often called, misleadingly, plain Hemlock, a name which strictly belongs to *Conium*. But this too is one of the few really dangerous wild plants, and Marquand's

warning should be universally heeded (some German soldiers didn't) – 'This species is one of the most poisonous of our native plants, and many deaths have occurred from eating the roots, which smell and taste (how did he know?) like parsnips' – and look so attractive. It is largely this attractiveness that increases the danger. Cattle have died from eating it, even in recent years. Very rightly it is officially a noxious weed. Gosselin's specimens are labelled *Phellandrium aquaticum*, and marked Plante Vénéneuse. Plants occur occasionally with stems, leaves and even flowers all of a dark brownish purple. J common. A eradicated a century ago. S frequent. H local.

FINE-LEAVED WATER DROPWORT *O. aquatica* (L.) Poiret (*O. Phellandrium*)
Gosselin's specimen labelled this as of the last species. J last collected 1930. A –. S –. H –.

FOOL'S PARSLEY *Aethusa cynapium* L. ssp *cynapium* Tue-Lapin
Not very common, but to be seen all over the island. It seems always to be of the typical subspecies, with the upper bracts much longer than the small umbels and the stalks of the outer fruits twice as long as the fruits. Ssp *agrestis* (Wallroth) Dostál has both much shorter and could occur. Gosselin marked his specimens Plante Vénéneuse. But does it kill rabbits? J uncommon. A rare. S frequent. H –.

FENNEL *Foeniculum vulgare* Miller ssp *vulgare* Fanoué
Quite frequent on the lower coasts, scarcer in the south, and inland, and possibly there due to cultivation. Andros wrote that Fennel – Fenaisie – seeds and leaves drunk with milk would kill worms, and others too used it medicinally. Gosselin collected it, noting it grew near the Maison de Bas, Maingy's at L'Epine, east of the Mare de Carteret, Grand Mielles and Hougue à la Père. J frequent. A locally common. S frequent. H rare.

(Dill, *Anethum graveolens* L., was recorded in Jersey in 1925.)

WILD ANGELICA *Angelica sylvestris* L.
This is in Gosselin's 1788 list, but there is no other record for this surprising absentee from all the Archipelago except J frequent. A –. S –. H –.

(Hog's Fennel, *Peucedanum officinale* L., has been claimed unsatisfactorily for Jersey.)

PARSNIP *Pastinaca sativa* L. ssp *sativa* Panais
Very scarce, and perhaps now only an escape from culture. MacCulloch said Parsnips seem to have been cultivated at a very early period in Guernsey and that tithe was paid in them before the Reformation, for example in 1331. By 1815 local Parsnips were remarkable for their bulk and goodness. They were grown for seed as well as for their roots which were used, unwashed and uncut, rather than Turnips for fattening cattle and pigs, as well as for human use, partly replacing Potatoes. Not long after, the Channel Islands became the centre of their commercial cultivation. A leading variety, the 'Guernsey', originated in the island about 1840 and is still listed. Although only 'semi-long', its roots were said to grow to a length of four feet. Farmers used to deep-dig for them in February and March with La Grand Querue, or Charrue, the heavy plough which might use a dozen horses and oxen. The process called for much local co-operation, and was accompanied by plenty of food and cider, and was still used in the

1920s. Yet the yield, despite all the heavy manuring, was at most 22 tons in 1837, and 20 tons per acre in 1859. The usual rotation in 1841 was Wheat, Barley, Clover and Parsnips. During the occupation Parsnips were used cut and roasted for coffee. J rare. A occasional. S rare. H –.

HOGWEED *Heracleum Sphondylium* L. ssp *Sphondylium* Tchlaise
An officially noxious weed but still very common. There is a specimen in Gosselin's scrapbook. J common. A common. S common. H common.

(Giant Hogweed, *H. Mantegazzianum* Sommier & Levier, is established in Jersey.)

CARROT *Daucus Carota* L. Carotte
Plants undoubtedly exist which seem to have read the books and show the distinctive characters of the usually inland ssp *carota* or of the seaside ssp *gummifer* Hooker f. But, partly perhaps because so much of Guernsey is under the influence of the sea and the species is common, many plants are difficult to place, as Marquand, Lester-Garland and the *Supplement to the Atlas* also found. Indeed Watson sowed seeds of the Channel Islands maritime form and the plants which resulted were even in the first generation indistinguishable from common wild carrots. Occasional plants could in addition come from a garden – for they were grown for seed too – and be ssp *sativus* (Hoffmann) Arcangeli, with the really edible root. Cultivated agriculturally a good crop was said in 1859 to produce about 27 tons per acre. But they were not much grown. Gosselin's specimens are of the inland form. J common. A common. S common. H frequent.

MELON FAMILY Cucurbitaceae

VEGETABLE MARROW *Cucurbita Pepo* L.
Always liable to appear on tips and the like from garden and kitchen rubbish, and so it did on the Mont Cuet dump in 1968, and most likely on other unrecorded occasions too. J -. A 1974. S -. H -.

(White Bryony, *Bryonia dioica* Jacquin, grows rarely in Jersey.

Squirting Cucumber, *Ecballium Elaterium* (L.) A. Richard, may still occur there.)

SPURGE FAMILY Euphorbiaceae

ANNUAL MERCURY *Mercurialis annua* L. Fouarolle
Generally a plentiful weed. Gosselin's specimens show both male and female plants, which he called Plantes Médécinales. J common. A common. S common. H occasional.

(Dog's Mercury, *M. perennis* L., is a rare native on the north and east coasts of Jersey.

The Castor-oil plant, *Ricinus communis* L., occurs occasionally there.)

PURPLE SPURGE *Euphorbia Peplis* L.
Gosselin knew this attractive but elusive plant, but only from Herm. Babington saw it however in great plenty in the Grande Havre on 26 August 1837. Yet there

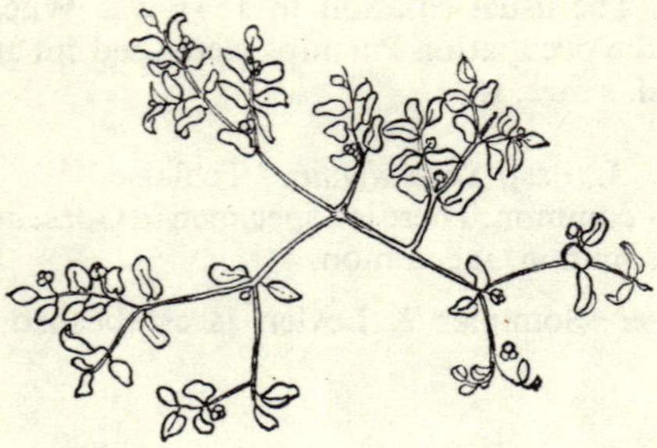

Purple Spurge ×⅔

have been only four records since. Watson collected it in 1850, More north of the Vale church on his brief visit in 1859, and Wolsey in 1861 at Perelle. Druce failed at the Grande Havre in 1877, and presumably everyone else until 1931, when it was recorded near L'Erée without a voucher. Its fruits are distributed by the sea in the same way as Sea Knotweed's, so it always has been uncertain in its appearance, due perhaps to changing currents. It has got much scarcer in the British Isles in recent centuries – Ray knew it plentifully in Cornwall in the 1660s. Nowadays the only place where it can usually be seen is Alderney. J last records 1928. A rare. S –. H last record 1968.

CAPER SPURGE *E. Lathyris* L.
A distinctive and architectural plant which has the habit of cropping up in gardens where it has never been seen, or noticed, before. It may go on doing this, as it did in a garden in St Saviour's for at least 30 years and it is still doing in several gardens elsewhere – there have been at least half a dozen such records since the *Flora*. But at least there is no need to plant it on Guernsey to try to keep moles away, which anyway it doesn't. J occasionally naturalised. A –. S –. H occasional.

SUN SPURGE *E. helioscopia* L.
A frequent weed with its broad yellowish umbel of flowers always looking at the sun – for this is the meaning of its specific epithet, which dates back to Pliny and Dioscorides in the first century A.D. Gosselin's specimens are labelled 'Reveille Matin'. J occasional. A locally frequent. S frequent. H frequent.

PETTY SPURGE *E. Peplus* L. Lait d'Souari. Herbe à verrue
A common and weedy weed, with however the fantastic detail in its flower common to all spurges. Gosselin collected it, noting it in kitchen gardens and rich cultivated soil. Its specific name is identical etymologically with that of the decorative Purple Spurge. J frequent. A rare. S occasional. H occasional.

DWARF SPURGE *E. exigua* L.
Gosselin collected fine specimens, and Marquand called this species frequent, but rare in the north. In 1913 it was said to be common on L'Ancresse. Since then there has been precisely one record, from the Icart area in 1951 by G. H. Morgan, and this despite many people specially looking out for it. J last record 1928. A –. S last record 1930. H –.

PORTLAND SPURGE *E. portlandica* L.
Common on the cliffs, and to be found also all round the coast, sometimes in flower in April. Its first record was by Finlay about 1780. Linnaeus named it after Portland in Dorset, but said this was in Devonshire. J common. A frequent. S locally common. H common.

SEA SPURGE *E. paralias* L.
Gosselin collected this and noted it grew at L'Ancresse, where it still does. It is still scarce and apparently decreasing, as it is in Jersey. It has also been recorded from near Bordeaux harbour, but from nowhere else since the *Flora*. J very local. A locally frequent. S last record 1872. H rare.

CYPRESS SPURGE *E. cyparissias* L. (*E.* '*Esula*')
Mrs McCrea reported in 1935 *E. Esula* from Richmond Avenue as a probable garden escape. Since there is little attraction to growing this in a garden, since 'Bentham and Hooker', which is likely to have been the book she used, lumps *E. cyparissias* with it, and since this latter is a very attractive plant (given room for its roots to roam!), the assumption must be that this is what she saw. Neither plant is to be seen in that Avenue now. J rare escape. A –. S –. H –.

(*E.* '*Esula* L.' was collected in Jersey in 1924 and recorded from Sark in 1958. The alien plant which can closely resemble it and has been called *E. uralensis* was seen above La Pulente in 1956. Its proper name is *E.* × *pseudovirgata* Soó (*E. Esula* × *E. virgata* Waldstein & Kitaibel) according to A. R. Smith.)

WOOD SPURGE *E. amagydaloides* L. ssp *amagydaloides*
A plant now known inland in Guernsey only in the Fauxquets Valley and near the Reservoir. Its main habitat has always been on the south cliffs, where it grows robustly, and perhaps more hairily. Gosselin's specimens came from the Forest School to Plaisance and on the Terres Gosselin, and he marked it Plante Vénéneuse. J common. A –. S 1838. H 1838.

DOCK FAMILY Polygonaceae

COMMON KNOTGRASS *Polygonum aviculare* L. P'tite S'nile. S'nile naeutchie
This is the Knotgrass with larger and broader leaves on the main stem than on the branches, and was collected by Gosselin. It seems much the commonest in Guernsey. The form frequently recorded as var *littorale* Persoon is no more than a seaside adaptation of it. J common. A common. S common. H common?

SMALL-LEAVED KNOTGRASS *P. arenastrum* Boreau
This is the Knotgrass which is particularly successful in surviving in trodden places, hard, wiry and with all the leaves small. For those who can see such things, it has 40 chromosomes, i.e. is tetraploid, while our other two are hexaploids with six sets of ten, 2n = 60. Either this one has been missed or it is rather scarce. But there has been little knowing recording – the earliest specimen is dated 1894. J ? A frequent. S occurs. H ?

NARROW-LEAVED KNOTGRASS *P. rurivagum* Jordan ex Boreau
Gosselin collected this, by chance. In recent years it has been claimed several times, eventually successfully by A. Leslie in 1970 from Mont Cuet, where it has

been seen since, confirmed by Dr B. T. Styles, whose account in *Watsonia* for October 1962 may be consulted. This has its leaves long and narrow, some large, some smaller. J –. A –. S claimed. H –.

RAY'S KNOTGRASS *P. Raii* Babington
First recorded on 12 August 1837 by the man who had given the species its name three years earlier, and said by Marquand to be not uncommon, indeed locally plentiful. But there have been few records since then. One was from Rocquaine in 1925, and then from Vazon, the last in 1961, where it was not all that rare after the war. The earliest collection from there is of two stems from the top of a plant which had 15–20 in all. Maybe it has been, is being, overlooked, but equally it is probably at least much scarcer, perhaps for the same reasons as the next species, as in Jersey. J last record 1926. A 1838. S 1838. H 1851.

SEA KNOTGRASS *P. maritimum* L.
Pollen of this or the last species was claimed from the Vazon peat. Gosselin listed this or the last species, as *P. marinum*, in his first draft. Haslam noted it in 1829, and Babington and two associates collected it at Grande Havre on

Sea Knotgrass ×⅓

14 August 1837. Watson misclaimed it in 1852 and 1865 (both were *Raii*), Syme got it in 1853, More in 1859, Blow in 1876 and finally Marquand found one plant in 1891 growing with the last species. Thereafter diligent search by him and others was without success, nor has anyone succeeded since. It starts flowering in May. This plant and the last and Purple Spurge are at least partly dependent on sea currents for what happens to their seeds, a difficult process for the keenest conservationist to control. J last record 1925. A –. S –. H very locally plentiful.

FLEECE FLOWER *P. amplexicaule* D. Don
A garden perennial from the Himalayas which may survive outside for a while. It has been noted two or three times thus in Guernsey. J rare. A –. S –. H –.

(Bistort, *P. Bistorta* L., was collected in 1928 in Jersey.)

AMPHIBIOUS BISTORT *P. amphibium* L.
Marquand called this rare, but it is nevertheless to be seen quite frequently in

moister or more watery places, where these are allowed to stay moister or more watery. It does not seem to be a weed of cultivated ground in Guernsey. Gosselin's specimens came from watery ditches. J frequent. A occasional. S 1947. H –.

REDLEG *P. Persicaria* L. Herbe traïtresse. Lange d'Ouaie. Rouage S'nile. Rouage Gambe. Courage
A common and variable weed, first collected by Gosselin, some forms, notably whitish ones, being mistaken for the next, glandular, species. Its pollen was found in the Vazon peat, which suggests either it had some status other than arable weed, or that there was then some arable in Guernsey. R. Hay in his book *Annuals* of 1950 says 'the leaves of this attractive plant have a crescent-shaped spot near their centre, whence the name Lady's Thumb.' In Guernsey this spot is attributed to a woman's blood-stained fingers, who was thus betrayed, hence its local name. Gosselin's notes on garden plants record that 'Arse-smart sows itself'. J common. A frequent. S frequent. H 1837.

PALE PERSICARIA *P. lapathifolium* L. (incl. *P. nodosum* (*P. maculatum*))
Marquand called this rare, and it is still at least unexpectedly scarce. In the words of *Flora Europaea* it is 'extremely variable, especially in habit, colour of foliar glands and of perianth and in indumentum' and the various states tend to get perpetuated by its normal self-pollination. Hence the modern tendency, foreshadowed by A. Briggs all but 100 years ago, to merge *P. nodosum* – cf Timson in *Watsonia* for November 1963, pp. 386–95. J frequent. A occasional. S 1872. H –.

WATER-PEPPER *P. Hydropiper* L.
Still rare, or rather scarce. The test is to chew a leaf which, after about half a minute, should produce a strong peppery taste. Gosselin was its first collector. J frequent. A rare. S occasional. H -.

TASTELESS WATER-PEPPER *P. mite* Schrank
Only Marquand's 'single specimen' of 1890, which has not been traced. J –. A –. S –. H –.

(*P. minus* Hudson was last collected in Jersey in 1851, and 1925.)

BLACK BINDWEED *P. Convolvulus* L. Langue d'Ouaie. Vâle
Frequent, but hardly now very common. Gosselin collected it as a garden weed. J frequent. A common. S occasional. H occasional.

RUSSIAN VINE *P. Aubertii* L. Henry (*P. 'baldschuanicum'*)
A rampageous clamberer, which will often last where it has been put, and so can look wild. It occasionally occurs thus in Guernsey. It comes from the hills of W. China and Tibet. J occasional. A –. S 1960. H –.

DONKEY'S RHUBARB *P. cuspidatum* Siebold & Zuccarini (*P. Sieboldii*)
The delightful vernacular name comes from Cornwall and seems preferable to the conventional Japanese Knotweed. It was originally grown for ornament – 'of sterling merit and of fine graceful habit, its creamy-white flowers borne in profusion' as William Robinson (1838–1935) described it, who encouraged its planting – and it brightens quite a number of waste sites in Guernsey in late summer. But it has tenacious spreading underground stems. It was first noted in 1947. J frequent. A occasional. S rare. H –.

BUCKWHEAT *Fagopyrum esculentum* Moench Sarrazin
'Occasional plants are to be found on roadsides and near houses, springing up from scattered poultry seed,' wrote Marquand, and his 1892 record is the last we have. Indeed there seem to be only four others, Babington 1838, Dupuy 1864, Hillhouse 1881, Dawber 1891. J occasionally escapes. A 1900. S 1902. H –.

WIRE PLANT *Muehlenbeckia complexa* (A. Cunningham) Meisner
A dioecious shrub with thin wiry stems which can interlace into large thickets, dense and high in hedges, and has done so in perhaps half a dozen places in the

Wire Plant ×½

island. There are smaller colonies too, including a remarkable one right out on the cliffs by Le Gouffre which produces female flowers and white seedless berry-like fruits in plenty. It comes from New Zealand. J scarce. A –. S –. H since 1911.

SHEEP'S SORREL *Rumex Acetosella* L. P'tite Surelle
Common, and decorative in its mature reds and browns. But it is also a garden weed on light soils, as Gosselin noted with his specimens. J common. A common. S common. H common.

COMMON SORREL *R. Acetosa* L. Surelle
Also common, and also decorative in its mature reds and browns. It was measured 7 ft. high in 1968. Gosselin collected his plants on pathsides beyond the Vauquiédor. Its root was used medicinally in the 18th century. Pollen of some species of *Rumex* is in the Vazon and Catioroc peats. J common. A common. S common. H common.

GREAT WATER DOCK *R. Hydrolapathum* Hudson Doque de Douit
A stately plant which is, rightly, sometimes planted by pools etc. But it is natural enough in the wet ditches (the habitat from which Gosselin got his specimens) north of the Château des Marais and near Les Goubeys, where Marquand knew it too. It has also been recorded recently at Perelle, Vazon and Mont Cuet. J rare. A –. S –. H –.

CURLED DOCK *R. crispus* L. Doque
Commonest where man has been most. All docks are officially mauvaises herbes

in Guernsey which must not be allowed to flower or seed. But this one and the next are the only two which deserve such condemnation, not that this law seems to have made much difference to their frequency. Gosselin labelled his specimens '*R. crispus* or *acutus*'. The maritime variety with three swollen tubercles, var *littoreus* Hardy (*trigranulatus*) occurs. J common. A common. S common. H common.

BROAD-LEAVED DOCK *R. obtusifolius* L. ssp *obtusifolius* Grande Doque
Common, perhaps not quite so common as the last, but an equally bad, or worse, weed. Gosselin wrote with his specimens that it 'grows everywhere'. From its habit of often growing with nettles comes the Guernsey version of the well-known antidote. 'Doque, doque, gueri me d'la pitchaeure qu' l'ortie m'a fait.' A decoction of dock and dandelion was once used to purify the blood. J common. A frequent. S common. H frequent.

(*R.* × *acutus* L. (*R. crispus* × *R. obtusifolius*) was noted in Jersey in 1963. *R* × *Dufftii* Haussknecht (*R. obtusifolius* × *R. sanguineus*) was recorded there in 1961.)

HYBRID DOCK *R.* × *ogulinensis* Borbás (*R. obtusifolius* × *R. pulcher*)
Recorded from Fontenelle Bay, L'Ancresse in 1953 with both parents, but the specimen seems not to have survived. J –. A –. S –. H –.

FIDDLE DOCK *R. pulcher* L. ssp *pulcher* Doque des rues
Widespread, but unrecorded from nearly half the island's squares – or is it overlooked? Yet its stiff squat panicle and usually fiddle-shaped basal leaves make it distinct enough to recognise. Gosselin collected his specimens from the roadside at Belgrave. J common. A frequent. S frequent. H frequent.

WOOD DOCK *R. sanguineus* L. Doque à sang
Linnaeus described this species from the variety which has the veins of the leaves, and often the stalks too, beetroot-red, very decorative; and added 'Habitat in Virginia' – where it can only have been a waif. Long before his time, it had been known as *Lapathum rubens*, Bloodwort, or *L. sanguineum*, which is the name Gosselin used when he collected it. Generally this is scarcer and found near habitations, where it was used as a vegetable. It comes true from seed. The variety with green veins, *viridis* (Sibthorp) Koch is, now at any rate, the usual one in Guernsey. J frequent. A rare. S occasional. H 1958.

CLUSTERED DOCK *R. conglomeratus* Murray
A thoroughly dull dock, even by dock standards, rather commoner than the last, from which it has not always been happily distinguished – and indeed it is likely that hybrids between them are to be found. J frequent. A frequent. S occasional. H 1958.

SHORE DOCK *R. rupestris* Le Gall
A plant of Atlantic coasts from S. Wales to N. Spain named in 1850 by the Breton judge commemorated in *Ulex Gallii*. It is often difficult to be sure when one has got it, for it can be so like forms of Curled Dock. Consequently it is very likely overlooked, as well as misclaimed, but few take much interest in this genus. At best however, it seems very scarce, its appearances perhaps also influenced by sea currents. It was first found by Marquand in 1889 in the Rocquaine/Pleinmont area, where it still turns up from time to time; and has

also been seen in recent years around St Sampson's and Bordeaux, vetted by J. E. Lousley. J rare. A 1858. S –. H rare.

(*R. maritimus* L. was collected in Jersey in 1924.)

(Garden Rhubarb, *Rheum* × *cultorum* Thorsrud & Reisaeter, was recorded in 1963 as a garden outcast in Alderney.)

NETTLE FAMILY Urticaceae

PELLITORY *Parietaria judaica* L. (*P. diffusa*) Paraietole. Palitole
Still frequent in all parts of the island, still dusty, still interesting in its attachment to the artificial habitat of walls, which is reflected in its generic and English names. Pellitory is derived from the Latin *parietarius*, which is the adjective of *paries* a wall. So the usual English name is tautologous 'of the wall of the wall'. It also grows on shingle. Mrs de Garis records that its leaves were used as a poultice for bruises and wounds. J common. A locally common. S rare. H local.

MIND-YOUR-OWN-BUSINESS *Soleirolia Soleirolii* (Requien) Dandy (*Helxine Soleirollii*)
A Corsican matformer, also called Mother of Thousands, which may be under-recorded for two reasons. For one, it is inconspicuous; but it is also so familiar to many garden owners in or outside their greenhouses, that they do not notice it elsewhere, or scorn it as a wild plant. But such it is, frequently maintaining itself on walls and in moist places all over the island, admittedly usually near houses or in garden paths, but indomitably persistent all the same. It was claimed as new to the island in 1954, but in fact it had been recorded as abundant on walls in 1947, and even earlier Chevalier had included it in his report on Guernsey wild flowers in 1933. No doubt it was about well before that. J frequent. A occasional. S occasional. H rare.

SMALL NETTLE *Urtica urens* L. Petite Ortie
Widespread and locally plentiful, perhaps mostly in the north and north-west. Gosselin's specimens are annotated as growing near the sea-shore at L'Ancresse and the Vazon etc. Marquand wrote that the sting of this annual species is more venomous than that of the next. The stings of both, but especially this one, wear down in the autumn, when old plants may often be freely and painlessly handled. J common. A frequent. S occasional. H frequent.

STINGING NETTLE *U. dioica* L. Grande Ortie
Gosselin was the first to collect this, saying it grew as a weed everywhere, adding in pencil 'médécinale'. It is now one of the official noxious weeds, but at one time was used for rope, cloth and as the excellent spring vegetable it is. Andros wrote in Tudor times – he called them Orties Grecques – 'liniment made with nettle leaves, salt and oil protects all parts of the body from cold and shivering'. Later on nettle tea was used as a blood purifier. One fruit was found in the Vazon peat. A narrow-leaved stingless form was collected in the Grande Mare in 1968. J common. A common. S common. H common.

(Roman Nettle, *U. pilulifera* L., was collected in 1926 in Jersey.)

Hemp Family Cannabaceae

Hemp *Cannabis sativa* L. Hans. Canivet. Chanvre
In many places a frequent casual, usually a survivor from bird seed, for which its oily qualities are valuable. It was grown in Guernsey in the Middle Ages for its fibre, hence Chanvrière place names. But there was no record of this plant wild there until 1969. Then a gigantic – 12 ft. (because manured) – female plant appeared in a garden at St Peter Port and got its picture in the *Guernsey Press* in September. It came from canary seed, but it was seized on as dangerous and destroyed. Yet it cannot produce proper Cannabis resin so far north. A 4 ft. male plant was in the Beaucamps Road in 1972. The species probably originated in Asia. J rare. A 1901. S –. H –.

Hop *Humulus Lupulus* L.
This is native in fens, and its pollen (or it might be that of Hemp) was found in the Vazon peat from the days when fens were widespread in Guernsey. MacCulloch in 1815 commented that wild Hop was luxuriant, but not cultivated. Nowadays it seems exclusively in, or rather on, hedges, but is not common. J not uncommon. A rare. S occasional. H –.

Elm Family Ulmaceae

Wych Elm *Ulmus glabra* Hudson (*U. montana*) Orme
Now rare and in the south only and always planted for amenity. But it is the most likely Elm to have left its pollen freely in the Rousse, Vazon and Catioroc peats. J scarce. A rare. S rare. H rare.

Guernsey Elm *U. minor* Miller 'Guernsey' (*U. sarniensis*)
N. Jee showed in the Société's *Transactions* for 1961, p. 95, that practically all Guernsey Elms belonged to one of two clones, that is stocks propagated vegetatively, see also his article in *Tree News* for summer 1972, and his *Guernsey's Natural History*. This one, which is called the Male Elm, he typifies as 'a stiffly erect Elm with the main axis perfectly straight, and the upper branches ascending, making a small angle with the axis. Lower branches may leave the trunk at right angles, but the bend is upwards at the end. Young shoots straight, with alternate buds strictly in a plane. This means that in young plants the whole tree is in a plane. Leaves small. It comes into leaf later and loses its leaves later.' The *General View of Agriculture* of 1815 said that the species of Elm in the island was of peculiar form, its branches tending upwards and giving the tree somewhat the appearance of a Lombardy Poplar. These pyramidal trees in Guernsey have been given varying names, but Dr R. H. Richens, who has taken a deep interest in the matter, advised using the broader Latin name *U. minor*, which covers those called Jersey, Guernsey and Cornish Elms, with the clonal name 'Guernsey'. This is the only form of the species in Guernsey. It has apparently been recently introduced into Jersey, where there is an allied form. The situation about the well-used name *sarniensis*, Dr Richens adds, is fraught with difficulty. G. Loddiges was the first to use it, in 1836, but gave no description with it. 101 years later it was validly used as a specific name by H. Bancroft. Her series of articles on Elms in the *Gardeners Chronicle* for 1934 may be consulted, notably that for 22 September. Melville published the name for a hybrid in the *Kew Bulletin* in

1960. It has also been used for a variety and a form. Whether all these are the same thing, and if so of which botanical rank or just one clone (B. K. Boom first used the name clonally, in 1959), and whether this is indeed the same as 'Guernsey', remains to be seen. Mrs de Garis quoted 'Quand tu vais la fielle a l'Orme, seume ton Orge' – when you see the Elm in leaf, sow your Barley. This Elm? J an allied form common. A occurs. S rare. H rare.

(*U. carpinifolia* Suckow (*U. nitens*) was named from Alderney in 1932, and *U. carpinifolia* × *U. Plotii* Druce from Sark in 1958 and from Herm in 1959. J. E. Dandy says these will come under the last species.)

HYBRID GUERNSEY ELM *U.* × *hollandica* Miller (*U. glabra* × *U. minor*). (*U. 'campestris'*)
This is the Latin name Dr Richens gives to the other common clone in Guernsey. Mr Jee describes it as 'an irregular tree, with the trunk inclined and bending, never upright, even in sheltered places. Trunk covered with bosses. Young twigs thin and unable to support their own weight, drooping. Lower branches drooping to the ground. Leaves larger.' Dr Melville thought there might be some *U. Plotii* in the parentage, and *U. minor*. No doubt the records for *U. procera* (*U. 'campestris'*) belong here. Both these clones are distinctive and can be recognised all over the island. Both are planted only and seed is at best rare, although this one may sucker somewhat. Dr Richens comments that there is no close affinity between the present Channel Island clones and those of the facing coast of England. He thinks there is every reason to believe that they were introduced from north-west France, whence the cider-apple culture was also introduced. He says it is rather characteristic of Elm plantings that they often consist of an admixture of more than one sort. The Hybrid Guernsey Elm he thinks is derived from the population of large-leaved hybrids that occur in northern France, at least those of Northern Brittany to Mont St Michel. These came ultimately from the Ardennes region, where native Wych Elm met *U. minor*, which is native in the southern half of France, and has undoubtedly been moved northward by Man. The ready advice of both Dr Richens and Dr Melville on this subject has been much appreciated. The non-aggressive strain of Dutch Elm disease, noted on two trees in 1972, was rampant by 1974. J frequent. A occurs. S ? H occurs.

MULBERRY FAMILY Moraceae

FIG *Ficus Carica* L. Figuier
Figs have been grown successfully in Guernsey for a long time. Knowlton in 1726 several times noted trees 'as large as apple trees' and saw them growing in the hedges in two or three places in great quantity. Mrs de Garis records that every farm in St Peter's in the 18th century had its couple of pigsties built solidly of granite shaded by a fig tree or two; a tree at Mont Plaisir was variously measured at different times, but about 1825 had a trunk of 7 ft. circumference, was 20 ft. high and its branches covered 40 ft.. In 1862 fig trees were still abundant, all standards, sometimes in Figgeries, chiefly purple-fruited but also green, and in 1874 they were described as universally planted, but are now nothing like so common. However garden fig trees cannot produce fertile fruit in the British Isles, because the special chalcid wasp which effects this in the Mediterranean cannot endure the climate. The astonishing process is described in *Pollination of Flowers* 1973. And yet fig trees appear in places where no human could plant

them, usually high on walls or rocks, with sometimes their roots not even reaching the ground. It seems the source of wildlings is the seeds in imported dried figs. Such plants have been reported from three or four places in St Peter Port and elsewhere. But even if they are self-sown, they will not be able to perpetuate themselves. A recipe written by James Carey on 11 March 1724/5 showed how to use the leaves for snuff. 220 years later they were being tried as a tobacco substitute. J ? A –. S –. H –.

WALNUT FAMILY Juglandaceae

WALNUT *Juglans regia* L.
A familiar and superb southern European tree, from which seedlings may arise. But are the trees in Guernsey more than fine, and scarce, persisters? J –. A –. S –. H –.

BIRCH FAMILY Betulaceae

SILVER BIRCH *Betula pendula* Roth (*B. alba*)
Babington wrote that this was frequent in hedges. Marquand castigated this as an error, since it is not found in hedges: what occurred were in enclosed grounds. So it is now, with no sign of natural regeneration. But why not? This is an enterprising and pioneering tree, whose pollen was freely recorded in the peats of the west coast, and even birch bark was found there in 1929 and 1930. Why did it die out? Why has it not returned? J rare. A rare. S rare. H –.

DOWNY BIRCH *B. pubescens* Ehrhart
This too is planted, but rarely. In fact this is the more likely species of Birch to have been in the wet Guernsey of the past, but both may well have been. J rare. A –. S –. H –.

ALDER *Alnus glutinosa* (L.) Gaertner
A typical tree of streamsides and fens, whose pollen has been found in all local peat samples. And yet Gosselin does not mention it. Babington commented it was probably planted (in hedges), and Marquand knew only very few trees, and some at least of these were evidently planted. Miss Guille collected it at Les Vauxbelets, status unknown. In 1940 Dr Falkener collected it on the cliff at Saints Bay. It is still a scarce tree, still at the Château des Marais and in about half a dozen other places and very fine at Havilland Hall. Being well suited to such places, it may be that it is regenerating in them. i.e. is naturalised, even if our trees are not aboriginal. J occasional. A rare. S rare. H rare.

HAZEL FAMILY Corylaceae

HORNBEAM *Carpinus betulus* L.
This delightful tree appears in Ansted's list of 1862, but Marquand knew it only in private grounds. Doubtless the very few trees there are now are all where they were put, but one at Sausmarez Manor is superb, and another down towards Pied du Mur is very fine too. J planted. A –. S –. H –.

HAZEL *Corylus Avellana* L.
Pollen of this shrub occurs in all the peat samples from the west coast, and Andros mentions it in Tudor times. Carré told Babington that nuts were found in the bogs. Lukis records them with the kernels still on after a great storm in 1847. Derrick knew them from L'Ancresse and Vazon, Marquand saw them and they are still in the peat. But today, as in Marquand's time, it is very rare, only the occasional shrub here and there, albeit usually in natural-looking places. What is there that prevents it being as frequent as one would expect? J occasional. A –. S planted. H planted.

BEECH FAMILY Fagaceae

BEECH *Fagus sylvatica* L.
This fine forest tree was yet another which Babington recorded from hedges. Marquand thought it might be native if it were true that beech mast had been found in the submarine beds at Vazon. Recent investigators have not found any, but its pollen has occurred there, which may indicate it grew locally in earlier times. There are good trees to be seen nowadays, but not commonly. J planted. A rare. S planted. H planted.

SWEET CHESTNUT *Castanea sativa* Miller (*C. vulgaris*) Castanier
Babington said this Mediterranean tree was naturalised in many places. Marquand said all the existing trees had been planted. Neither probably knew that this tree may well have been in the British Isles much longer than was once thought. Today it thrives in several areas in Guernsey and there are some specimens of large girth. J common. A occasional. S planted. H planted.

TURKEY OAK *Quercus cerris* L.
Unmentioned by Marquand and in those days hardly even considered as a wild plant. But it was said by Ansted in 1862 to be 'sufficiently common' and was collected in Guernsey in 1866 by Marriott. It was noticed on the Fort George cliffs in 1958, and on those at Le Gouffre in 1973. It is indeed quite widespread and there are some fine trees to be seen. It can naturalise quite readily, so some at least of the trees have no doubt arisen from local acorns. It is indeed a native of Turkey. J 1971. A –. S planted. H planted.

HOLM OAK *Q. Ilex* L. Vert Tchêne
A prominent feature of the island's landscape, not mentioned by Marquand as more than planted – which it certainly has been, widely. Beauvoir was writing for acorns of this in 1724, implying none were then available in the island, but Ansted in 1862 said that it was one of the most frequent of trees. It has so settled down, that its seedlings may spring up quite readily in some places, perhaps most notably on the cliffs, where this ancient tree holds its own so magnificently. Holm is a corruption of Holly, from a supposed resemblance of its leaves, which can be somewhat spiny: it shares its specific epithet with the generic name of the Hollies. It is native in southern Europe now, but its pollen has been listed from the Vazon and Catioroc peats. J frequent. A –. S occasional. H planted.

OAK *Q. Robur* L. Tchêne
Quite a frequent tree. Oak pollen occurs freely in the west coast peat, and acorns have been found preserved in it, for example after the 1847 gales. Fresh ones

were used for coffee during the occupation. J common. A rare. S occasional. H occasional.

DURMAST OAK *Q. petraea* (Mattuschka) Lieblein (*Q. sessiliflora*)
Noted by Marquand as planted, but it has not been recorded at all since. J rare. A –. S –. H –.

(*Q.* × *rosacea* (*Q. petraea* × *Q. Robur*) Bechstein occurs in Jersey. The American *Q. borealis* Michaux may sow itself there.)

WILLOW FAMILY Salicaceae

WHITE POPLAR *Populus alba* L.
No doubt still 'probably always planted' – Ansted recorded it made fine trees in a short time. But it is no longer frequent, although it can last well, especially in sand, with its persistent suckering. J frequently planted. A planted. S planted. H planted.

GREY POPLAR *P. canescens* (Aiton) Smith
Another southern European, also only planted, but perhaps rather less rare. But it has not always been reliably told from the last species. J rarely planted. A planted. S –. H planted.

ASPEN *P. tremula* L.
Another vigorous suckerer, whose status is hard to judge. It is rather less scarce than the last two species – or has it been overlooked? Poplar pollen was in the Vazon peat, but it is impossible to say of which species. J rare. A –. S –. H –.

BLACK ITALIAN POPLAR *P.* × *canadensis* Moench (*P.* '*nigra*') Peupillier
Locally planted, sometimes in hedges, but unable to persist beyond its natural span. This hybrid name covers several clones, all of which will be of one sex only, but the only such note is that some trees by the Reservoir were female. In Marquand's time these Poplars were not often distinguished from the true Black Poplar, which is one of the parents of these hybrids. They are not Italian and probably arose in France in the mid 1700s. J planted. A last record 1900. S planted. H planted.

[*P. nigra* L. The clone 'Italica', the Lombardy Poplar, was recommended by the Guernsey Growers Association in 1900 for windbreaks and is still planted.]

BALSAM POPLAR *P. Tacamahacca* Miller
The earliest known specimen of any plant from Guernsey is of this species. It was sent to Sir H. Sloane by Parey in 1734 as 'the leaves of the Tree of the Balsam of Peru, growing in that island'. (The real Balsam of Peru comes from a leguminous shrub *Myroxylon balsamum* (L.) Harmsworth var *Pereirae* (Royle) Baillon.) But this scrap evidences one of the oldest records in Europe for this species – the story, largely in Parey's own quaint words, is set out in the *Quarterly Journal of Forestry* for April 1973. Knowlton had seen this tree eight years before and recognised it as 'the Tachamahca of Plucknett'. How did he know? Nowadays this is a rare tree, its western counterpart, *P. trichocarpa* Torrey & Gray ex Hooker being the usual Balsam poplar, although introduced 200 years later. J –. A –. S –. H –.

(*P. gileadensis* Rouleau is occasionally planted in Jersey.)

(Bay Willow *Salix pentandra* L. is planted in Jersey.)

WHITE WILLOW *S. alba* L.
Could be native, but it is a rare tree. J rare. A –. S –. H –.

HYBRID CRACK WILLOW *S.* x *rubens* Schrank (*S. alba* × *S. fragilis*)
Recorded in 1971 by E. Milne-Redhead as 'the *S. fragilis*-like hybrid usually more commonly planted than *S. fragilis*'. No specimen was collected. J 1933, 1967. A –. S –. H –.

CRACK WILLOW *S. fragilis* L. Saue
This, or something like it, is not infrequently planted, especially in the variety *Basfordiana* (Scaling) Bean with the dull orange-brown twigs. Mr and Mrs Howitt indeed consider no trees in the island to be true *fragilis*, but most rather the var *Russelliana* (Smith) Koch, the Duke of Bedford's Willow. For an excellent account of this and all our willows, see *British Trees and Shrubs* by R. D. Meikle 1958. J occasional. A planted. S planted. H planted.

ALMOND WILLOW *S. triandra* L. ssp *triandra*
Recorded from the Grande Mare in 1900, with no specimens. J rare. A –. S planted. H –.

HYBRID WILLOW *S.* × *mollissima* Ehrhart (*S. triandra* × *S. viminalis*). (*S. undulata*)
Also found in 1900 in the Grande Mare, but again no specimen has been traced. J –. A –. S –. H –.

(*S. purpurea* L. grows rarely in Jersey and has been recorded planted in Alderney.)

VIOLET WILLOW *S. daphnoides* Villars
Three old trees with the characteristic plum-coloured twigs grow in a row out in a field at Les Maingys. They are female. The species received an Award of Merit in 1957. J –. A –. S –. H –.

COMMON OSIER *S. viminalis* L. Osier
Very little recorded, but apparently now only in the north, which might suggest it was only a planted shrub in the island – indeed Gosselin wrote 'cultivated in moist ground'. And yet one would have expected it to have grown readily in the wet areas of the west. Osiers were at one time planted commercially at Rocquaine, in Saudrées, but there is no record which species was, or were, used. J common. A planted. S planted. H –.

WIMMER'S OSIER *S. calodendron* Wimmer
There is a good clump of this large, puzzling and scarce osier by the site of the Mare de Carteret, first noticed only in 1968. Here it is unusually glaucescent, according to Mr Meikle, and female – if the male exists at all, it is extremely rare. For a discussion of this and the last taxon, see R. D. Meikle in *Watsonia* for October 1952, pp. 244–7. J –. A –. S –. H –.

GOAT WILLOW *S. caprea* L.
Surprisingly, a real rarity, of which no voucher specimens are known. Guernsey's first record was made by a critical botanist, Rogers, in 1897. The plant has been

subsequently claimed on many occasions, usually by visitors unaware how exciting a voucher would be, but 'feel sure they saw it'. J rare. A last records 1900. S error. H –.

COMMON SALLOW *S. cinerea* L. ssp *oleifolia* Macreight (*S. atrocinerea*)
P'tits Cats, Cattons (the catkins)
Quite the commonest Pussy Willow of Guernsey, unless it be the Hybrid Sallow. Its leaves are often sadly blackened by a species of *Cladosporium* fungal mould. J common. A frequent. S frequent. H occasional.

SMITH'S OSIER *S.* × *Smithiana* Willdenow (*S. cinerea* × *S. viminalis*)
Claimed by Marquand in 1891, but no specimen is known. Dr H. Bowen collected it at Fermain Bay in 1968, when the name was confirmed by R. D. Meikle, and also north of the Mare de Carteret. J 1958. A –. S 1957. H –.

(*S.* × *stipularis* Smith (*S. viminalis* × ?) was recorded from Alderney by Babington, assisted by W. Borrer.)

HYBRID SALLOW *S.* × *multinervis* Doell (*S. aurita* × *cinerea*)
Specimens from the Grande Mare in 1957 were named as this hybrid by R. D. Meikle. In 1969 Mr and Mrs Howitt considered that the majority of the Sallows were this. They characterised them by being smaller bushes, with twigs making a wider angle with the stem, smaller catkins, reddish stamens and a twisted tip to the leaf. J –. A –. S –. H –.

EARED SALLOW *S. aurita* L.
Mr Meikle named a bush from the Grande Mare in 1957 as this, but it has never been refound. J 1928. A last good record 1900. S –. H –.

CREEPING WILLOW *S. repens* L.
Still only in the Grande Mare (except for Babington's record of 'var *ascendens*' from Les Landes), but in very small quantity now. Mr Meikle noted two forms; and Ansted in 1862 wrote that 'a peculiar dwarf variety covers the fields in some parts of Guernsey', but there is no clue just what he meant by this. J rare. A –. S –. H –.

CREEPING HYBRID WILLOW *S.* × *ambigua* Ehrhart (*S. aurita* × *S. repens*)
Named from specimens from the Grande Mare in 1957. J –. A –. S –. H –.

HEATH FAMILY Ericaceae

RHODODENDRON *Rhododendron ponticum* L.
Never seems to get going in Guernsey and certainly no pest. There are some straggling bushes in the undergrowth by the car park above Moulin Huet, and it may be seen similarly in a few places elsewhere. But that seems all. It is native in the region of Pontus, the Black Sea, and in S. Spain. J local. A –. S rare. H scarce.

(*Gaultheria Shallon* Pursh is naturalised in Jersey.)

(The Strawberry Tree, *Arbutus unedo* L., has established itself in Jersey.)

HEATHER *Calluna vulgaris* (L.) Hull
Locally common, mostly on the cliffs. Gosselin collected it, saying it grew 'on the

hedges in the lower grounds of the Câtel and St Sampson'. Marquand records finding it in flower in December. If he had propagated this, it might have proved a useful late form for gardens. Salwey picked a double-flowered sprig in 1847, but there is no indication whether it was wild. A recent plant from L'Ancresse is now in cultivation which has deep crimson flowers, white at the base in bud. Pollen of this species was in the Vazon peat. J locally common. A frequent. S frequent. H –.

BELL HEATHER *Erica cinerea* L. Beruelle. Bervière
Commoner than the last and locally gloriously plentiful, but apparently gone from some of its old localities. Gosselin noted on his specimens that it grew 'on the hedges and in the furze fields at St Sampson's; and lower grounds of the Câtel; also near the Rocque du Guet'. Marquand recorded white flowers at Cobo, but nobody else has mentioned these in Guernsey. The flowers of Bell Heather in Guernsey are usually of a particularly rich purple (Doge Purple HCC 732/3), and on the cliffs its habit is dwarf and spreading, characters induced genetically by the exposed habitat and retained by cuttings. Four such prostrate plants from the Bailiwick are on the market as 'Guernsey Plum', 'Guernsey Purple' (Orchid Purple HCC 31/1), 'Guernsey Pink' (Fuchsine Pink HCC 627/1) and 'Guernsey Lime', with lime-yellow (Scheeles Green HCC 860/3) foliage. Colour photographs of two of these are in *Heathers in Colour* 1974, Plates 56 and 121. Bell Heather is liable to start flowering early, often in April; Marquand wrote that it may continue to blossom all through the winter months. Ericaceous pollen has been found in the Rousse and Catioroc peat deposits. J frequent. A common. S locally plentiful. H common.

CROSS-LEAVED HEATH *E. Tetralix* L.
This was claimed from Saints Bay in 1951, but surely erroneously – there is no voucher. J rare. A –. S –. H –.

(Dorset Heath, *E. ciliaris* L., is wrongly attributed to Jersey in the *Armorican Flora* by misquoting Lester-Garland. Cornish Heath, *E. vagans* L., has been collected in Jersey and is an established garden escape in Sark.)

[Tree Heather, *E. arborea* L., was reported in the *Gardening World* for 18 October 1890 to be growing 25 ft. high at the Rohais Nursery. This is nearly matched by a specimen in the Candie Road said to be nearly 100 years old, which has three trunks, one 33 in. in circumference, and a fourth cut off. The species can be seen doing very well elsewhere too. In Grindon's herbarium at Manchester are dried plants bought in the market there from Guernsey in 1885.]

(Bilberry, *Vaccinium Myrtillus* L., is a rare native of Jersey.)

WINTERGREEN FAMILY Pyrolaceae

ROUND-LEAVED WINTERGREEN *Pyrola rotundifolia* L.
First collected on 23 August 1837 in the marshes of Vazon Bay by Babington, and well-known there until the time of Marquand's *Flora*. Since then all efforts to find it have failed. A discussion on the subspecific name for this special Guernsey plant, the only Wintergreen definitely known in the Channel Islands, is on p. 127 of the *Flora*. J once claimed. A –. S –. H –.

Pepper-bush Family Clethraceae

Lily of the Valley Tree *Clethra arborea* Aiton
This is not only very fine in Guernsey gardens, but has seeded itself on to walls. J self-seeds. A –. S –. H –.

Sea-lavender Family Plumbaginaceae

Common Sea-lavender *Limonium vulgare* Miller ssp *vulgare* (*Statice Limonium*)
Another plant extincted by the drainage of the Braye du Valle. Gosselin, Trevelyan, Babington and Newbould all knew it; so did Knowlton in 1726 if he meant this species by '*Limonum*'. The last specimen was from Miss Guille in 1850. The claim on p. 310 of the 1898 *Transactions* is an error for Rock Sea-lavender. J rare. A –. S –. H –.

Lax Sea-lavender *L. humile* Miller
Under the name of *Statice bahusiensis* this was recorded from the Braye du Valle by young Newbould in August 1841. But his specimens are of the form *pyramidale* C. E. Salmon of the last species. J –. A –. S –. H –.

(*L. bellidifolium* (Gouan) Dumortier (*Statice* '*reticulata*') was collected in Jersey in 1840.)

Alderney Sea-lavender *L. auriculae-ursifolium* (Pourret) Druce ssp *auriculae-ursifolium* (*Statice lychnidifolia*)
Recorded for Guernsey by Chevalier in 1933, a record repeated in the *Armorican Flora* – an error for the next species? J very local. A rare. S –. H –.

Rock Sea-lavender *L. binervosum* (G. E. Smith) C. E. Salmon (*Statice occidentalis*. *S.* '*spathulata*')
Spread all along the south cliffs, although rarely in much quantity, and not recently noted west of Le Gouffre. J local. A occasional. S occasional. H –.

Thrift *Armeria maritima* (Miller) Willdenow ssp *maritima* Eillet d'banque.
'Grows all along the sea-shore', wrote Gosselin by his specimens. Rather is it common all round the coast, rare inland, the odd clump with white flowers. It is known from the peat of Catioroc, and was seen by Knowlton at the Saltpans in 1726. A large tuft found at Albecq in 1958 has proliferating and oddly-formed flower heads, and retains this characteristic in cultivation. It was shown to the RHS Scientific Committee on 29 June 1965. Miss Muirhead considered specimens from the rocks by the foghorn at St Martin's Point in 1969 to match var *pubigera* (Desfontaines) Boissier. They had sheaths and bracts as well as the leaves hairy, but the status of these plants is uncertain: see *BSBI Proceedings* for September 1966, p. 279. J common. A common. S common. H common.

(*A. alliacea* (Cavanilles) Hoffmannsegg & Link (*A. arenaria*. *A. plantaginea*) is native in Jersey and appeared on their 5p stamp in 1972. Its hybrid with *A. maritima* also occurs there rarely.)

Primrose Family Primulaceae

Cowslip *Primula veris* L. ssp *veris*
At the time Marquand wrote his *Flora* this attractive plant was known to have occurred in St Martin's parish in former times. Sir H. de Sausmarez in 1924 said many plants had been growing in a field in that parish for 40 years, i.e. before they were reported there by Derrick in 1895. They continued to be seen in the grounds of Sausmarez Manor until 1969. In addition Marquand heard tell they once grew in the Petit Bot area, and N. D. Simpson gathered them in the Grande Mare in 1923. In 1973 two plants were seen by the pond in Saumarez Park. Other records were probably of the umbellate form of Primrose. J rare. A rare. S –. H –.

(*P.* × *Tommasinii* Grenier & Godron (*P. veris* × *P. vulgaris*) (*P.* × *variabilis*) occurs in Jersey.)

Primrose *P. vulgaris* Hudson ssp *vulgaris* Pâquerolle
Still happily a rich and plentiful ornament of Guernsey lanesides and banks, which received an Award of Garden Merit in 1959. At least three local sayings show that it was, is, normal for it to be in flower at Christmas, e.g. Noué n'est pas Noué sans pâquerolle, and it was also seen flowering in August 1953. In Gosselin's scrapbook there are three specimens, one marked common, one white and one reddish. Marquand records it with white and liver-coloured flowers, and N. Jee had it with pink flowers at La Houguette in 1969, where also have been Jack-in-the-Green forms (which sow themselves freely in Miss N. Hichens' garden in the Fort Road). The umbellate form, *caulescens* (Koch) Schinz & Thellung, occurs, and has at least once been mistaken for a Cowslip. These may all show the influence of garden plants. Before 1941 Dr Falkener found many plants near a stream above La Bette Bay without a corolla, the calyx much enlarged. A plant with a double corolla was found by Miss H. Roussel in 1973. Other variations have been noted as well. Marquand wrote a paper in the 1907 *Transactions*, pp. 323–8, recording his and his son's counting 5,289 flowers. This showed that 2,653, 50.16% had pin, and 2,636, 49.84% thrum eyes. An old Guernsey cure for rheumatism was rubbing the affected parts with fresh lard in which primrose flowers had been boiled. J common. A occasional. S common. H common.

Hybrid Primrose *P. polyantha* Miller × *P. vulgaris*
Dr S. R. J. Woodell placed here a white-flowered caulescent specimen collected far from a garden in St Peter's in 1969. J –. A –. S –. H –.

Spring Cyclamen *Cyclamen coum* Miller
This Mediterranean species was planted out in Saumarez Park about 1920 in what might have been thought a most unsuitable place, rough grass. Yet there it still was when P. Girard lit on it in 1968, unaware of its origin, and there it still is, flowering when it is given the chance. It received an Award of Merit in 1956. J –. A –. S –. H –.

Autumn Cyclamen *C. hederifolium* Aiton (*C. neapolitanum*)
This Neapolitan plant too was found by P. Girard, in 1967, among bracken under pines at the Guet. There was very little, but it must have been there a long time, and is thriving. It has also long survived in grass in the Fermain Valley. The

source of the record in the *Atlas* is lost. Gosselin grew it as Sowbread in the 18th century. J three localities. A –. S –. H –.

CREEPING JENNY *Lysimachia Nummularia* L.
Known for at least a quarter of a century up to about 1896, from the Rue du Pont Vaillant. Its only other record was from Vazon way. No doubt it was a garden outcast in both places: as such it can do quite well vegetatively, for the different clones of its commoner chromosome race (2n = 45) are all sterile in the British Isles, and the rarer 2n = 30 is probably self-incompatible. It is still to be seen in Guernsey gardens, and could well survive outside again. J rare. A –. S –. H –.

(Yellow Pimpernel, *L. nemorum* L., grows in Jersey and Sark.)

YELLOW LOOSESTRIFE *L. vulgaris* L.
A flourishing colony was found in 1954 by P. Girard in a marsh below Les Lohiers. It is not identical with the usual wild plant and seems to be var *Klingraefferi* Abromeit with a blotch at the base of the petals. A similar patch was found in 1970 near La Croix in the Forest, where it also still is. J rare. A –. S –. H –.

(*L. punctata* L. was seen in Jersey in 1966.)

BOG PIMPERNEL *Anagallis tenella* (L.) L.
A gem anywhere, which happily is still to be seen in several damp places from north to south of the island. A form no different from what may be seen in Guernsey was given an Award of Merit by the RHS in 1951. J local. A locally frequent. S locally frequent. H local.

SCARLET PIMPERNEL *A. arvensis* L. Pimpernelle
Generally common and generally a favourite. The form with the typical scarlet flowers is the commonest, and was depicted on a 9p stamp in 1972. But especially near the sea the f. *carnea* (Schrank) Hylander with pale pink flowers is not infrequent. Also to be seen are the almost white f. *pallida* (Hooker) Hylander, the probable source for claims of white pimpernels, which have never been proved, the f. *vinacea* Marsden-Jones with wine-coloured flowers and the f. *azurea* Hylander with blue ones, which Gosselin knew near the Mare de Carteret. There are a dozen or more records of the last, which is liable to be thought to be the next species. J common. A common. S common. H common.

BLUE PIMPERNEL *A. foemina* Miller
Marked for Guernsey in the *Supplement to the Atlas*, based on Carré's record in *Flora Sarnica*. But was he right? There is no specimen: other unproven or incorrect claims have been made. This species differs from the f. *azurea* of the last in having its flower-stalks shorter than the leaves and its petals not, or hardly, fringed with glands. J last claim 1847. A –. S claimed 1879. H –.

CHAFFWEED *A. minima* (L.) E. H. L. Krause (*Centunculus minimus*)
Marquand wrote that this was abundant in many parts of L'Ancresse. Despite recent close search, it has been seen in only two spots and in no plenty. Nor has it been seen in other recorded areas such as L'Islet, Cobo, Vazon or Petit Bot. It must surely have decreased in quantity, although it will surely also have been overlooked, for Guernsey plants seem rarely to reach 1 inch high. J rare. A rare. S –. H 1894.

SEA MILKWORT *Glaux maritima* L.
No longer 'common in brackish marshes' as these become ever scarcer, nor has it been reseen at Vazon. But it is still where Knowlton presumably saw it in 1726 and Gosselin collected it, near the Vale bridge, (and in the Mare Pirouin), and at Fontenelle Bay, Pulias, Lihou, Rocquaine Bay and Petit Port. J rare. A rare. S 1847. H rare.

BROOKWEED *Samolus Valerandi* L.
Very locally plentiful, where the conditions it so typically likes are to be found, above all wet cliff trickles near the sea. But it is also occasionally seen inland. Gilbert-Carter tells us that Valerand was a 16th-century botanist who thought that this plant was the *Samolus* of Pliny. Several different guesses have been made of the origin of this generic name. J local. A occasional. S occasional. H local.

MYRSINE FAMILY Myrsinaceae

MYRSINE *Myrsine africana* L.
An African and Asiatic shrub which was planted as long ago as 1860 under the cliffs of Fort George. It is still used occasionally for hedging and may outlast the tidiness of a garden. It received an Award of Merit in 1927. J –. A –. S –. H –.

BUDDLEIA FAMILY Buddlejaceae

BUDDLEIA *Buddleja Davidii* Franchet
A now familiar Chinese shrub unmentioned by Marquand. This is not surprising, since it was effectively introduced from China only early in the present century. Soon its winged seeds began to spread, and now it decks many a wall, quarryside or waste patch, its violet flowers a lure for butterflies and day-flying moths. Although it must have been about earlier, it was first formally noted only in 1952, in the Rue des Frères and elsewhere. It is now to be seen much more widely and may well spread further. It received an Award of Merit in 1941. J common. A rare. S rare. H rare.

GOLDEN-BALL TREE *B. globosa* Hope
This survived for some time in a long-neglected garden below Pleinmont. It attracted attention, but had no claim to be considered naturalised. It comes from South America. J –. A –. S –. H –.

OLIVE FAMILY Oleaceae

ASH *Fraxinus excelsior* L. ssp *excelsior* Frêne
A frequent tree and doubtless an aboriginal one, for its pollen is in the Vazon peat. J frequent. A occasional. S frequent. H local.

LILAC *Syringa vulgaris* L. Lilas
A southern European shrub which has been cultivated for centuries. It can persist well where it has been put by suckering freely. It does ripen seed, but seedlings are at best rare. In Guernsey it never looks more than a survivor. J recorded. A –. S Brecqou. H –.

WILD PRIVET *Ligustrum vulgare* L.
A tough fragrant-flowered native on the south cliffs. Gosselin collected it without giving a locality, but his early list notes it 'sur les Hayes de St Martin', where it is today. J local. A rare. S occasional. H local.

JAPANESE PRIVET *L. ovalifolium* Hasskarl
A Japanese shrub long planted for hedging, surviving after the original need has ended. It was recommended for windbreaks by the Guernsey Growers Association in 1900. J planted. A frequent. S Brecqou. H –.

JASMINE *Jasminum officinale* L. Jasmin
Twice known surviving on an old wall, succumbing only when the wall was pulled down. But it is hardly a wild plant. J –. A –. S –. H –.

PERIWINKLE FAMILY Apocynaceae

LESSER PERIWINKLE *Vinca minor* L.
A native of Central Europe found at Beaucamps de Bas in the Catel by P. Girard. It has no hairs at the edge of its, smaller, leaves. J local. A –. S claimed. H –.

GREATER PERIWINKLE *V. major* L. ssp *major* Pervenche
Collected at Fort Bay by Dupuy in February 1864 and there and at Moulin Huet (it is still in both places) in 1879 by Hillhouse. Marquand knew it in three other places. Now it is on record from 27 squares. It is a southern European plant long known as naturalised in the British Isles. J frequent. A occasional. S occasional. H –.

GENTIAN FAMILY Gentianaceae

SLENDER CICENDIA *Cicendia filiformis* (L.) Delarbre
A neat delightful miniature hardly to be seen except on hands and knees, although Guernsey plants may, rarely, reach 4 in. high. 1 in. plants usually reward such searchers in various slacks on L'Ancresse (where Gosselin collected it north of the Clôture fields); and it was unexpectedly but happily rediscovered in 1970 on the cliff just west of Saints Bay, and Albecq added in 1973. Cobo Castle hill is no longer suitable. It was also recorded from Hommet in 1913. J rare. A –. S –. H –.

GUERNSEY CENTAURY *Exaculum pusillum* (Lamarck) Caruel (*Cicendia pusilla*)
A supreme Guernsey rarity, a native plant unknown elsewhere in the British Isles, It is even harder to spot than the last, being rarely so tall, although wider-branched, and its flowers are not a pale yellow in the form, *Candollei* Bastard, in Guernsey, but a pale fawny pink. This species always grows with the last. It was first gathered by Capt. J. C. G. Gosselin, then a Commander, a grandson of Joshua, in 1850 near Paradis, and in September of that year it was collected there by Miss Guille. Townsend, who identified Gosselin's plant, published the record. The locality was given as 'waste broken ground', whereas it is now to be seen only in the fine short moist turf of dune slacks – Wolsey collected it at the 'margin

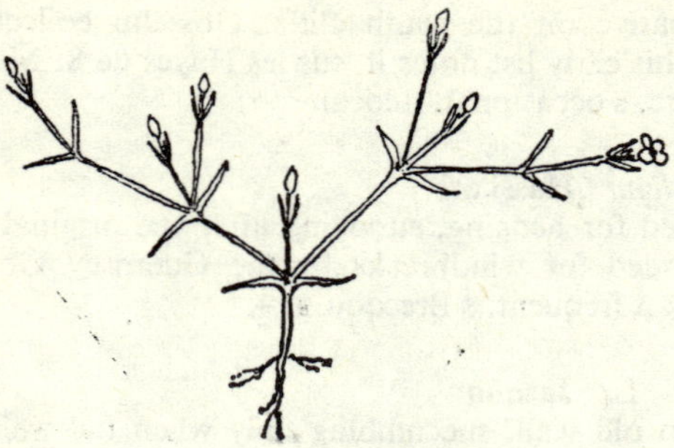

Guernsey Centaury ×2

of hollow'. This original spot was just south of Fort Doyle, and has now been turned by human interference into almost waste broken ground. The plant was known there until at least the 1920s, in two spots a short distance apart, but close search has failed to find it since. Nevertheless it does vary greatly in quantity from year to year and can fail to appear at all in some years. In 1900 its second distinct locality was discovered, by Miss Agnew, south of Fort le Marchant. Here its very existence was threatened by sand quarrying in 1961 – see the *Transactions* for that year, p. 96, where there is a list of accompanying plants. The difficulty of preserving it was, is, the greater because no one knows its ecological needs. However Dr Bowen helped by finding a fine colony a mile to the west in a slack which had been searched more than once before; and in 1972 Miss R. de Sausmarez found it growing exceptionally large in a new place near by. But unknown to everyone, there was a letter from Wolsey dated 18 February 1862 at the British Museum. In it he 'feared the original site would soon be destroyed for stones were being carted to the hollow to level it'. He went on 'I found *one* plant at the base of the hill on L'Ancresse Common where the Cromlech is situated' – which must surely be this westerly area. Bevan's *Tourist Guide* of 1884 said it grew by the Dolmen Te Dehus, a kilometre to the south of Fort Doyle. Marquand never mentions this locality but did write in 1908 of it growing 'in 2/3 places'. Plate 911 of the 3rd edition of *English Botany* was apparently drawn from a Guernsey specimen. J –. A –. S –. H –.

SLENDER CENTAURY *Centaurium pulchellum* (Swartz) Druce (*Erythraea pulchella*)
Seen in recent years still on Lihou, near Fort Hommet (where the minute f. *Swartziana* Wittrock of *E. pulchella* has been collected: but compare B.E.C. 1916 *Report*, p. 578), at Grandes Rocques and on L'Ancresse, and also at Pulias. It is in Gosselin's herbarium, and has in the past also been collected at St Sampson's, Grande Havre and the Vale Pond, and by the Château des Marais. It remains rare. A condensed form from Guernsey is also referred to in *English Botany* 3rd Edition, Vol. VI, p. 69. J rare. A rare. S –. H –.

CHANNEL CENTAURY *C. tenuiflorum* (Hoffmannsegg & Link) Fritsch
There is a specimen at Cambridge collected by Babington at the Braye du Valle on 14 August 1837 originally labelled *C. pulchellum*, which he altered to *ramosissimum*, in effect a synonym. But this is *C. tenuiflorum*, a species not known to be British until 41 years later, and the only record for the island. J 1837. A –. S –. H –.

BROAD-LEAVED CENTAURY *C. latifolium* (Smith) Druce (*E. latifolia*)
Babington's records for this referred, as he later realised, to broad-leaved forms of Common Centaury. J error. A error. S –. H –.

COMMON CENTAURY *C. erythraea* Rafinesque ssp *erythraea* (*E. 'Centaurium'*) Centurée. Déblôimâie
Quite frequent and sometimes to be seen with white flowers – Gosselin collected it thus. He considered it a medicinal plant. Some of its forms mimic other Centauries and have been misclaimed for them. It was in flower already on 20 April 1957. J frequent. A frequent. S frequent. H frequent.

DUMPY CENTAURY *C. erythraea* Rafinesque ssp *erythraea* var *capitatum* (Willdenow) Melderis (*E. capitata*)
On 1 July 1876 Matthews collected in the north of Guernsey, presumably on L'Ancresse, a Centaury – the specimen has not been traced. Four years later Townsend recognised Dumpy Centauries, with the stamens attached only right at the bottom of the corolla tube instead of half way up, as they are in all our others, as *E. capitata*. This was the name which was given in 1815 by Willdenow to specimens from near Berlin, although he had failed to remark on the decisive stamen character which it proved these specimens possessed. Nevertheless it seems they tallied in other respects as well with Townsend's plants. The Berlin plant has never been seen again. In 1884 Matthews, from the slender evidence of its single flower, recognised his specimen as the same as Townsend's, and Townsend agreed. 42 years later a party of amateur botanists consisting of Lady Davy, Miss C. Vivian, Miss G. Bacon and Foggitt (who later married, *en secondes noces*, Miss Bacon), collected this plant at Fort le Marchant. No one else has succeeded in finding it in Guernsey – or in the Armorican Peninsula. But was Townsend right in considering it a species? Surely it is no more than a sometimes rather chancy variety, liable to come and go, and never seen except with Common Centaury. It differs only in this single character, which in other genera is treated only as a dimorphism within the species. It is a character quite inadequate to found a new species on, but Grisebach, the taxonomist of the Gentian family, had only 35 years before Townsend wrote, chosen stamens joined high on the corolla as one of the distinguishing characters of Centauries. To have them joined at the bottom therefore put them into a different genus! The fault was of course his unfortunate choice of detail. This plant clearly is not of a different genus, being only certainly distinguishable from dumpy forms of Common Centaury by splitting the corolla tube open. It is surely a mutant which the genes of the Common one may throw from time to time, and when they do, the resultant offspring may reproduce themselves similarly from seed: Townsend in 1881 sowed seed from a Dumpy Centaury and found it came true. Cunnack however in 1884 wrote to Sir J. D. Hooker, saying he had carefully examined a number of coast forms in Cornwall and found a number of specimens with some stamens inserted at the base of the tube and a very few with the whole of the stamens so inserted: he had held the opinion for some time that this was a heteroclite form of the Common species. Perhaps the Guernsey finds were of chance productions which could not perpetuate themselves, at least for long, but may arise again. There are analagous forms in other species of Centaury on the Continent. (Since the above was written, Melderis in *Flora Europaea* has downgraded this taxon to a variety.) J 1906, 1936. A –. S –. H –.

SEASIDE CENTAURY *C. littorale* (D. Turner) Gilmour (*E. 'linariifolia'*)
Babington's specimens so labelled are of Common Centaury. J –. A –. S –. H –.

(Yellow-wort, *Blackstonia perfoliata* (L.) Hudson, has been recorded in two localities in Jersey; and Field Gentian, *Gentianella campestris* (L.) Börner, there once.)

BOGBEAN FAMILY Menyanthaceae

BOGBEAN *Menyanthes trifoliata* L. Faive de Douit
Doubtless an ancient inhabitant of Guernsey, its pollen in the Vazon peat. As a living plant it was collected by Gosselin, who called it a Plante Suspecte, and Miss Guille, and known to Carré too from ditches behind the Château des Marais, until about 1850. There is a specimen from Dupuy from St Saviour's in 1864. Marquand records it as at one time plentiful in the Grande Mare, where 'an enthusiastic collector' (who ?) exterminated it about 1870. He knew it in a marshy corner of a field at Cobo, where it was found in 1892. In 1907, when he thought it very nearly extinct, Hocart found it in the Douit des Barras. between Noirmont Mill and Grandes Rocques. Since then it has been searched for, but found nowhere. J last collected 1928. A –. S –. H –.

(*Nymphoides peltata* (S. G. Gmelin) Kuntze was once recorded in Jersey.)

NEMOPHILA FAMILY Hydrophyllaceae

BABY BLUE EYES *Nemophila Menziesii* Hooker & Arnott
A garden annual from California, which was found in arable in the Rues Frairies in 1970 by H. Nicolle. J –. A –. S –. H –.

JACOB'S LADDER FAMILY Polemoniaceae

(The Californian annual *Gilia multicaulis* Bentham was collected in Jersey in the 1920s. So was also the originally American *Phlox paniculata* L.)

BORAGE FAMILY Boraginaceae

HOUND'S-TONGUE *Cynoglossum officinale* L.
Surprisingly elusive, with few records this century, and never noted in the same place two years on end, except in the Port Soif/Portinfer area, where it persists in small quantity. Marquand called it rare, but Gosselin wrote with his specimens that it grew at L'Ancresse and near the seashore in divers parts of the island – and it is not rare just across the Russell in Herm. J last record 1928. A claimed. S –. H common.

GREEN HOUND'S-TONGUE *C. germanicum* Jacquin
This was recorded by the eminent eventual centenarian Ridley on p. 594 of his great work *The dispersal of plants and animals throughout the world* of 1930, as growing against the walls of the ruined chapel on Lihou, where sheep had been constantly resting, saying he found it there himself. But even he had nodded,

and his plant was doubtless the last species which has similar bur fruits and Marquand knew from there. But Ridley's observations are equally valid for either species. Rabbits preen their pelage of burs before going down their burrows, but sheep into whose thick wool the burs get deeply entangled do not preen. Their coats have been artificially developed by man, and it is precisely the fur of man's congeners which carries seeds and the like over distances, for they have been artificially selected over long ages for man's benefit and not to fit them for the wild. Our native animals have been naturally selected for smooth coats, which avoid the irritation of burs, or at least make them easier to dislodge. So perhaps in the earliest times, Hound's-tongue and the like were less widespread, until man's animals came on the scene to aid in the dispersal of their fruits. J –. A –. S –. H –.

COMMON COMFREY *Symphytum officinale* L. ssp *officinale* Grande Console

At the time Marquand wrote his *Flora*, very few people knew how to tell this species from the next, indeed even knew that it existed. This one does grow in Guernsey, and without doubt has been there in wetter places since time immemorial. It was also grown as a herb above all for poultices for lumbago. But nowadays it is rare. J scarce. A rare. S 1905. H Jethou 1890.

RUSSIAN COMFREY *S.* × *uplandicum* Nyman (*S. asperum* × *S. officinale*)

This differs from the last in having its stems less winged, or finned, from the leaf bases continuing a shorter way down the stem, and in growing in drier places. It was successfully introduced from Russia in the early 1870s and for two decades thereafter was popular for fodder; and has had fitful resurgences since, even to the extent of there being a Russian Comfrey Society. Once established it is a difficult plant to eradicate with its deep thick roots, said to reach 8ft. Consequently it is a good persister – it seems rarely to set seed. It is now generally widespread in two chromosome races and generally commoner than the last species, one of its parents. It is commoner in Guernsey, but that still means only about half a dozen stations. Its first record was made in 1957, but subsequently one was traced from Miss M. Martin from Icart in 1923. The Guernsey plants, Dr Perring agrees, seem to be of the $2n = 36$ race, with pinkish buds and hardly decurrent leaf stalks. J scarce. A locally frequent. S –. H –.

(*S. asperum* Lepechin and *S. orientale* L. have been collected in Jersey.)

(*Lappula squarrosa* (Retzius) Dumortier ssp *squarrosa* (*Echinospermum Lappula*) was in Jersey in 1898/9.)

BORAGE *Borago officinalis* L. Bourrage

A decorative Mediterranean annual that goes on cropping up, all the more welcome since flowers of a good blue are scarce – pink and white are recorded. It has however been perhaps less grown for its rough beauty than as an adjunct to cooling drinks. Indeed it is said to have been collected quite recently for claret cup at official banquets, and no doubt not only at banquets. In 1862 a visitor noted that its abundance in cottage gardens was because it was a favourite flavouring of the soup, which was the prominent dish of every Guernsey cottager's daily bill of fare (cf p. 59). In August heaps of it were to be seen drying by each cottage wall preparatory to storage for winter use. Its leaves were used herbally too. Whatever its current source may be, a few plants may be seen in various places over the island in most years. Gosselin's specimen is annotated 'grows in gardens'. J quite frequent. A occasional. S locally frequent. H –.

(*B. pygmaea* (DC) Chater & Greuter (*B. laxiflora*) has been known for some time naturalised on heathy ground on Jethou.)

ABRAHAM, ISAAC AND JACOB *Trachystemon orientalis* (L.) G. Don
A startling name which has been applied to other plants of this family with flowers of many colours, as Joseph's Coat is also used. This one has the oddest corolla, like a jester's cap, whose natural position can be seen only on fresh plants. This species comes from the Near East, and can get well established in shadier places with its rhizomes, and has done just that in the Caledonia Nursery and Sausmarez Manor. J –. A –. S –. H –.

GREEN ALKANET *Pentaglottis sempervirens* (L.) Tausch ex L. H. Bailey (*Anchusa sempervirens*)
Another good persister from farther south, and another plant with fine blue flowers. It was first noted in Guernsey above Fermain in 1883 by Lomax, then aged 22. It is still to be seen in odd places in that area, and in that area only, although it was noted at Pleinmont in 1958. J frequent. A –. S rare. H –.

SMALL BUGLOSS *Anchusa arvensis* (L.) Bieberstein ssp *arvensis* (*Lycopsis arvensis*) Bourrage sauvage
Not very common but quite often to be met with, chiefly in the north and west. Gosselin collected it by the Hougue à la Père. Andros in 1589 wrote that wine in which Bugloss leaves had been steeped would take away all sadness. J frequent. A frequent. S occasional. H frequent.

COMMON ALKANET *A officinalis* L.
This was claimed without supporting evidence from Vazon Bay by a visitor in 1951. Her other, alas published, records were equally dubious. J 1847. A –. S –. H –.

WATER FORGET-ME-NOT *Myosotis scorpioides* L.
The sole evidence for the occurrence of this species in its restricted sense in Guernsey is one sheet dated 13 June 1866 from Marriott, now in the British Museum. J doubtful. A –. S –. H –.

CREEPING WATER FORGET-ME-NOT *M. secunda* A. Murray (*M. repens*)
'Common' to Marquand, if he was naming his Forget-me-nots right – who finds them easy? – but nowadays at best extremely elusive, despite wide-open eyes. Indeed there are only five records of this species since the *Flora*. J occasional. A frequent. S rare. H –.

TUFTED WATER FORGET-ME-NOT *M. laxa* Lehmann ssp *caespitosa* (C.F. Schultz) Hylander ex Nordhagen Herbe d'Azur
First collected by Gosselin, as *M. scorpioides*, which was then the general name for Water Forget-me-nots. It was subsequently collected by Babington, Watson and Hillhouse (as *M. strigulosa*), all before Marquand claimed it as new in 1891. He called it local and rare, but even if he was right, it is now the most seen of the group. J frequent. A –. S –. H –.

(*M. sicula* Gussone is a very special native of Jersey.)

WOOD FORGET-ME-NOT *M. sylvatica* Hoffmann Tricotin
A few plants of this species were found in arable to the east of the Airport in 1969 by A. Leslie and confirmed by A. E. Wade. Forms are grown in gardens, and somehow this must have been the source of this occurrence. The field has since been down to grass. J garden escape. A –. S –. H –.

COMMON FORGET-ME-NOT *M. arvensis* (L.) Hill ssp *arvensis*
Apparently no more than occasional now. J rare. A occasional. S rare. H 1889.

CHANGING FORGET-ME-NOT *M. discolor* Persoon (*M. versicolor*)
Not infrequent, but not to be seen by the late comers, for it is one of those ephemerals that soon dry up and vanish. It occasionally has all-yellow flowers, when it has been called *M. Balbisiana*: the true *M. Balbisiana* Jordan is a different plant. White flowers have also been seen, the var *pallida* Brébisson. J common. A occasional. S frequent. H frequent.

EARLY FORGET-ME-NOT *M. ramosissima* Rochel ssp *ramosissima* (*M. 'collina'*)
Locally frequent, especially on the cliffs, its flowers normally of the richest blue, but is seen also with white flowers (var *Lebelii* Godron & Grenier?). First recorded by Newbould in 1841/2 in St Martin's. J frequent. A frequent. S frequent. H frequent.

COMMON GROMWELL *Lithospermum officinale* L.
Never a sign of this since Marquand's time, until J. Flint reported one plant at Cobo in 1970. But it seems always to have been rare and in small quantity. J –. A –. S –. H –.

(*L. purpurocaeruleum* L. was collected in Jersey in 1971.)

CORN GROMWELL *Buglossoides arvensis* (L.) I. M. Johnston ssp *arvensis* (*Lithospermum arvense*)
Marquand's find, in 1890, was the last, not the first, of this annual, for Derrick recorded it in flower in April 1885 in a field near the cliff by La Villette. J last record 1925. A 1900 and 1971. S –. H –.

VIPER'S BUGLOSS *Echium vulgare* L.
Curiously scarce, since there seems plenty of ground suitable for it. Gosselin's specimens, labelled *E. anglicum*, came from 'Erm'. It was rare in Marquand's time and is even rarer now with only two records since 1942, from opposite ends of L'Ancresse. Yet, close by in Herm there is plenty. J last seen *c.* 1965. A locally frequent. S rare. H frequent.

PURPLE VIPER'S BUGLOSS *E. plantagineum* L.
First collected by Miss Dawber in 1886 near the Vale Castle, where aliens were gathered, and where other people also collected it in 1891 and 1894. But that is all. And yet in Jersey it is not at all rare, and it was depicted on their 9p stamp in 1972. J locally frequent. A –. S error? H error ?

GIANT ECHIUM *E. Pininana* Webb & Berthelot
These striking 'Rocket Plants' from the Canaries can seed themselves in wild places, such as bramble thickets and on the tops of walls, as well as excessively

Giant Echium $\times\frac{1}{72}$

in gardens. They have been noted in Guernsey on two or three recent occasions thus, the name confirmed by Dr D. Bramwell. There is a photograph in the R.H.S. *Journal* for December 1956 of Warry with a 23 ft. specimen in his garden. Their success here is remarkable in view of their very specialised ecological requirements in their native areas on the east side of La Palma. There they grow at between 500 and 1000 metres in cloud-zone laurel forests or Tree Heather heaths. J –. A rare. S rare. H rare.

BINDWEED FAMILY Convolvulaceae

FIELD BINDWEED *Convolvulus arvensis* L. Vâle
Common. Gosselin collected it in his gardens at Le Truchot and Glateny as a weed, calling it a Plante Médécinale. J common. A common. S common. H frequent.

GREAT BINDWEED *Calystegia sepium* (L.) R. Brown ssp *sepium*
(*Convolvulus sepium*) Grande Vâle
Gosselin collected the usual white form of this species, which is not uncommon. Its stamens are under 23 mm long. The pink-flowered form *colorata* Lange is also in several places, but is not easy to tell from the next sub-species into which it seems to merge. Lady Anne Brewis in 1971 found it near Perelle in an apparently hitherto unrecorded form with the corolla divided into lobes, which has been seen by Dr C. Stace as well as by Dr Brummitt. It is the pink counterpart of the white form *schizoflora* (Druce) Stace – there is a note on such plants in *Watsonia* for July 1973. She found the white form there as well and also a mile away at Sous l'Eglise in 1973. J common. A locally common. S occasional. H occasional.

ROSY BINDWEED *C. sepium* (L.) R. Brown ssp *roseata* Brummitt
This name was published in 1967 for pink-flowered bindweeds with their stems and leaf stalks usually pubescent and the leaves much longer-pointed. Various gatherings from Guernsey have been said by Dr Brummitt to be of this subspecies. Who is to say if this was the plant recorded by Bromfield on p. 561 of the *Phytologist* of 1848 as a 'maritime form' with '*fl incarnatis*', the earliest Guernsey record for a pink-flowered plant? J –. A –. S –. H –.

DOWNY BINDWEED *C. pulchra* Brummitt & Heywood
Another pink-flowered plant recently distinguished, and nowhere known as a native plant. It is to be told by its always pink flowers intermediate in size between the last and the next species, by the slightly downy stems and sometimes lower bases of the leaves, which are U-shaped below and have roundish tips. Plants like this were collected in 1970 and 1971. J 1960. A –. S –. H –.

HYBRID PINK BINDWEED *C. pulchra* × *C. sepium*
Several pink-flowered plants are thought by Dr Brummitt (who has given much help with the Guernsey plants) to be possibly of this cross. But the pink-flowered Bindweeds of Guernsey are difficult to name with certainty. J –. A –. S –. H –.

HYBRID WHITE BINDWEED *C.* × *lucana* (Tenore) G. Don (*C. sepium* × *C. silvatica*)
Both the parents of this hybrid may vary in size, especially the latter, but some white-flowered plants in Guernsey are likely to be this cross – one at least certainly is. J ? A ? S ? H –.

AMERICAN BELLBINE *C. silvatica* (Kitaibel) Grisebach ssp *silvatica*
The largest of the Bindweeds, with stamens at least 26 mm long and broadly spreading leaf bases – not rounded as in Great Bindweed. It is now very well naturalised from, not America, but S. E. Europe. It has been noticed only with white flowers in Guernsey, where it is not infrequent, although unrecorded until 1958. J occasional. A locally common. S occasional. H –.

SEA BINDWEED *C. Soldanella* (L.) R. Brown (*Convolvulus Soldanella*)
Not so common now on the harried coasts, but to be seen in the sandier areas of the north and west coasts. Its record goes back to the peat deposits of Vazon Bay, where Gosselin collected it and it still is. Bellamy in 1850 wrote that it had become much less used herbally, but grew abundantly in sandy places. J local. A locally common. S –. H common.

COMMON DODDER *Cuscuta epithymum* (L.) L. ssp *epithymum* Herbe d'Emeute
In 1866 this was said by Bailey to be called Fairies' Hair and to be covering Gorse everywhere. In 1883 Lomax reported all the bushes thick with it. Marquand called it frequent. It seems scarcer now, and recorded only from the south coast and the north-west. But locally it can festoon the cliff Gorse thickly, up to 3 or 4 feet above the ground. It may also be seen on Heather and low herbaceous plants, notably Clovers and the like, when it used to be considered a distinct species *C. Trifolii* Babington. The large Dodder of p. 162 of the 1938 *Transactions* will have been this species and not the true Greater Dodder, *C. europaea* L. Gosselin's specimens are labelled as this latter species, but he was following Hudson's *Flora Anglica* which united the two species. Gosselin's English names, Hellweed and Devils Guts, also come direct from Hudson. Metivier quotes from 'Un Câtelain', author of *Rimes Guernesiaises* of 1831, of a woman, Dame Toumesse, who had had seven husbands and had lost her speech, that 'I fallut llî bouidre, vraiment ... d' l'Herbe d'Emeute, d' la Squinaisie, de rouages Paquerolles et du Piment'. J locally common. A frequent. S occasional. H occasional.

Nightshade Family Solanaceae

Apple of Peru *Nicandra physalodes* (L.) Gaertner

This South American annual appeared simultaneously in 1965 in two fields of Kale, at Havilland Hall and at Les Quartiers, and about the same time in another field at Le Douit, St Peter's, where it persists. It does not seem to have been imported with the seed, as in one case at least the seed was Guernsey grown. But this plant does just this – appears. It can come in grain; it can come with wool waste, shoddy; and it is grown in gardens as undoubtedly decorative – and even by some for its alleged reputation as a 'Shoo-fly' plant. J occasional. A 1969. S –. H –.

Duke of Argyll's Tea Tree *Lycium barbarum* L. (*L. halimifolium*. *L.* '*chinense*') Epäenne d'Auriny

A hedging plant which can persist almost indefinitely thanks to vigorous suckering. It has been known at the road junction by the Vale Pond for at least three-quarters of a century, and can be seen in three or four other places. Hocart records that it got its Guernsey name from having been introduced from Alderney in the 1850s by Mrs Bougourd of La Lande, Paradis. It is a native of China. J local. A occasional. S –. H –.

Petunia *Petunia* × *hybrida* (Hooker) Vilmorin (*P. axillaris* (Hooker) Schinz & Thellung × *P. integrifolia* (Lamarck) Britten, Sterns & Poggenburg)

This is the familiar bedding annual, selected from the crossing of two Argentine species, first made in 1835, and from subsequent mutations. It may appear fleetingly but attractively on rubbish tips and in waste places. There are three such records from Guernsey, in 1957, 1971 and 1973. J –. A –. S –. H –.

Wild Tobacco *Nicotiana rustica* L.

This is the original North American tobacco plant introduced into France by Jean Nicot, which contains more nicotine than the usual *N. Tabacum* L. It is occasionally grown in gardens, not always for its flowers, and can appear outside them for a season. There is one Guernsey specimen, from a field near Les Hubits in 1917 found by Mrs Hichens and named by Druce. Andros recommended tobacco as a balm in his Notebook in 1589. This may have been this species or *N. Tabacum*, but either way it is remarkable that it was known in Guernsey so early, for this species was brought from America only in 1560 and the latter species in 1557. J –. A –. S –. H –.

(*N. Tabacum* L. was collected in Jersey in 1928.)

Sweet Tobacco *N. alata* Link & Otto

A decorative annual from South America fragrant and attractive to moths in the evening. It may similarly appear 'wild' and is once recorded thus in Guernsey, on the Mont Cuet tip in 1968. J 1926. A –. S –. H –.

Mountain Tobacco *N. silvestris* Spegazzini & Comes

Tobacco was grown during the occupation and the odd plant has persisted since. This species was found growing out of a wall of a car park in St Peter Port in 1971. J –. A –. S –. H –.

DEADLY NIGHTSHADE *Atropa Bella-donna* L.
A plant much overclaimed by the less expert, who confuse it with Bitter-sweet or Black Nightshade. It has been planted, for good rather than evil, for many centuries, and no doubt reached Guernsey this way. In any event there are only five records of it, four from the area from Paradis to Mont Crevelt, all but Gosselin's (he knew it as a poisonous plant) in the 1840s. The fifth, reported by Ansted, grew 'accidentally' in a garden in St Peter Port and 'attained the proportion of a tree'. J last wild record 1899. A –. S –. H –.

(Bladder Cherry, *Physalis Alkekengi* L., has been recorded for Jersey.)

HENBANE *Hyoscyamus niger* L. Hanebâne
Henbane seems to have been known in the L'Ancresse area for many a long year, indeed since Gosselin's time, until its final recorded appearance in 1933 – it was there in 1913 but thought to be gone in 1922. Marquand wrote in his *Flora* that the plants were intentionally dug out by the owners of sheep grazing on the Common, for fear of poisoning. This might account for its diminution from 'by no means rare' 20 years earlier. There is only one other record, very common as a weed in the garden of La Chaumière, Câtel in 1913 and by the Câtel Cemetery. Gosselin knew it as a Plante Vénéneuse. J last record 1926. A last record 1900. S –. H 1889 and 1922.

BITTERSWEET *Solanum Dulcamara* L. Amerdaön. Morelle
Quite frequent. Its pollen is in the Vazon peat, and Gosselin, who considered it poisonous, collected it near the Longstore and Hougue à la Père. Var *marinum* Babington is the normal form on shingle and by the sea. White flowers have been reported, for example at Mont Crevelt. A variegated plant with rich creamy margins to the leaves was found at Fort Saumarez in 1971. J. K. Burras, the Curator, says a similar chimaera was being grown at the Oxford Botanic gardens around 1650. J frequent. A occasional. S frequent. H frequent.

BLACK NIGHTSHADE *S. nigrum* L. ssp *nigrum* Crève-coeur
A frequent, if not common, weed. Gosselin, who knew it as poisonous, called his specimens 'Garden Nightshade'. Tall plants with very narrow corolla lobes from the Vaux de Monel, which Dr Edmonds at first sight thought looked like *S. americanum* Miller, she decided were in fact a form of *S. nigrum*. J common. A occasional. S frequent. H frequent.

RED NIGHTSHADE *S. luteum* Miller ssp *alatum* (Moench) Dostál (*S. miniatum*)
The form with scarlet berries was known to Newbould and Syme from Icart and Jerbourg, and the one with yellowish ones, to Marquand from between these two places. There have been no records since. J last record 1927. A –. S – H –.

TALL NIGHTSHADE *S. sublobatum* Willdenow ex Roemer & Schultes (*S. Ottonis*)
Somehow this perennial from S.E South America managed to get a footing in the Channel Islands – there are only two other records from the British Isles, both fleeting, in 1925 and 1935, according to Dr J. Edmonds. But in Guernsey man's hand has been inadvertently against it and its hold is tenuous. It is like a tall – 4 ft. to 5 ft. – grey-downy Black Nightshade with narrower leaves and

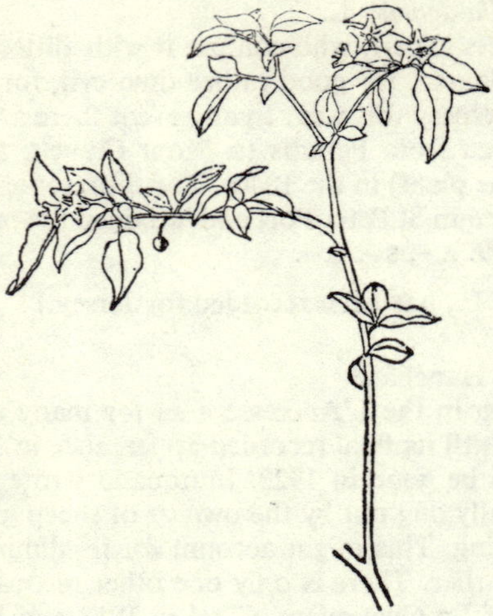

Tall Nightshade ×⅓

sweet berries. It was first noticed, several plants, along a wall by Manuelle's yard south of St Sampson's harbour on 17 August 1958. Shortly after, the wall was demolished, and the plants overwhelmed by a pile of road metal. Nevertheless two even taller ones were found not far away, only in due course also to be similarly lost. It had been seen in four or five places in that area when by 1970 all seemed gone. But in 1971 it was rediscovered, is still there, and has been successfully grown from its seed in gardens. J –. A –. S 1961. H –.

KANGAROO APPLE *S. laciniatum* Aiton
This fine Australasian was found by Miss R. de Sausmarez on clearing undergrowth at the Vaux de Monel in 1973. It proved to have been brought there by Miss Bonamy Collings in 1919 from New Zealand, but not only has it persisted on its own, it has spread right to the top of the slope. In 1973 too, a single fine plant was seen in the Bordeaux quarry tip – whence? J rare. A –. S –. H –.

(*S. sarrachoides* Sendtner from America was seen in Alderney in 1969 and 1973, and Sark in 1956; and is now locally frequent in Jersey, where too the Madeiran *S. pseudocapsicum* L. has been reported.)

POTATO *S. tuberosum* L. ssp *tuberosum* Patate
Raw potato scraps thrown out are always liable to sprout if they contain an eye. Hence, and from whole potatoes, come potato plants on rubbish tips etc. As such they have a low status as a wild plant. But sometimes 'this esculent vegetable', as it was described in 1859, may appear elsewhere, for example on sandy ground, and stay for longer than just until the next frost. The Guernsey climate allows it to do this, and so it may persist awhile vegetatively. At one time potatoes were extensively grown, yielding some 22 tons per acre; and 10,000 tons were exported in 1839–40. They originated in S. America. J recorded. A 1956. S 1961. H 1957.

TOMATO *Lycopersicon esculentum* Miller Toumate
Another vegetable in general scorned as wild, with reason. But it too may persist by its own seed. One place where it does this is near trickles of water by the sea-

shore, where frosts are less and competition absent. It has done this for several years by the slipway north of Fort Saumarez, and has done the same elsewhere; and in Guernsey it need never lack for sources of seed. J –. A 1956. S occasional. H Longue Pierre 1969.

COCKS-EGGS *Salpichroa origanifolia* (Lamarck) Baillon
This South American perennial now sprawls over wide areas north of the Grandes Rocques Hotel and by the yard at the south-east corner of Les Dicqs. It

Cocks-eggs ×½

has also been seen in a small quarry by the Route du Vaugrat to the south-west, by St John's Church, and in a sand pit south of the Golf Clubhouse. Warry was the first to record it, in 1946. J –. A –. S –. H –.

THORN APPLE *Datura Stramonium* L. Pommier du Djable. Graines du Djable
Although there are only about a score of definite recorded occurrences, this plant seems always to have been cropping up and still does so regularly – indeed Derrick wrote in 1902 that he had met with it in almost all the country parishes. Gosselin noted it from rubbish and dunghills. It is rather a mystery where the seeds come from for these spasmodic appearances, but they can undoubtedly remain dormant in the soil for decades. Thorn Apple is currently being used as a test plant for potato disease. It may be of American origin. J occasionally persisting. A once. S 1953. H –.

FIGWORT FAMILY Scrophulariaceae

COMMON MULLEIN *Verbascum Thapsus* L. ssp *Thapsus* Moleine
Local, never in quantity and sometimes misclaimed for the next species. There is a rosette in one of Gosselin's scrapbooks, and his early notebook recorded it 'dans mon jardin & aux cotins'. J occasional. A rare. S rare. H rare.

(*V. densiflorum* Bertolini (*V. thapsiforme*) has been claimed from Jersey.)

ORANGE MULLEIN *V. phlomoides* L.
This is the species Marquand collected in 1892 and called *V. pulverulentum*. The next year Miss Dawber collected it and called it *V. Thapsus*. It has been seen at least six times since 1958, once with white flowers. It is native farther south. J rare. A –. S 1958. H rare.

(White Mullein, *V. lychnitis* L., was collected in 1925 from Jersey.)

HOARY MULLEIN *V. pulverulentum* Villars
Its only record, in the *Flora*, is proved by Marquand's specimen to belong to the last species. J 1885. A –. S –. H –.

BROUSSA MULLEIN *V. bombyciferum* Boissier
Two plants appeared near the Golf Clubhouse in 1971 where it still is. This is a striking extremely white-woolly biennial introduced into gardens – in Guernsey too – since the last war. It comes from Bursa or Brusa in Asia Minor. J –. A –. S –. H –.

(*V. speciosum* Schrader was seen in Jersey in 1960.)

PURPLE MULLEIN *V. phoeniceum* L.
A fine plant of this on the rubbish tip at Candie gardens was independently noticed by three visitors in 1968. J 1960. A –. S –. H –.

BLACK MULLEIN *V. nigrum* L. ssp *nigrum*
Six records, the last in 1947 at Vimiera. Mrs de Garis records that 'Great or Black Mullein' was used once medicinally. Gosselin was the first to collect it, 'proche Les Rouvets'. J occasional. A rare. S rare. H rare.

MOTH MULLEIN *V. Blattaria* L.
Collected by Gosselin in two places, as Balm-leaved Figwort. But his specimens are indubitably of this species. Claimed by Carré in the 1830s, but there is no vouching specimen. Claimed in 1864 by Dupuy with a specimen, which proves it was the next species. J last record 1950. A –. S 1872. H –.

LARGE-FLOWERED MULLEIN *V. virgatum* Stokes
The records are Babington 4 July 1838, Dupuy 1864 (as the last species), Marquand 1891, and Druce in 1906 ('but not typical'). It was also claimed in 1944 by Warry from Bouet, but his plant is more like *V. phlomoides*. J –. A –. S –. H –.

LESSER SNAPDRAGON *Misopates Orontium* (L.) Rafinesque ssp *Orontium* (*Antirrhinum Orontium*)
Fairly frequent. Gosselin collected it, noting it grew in gardens as a weed, as well as in cultivated grounds and cornfields. J locally frequent. A 1970. S common. H local.

COMMON SNAPDRAGON *Antirrhinum majus* L. ssp *majus* Goule d' llaon
Rather scarce – and yet one might have thought the local walls would have suited this Mediterranean plant. A remarkable fully peloric form, yellow and red, was collected from the St Sampson's dump in 1971. J occasional. A last record 1900. S rare. H 1958.

PURPLE TOADFLAX *Linaria purpurea* (L.) Miller
To be seen upstanding on quite a number of walls here and there, which is a

habitat that it often affects in our islands. It was first noted only in 1957/8, but clearly had been naturalised much earlier. It occurs also with pink flowers. It is South European. J occasional. A –. S rare. H –.

PALE TOADFLAX *L. repens* (L.) Miller
Marquand was not the first person to record this plant in Guernsey – Watson was, in 1852, but he called his specimen *L. minor*. Further, Miss Dawber had collected a specimen in 1886 and Derrick reported in 1888 that it had been found for three years at St Sampson's, St Andrew's and the Forest. Green noted it also in 1893 at Moulin Huet. But the only records since those days are from A. Leslie in 1970 at Calais, and in a wall by Les Câches in 1971, where it had presumably run from a garden. J rare. A –. S 1841. H –.

COMMON TOADFLAX *L. vulgaris* Miller
Not rather common now, but local. But there seems no reason why it should have become scarcer. Gosselin collected it as a Plante Médécinale. J frequent. A rare. S frequent. H last record 1962.

PROSTRATE TOADFLAX *L. supina* (L.) Chazelles
Wolsey, in the company of the Jersey botanist J. Piquet, collected this among rubbish near St Sampson's harbour in 1858, its only C.I. record. J –. A –. S –. H –.

(*L. Pelisseriana* (L.) Miller is a famous Jersey rarity, not seen for several years. *L × sepium* Allman (*L. repens × L. vulgaris*) was collected there in the 1920s. *L. maroccana* Hooker f. was seen in Alderney in 1973.)

SMALL TOADFLAX *Chaenorhinum minus* (L.) Lange (*Linaria minor*)
Recorded by Watson from among *Ulex* and *Calluna* near Petit Bot in August 1865. But the habitat is wrong, and his small specimen is of *Linaria repens*. J last record 1925. A –. S –. H –.

ROUND-LEAVED FLUELLEN *Kickxia spuria* (L.) Dumortier ssp *spuria* (*Linaria spuria*)
Two records, by Babington in 1837/8 and his friend Newbould in 1841/2 from St Martin's Point; no specimens. J only specimen 1927. A –. S 1892. H –.

SHARP-LEAVED FLUELLEN *K. Elatine* (L.) Dumortier ssp *Elatine* (*Linaria Elatine*)
Rather common to Marquand. It is still widespread, but definitely scarcer now. Gosselin collected it as a Plante Médécinale, commenting it grew in cornfields and gardens as a weed. J rare. A very rare. S occasional. H occasional.

IVY-LEAVED TOADFLAX *Cymbalaria muralis* (L.) Gaertner, Meyer & Scherbius ssp *muralis* (*Linaria Cymbalaria*)
Happily common on walls. This completely naturalised, originally Mediterranean, plant is very rarely to be seen in any but this artificial habitat, but there is one record of it on rocks, in 1930. Who is to say when it reached Guernsey? – well before Marquand listed it in 1891. It is a plant people assume is recorded and so fail to note. The white-flowered form was noted from Fort George in 1935 and has been seen in two or three places in Town. J common. A occasional. S rare. H local.

COMMON FIGWORT *Scrophularia nodosa* L. Herbe de Crampe
Once used as a remedy for cramp but by no means the common Figwort of Guernsey: indeed it is unexpectedly rare. There are only two recent records, and no others since the *Flora*. Gosselin collected it and noted it from 'moist and shadowy places in the lower parts of fields and meadows, as found at the foot of the upper hedge of my orchard at L'Hyvreuse'. J rare. A –. S rare. H rare.

WATER FIGWORT *S. auriculata* L. (*S.* '*aquatica*' incl. *S. Balbisii*) Orvale
Collected by Gosselin, and still quite frequent in wetter places. It was used locally for skin, and many other, troubles. J rare. A occasional. S occasional. H rare.

BALM-LEAVED FIGWORT *S. Scorodonia* L.
This is the most plentiful Guernsey Figwort, to be seen in all sorts of places – it has been seen in flower in March. It is unquestionably native and no colonist, as Marquand himself later conceded. Gosselin sent Sir J. Banks seed of this on 16 January 1792. J common. A –. S –. H frequent.

MUSK *Mimulus moschatus* Douglas ex Lindley
This American was reported in *Science Gossip* in 1890, as having been found in 1885, the locality too secret to be put into print. It proved to be native Yellow Bartsia. J –. A –. S –. H –.

(*M. guttatus* DC was found in Jersey in 1962, and may spread.)

CORNISH MONEYWORT *Sibthorpia europaea* L.
Currently known in only two places, and seen since the war in only one other, all in the south. In total it has been known in perhaps ten, but it is easy to overlook. The first records are from Newbould in 1841 from Saints Bay and Dupuy in 1864 from Petit Bot. J frequent. A –. S rare. H –.

FAIRY FOXGLOVE *Erinus alpinus* L.
A Central and Southern European plant which has presumably seeded itself from rockeries and has made itself at home on walls over a wide stretch of the British Isles. It was on the side of a wall at Saumarez Park in 1967 and is atop another by the Les Câches crossroads. J occurs. A –. S –. H –.

FOXGLOVE *Digitalis purpurea* L. ssp *purpurea* Cllatchets
Never really plentiful – hardly common now, but still chiefly in the southern half. Gosselin collected it 'about the south part of this island', and knew it with white flowers, which still occur. He knew it too as poisonous. This is noteworthy, for it was only in 1785 that Withering published his *Account of the Foxglove*, where its properties were set out for the first time. Perhaps Gosselin was aware of some of the fatal results of using it herbally before then, for it is one of our most dangerous plants, beneficial to the heart only when properly used. J common. A locally frequent. S locally common. H common.

BROOKLIME *Veronica Beccabunga* L.
Common to Marquand, but scarce now, apparently. Gosselin collected it from small standing waters. An 18th-century Mrs Carey used it in a recipe for scurvy. J common. A occasional. S rare. H –.

WATER SPEEDWELL *V. Anagallis-aquatica* L. (*V.* '*Anagallis*')
All the records for this species seem to belong to the next one, qv. J –. A ? S –. H –.

PINK WATER SPEEDWELL *V. catenata* Pennell (*V. 'Anagallis'*)
In Marquand's time, and indeed until after the last war, this species was rarely if ever separated from the last. Specimens prove that Gosselin's Grande Mare plant from the 18th century and Marquand's Cobo one a century later are both of this species, as is Dupuy's from Vazon in 1864. Add to this that the three stations at present known for it, at Les Maingys, Port Soif and the Mare de Carteret, all have this species only, and it may be surmised that the two remaining unvouched localities were probably the same. But it is still a rare plant, in small quantity anywhere. J 1912. A ? S –. H –.

MARSH SPEEDWELL *V. scutellata* L.
Gosselin collected this nearly 200 years ago, but no one has seen it since. J last record 1926. A –. S –. H –.

HEATH SPEEDWELL *V. officinalis* L.
Many books call this the Common Speedwell, but that it is in few areas and certainly not in Guernsey: there has been no record since the *Flora*. Yet, once again, only four miles away in Herm it is indeed common. It was the Male Speedwell to Gosselin, who got the name from Hudson. J rare. A rare. S rare. H common.

BIRD'S-EYE SPEEDWELL *V. Chamaedrys* L. ssp *Chamaedrys* Herbe Terraie. Veronique
Hardly 'very common' now, but nevertheless happily frequent, especially in the south. Gosselin collected superb specimens. It was used at one time to cure indigestion and the like. Dr Dony in 1970 noticed a plant with pale flowers at La Fosse. J common. A frequent. S common. H frequent.

LONG-LEAVED SPEEDWELL *V. longifolia* L.
A common garden plant from Central Europe which can persist a while outside. It was seen thus in 1971 in St Andrew's. J on record. A –. S –. H –.

THYME-LEAVED SPEEDWELL *V. serpyllifolia* L. ssp *serpyllifo'ia* Veronique
Perhaps commoner than it seems, because of its unobtrusiveness. Gosselin gathered it as a garden weed, which it still can be. He used Hudson's name Paul's Betony, a name going back in print to Turner in 1548, as *Betonica Pauli aeginete*, who used it for Heath Speedwell. Paul Egine was a 7th-century Greek who made a great name for himself in the Arab world for his medical writings. J common. A error. S frequent. H frequent.

NECKWEED *V. peregrina* L.
At the meeting of the Thirsk Natural History Society in July 1859, specimens of this American annual were exhibited raised from seed stated to have been procured from wild Guernsey examples. Rather later in the same issue of the *Phytologist*, which reported this, is written 'Mr Wolsey's Sarnian station before adverted to is an apple orchard or nursery at St Saviour's Jersey' – where indeed it was known then. Here is yet another muddle between the islands, and there is no other claim for this plant in Guernsey. The American name comes from its use as a charm hung round the neck. J rare. A –. S –. H –.

WALL SPEEDWELL *V. arvensis* L. Veronique
Common. It can be very small in short sandy turf – var *nana* Poiret? Gosselin

collected it and called it Chickweed, or Corn Speedwell. J common. A frequent. S common. H common.

IVY-LEAVED SPEEDWELL *V. hederifolia* L. ssp *hederifolia* Herbe au Bourdon

Ivy-leaved Speedwells were recently split and the records have not been sorted to decide which might belong where – the distinguishing features are not easy to make out in practice. This one definitely occurs but possibly is the scarcer of the two in the island. J occurs. A ? S ? H ?

LESSER IVY-LEAVED SPEEDWELL *V. hederifolia* L. ssp *lucorum* (Klett & Richter) Hartl (*V. sublobata*)

Possibly this is commoner than the last in Guernsey, but the knack of telling the two apart has hardly been achieved yet. The species in the aggregate is common. J ? A ? S ? H ?

COMMON FIELD SPEEDWELL *V. persica* Poiret (*V. Buxbaumii*)

A Near Eastern, Persian indeed, annual which first reached the British Isles probably early in the last century, and has succeeded in being the commonest such Speedwell for about a century now. Dupuy first collected it in Guernsey – from Les Hubits in 1864. It has been seen with white flowers. J common. A frequent. S common. H frequent.

GREY FIELD SPEEDWELL *V. polita* Fries

'Frequent' in 1901. 'Common' in 1936. Very scarce now. But was it always correctly identified? There are specimens of this from Gosselin mixed with those of the next species. J frequent. A rare. S 1958. H last record 1894.

GREEN FIELD SPEEDWELL *V. agrestis* L.

Collected by Gosselin as a garden weed, and considered common generally at the time Marquand wrote his *Flora*. But either it was misclaimed, perhaps for the Common one, or it has most markedly declined everywhere. It is now very scarce in Guernsey too – apparently always with pink and white flowers. J scarce. A rare. S last record 1896. H rare.

SLENDER SPEEDWELL *V. filiformis* Smith

Chevalier in 1933 noted this species as naturalised on roadsides. Nothing more was seen of it, by recognising eyes anyway, until 1958, when a little was noticed in two places at Fermain. It has since been seen in about half a dozen other sites. In some five of these it has ramped into the lawns in its special way, but perhaps there are other gardens where it also is doing this unreported, or will do, for it is easily taken from one garden to another. It seems never to set seed, but any morsel can take root. There is a drawing of it in the *Transactions* for 1958, pp. 315–16. J locally frequent. A –. S 1933 only. H 1932.

HEDGE VERONICA *Hebe* × *franciscana* (Eastwood) Souster (*H. elliptica* Forster f × *H. speciosa* R. Cunningham ex A. Cunningham) (*H.* '*Lewisii*')

This is the common shrub with spikes of rich purple flowers. It is ultimately of New Zealand origin, although first named from San Francisco. Its history is set out in the RHS *Journal* for November 1956, pp. 495–8: see also *Watsonia* for July 1973. It is well naturalised in the warmer south-western parts of Britain, as it is in Guernsey, where seedlings are frequent. It was no doubt what Carré recorded in 1862 as generally flowering freely the whole winter, seeding abundantly and producing seedlings in the open ground. In the same year it was referred to as *Veronica Andersonii*, which is in fact *V. salicifolia* × *V. speciosa*, and said to be common. Chevalier in 1933 called what must have been this plant *V. elliptica*, but the naming of these shrubby Veronicas has never been easy. It only got firmly on the Guernsey list in 1967, no one before having noticed that it was missing. Its record from the Vauvert Road with pink flowers needs verifying. J occasional. A occasional. S occasional. H occasional.

NARROW-LEAVED HEDGE VERONICA *H. salicifolia* (Forster f.) Pennell
This shrub may seed itself and has done so on a wall at Saumarez Park, abundantly, and also at Les Rocquettes. J recorded. A –. S –. H –.

RED RATTLE *Pedicularis palustris* L. ssp *palustris*
Only Babington has ever recorded this. He may have been right, but he collected no proof. J 1839. A –. S –. H –.

LOUSEWORT *P. sylvatica* L. ssp *sylvatica*
Another plant which seems to have got rarer since Marquand's time, for it is only locally to be seen nowadays. It has not been noted south of a line from Mont Hérault to Fort Doyle. J local. A occasional. S common. H –.

YELLOW RATTLE *Rhinanthus minor* L. (*R. Crista-galli*) Herbe à Sonnettes
Also apparently scarcer than it used to be. Gosselin noted it near the coast and implied it was not uncommon. Currently it has been in six squares, all on the west coast. The plants in the Grande Mare were said by Druce to be var *stenophyllus* (Schur) O. Schwarz, which may be no more than an autumnal state. Dr Perring has recently opined that they were between this and the var *minor*. An apt English name for this species is the Chick and Egg plant. J rare. A –. S –. H –.

(Common Cow-wheat, *Melampyrum pratense* L., was collected in the 1920s in Jersey.)

SMALL-FLOWERED EYEBRIGHT *Euphrasia micrantha* Reichenbach
Elegant, unbranched plants from the Grande Mare, called var *gracilis* of *E. officinalis* L. belong here, according to Dr Yeo. Two other records, in 1866 and 1914, have been referred to other species. J –. A –. S –. H –.

SHORT EYEBRIGHT *E. curta* (Fries) Wettstein
The var *glabrescens* Wettstein was recorded by Druce in 1906, but the specimens are *E. nemorosa*. J similar error? A similar error? S similar error? H –.

WESTERN EYEBRIGHT *E. tetraquetra* (Brébisson) Arrondeau (*E. occidentalis*)
The commonest eyebright, but in a less stout and stocky form than in England: one gathering, Dr Yeo said, resembled plants he had collected north of Morlaix in Brittany. Several gatherings have been put under var *calvescens* Pugsley, for what that may be worth. J frequent. A frequent. S frequent. H common.

A HYBRID EYEBRIGHT *E. nemorosa* × *E. tetraquetra*
Collected at Grandes Rocques in 1958, specimen mislaid. J –. A –. S –. H –.

A HYBRID EYEBRIGHT *E. stricta* × *E. tetraquatra*
Possibly this at Calais in 1958 – cf *Proceedings* of BSBI December 1968, p. 383. J –. A –. S –. H –.

COMMON EYEBRIGHT *E. nemorosa* (Persoon) Wallroth (*E. nitidula*)
Occasional. Specimens from Saints Bay in 1970 were noted by Dr Yeo as strongly glandular. He has written that the characteristic combinations of features of this and other species are rarely fully realised in the Channel Islands. He determined Gosselin's specimens as belonging to this species, who called all Eufrasias (sic), which included Red Bartsia, Medicinal Plants. J occurs. A occasional. S occasional. H –.

CONFUSED EYEBRIGHT *E. confusa* Pugsley
A confused species indeed, confirmed from Herb: Marriott in 1866 and from L'Ancresse in 1968 from Dr Bowen. But Dr Yeo writes that Channel Island plants are difficult to determine. He has seen all the specimens of this genus, and greatly assisted with them. J –. A 1963. S 1928. H –.

(*E. arctica* Lange ex Rostrup ssp *borealis* (Townsend) Yeo (*E.* '*brevipila*') has been misclaimed from Jersey: it was *E. nemoralis.* So has *E.* '*Kerneri*'.)

UPRIGHT EYEBRIGHT *E. stricta* D. Wolff ex J. F. Lehmann
Several records have been made of this species, not only in Guernsey, but all were discredited. In 1958 however Dr Yeo recognised it in collections from Calais, and grew on more from its seeds. The colony was still there in 1961, but could not be seen in 1969. Silhouettes of these plants are on p. 384 of the *Proceedings* of the BSBI for December 1968. It now proves however that this species was first collected in 1893 on L'Ancresse by Miss Dawber, where similar collections were made by Wilmott in 1928, and in 1971; and Dr Bowen also got it on a cliff-top at Pleinmont in 1968. J errors. A –. S –. H –.

SHRUBBY CALCEOLARIA *Calceolaria integrifolia* L.
A garden shrub from South America which has been seen thrice, in 1953, 1967 and 1973, self-sown on walls. Carré in 1862 had recorded that it seeded abundantly. J –. A –. S –. H –.

RED BARTSIA *Odontites verna* (Bellardi) Dumortier ssp *serotina* (Dumortier) Corbière (*O. rubra*)
Fairly frequent, and typically the autumnal race of the species. But the distinctions are not clear in the field, and Marquand too noted forms intermediate to the next subspecies. J rare. A occasional. S –. H –.

EARLY RED BARTSIA *O. verna* (Bellardi) Dumortier ssp *verna*
Gosselin's specimens of this were said to verge on to the last subspecies. Marquand claimed to know this plentifully in Moulin Huet, and Dupuy's specimens from the Grande Mare in 1864 resemble it. Typically this is a race of arable weeds, but the distinctions do not seem to hold good in Guernsey. J –. A claimed. S –. H –.

YELLOW BARTSIA *Parentucellia viscosa* (L.) Caruel (*Eufragia viscosa*)
This is quite widespread, if hardly frequent any longer. But it still comes up strongly (4 ft. 4 in. high on L'Ancresse in 1958) and decoratively, not only in moist meadows, but even on the now barish ground of the old coal yard north of

Vale Castle. Woods was its first recorder, on 28 July 1836. T. Parentucelli (1398–1455) was later Pope Nicholas V. J local. A occasional. S frequent. H 1889, Jethou rare.

BROOMRAPE FAMILY Orobancheaceae

YARROW BROOMRAPE *Orobanche purpurea* Jacquin (*O. caerulea. O. arenaria*)
The records are 1837/8 from St George, where it was also seen in 1894; from the nearly eponymous Fort George cliffs 3 miles distant about 1850; 1884 (no locality); and 1971-4. Two small colonies were found in 1971, one just off Bulwer Avenue, the other 200 yards to the north by the St Sampson's quarry, by Mrs Garratt and R. English. Both had pale yellow stems and lavender blue flowers, and their identity was confirmed by Dr Hambler. J local. A frequent. S 1847. H –.

(*O. ramosa* L. was collected in Jersey in 1913, and recorded from Sark in 1835.)

GREATER BROOMRAPE *O. Rapum-genistae* Thullier *O.* '*major*'
This is in Gosselin's list, but no one else's and his specimens resemble *O. Hederae*. This is somewhat surprising, for conditions on the south-west cliffs seem like those on Jersey and Alderney where it parasitises the prostrate subspecies of Broom quite plentifully locally. J locally frequent. A very locally abundant. S –. H –.

(*O. alba* Stephan ex Willdenow has been claimed from Jersey, and was collected on Sark in 1892. *O. elatior* Sutton has been collected in Jersey.)

CLOVE-SCENTED BROOMRAPE *O. caryophyllacea* Smith
There is a sheet at Newcastle-on-Tyne Museum dated 1833 from Trevelyan claiming this species for Guernsey. But it is a mixed gathering, and the Guernsey specimen on it is *O. maritima*, Dr Hambler reports. There is also a fine painting, now at St Peter Port, of unknown provenance dated 24 June 1863 from Cobo and named as this species, but this too he considers to be *O. maritima*. J. –. A –. S –. H –.

COMMON BROOMRAPE *O. minor* Smith (*O. apiculata*)
Not the common Broomrape of Guernsey, and not always readily to be told from the next three species. It varies in appearance, partly perhaps in response to the varying plants it grows on. Those mentioned include Hop Trefoil, Spotted Medick, Red Clover, Yellow Vetch, Buck's-horn Plantain, Common Cat's-ear and Autumn Hawkbit, but the records are incomplete, and indeed it is frequently difficult to be sure just what the host is. *O.* '*amethystea*' on Sea Holly in the Channel Islands is said by Prof. Clapham to be *O. minor*. Dr Le Poidevin noted in the 1951 Report a specimen with 61 flowers near Ile de la Chapelle. The var *flava* Regel (*flavescens*) recorded by Marquand and others was queried by Pugsley in 1940. Plants from Albecq, Rousse and Pleinmont have been recently referred to his var *compositarum*. J frequent. A frequent. S rare. H rare.

OX-TONGUE BROOMRAPE *O. loricata* Reichenbach (incl. *O. picridis*)
Miss Dawber's specimens of *O.* '*amethystea*' from Bon Repos in 1892 were recognised by Graham as belonging to this rare species, its only C.I. proven record. J recorded. A –. S –. H –.

IVY BROOMRAPE *O. Hederae* Duby (*O.* '*barbata*')
This is the common Broomrape of Guernsey, locally plentiful. Knowlton in 1726 saw 'upon roots of Ive' at the Château des Marais ('Ivy Castle') 'orabranca or Kapi', quite its earliest record for the British Isles. A scrap in Gosselin's scrapbook called '*O. major*' is probably of this species. It was next recorded by Gay in 1832. Its appearance apparently some distance from an Ivy merely shows how the Ivy's roots spread. The form *stenantha* Beck was named by Prof. Beck himself from specimens from Ruettes Brayes from Miss Dawber dated 1888. Dr N. Le Poidevin recorded also f. *typica* Beck and f. *monochroa* Rouy. J rare. A rare. S frequent. H rare.

CARROT BROOMRAPE *O. maritima* Pugsley (*O.* '*amethystea*')
Several gatherings appear in folders in herbaria under one or other of these names, and there are other possibly acceptable records. But it is now either rare or elusive or overlooked or, contrariwise, over-recorded. It is difficult to discriminate satisfactorily, and may indeed be no more than a variety of *O. minor* q.v. Dr Hambler says this species has a dense spike and distinctly purple stem, while *O. minor* has a much laxer inflorescence especially near the base and its stigma lobes are separated, and spread far apart as the flower dies. The host in Guernsey has been Carrot, with the exception of a record by Ward, one of whose specimens in the British Museum, from Pleinmont in 1894, is said to have been on Sea Plantain. J rare. A occasional. S rare. H last record 1925.

BUTTERWORT FAMILY Lentibulariaceae

(Common Butterwort, *Pinguicula vulgaris* L., and *P. lusitanica* L. were recorded unvouched from Jersey in the 1830s.)

GREATER BLADDERWORT *Utricularia vulgaris* L.
A glance at the specimen vouching this in 1923 will show that it was Water Milfoil. J error? A –. S –. H –.

LESSER BLADDERWORT *U. minor* L.
Gosselin collected this in two places in 18th-century Guernsey. J –. A –. S –. H –.

ACANTHUS FAMILY Acanthaceae

BEAR'S BREECH *Acanthus mollis* L.
This curious English name for an ancient denizen of our gardens goes back at least 350 years. Before that, as long ago as 1538, Turner called it Brank Ursine, and in 1548 (even this is three years before its first reference in the *Oxford Dictionary*) wrote that it grew 'in many places in Englande in gardines'. Abroad, where it was *Branca ursina*, this name was also used for Hogweed, which it has been in this country and is today in France. The leaves are said to have inspired the ornamentation of Corinthian capitals – the plant is a native of Greece. The cultivated form is var *latifolius* (Goese) Grönland & Rümpler, which received an Award of Merit in 1973. Once established it gets its roots well down and lasts. It did so for some time on a roadside north of the Câtel church, until the early 1960s, and is doing so in some quantity off Mount Durand, on waste ground above St Martin's Point, in the Fermain Valley, by La Haye du Puits, and can exceed its welcome in gardens elsewhere. J occasional. A –. S –. H –.

Verbena Family Verbenaceae

Vervain *Verbena officinalis* L. Vervaïne
Still rather scarce and never in plenty. On Gosselin's sheet he wrote 'Grows by hedges and park-sides' and noted it also 'dans nos parterres'. He knew it as a medicinal plant. It was grown in herb gardens and considered a general cure-all, for it had magical properties as well and was used in counterspells, as Mrs de Garis relates. J frequent. A rare. S last recorded 1892. H –.

Thyme Family Labiatae

Pennyroyal *Mentha Pulegium* L. Pouillet
This has been known in three areas in the north of the island: from Paradis in the 1830s, from the Braye du Valle until 1854, and from west L'Ancresse until 1924. But there is still not unsuitable ground and it can merge unflowering and unnoticed in damp turf. Andros, who called it also *Statis aigre*, wrote in his notebook in the 16th century 'Penny Royal soaked in vinegar and held in the mouth will relieve toothache'. It was also believed to be efficacious in clearing children's heads of vermin. J very rare. A –. S 1902. H –.

Corn Mint *M. arvensis* L.
The only records for this plant since 1900 were made by Warry in 1944 from the Rue des Marettes and by Mrs Page in 1974 in the forest. J rare. A –. S rare. H –.

Bushy Mint *M.* × *gentilis* L. (*M. arvensis* × *M. spicata*)
One of the three most usual garden mints, which was noted by Dr Bowen in 1968 at Les Terres. J 1966. A –. S –. H –.

Water Mint *M. aquatica* L. (incl. *M. 'hirsuta'*) Mente
Still as frequent as Gosselin's specimens and notes imply. J common. A frequent. S occasional. H local.

Whorled Mint *M.* × *verticillata* L. (*M. aquatica* × *M. arvensis*) (*M. sativa*)
There is a good stretch of this on the artificial south bank of the eastern prong of the Reservoir, found in 1963 by Mrs Russell. J rare. A –. S 1892. H –.

Peppermint *M* × *piperita* L. (*M. aquatica* × *M. spicata*) Pepermàn
Five records, the last in 1926, three said to have been of var *piperita* (*officinalis*), one of var *vulgaris* Sole, and one, in 1899, of *M.* × *dumetorum* Schultes (*pubescens*), which is in effect a downy Peppermint. It was vouched for by Bennett, but the specimen has not been traced. J 1926. A occasional. S 1957. H –.

(*M. piperita* L. 'Citrata', the Bergamot Mint, grows in Jersey. So did *M.* × *Maximilianea* F. W. Schultz (*M. aquatica* × *M. suaveolens*) in 1957.)

Spearmint *M. spicata* L. (*M. viridis*, incl. *M. cordifolia*)
The usual, hairless, Mint Sauce, form of this polymorphic species has been recorded on half a dozen or so occasions. A plant collected in 1958 4 ft. high in a hedge was at the time expertly named *M. cordifolia*, but is, Dr R. Harley reports,

a tetraploid form of this species; another of 1958 is also of this species. Useful details are in his paper in BSBI *Proceedings* for May 1967, pp. 369–72. J scarce. A last record 1900. S rare. H 1957.

A LONG-LEAVED MINT *M. longifolia* Hudson × *M. spicata*
'Probably this', wrote Dr Harley on an uncultivated specimen persisting in a shrubbery at Mont Saint in 1969. A similar plant was recorded from Jerbourg in 1971. True *M. longifolia* is wild no nearer than the Alps. J –. A –. S –. H –.

A HYBRID MINT *M.* × *villosa* Hudson (*M. spicata* × *M. suaveolens*)
A well-established patch away from houses near Niaux in 1970 was named this by Dr Harley, who has helped greatly with the Guernsey mints. J –. A –. S –. H –.

APPLE MINT *M.* × *villosa* Hudson (*M. spicata* × *M. suaveolens*) (*M. 'sylvestris'*)
This has been given many names, most often *M. alopecuroides*, or more recently *M. niliaca*, which however refers to another hybrid. As usually seen, it is, in great part at least, a clone passed from garden to garden and thence to rubbish heaps and roadsides, by separating its runners, as with other garden mints. Its aptest appellation therefore is precisely by such horticultural nomenclature as its status calls for, i.e. as a cultivar 'Alopecuroides'. It was first recorded in Guernsey by Hillhouse in 1879 from Moulin Huet – correctly ? – and there have been five records since. It has on various occasions been erroneously claimed from the southern valleys, and can be hard to tell from luxuriant forms of the next species. This one has the teeth round the edge of the leaf pointing much more distinctly towards the apex, and differs in smell. J rare. A –. S –. H –.

ROUND-LEAVED MINT *M. suaveolens* Ehrhart (*M. 'rotundifolia'*)
This is the mint locally frequent by the streams running down the valleys to the sea in the south, especially towards the east. Gosselin got his specimens from 'the side of the brook that runs from the Forest to Petit-bo'. There are no records of it elsewhere. J local. A –. S 1841. H 1920 – error?

ROSEMARY *Rosmarinus officinalis* L. Rosmarin
Seedlings have been seen on walls and waste ground – but there is none now in Rosemary Lane. Andros said its charcoal was used for drawing pictures. It was also grown as a herb, but to be efficacious it must have been given, not bought. It received the AGM in 1973. J –. A –. S –. H –.

GIPSYWORT *Lycopus europaeus* L.
Still rare, or at least very scarce. Gosselin collected it from either the Campdurand or St Sampson's. J locally frequent. A –. S –. H –.

MARJORAM *Origanum vulgare* L. Marjolaine
Always very rare and last seen on the wall of St Martin's churchyard, in the 1890s. It is no longer in that precarious situation. No doubt its three known occurrences all derived from herb gardens, in which it was grown. J last record 1900. A 1966. S –. H –.

WILD THYME *Thymus praecox* Opiz ssp *arcticus* (E. Durand) Jalas (*T. Drucei. T. 'Serpyllum'*) Cassidone
A variable plant, recently dubbed with a mouthful of a new Latin name. Earlier

in this century it was split into perplexing microspecies – *T. britannicus* Ronniger and *T. neglectus* Ronniger were named from Guernsey before the First World War. Thyme is now hardly very common, but rather frequent, and chiefly round the coast. It may have white flowers. Gosselin's specimens and notes call it 'Mother of Thyme', which name was quite freely used from at least Tudor days, perhaps because of its reputation in dealing with the womb – mother. J common. A common. S common. H common.

(There are two gatherings of *T. pulegioides* L. labelled Jersey. *T. vulgaris* L. was seen there atop a wall, as usual, in 1961 and 1973.)

(*Satureia montana* L. was collected in Jersey in 1911. *S. hortensis* L. was claimed there in 1924.)

Common Calamint *Calamintha sylvatica* Bromfield ssp *ascendens* (Jordan) Ball (*C. 'officinalis'*)

It is uncertain if this has ever occurred in Guernsey. Marquand mentions a specimen of Gosselin's from the Maison Sohier, which is the next species. A specimen Marquand himself collected there is Balm, and not Calamint. Then in the 1890s a plant was seen in the Les Pelleys area, which was said to have been of this species and to match its var *Briggsii* Syme. Later, the *Journal of Botany* in 1922 made it conspecific with Pugsley's *C. baetica* from Corfe Castle, Dorset, which is now realised to be a form of this. The complications of the nomenclature of this plant are summarised in the *Botanical Journal of the Linnean Society* for October 1972. But the relevant specimens have not yet been traced, nor has anyone succeeded in refinding any Calamint at Les Pelleys. J 1961. A –. S –. H claimed.

Lesser Calamint *C. Nepeta* (L.) Savi

Nobody could call this very rare nowadays, although it is plentiful only in one area, where indeed Marquand knew it in abundance, in the Rue des Hougues, and Royle knew it near by. It is also plentiful on the roadside banks to the south, towards the Reservoir, and grows to the west in the Rue à l'Or. Gosselin collected it, as Basil Thyme, in a furze field near the Maison Sohier. On his specimens he said it was to the east, in his notebook to the west of it! Dupuy got it at the Vale in 1866, and Tomlin at Fort Doyle in 1924. It was at Mont Crevelt in 1958 and recently reported as still at Bordeaux in the north. Finally Dr Campbell picked it in 1970 in quite a new area, at Fort Hommet. J claimed. A –. S –. H frequent.

(Basil Thyme, *Acinos arvensis* (Lamarck) Dandy, has been claimed from Jersey. Wild Basil, *Clinopodium vulgare* L. ssp *vulgare*, was collected there in 1898 and in Alderney in 1900.)

Balm *Melissa officinalis* L. Piment

A South European plant used as a herb for a very long time. It can persist quite readily and seed, but rarely in much quantity. It has been known in Guernsey in half a dozen or so places. J occasional. A 1956. S –. H –.

Whorled Sage *Salvia verticillata* L.

Another South European plant, collected by the conchologist Tomlin from Fort Doyle in 1923. J claimed. A –. S –. H –.

(*S. pratensis* L. was in Alderney, and has been twice claimed from Jersey.)

SAGE *S. officinalis* L.
There are specimens of this Southern European herb collected by Gosselin as Clary. J claimed. A –. S –. H –.

GARDEN SAGE *S.* × *sylvestris* L. (*S. nemorosa* L. × *S. pratensis*)
The *Flora* says two plants of this were found in July 1898, but the finder, Andrews, said August and the two specimens at the British Museum are dated 9 August. Never mind. They will have been no more than garden outcasts. J 1882. A –. S –. H –.

HOARY SAGE *S. canescens* C. A. Meyer
Recorded from Rocque Poisson by M. Torode in 1934. No specimens have been seen to check the identification of this Caucasian species. J –. A –. S –. H –.

CLARY *S. Verbenaca* L. (incl. *S. horminoides*) Saouche
Occasional on warm dry banks. Gosselin collected it and knew it at Hougue à la Père, near the Mare de Carteret and on the south cliffs. J frequent. A frequent. S –. H rare.

MARQUAND'S CLARY *S. Marquandii* Druce (*S.* '*clandestina*')
This is a much discussed and often misunderstood taxon, not readily to be told from other forms of Clary. It has been seen since before Babington's *Flora* – his specimen dated 18 July 1837 is, however, ordinary Clary – for Trevelyan collected it in Vazon Bay on 1 August 1835. Druce had it in 1877 and other collectors

Marquand's Clary ×⅓

followed e.g. in 1886, 1889 and 1890. Druce revisited it, with Marquand, in 1906 and in December of that year formally named it in the *Journal of Botany S. Marquandii*, but said it could be that 'some might prefer to write *S. Verbenaca* var *Marquandii*'. The paper and drawing are reproduced in the *Transactions* for 1906, pp. 226–8 – cf also page 131. Druce wrote that it may be distinguished 'at a glance' by its lighter blue flowers, paler foliage, narrower leaves, few glandular hairs and different odour, but in practice it is not nearly as easy as that! It was then said to grow in fair quantity, but in 1914 Pugsley reported it to be on the verge of extinction. Fortunately it was not, and was seen by many others in the succeeding 40 years. In 1926 it was noted as growing on both sides of the entry to the Grande Mare farm, with one plant in the field at the back, which is the very restricted area from which all the reliable records have come. It had apparently vanished during the 1960s, but was refound in very small quantity in 1971. What seems to have been the right plant was collected in 1894 by Gray on a hillside above Moulin Huet Bay, if his label was correct. Or was it an indication that this difficult taxon is only a form of Clary? For the consensus of opinion now is that it is conspecific with *S. Verbenaca*, which is a very variable species, the forms in the Channel Islands coming nearer to those in the rest of Europe rather than to those in the rest of the British Isles. J errors. A –. S –. H –.

(Bastard Balm, *Melittis Melissophyllum* L., was collected in Jersey in 1925.)

SELF-HEAL *Prunella vulgaris* L. ssp *vulgaris*
Gosselin's comments with his specimens 'grows in orchards, fields and hedge-sides' suggests it was not then rather uncommon, as it is now; it is scarcest in the north. It occurs from time to time with white flowers. J common. A frequent. S frequent. H occasional.

(*P. laciniata* (L.) L. was collected in Alderney in 1932.)

BETONY *Stachys officinalis* (L.) Trevisan (*S. Betonica*)
Who is to say if this was ever a Guernsey plant? It could have been, but its only recorder, Carré, for all he was a useful plantsman, was primarily a senior official of the island, and no specimens of his are known. The plant so labelled in Dupuy's herbarium is Hedge Woundwort. J locally frequent. A –. S –. H –.

FIELD WOUNDWORT *S. arvensis* (L.) L.
Perhaps still common. Gosselin collected it as a corn and garden weed at the Grange. J frequent. A occasional. S occasional. H occasional.

(*S. annua* (L.) L. has been thrice claimed for Jersey, and *S. germanica* L. once; and *S. olympica* Poiret (*S. lanata*) collected on Brechou in 1957.)

MARSH WOUNDWORT *S. palustris* L.
Only fairly frequent now as wet areas get scarcer. Gosselin's specimens and notes quote several places for it. He uses Hudson's name of Clown's Allheal, which was invented by Gerard, because a country man (Clown) who had cut himself to the bone with a scythe healed the wound with it in seven days. Clown took on its present meaning only after Gerard's time. J locally frequent. A occasional. S rare. H –.

HYBRID WOUNDWORT *S. × ambigua* Smith (*S. palustris × S. sylvatica*)
Colonies, not all identical, continue to be found attributed to this by Dr Perring, often in the absence of at least one parent. J occasional. A –. S –. H –.

HEDGE WOUNDWORT *S. sylvatica* L. Ortie puante
Frequent, and as smelly, when rubbed, as the Guernsey-French name implies. J common. A frequent. S frequent. H –.

BLACK HOREHOUND *Ballota nigra* L. ssp *foetida* Hayek
Hardly common as Marquand found it in the north, but rather thinly spread from Fort Doyle to Pleinmont and rare in the south-east. It has been seen with

white flowers. Gosselin's specimens are annotated 'grows in the lane before the Beauregard and on the east bank of the Mare Pirouin', to which his notes add Camp-duré. It was a medicinal plant to him. J locally frequent. A rare. S rare. H occasional.

(Yellow Archangel, *Lamiastrum Galeobdolon* (L.) Ehrendorfer & Polatschek (*Lamium Galeobdolon*), is rare in Jersey.)

HENBIT *Lamium amplexicaule* L. ssp *amplexicaule*
Not so frequent as in Marquand's day, and scarce in the south-eastern parts. J frequent. A occasional. S rare. H common.

CUT-LEAVED DEAD-NETTLE *L. hybridum* Villars (*L. incisum*) Herbe au Bourdon
Probably the commonest Dead-nettle in the island, but still hardly 'rather common' as Marquand noted it. J not uncommon. A occasional. S occasional. H frequent.

RED DEAD-NETTLE *L. purpureum* L. Rouâge Ortie
Also less frequent than in Marquand's time, although still widespread. Gosselin collected it, saying it grew in the corn and as a weed in the garden of the Grange. In his early list he noted it twice under *Lamium* and once under *Sideritis*. J common. A common. S occasional. H last record 1890.

(White Dead-nettle, *L. album* L., is in Jersey, but very rare.)

SPOTTED DEAD-NETTLE *L. maculatum* L.
Survives in a long overgrown ex-garden near the Grande Mare. J rare. A –. S –. H –.

MOTHERWORT *Leonurus Cardiaca* L. Picot
'Noted in many parishes' in Marquand's time, but not as wild since – it comes from farther south in Europe. Gosselin wrote on his herbarium sheet 'grows in and near some gardens in the country', but his early notes say 'dans nos parterres', and it was used medicinally in his time and after – and again in 1942, from cultivated plants. In 1884 its reputation was for 'certain eruptions which arise from the heat of summer'. J last record 1961. A –. S rare. H –.

COMMON HEMP-NETTLE *Galeopsis Tetrahit* L. s.s.
A Guernsey extreme rarity, collected by Gosselin at Mont Plaisir and Rohais and only once – in 1897 – between 1838/9 and 1969, when a few very fine plants intruded into Martel's Nursery. J rare. A occasional. S –. H –.

(*G. angustifolia* Ehrhart ex Hoffmann was in Jersey in 1907 and 1925, and *G. speciosa* Miller in 1928.)

GARDEN CATMINT *Nepeta × Faasenii* Bergmans ex Stearn (*N. Mussinii* Sprengel × *M. nepetella* L.)
The usual, sterile, Catmint of garden borders, which can survive outside for a while. It was reported thus in 1958 from Rohais by M. English. Its history is in the RHS *Journal* for 1950 pp. 403–8. J. H. Faasen ran a tree nursery at Tegelen in Holland. J rare. A 1972. S –. H –.

(Catmint, *Nepeta cataria* L. has been claimed from Jersey.)

GROUND IVY *Glechoma hederacea* L. (*Nepeta Glechoma*)
Not common, perhaps still at its best under hedges (whence Gosselin's specimens came) or scrub on the south cliffs. He called it a medicinal plant. It has been seen with white flowers. J uncommon. A occasional. S frequent. H occasional.

WHITE HOREHOUND *Marrubium vulgare* L. Orâne
Gosselin collected this, noting it 'au pied des Rochers aux Jaons', and Carré knew it. But it was rare to Marquand – Hillhouse collected it at Mont Cuet in the 1880s and since the *Flora* it has been seen only in 1922, 1926 and 1971 (one plant on a wall at La Porte Hotel). Its decline coincides with the decline of its use as a herb: it used to be prized as a tonic and for coughs and colds. The 'hore' in the name is a corruption of 'hoar' from the white hairs with which it is covered. J occasional. A rare. S rare. H –.

COMMON SKULL-CAP *Scutellaria galericulata* L.
Rare, unless it is passed by unnoticed, for all its four old stations could still hold it. It was in quantity at the Grande Mare in 1926, but has not been noted there since by any of its numerous searchers. It is still however in small quantity in the Marais north of the Château des Marais, where Gosselin collected it (he called it a medicinal plant), and there is rather more in the Vale Marais. J rare. A –. S –. H –.

LESSER SKULL-CAP *S. minor* Hudson
The cliff stream at Le Jaonnet, where alone this has been seen since the 1830s, and it was fairly plentiful in 1900, is now so rankly overgrown that so small a plant must be stifled. J rare. A –. S –. H –.

(*Teucrium Chamaedrys* L. was collected in 1926 in Jersey.)

WATER GERMANDER *Teucrium Scordium* L.
Listed by Gosselin from 'le long des Barras'. Discovered in considerable quantity near Grandes Rocques in 1900, where it seems still to have been in 1925. But the area has been very much altered for the worse, and it seems unlikely to have been able to survive. In the *Armorican Flora* the plant is said to belong to ssp *scordioides* Rouy. J only specimen 1926. A –. S –. H –.

WOOD SAGE *T. Scorodonia* L. ssp *Scorodonia* Ambrouaise
Still quite common and to be seen all over the island. Gosselin's specimens have the alternative name of Sage-headed Germander. J common. A common. S common. H common.

BUGLE *Ajuga reptans* L.
Gosselin's vouchers record that it grew in many meadows, but now it is not more than fairly frequent. It has been seen with white flowers. J garden escape. A –. S –. H –.

(Ground Pine, *A. Chamaepitys* (L.) Schreber, was collected in Jersey in 1876.)

PLANTAIN FAMILY Plantaginaceae

RAT'S-TAIL PLANTAIN *Plantago major* L. ssp *major* Pllantain
An old inhabitant of Guernsey, its pollen having been detected in the Vazon peat.

It is still quite frequent all over the island. A remedy for burns in Tudor times was leaves of Plantain powdered with white of egg. 'Eau plantis' or Plantin water was used as a mouth wash. J common. A frequent. S frequent. H occasional.

HOARY PLANTAIN *P. media* L.
Babington claimed this in his *Flora* for Jersey and Guernsey. But later in his own copy he deleted Jersey and put a question mark after Guernsey. Well he might, for no one else has even claimed it, except his pupil Hillhouse in 1881, who also omitted to preserve a specimen in support. J very rare. A –. S –. H –.

RIBWORT PLANTAIN *P. lanceolata* L. Amourette
Common, known from the Vazon peat and probably one of the species recorded by Gerard in 1597 and his successors (cf p. 23). Var *sphaerostachya* Mertens & Koch is on record from 1906. J common. A common. S common. H common.

SEA PLANTAIN *P. maritima* L.
Rather local on the lower parts of the south cliffs, and known also from the Vale Pond, Fort Richmond and Fort George. J frequent. A –. S locally frequent. H –.

BUCK'S-HORN PLANTAIN *P. Coronopus* L.
The story of this starts in the Vazon peat, and is continued, as with Ribwort Plantain, in Gerard's *Herbal* of 1597, where it is clearly illustrated on p. 343, the record being copied with small variations down to Salmon's *Botanologia* of 1710 (cf. p. 23). It is still plentiful. In the *Guernsey Evening Press* for 8 September 1928 there was a complaint that the golfing greens at L'Ancresse were infested with 'Starweed, a nasty plant that rises and baulks the true course of the ball'. The poor innocent proved to be this Plantain. J common. A common. S locally common. H common.

(*P. arenaria* Waldstein & Kitaibel (*P. indica*) and *P. sempervirens* Crantz (*P. cynops*) have been known in Jersey, last collected in 1925 and 1928.)

(Shoreweed, *Littorella uniflora* (L.) Ascherson, was last seen in Jersey in the 1950s.)

BELLFLOWER FAMILY *Campanulaceae*

IVY-LEAVED BELLFLOWER *Wahlenbergia hederacea* (L.) Reichenbach
The only suggestion, let alone proof, that this delightful flower ever grew in Guernsey rests on a specimen collected by Miss Guille in St Andrew's in 1858. J last collected 1928. A –. S –. H –.

(Harebell, *Campanula rotundifolia* L., is one of the strange absentees from the Channel Islands. Gosselin wrote in his manuscript '*Campanula*, none'. *C. patula* L. has been claimed from Jersey.)

ADRIA BELLFLOWER *C. Portenschlagiana* Schultes
A common rockery plant from Dalmatia with underground stems which thread their way readily into the interstices of rocks. As a result it can make itself very much at home in stone walls, its roots in the cool, its flowers basking in the sun long after it has ceased to grow in the garden whence it started. It can be seen thus in several places in Guernsey. J occasional. A –. S –. H –.

CHIMNEY BELLFLOWER *C. pyramidalis* L.
Another South European plant, but this time a biennial, to be seen on walls in Guernsey, often many feet up and in places where it could have been put only with great difficulty and a ladder. It will have sown itself in these positions, but whence? It has not yet been noted inside any garden. But there are at least five records of it outside them, the first in 1953, with both white and purple flowers. J –. A –. S –. H –.

THROATWORT *Trachelium caeruleum* L.
A Mediterranean perennial which has been well naturalised, also on walls, for a century in Guernsey, and until very recently was known nowhere else in the British Isles. Its original station was in the Rue des Frères, where it continues to

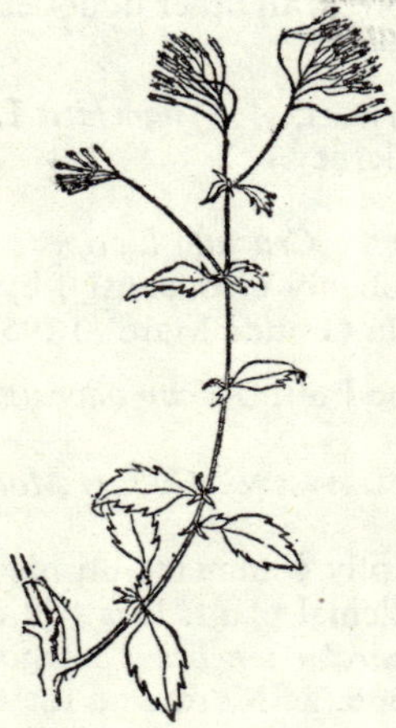
Throatwort ×⅛

urish, and in 1969 was noticed by C. David on another wall in St Peter Port by the Guille-Allès Library. Eight years earlier Lt.-Col. J. Codrington had spotted it on both sides of the road at Câtel Hill, where it is annually shaved, but manages to survive. In 1971 it was noticed high on the wall of Mount Durand, where it proved to have been for many years. J one locality. A –. S–. H –.

(*Legousia Speculum-veneris* (L.) Chaix has been claimed for Jersey.)

SHEEP'S-BIT *Jasione montana* L. Eillet d'côti. Pain d'Orvé
Still generally plentiful round most of the coast, where it can grow very fine indeed: one plant was 18 in. high in 1947. H. Nicolle has watched its spread inland since the First World War, where it is now often common on dry banks. Gosselin made two gatherings, noting it from the Terres Gosselin and implying that it was common. It occurs with white, very pale blue and mauve flowers. The var *littoralis* Fries was recorded in 1922/3. Stout plants have been erroneously attributed to *J. laevis* Lamarck (*J. perennis*). There was a fasciated one at Les Tielles in 1973. It has been mistaken by visitors for Field or Small Scabious. J common. A common. S common. H common.

LOBELIA *Lobelia Erinus* L.
This is the familiar bedding annual, usually dark blue, originally from South

Africa. Odd plants are always liable to appear outside gardens, and have done so in Guernsey. J occurs. A –. S –. H –.

BEDSTRAW FAMILY Rubiaceae

FIELD MADDER *Sherardia arvensis* L.
Although Marquand called this very common, it seems now rather scarce, on cliff tops and in arable. Gosselin's specimens are annotated 'Grows in Clover fields'. White flowers have been seen on several occasions. J frequent. A frequent. S common. H common.

BLUE WOODRUFF *Asperula arvensis* L.
Found, along with other doubtless grain casuals, in 1900. J three casual records. A –. S –. H –.

(Squinancywort, *A. cynanchica* L., was last collected in 1926 in Jersey and is rare in Alderney.)

CROSSWORT *Cruciata laevipes* Opiz
Listed, probably erroneously, by Gosselin in his first draft from 'le long des Barras de la Grande Mare'. J 1958. A 1962. S –. H –.

(Sweet Woodruff, *Galium odoratum* (L.) Scopoli, occurs rarely in Jersey.)

HEDGE BEDSTRAW *Galium Mollugo* L. ssp *Mollugo* Pain d' Paenpaen. Contreprinse
Gosselin aptly comments on his specimens 'Grows in the Hedges' and said it was a medicinal plant. It is still quite common. Paenpaen is the Bloody-nosed beetle *Timarcha tenebricosa* whose larvae feed on this plant and can exude caustic blood, as Marquand relates on p. 108 of his *Flora* and on p. 44 of the 1905 *Transactions*. J common. A rare. S common. H occasional.

UPRIGHT HEDGE BEDSTRAW *G. Mollugo* L. ssp *erectum* Syme
Plants which seem to many people to tally with the specification of this subspecies have been collected on the cliffs, at least at Icart and Saints Bay, and have been noted at Mont Cuet, but not everyone agrees. J recorded. A 1932. S error. H –.

HYBRID BEDSTRAW *G.* × *pomeranicum* Retzius (*G.* × *ochroleucum*)
Recorded from Vale Church in 1883 by Fawcett and collected in the Vale by Druce in July 1907. J rare. A –. S –. H –.

LADY'S BEDSTRAW *G. verum* L.
Not as common as might have been expected on the sandy coasts, rare elsewhere. Gosselin collected it east of the Taye Marquand. J common. A common. S occasional. H common.

HEATH BEDSTRAW *G. saxatile* L.
There are few records of this and none are undoubtedly right. Babington's is not (and was corrected by him). Marquand's is not. But he later vouched for the correctness of a specimen dated 1839 from Saints Bay, and himself noted several small patches in flower on the cliffs there in 1909. But there are no vouchers, nor

has the specimen been located which Gathorne Hardy had confirmed at Kew from Fort Doyle in 1947. There seems plenty of suitable ground for this plant in Guernsey, but search has failed to find it. J locally frequent. A occasional. S twice. H scarce.

MARSH BEDSTRAW *G. palustre* L.
Still to be seen locally – 'a vast quantity, a fine sight' was reported by C. Hare from the Château des Marais in 1971. Gosselin knew it at the Grande Mare, Marais etc. and collected it. But there is uncertainty to which subspecies Guernsey plants belong. Dr K. Goodway has measured the stomata of plants from Cobo and the Château des Marais and found them between 40 and 43μ; yet their flowers are 3.5 to 4 mm in diameter. They need to have their chromosomes counted. J frequent. A occasional. S rare. H rare.

SLENDER MARSH BEDSTRAW *G. debile* Desvaux
This is what both Babington on 27 June 1838 and Marquand in 1891 collected near Fort Doyle as Heath Bedstraw. Babington however later noted on his

Slender Marsh Bedstraw $\times\frac{2}{3}$

specimen '*G. debile* Desv. probably' and so it was. This is by 67 years the first record for it in the British Isles, much antedating Druce's claim for it when he got it in 1906 on L'Ancresse and in Jersey. But it has not been refound. J 1906, 1924. A –. S –. H –.

FEN BEDSTRAW *G. uliginosum* L.
This was listed in Ansted in 1862, based perhaps on a record by Watson in 1852. But no one has mentioned it since, and no voucher is known. J only specimen 1926. A –. S –. H –.

GOOSEGRASS *G. Aparine* L. Gratteron. La Coue. Herbe d'Satan
Still rather common all over the island. Gosselin spelt its name Cleavers on his specimen and Clivers in his list, and called it a medicinal plant. La Coue refers to the effect of sticking it on anyone's back. J common. A common. S common. H occasional.

WILD MADDER *Rubia peregrina* L.
Marquand recorded this plant as being in Guernsey until about 1870, but with no details, and Babington collected no specimen. Yet it could occur. J locally frequent. A rare. S rare. H –.

Honeysuckle Family Caprifoliaceae

Dwarf Elder *Sambucus Ebulus* L. Yèble
A small patch survives by a track and house at Paradis, quite likely where Carré knew it a century and a third ago, and possibly where Gosselin knew it nearer two centuries ago, happy links with past days. But it has not been refound in the three or four other places where it has been recorded. J only specimen 1926. A –. S –. H –.

Elder *S. nigra* L. Seue
Widespread, but not very common now. Every farmhouse used to have its Elder bush, often by the dairy window. It was there not only for its leaves, flowers, fruits and bark, but also as a protection against witches, suicide and lightning. Its leaves were used, as Elder Tea, for influenza by Rev. P. de Putron on 9 October 1851; and it also eased stomach pains. A decoction of its flowers improved the complexion and removed freckles. The berries were soothing for sore throats; and the inner bark soothed burns. The dried fruits were used as currants during the occupation. A recipe copied out in the 18th century used the soft end of an Elder branch to cure warts. The branch had as many notches made in it as there were warts to cure. This was then wrapped in paper on which had been written the name of the sufferer and the number of his warts and the whole buried. 'Et les verrues s'en iront comme le tout pourira'. J common. A frequent. S frequent. H frequent.

(Laurustinus, *Viburnum Tinus* L., is naturalised in Jersey. Guelder Rose, *V. Opulus* L., has been collected there in 1926 and 1958 and Wayfaring Tree, *V. Lantana* L., in 1926.

Snowberry *Symphoricarpos rivularis* Suksdorf
A familiar North American shrub seen twice, in 1957 and 1970, as a relic. J occasional. A –. S –. H –.

Japanese Honeysuckle *Lonicera japonica* Thunberg
Survived in a neglected garden at Pleinmont, and to be seen in odd hedges elsewhere. But it does no more and is never the pest it can be, for example in the USA. It is Far Eastern in origin. J occasional. A –. S –. H –.

(Fly Honeysuckle, *L. Xylosteum* L., was collected in 1928 in Jersey.)

Honeysuckle *L. Periclymenum* L. Suchets
Still common in all sorts of places. Some of the leaves on a plant by the Moulin Huet car park tallied with the form *quercina* (Weston) Rehder. A handful of Honeysuckle blossom was included in a mid-19th century recipe for soreness of the gums. The stems have been used to make fishermen's baskets. J common. A occasional. S common. H frequent.

Hedging Honeysuckle *L. nitida* E. H. Wilson
A relic of old hedges, which lingers forlornly in a few spots. It was introduced from China during the present century. J occasional. A –. S –. H –.

Himalayan Honeysuckle *Leycesteria formosa* Wallich
An Indian shrub which can sow itself and get well established. It was at the foot of a wall near Fort George in 1958. J occasional. A –. S –. H –.

Valerian Family Valerianaceae

Cornsalad *Valerianella Locusta* (L.) Betcke (*V. olitoria*)
Not very common, not common at all probably. But it is not possible to tell it from the next species without examining its fruits, which few trouble to do, or do effectively. So reliable data are few. J locally frequent. A occasional. S occasional. H occasional.

Keeled Cornsalad *V. carinata* Loiseleur Bruxette. Pourselle
Cornsalads, or Lamb's Lettuces, are common in Guernsey, and most prove on examination to be of this species. Gosselin noted 'it sows itself in gardens when once it is introduced'. J common. A common. S frequent. H occasional.

(*V. eriocarpa* Desvaux is a rare plant in Alderney, and was last collected in Jersey in 1928.)

Narrow-fruited Cornsalad *V. dentata* (L.) Pollich
Recorded only in 1888 at Ruettes Brayes. No specimen known. J only specimen 1926. A 1900. S –. H –.

(There are specimens of Common Valerian, *Valeriana officinalis* L., from Jersey dated 1875 and 1926.)

Red Valerian *Centranthus ruber* (L.) DC
A Southern European not infrequent on old walls and quarry sides. Gosselin knew it on the walls near Truchot Lane. Its flowers may be dark red, f. *coccineus*, mid-red f. *ruber*, or white f. *albiflorus*. J common. A frequent, S occasional. H occasional.

(*C. macrosiphon* Boissier was collected in 1926 in Jersey.)

Teasel Family Dipsacaceae

Wild Teasel *Dipsacus fullonum* L. ssp *fullonum*
A rare plant in the Channel Islands, recorded in Guernsey about half a dozen times since the war. Gosselin listed it, as Chardon or Foulon Sauvage, most suitably, from 'Le long du Chemin du Foulon'. J local. A rare. S rare. H local.

(Fullers Teasel, *D. fullonum* L. ssp. *sativus* (L.) Thellung, has been seen in Jersey and Alderney.)

Field Scabious *Knautia arvensis* (L.) Coulter ssp *arvensis*
There are very few proven records of this since the war, and one unproven – from the Calais area: it is not infrequently muddled with Sheep's-bit. Miss Mauger and H. Nicolle have known it for some time around the Blicqs; and Mrs Ryan found it in 1972 – or refound it? – not far from the old Coudré Mill in St Peters. J collected 1898, 1929. A occasional. S rare. H –.

Small Scabious *Scabiosa columbaria* L.
Another of Babington's unconfirmed records. J Babington only. A –. S –. H –.

Sweet Scabious *S. atropurpurea* L.
Recorded by Spreadbury in 1925 on almost bare sand on the west coast, doubt-

less from a garden. In 1971 Hon. R. Palmer found it in the valley just below the Gouffre Hotel, in whose grounds it had not grown, in recent years anyway. In both cases the plants had dark purple flowers. J gone. A –. S –. H –.

DEVILS-BIT SCABIOUS *Succisa pratensis* Moench (*Scabiosa Succisa*)
Listed by Ansted. J locally abundant. A –. S –. H –.

DAISY FAMILY Compositae

TRIFID BUR-MARIGOLD *Bidens tripartita* L.
A specimen of Gosselin's attests the former existence of this annual, in a horse pond at Les Landes in the Câtel, but there have been no other records. J rare. A –. S –. H –.

(Common Bur-marigold, *B. cernua* L., and the pan-tropical weed *B. pilosa* L. were last collected in Jersey in 1926 and 1927/8.)

GALLANT SOLDIER *Galinsoga parviflora* Cavanilles
This Peruvian weed, which is spreading widely, was noted by Chevalier from a sunken road near an old mill in 1933. It was at the Côte des Vardes, St Peter Port before the war, where Mrs de Jersey execrates it. In 1958 it proved to have been in the Duvaux area of St Sampson's for some time – since at least 1952 – and it was at Mont Cuet too. Since 1968 it has been seen in several other places, including nurseries, whence it may well reach other gardens. But it is still uncommon, if abundant locally. J local. A –. S –. H –.

SHAGGY SOLDIER *G. ciliata* (Rafinesque) Blake
Another Peruvian annual, first noted by N. Jee by the Grande Mare in 1960, and since seen in half a dozen places. These two plants were the subject of an article in the *Transactions* for 1958 pp. 315–16, where they are illustrated. J local. A –. S –. H –.

PERENNIAL SUNFLOWER *Helianthus rigidus* (Cassini) Desfontaines
One of the tall yellow garden daisies of autumn from North America, which can survive for a while outside, and has been recorded thus on a few occasions since 1958. J –. A –. S –. H –.

SUNFLOWER *H. annuus* L. ssp *annuus* Tourne-Soleil
An American annual grown as a stupendous garden plant, but common also as a source of food for larger cage birds. It is surprising it has been recorded only twice from Guernsey, for it is usually of regular occurrence on rubbish tips etc.; and may surprise garden owners, who suddenly find this vast plant appearing where they had fed the birds the previous winter, which gets its photograph in the paper. A plant sown from parakeet seed in 1973 attained 15 ft. 5 in. J common. A –. S –. H –.

JERUSALEM ARTICHOKE *H. tuberosus* L.
An originally American vegetable reported in 1970. J occasional. A –. S –. H –.

RAGWEED *Ambrosia artemisiifolia* L.
Another American, the sole known occurrence of which was one 3 ft. plant at N. Jee's house in the Câtel in 1963. J rare. A –. S –. H –.

COCKLEBUR *Xanthium strumarium* L.
A single plant of this pan-tropical weed appeared in 1890 on the ballast heap near Bordeaux harbour. The specimen has not been seen. J last record 1926. A –. S –. H –.

(*X. spinosum* L. was last collected in Jersey in 1926: *X. macrocarpum* DC in 1926 only.)

SPILANTHES *Spilanthes decumbens* (Smith) A. H. Moore (*S. leptophylla*)
A Brazilian plant which was collected from at least 1923 to 1926 at Fort Doyle. Mrs McCrea thought it was still there in 1947, but it wasn't. J 1926. A –. S –. H –.

(*Guizotia abyssinica* (L.F.) Cassini was in Jersey in 1969.)

RAGWORT *Senecio Jacobaea* L. Mèque
Gosselin wrote that this was 'almost everywhere', and it is still common, very occasionally in the var *flosculosus* DC (*discoideus*) with no ray florets. J frequent. A common. S common. H common.

MARSH RAGWORT *S. aquaticus* Hill
It seems this was never common, rather surprisingly, although recorded by Gay ('fort rare') and Babington (both called it *S. erraticus* 'the lyre-leaved Groundsel', a misidentification which lasted for a century), Newbould and Watson. All of these preceded Marquand's 'first' record of 1891, and the plant has not been claimed since. Specimens are known only from Newbould in 1841 and Marquand. J claimed. A –. S –. H –.

HOARY RAGWORT *S. erucifolius* L.
Gosselin listed this from three places, but the plants are much more likely to have been Common Ragwort. He collected no vouchers. The single plant found on shingle by Marquand in 1891 proves to be the Mediterranean *S. Cineraria*. Was not the 1898 singleton the same? – for it was also in the sort of place where *S. Cineraria* might be, which can naturalise near the sea. J claimed. A –. S –. H –.

OXFORD RAGWORT *S. squalidus* L.
This at least succeeded in reaching Guernsey by the late 1940s – or rather that is when it was first found, in 1949 by N. D. Simpson at St Sampson's. It is still to be seen there, to the north of the harbour, but only in small quantity. It seems extraordinary it has not spread farther on what seems just the right sort of ground. It has also been seen just west of the harbour at Delancey Park, and to the north by the Vale Castle dump. The farthest it has got so far is near St John's Church, in 1970. There is an account of it, and a drawing, in the *Transactions* for 1958, p. 315. J rare. A –. S –. H –.

HEATH GROUNDSEL *S. sylvaticus* L.
Marquand called this common, but it is rather scarce now, and perhaps best on the south cliffs, where he said it was abundant. Its decrease may be attributable to the cliffs being now so much more thickly overgrown with scrub. J common. A locally common. S occasional. H frequent.

STICKY GROUNDSEL *S. viscosus* L.
This is not infrequently claimed but, when evidence is produced, it always

proves to be the last species; and yet at least one unproven claim was made by an able recorder who may have been right. J –. A –. S –. H –.

GROUNDSEL *S. vulgaris* L. Snichäon
A common and variable annual, which Gosselin said with his specimens grew as a weed everywhere, and was a medicinal plant. A note of his day says 'We are assured on good authority that the roots and branches of groundsel have cured a great number of persons of all ages of an ague and fever now very prevalent.' In the early years of this century this species was split into several segregates by Prof. A. H. Trow – cf BEC *Report* for 1908, pp. 379–82. Marquand sent him from Guernsey his *S. lanuginosus*, a constantly densely floccose plant, which can be seen, for example, on the south cliffs and by the Hermitage. A variety which attracts attention is var *denticulatus* (O.F. Müller) Hylander with rayed florets, which seems to be getting commoner round the coasts. Babington called this var *radiatus* (*hibernicus*), but in a letter dated 19 February 1876 said it should rather be *denticulatus*. Syme a century ago said he had seen rayed forms only in the Channel Islands. Trow should be consulted in the *Journal of Genetics* for 1912, p. 246, on the radiate groundsels of the Channel Islands; and on *S. lanuginosus*. For modern comment see D. E. Allen in *Watsonia* for June 1967. J common. A common. S frequent. H frequent.

FEN RAGWORT *S. paludosus* L.
Babington curtly lists this for 'Guernsey' on the authority of Prof. La Gasca of Madrid. In this lie two weaknesses. For one thing it was in Jersey and not in Guernsey where La Gasca lived as an exile from 1831–4, and for another his List, surprisingly for so presumably expert an observer, contains too many mistakes to be relied on. J –. A –. S –. H –.

GERMAN IVY *S. mikanioides* Otto ex Walpers
Has run well out of a garden on to the ground near the Vale church car park. It is a South African with fragrant white flowers in winter, quite often grown as a house plant, originally so in Germany. J occasional. A –. S –. H –.

SILVER RAGWORT *S. Cineraria* DC
An attractive perennial from Southern Europe which is grown in gardens for its silvery foliage and can naturalise near the sea. It hardly seems to have done this in Guernsey, for both its known occurrences have been of single plants, and both were called at the time Hoary Ragwort. J last collected 1924. A –. S –. H –.

(*S. Cineraria* × *S. Jacobaea* was recorded in 1923 from Jersey.)

A GARDEN SENECIO *S. grandiflorus* Berg
A gay South African which has sown itself out of gardens in two or three places between Hauteville and Fermain, in one in quantity. J –. A –. S –. H –.

LEOPARD'S-BANE *Doronicum pardalianches* L.
'What appears to be a variety' of this was recorded in 1922, sans specimen. J –. A –. S –. H .

(TRUE) COLTSFOOT *Tussilago Farfara* L.
One of the surprising rarities of the Channel Islands. Only three records of it

were made in Guernsey in 56 years after the *Flora*, which called it rare. There were then two, followed by five in 1969–71. Most of its stations are fleeting, but there was nearly an acre of it on the site of old greenhouses, later built on, just east of the Câtel church. One of Gosselin's localities for it was north-east of this church. He called it a Plante Médécinale. It is so little seen, or noticed, that it has no name in English or Guernsey-French in the island. J rare. A rare. S –. H –.

(GUERNSEY) COLTSFOOT *Petasites fragrans* (Villars) C. Presl Pâs d'Ane
This is the plant now universally known as Coltsfoot in the Channel Islands – Marquand records it as Wild or Winter Heliotrope; the Guernsey-French name is that of true Coltsfoot in French. It is now 'Coltsfoot' also in Scilly, Cornwall and parts of Devon. Yet this is an alien plant, having been introduced to gardens from Italy via France. It is written that it 'first cast its odours on the British shore in the year 1806'. Guernsey can claim one of its earliest wild records, when Babington noted it on 6 June 1838. It is now to be seen on banks over nearly all the island. Metivier presumably referred to this species when he wrote 'Sen mesuage est pavai d'Pâs d'Ane'. Its leaves were used for tobacco during the last war. J common. A local. S occasional. H locally frequent.

(Butterbur, *P. hybridus* (L.) Gaertner, Meyer & Scherbius, is known locally in Jersey.)

POT MARIGOLD *Calendula officinalis* L. Sousique
This has been cultivated since at least the Middle Ages for medicinal and culinary reasons, and is familiar as an easy and gay garden annual. Being easy, its seeds germinate readily on rubbish tips etc. and the plants may persist for a while. Yet it was mentioned as such by nobody until 1893 – Green's record is dated 27 October. And only a few others have noted it since, perhaps because it is one of those plants people do not consider 'wild'. But it is to be seen most years. J frequent. A occasional. S rare. H 1957.

FIELD MARIGOLD *C arvensis* L.
This differs from the last in its taller more branched stature with rather smaller more numerous flower-heads. It seems first to have been collected, to the collector's surprise it was confirmed by Bennett, in 1890 at St Sampson's. But no other record has been traced until the 1950s, when it was found in some plenty

Field Marigold ×½

in the north-west. It is now in various parts of the island, locally plentiful, and seems to have spread considerably in recent years, and yet is practically never seen elsewhere in the British Isles. It comes from farther south in Europe. A recent French book says of it 'Médécinale de premier order bien méconnue'. But it was noted in 1957 that its petals were used medicinally. Is this a source of its introduction? J 1926. A –. S –. H –.

GAZANIA *Gazania rigens* (L.) Gaertner
This rich orange carpet bedder from South Africa grew by Fort le Marchant from at least 1947 to 1956, planted no doubt, but surviving magnificently on that bleak headland. J rare. A –. S –. H –.

ELECAMPANE *Inula Helenium* L. Campana
A stately medicinal herb probably native in Central Asia, grown since classical times, and persisting well with its deep root-stock. Marquand knew it in two places, neither of which has been refound. Druce got it at L'Erée in 1906; there was one plant at the Château des Marais in 1968 and there is a small patch at La Vallée, the only locality currently known for it. Mrs de Garis records that a love potion valid only at midsummer consisted of Elecampane leaves dried in the oven and pounded to powder. This was then mixed with ambergris, and the mixture worn next to the heart for nine days. Then somehow you had to get the person you loved to swallow some of it! J extinct. A –. S –. H –.

PLOUGHMAN'S SPIKENARD *I. Conyza* DC
One of the plants never seen outside the extreme south-east – it is still at Fort George and the Bec du Nez. Gosselin called it Médécinale. J rare. A occasional. S rare. H local.

GOLDEN SAMPHIRE *I. crithmoides* L.
Marquand called this rare, so either he did not get to the parts of the coast where it occurs or it has spread, probably the former. Nowadays it can be seen, in some plenty, at Fort Doyle, Jerbourg, Petit Port, Saints Bay, Le Gouffre, Bon Repos, Les Crêtes, Pleinmont, Pezeries and Rocquaine, and there is a record from Moulin Huet. Gosselin collected this and on his specimens says it grew at Mr Mansell's Saltpans; in his first notebook Mad: Mansell's; in his later one Pont Coliche; the plant was in that area until at least 1867. Ansted called it a useful plant – muddling it with Rock Samphire? J local. A occasional. S rare. H –.

COMMON FLEABANE *Pulicaria dysenterica* (L.) Bernhardi Coummaïre
Still widespread, but now frequent rather than common. Gosselin's specimens came from the Camp Collette. J frequent. A frequent. S frequent. H frequent.

SMALL FLEABANE *P. vulgaris* Gaertner
Gosselin's specimen of this is glued on the same sheet at the last, both being medicinal plants. It is now decreasing almost everywhere. Marquand's *Flora* gives only Gosselin's and Haslam's records, but it was collected at least three times after then, in 1843, 1850 and finally by Druce in 1877. J extinct since 1862. A –. S 1872. H –.

COMMON CUDWEED *Filago vulgaris* Lamarck (*F. germanica*)
Still 'rather rare and somewhat local'. Gosselin got it in a field by the Câtel churchyard. J rare. A rare. S rare. H rare.

(*F. pyramidata* L. (*F. spathulata*) was collected in Jersey in 1881 and 1931. *F. gallica* L. extinct in Jersey – last collected in 1924, has been known in Sark since 1902.)

SMALL CUDWEED *F. minima* (Smith) Persoon
Rather scarce now, chiefly on the south cliffs, not noted on L'Ancresse since the *Flora*. J common. A locally frequent. S occasional. H frequent.

WAYSIDE CUDWEED *Gnaphalium uliginosum* L.
Marquand called this rather common, but that it hardly is now, and never in quantity. Gosselin collected it from his garden. J common. A rare. S frequent. H occasional.

(*G. sylvaticum* L. was twice claimed from Jersey.)

JERSEY CUDWEED *G. luteo-album* L. Cottonière
A much misrecorded rarity, being constantly mistaken for the next species. It can be told by its unbranched stems often horizontal at the base, fewer and larger flower-heads close together, by being greyer, and lacking the unpleasant smell the other gives when rubbed. Gosselin sent it to Sir J. Banks in 1790 and 1791 –

Jersey Cudweed ×½

the first specimen is in the British Museum, saying it was very scarce, and it has been collected by many visitors and residents since, but Druce could see none in 1877. On the superb specimen in Gosselin's herbarium he noted it grew in a ditch on the Jaones near the house of La Moye and from there to the Clôture, also against a stable near the Camp-duré. He labelled it Guernsey or Jersey Cudweed, but in the printed list Guernsey has dropped out. It was found in Jersey in the 17th century, and that name is used as far afield as South Africa. It seems always to have been sporadic, but Marquand once saw a potato field completely filled with it, some specimens being 18 in. high. It may still crop up almost anywhere usually in the north and west, and usually with only a few plants in any one place. J rare. A –. S –. H –.

CAPE CUDWEED *G. undulatum* L.
Now the common Cudweed of the Channel Islands, inexplicably not mentioned by Marquand in his *Flora*, for only four years later he wrote that it sometimes occurred abundantly. Moreover it had been collected by his close collaborator Miss Dawber at the Hermitage in 1891 and by Gray in 1894, when he called it

Cape Cudweed ×¼

new. Babington at the end of that year wrote 'How it came is a curious question'. Brébisson in his *Flora of Normandy* of 1859 said it was naturalised round Cherbourg, Corbière in his *New Flora of Normandy* in 1894 that it had been naturalised there for about a century, and Lloyd in his *Flora of the West of France* in 1876 knew it in at least three places in Brittany. Yet it was claimed by the Société first for the island only in 1923. One must assume it was relatively scarce then, for not even misnamed specimens survive; and it would seem to have spread from the north, for all the records were from L'Ancresse until after the war. It is now widespread and often abundant, an early coloniser of burnt ground. J since 1888. A since 1956. S since 1902. H since 1957.

PEARLY EVERLASTING *Anaphalis margaritacea* (L.) Bentham (*Antennaria margaritacea*)

By no means 'naturalised in the Channel Islands', despite successive editions of Hooker's *Students Flora* saying this right down to 1937. There is a total of two records, and no specimen has been seen in support of the single Guernsey plant of 1898. It comes from North America, and it and similar species are also grown in gardens. J 1847 only. A –. S –. H –.

CANADIAN GOLDEN-ROD *Solidago canadensis* L.

An increasing weed in the British Isles, also from North America, also originally coming from gardens. It is on record from Guernsey in at least four places since 1958, one on top of a 12 ft. wall. J occasional. A 1963. S 1961. H –.

EARLY GOLDEN-ROD *S. gigantea* Aiton

A similar garden escape, noted in 1957 and 1968. J occasional. A –. S –. H –.

(Common Golden-rod, *S. virgaurea* L., is locally frequent in Jersey, but unknown in the other Channel Islands.)

SEA ASTER *Aster Tripolium* L.

Despite the existence of salt marshes all along the Braye du Valle, where Gosselin collected it and Babington noted it, there are no other mentions of this typical salt marsh plant except at what was its western end, now the Vale Pond, where it still is. J claimed. A rare. S –. H –.

MICHAELMAS DAISY *A. novi-belgii* L. agg.

Gosselin grew this North American plant (its name comes from an early name for New York) as Starwort in the 18th century. All over the rest of the British Isles it is now well established in the wild. Yet in Guernsey there have been only four records, all since 1967, two on walls; and at least one apparently of this species in its strict sense. It also persists in overgrown gardens. J frequent. A –. S –. H –.

(*Crinitaria Linosyris* (L.) Lessing was collected in 1840 from Jersey.)

BLUE FLEABANE *Erigeron acer* L.
Still rare, and known only in the area of Portinfer and the Mare de Carteret. J locally frequent. A rare. S –. H –.

ST PETER PORT DAISY *E. mucronatus* DC (*E. Karvinskianus*)
A dainty plant from Mexico, which is specially Guernsey's, for it was first recorded in the British Isles from St Peter Port, having been known there since

St Peter Port Daisy ×⅓

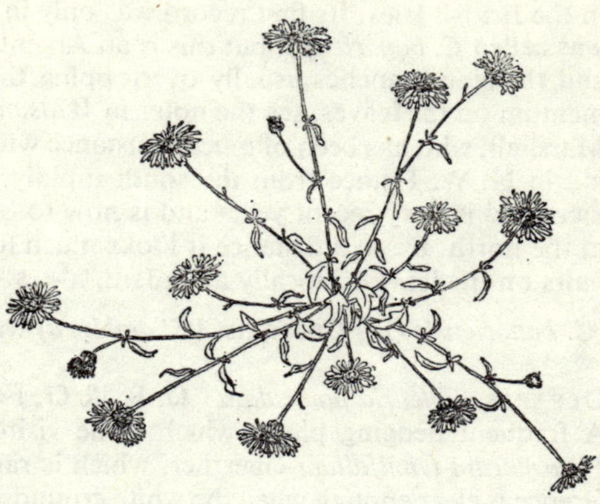

at least 1860, and being locally abundant already in the 1890s. It has spread over much of the island for many years now, always on walls, which it decorates delightfully, and so grows chiefly inland. J common. A 1970. S occasional. H –.

BEACH ASTER *E. glaucus* Ker-Gawler
A prostrate perennial from the Pacific coast of North America, useful for seaside gardens. It can do well outside them too, but usually, as in Guernsey, only where planted. J planted. A –. S –. H –.

(*E. philadelphicus* L. occurs in Jersey.)

CANADIAN FLEABANE *Conyza canadensis* (L.) Cronquist
A weedy Canadian annual which reached Europe, and Britain, in the 17th century, but Guernsey apparently only 200 years later. The first record is by Melville from the Braye du Valle in 1876, but no more was heard of it until 1947, when it seemed not all that rare. It is still not very common but may be met with anywhere in the north. J common. A locally frequent. S –. H –.

GUERNSEY FLEABANE *C. sumatrensis* (Retzius) E. Walker (*C. floribunda. C. Naudinii*)
It seems to have been in Guernsey that this plant from Peru first got established

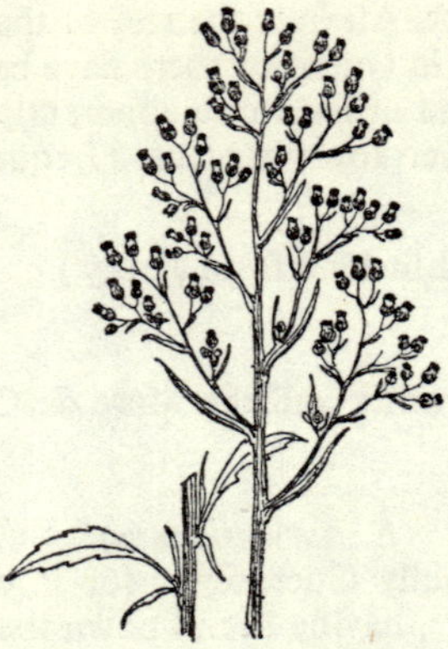

Guernsey Fleabane ×¼

in the British Isles. Its first record was only in 1961, from Mont Crevelt when it was called *C. bonariensis*, but this is an Argentine plant with larger flower-heads and the side branches usually overtopping the central one, and rougher indumentum on the leaves, see the notes in *Watsonia* for July 1973 and 1974 by J. B. Marshall, who has been of much assistance with these plants. It has been spreading in N. W. France from the south rapidly. In Guernsey it has undoubtedly increased in very recent years and is now to be seen in several localities, chiefly in the north. From a distance it looks much like the last species, but lacks long hairs on the leaves. J locally abundant. A –. S –. H –.

(*C. bonariensis* (L.) Cronquist (*C. ambigua*) was collected in Jersey in 1926.)

OLEARIA *Olearia paniculata* (J. R. & G. Forster) Druce (*O. Forsteri*)
A frequent hedging plant, which some visitors take for the slenderer greyer *Pittosporum tenuifolium* Gaertner, which is rarely grown in the island. The difference is clear enough when the white groundsel-like flowers appear, but at other times the more leathery, yellower, scurfier, wavy-edged leaves are distinctive. It can seed itself on walls or waste ground, and the seedlings attain full stature. It is from New Zealand. J –. A –. S –. H –.

NEW ZEALAND HOLLY *O. macrodonta* Baker
This is the fine Olearia, also from New Zealand, with broad well-toothed leaves, also capable of seeding itself, but only once definitely noted as doing so. J –. A –. S –. H –.

TRAVERS'S OLEARIA *O. Traversii* (F v Müller) Hooker f.
This has been seen away from gardens, but no doubt planted – it makes a good windbreak. It comes from Chatham Island, whose exploration was mainly accomplished in the 1860s through the generosity of W. T. L. Travers (1819–1903). J –. A –. S –. H planted.

KINGFISHER DAISY *Felicia Bergeriana* (Sprengel) O. Hoffmann
A pretty South African annual, one small example of which was seen on a rubbish tip in 1971. J –. A –. S –. H –.

DAISY *Bellis perennis* L. Berbiette
Gosselin wrote on his herbarium sheet 'Grows in every meadow and pasture

ground'. Happily it still does. He called it a medicinal plant. Some clumps with richly yellow-variegated leaves were found in 1972 at St George and exhibited at the Chelsea Flower Show that year. J. K. Burras said they were infected with a vein-clearing virus, which can appear on a wide range of hosts, and produces the yellowing of the vein tissues of the leaf. J common. A common. S common. H common.

HEMP AGRIMONY *Eupatorium cannabinum* L.
Widespread but not plentiful. Gosselin was the first to collect it. J local. A –. S frequent. H –.

STINKING CHAMOMILE *Anthemis Cotula* L. Méroque.
Marquand found this rather common. If he was right, either it is nowadays overlooked, which is easy, or much scarcer, perhaps both. Gosselin collected it near Saumarez at St Martin, and noted it from cornfields at the Camps du Moulin and roadsides and borders of dunghills. But did he know it? In his early List he combined the records for this with those for Scented Mayweed. J rare. A 1899. S occasional. H –.

CORN CHAMOMILE *A. arvensis* L.
This is another decreasing plant, possibly also always somewhat rarer than the books indicated. The only specimen known from Guernsey is from 1894, from Bordeaux harbour, by Royle. J rare. A 1838. S 1897. H –.

(*A. tinctoria* L. occurs in Jersey, and *A. ruthenica* Bieberstein claimed there.)

COMMON CHAMOMILE *Chamaemelum nobile* (L.) Allioni (*Anthemis nobilis*) Camière
Still locally common, one of the delights of short heathy turf, especially near the sea, natural chamomile lawns. Gosselin's specimens came from 'dry hillocks'. J common. A locally frequent. S common. H 1837.

(*C. mixtum* (L.) Allioni (*Anthemis mixta*) has been claimed for Jersey.)

YARROW *Achillea Millefolium* L. Tcherpentière
Still common. The flowers are sometimes pink, deep pink at La Fosse in 1958. Gosselin's specimens noted this as Médécinale. J common. A common. S common. H frequent.

(Sneezewort, *A. Ptarmica* L., has been seen as a garden escape in Jersey.)

COTTONWEED *Otanthus maritimus* (L.) Hoffmannsegg & Link (*Diotis maritima*)
There is a specimen of this collected by F. A. Hanbury in 1862 marked Guernsey. It might be right: it might be the usual confusion of Jersey with Guernsey. There are no other claims. J last specimen 1926. A 1838. S –. H –.

SEA MAYWEED *Tripleurospermum maritimum* (L.) Koch (*Matricaria inodora* var *maritima*)
This is the short-lived perennial of rocks and bare ground usually near the sea, although the sea is never far away in Guernsey. It is frequent. A paper on it is in *Watsonia* for July 1972, pp. 81–107, by Dr Q. Kay. J common. A common. S frequent. H scarce.

SCENTLESS MAYWEED *T. inodorum* (L.) Schultz Bip. (*M. inodora*)
This is the annual weedy counterpart of the last species, which occurs throughout the island in cultivated and waste ground. It was first noted by Gay in 1832. A form with double flowers was collected in 1922, doubtless from a garden. J common. A frequent. S frequent. H scarce.

SCENTED MAYWEED *Matricaria recutita* L. (*M.* '*Chamomilla*') Amroque
Quite common. Gosselin's specimens labelled this are Scentless Mayweed. J frequent. A –. S error? H last record 1893.

PINEAPPLE-WEED *M. matricarioides* (Lessing) Porter
An annual of waysides and trodden ground and arable, from western North America or Eastern Asia, which has spread rapidly since it was first collected in the British Isles in 1871. It was remarked by Chevalier in 1933 that it did not seem to exist in the Channel Islands, but was noted as frequent in Guernsey in 1947, its first record there, and so it still is all over the island. J common. A frequent. S occasional. H –.

CORN MARIGOLD *Chrysanthemum segetum* L. Murlu
This golden weed of arable still brightens fields in several parts of Guernsey, and may crop up anywhere, but is very susceptible to herbicides. Marquand found it rather rare, but it was said in 1939, just before the herbicide era, to be very common. Gosselin grew it in his garden from seed in 1767, and a hundred years later its leaves were being used in a herbal remedy. J common. A occasional. S frequent. H rare.

ANNUAL CHRYSANTHEMUM *C. carinatum* Schousboe
A gay garden annual originally from North Africa, which can sow itself outside, and was seen thus in 1958. J –. A –. S –. H –.

(*C. macrophyllum* Waldstein & Kitaibel is on record from Jersey.)

OX-EYE DAISY *Leucanthemum vulgare* Lamarck (*Chrysanthemum Leucanthemum*) Marguerite. Bllanc Murlu
Frequent and variable – no doubt work could usefully be done on the various forms. Already in 1832 Gay called one common near the sea in the east *multiflorum-corymbosum*, and another at St Martin's *corymbosum*; and in 1874 *muscosum* was used for 'the only form seen, branched and many-headed'. Such a form still grows on the south cliffs. Others have highly dissected leaves. Gosselin labelled his specimens Médécinale and grew it in his garden in 1767. J common. A common. S common. H occasional.

SHASTA DAISY *L. maximum* (Ramond) DC
This garden perennial originally from western North America has twice been recorded outside, once on a wall. It can persist a while. J garden escape. A –. S ? H –.

FEVERFEW *Tanacetum Parthenium* (L.) Schultz Bip. (*Matricaria Parthenium*) Epergoutte
A long cultivated herb, which can sow itself on walls etc. and may be seen doing

so quite widely in Guernsey. Its leaves were used for toothache and earache in Tudor times. Its first record is a note inserted by Babington in his own copy of his *Flora*. J frequent. A occasional. S frequent. H rare.

TANSY *T. vulgare* L. Tenaisie
Another aromatic herb occasionally to be seen. It was grown as such and may still be used for flavouring. J occasional. A occasional. S rare. H –.

(*Cotula dioica* (Hooker f.) Hooker f. from New Zealand grows in Jersey.)

MUGWORT *Artemisia vulgaris* L. Herbe d'Saint Jean
Hardly now 'rather rare', indeed recorded from over half the squares, mostly in the north and west, and yet not plentiful. *Artemisia* pollen is in the Vazon peat. Gosselin, who called it Médécinale, collected it near the Mare Pirouin. J common. A rare. S last record 1892. H rare.

WORMWOOD *A. Absinthium* L. Iaune.
Still rather rare, but still seen. It was grown as a herb and used for stomach pains, but Gosselin did not mark his specimens as medicinal. They came from the Maison-de-Bas at L'Epine. J rare. A occasional. S occasional. H –.

(*A. annua* L. was collected in Jersey in 1961, and *A. maritima* L has been recorded thence doubtfully.)

CARLINE THISTLE *Carlina vulgaris* L.
Now a surprising Guernsey rarity, little collected since Gosselin's time. He collected it on dry hills at Petit Bot, Moulin Huet and Saints Bay. In 1891 it was said to be frequent at L'Ancresse, but Marquand called it rare ten years later. It was last seen in its main area, near Fort le Marchant, in 1924, where the ground still seems suitable; but was rediscovered, a small colony, on the cliffs west of Saints Bay in 1969. J locally frequent. A frequent. S frequent. H frequent.

COMMON BURDOCK *Arctium nemorosum* Lejeune (*A. intermedium*) Boûillas
Burdocks are difficult to name satisfactorily, but this one seems to occur occasionally. J –. A last record 1932. S 1892. H –.

BABINGTON'S BURDOCK *A. pubens* Babington
This has been recorded twice, in 1951 and 1958, the latter checked by Dr Melderis. J –. A –. S –. H 1958.

LESSER BURDOCK *A. minus* Bernhardi
Probably the commonest Burdock, but still not very common. Gosselin's specimen is possibly of this species. All Burdocks were at one time lumped under *A.* '*Lappa*'. J uncommon. A frequent. S frequent. H occasional.

SEASIDE THISTLE *Carduus tenuiflorus* Curtis
To be seen round most of the coast, occasionally inland. Gosselin was its first collector, but called his specimens Welted Thistle. J common. A frequent. S common. H common.

MUSK THISTLE *C. nutans* L. ssp *nutans*
Local round the island, chiefly near the sea, rarely plentiful. There are specimens in Gosselin's herbarium. J rare. A frequent. S 1872. H 1889.

WELTED THISTLE *C. acanthoides* L. (*C. crispus*)
Gosselin's specimens are not this, as Marquand said, but were recognised by Dr W. A. Sledge to be fine ones of Seaside Thistle. There is no other claim for this as a Guernsey plant. J claimed. A –. S –. H –.

WOOLLY THISTLE *Cirsium eriophorum* (L.) Scopoli (*Carduus eriophorus*)
Listed by Gosselin, but his specimen is of the next species. Listed in 1922, with the same misidentification. J –. A –. S –. H –.

SPEAR THISTLE *C. vulgare* (Savi) Tenore (*Carduus lanceolatus*) Grand Cardaon. Cardaon beni
One of the official injurious weeds, collected by Gosselin and still common. J common. A common. S common. H common.

MARSH THISTLE *C. palustre* (L.) Scopoli (*Carduus palustris*) Cardaon
Frequent, chiefly inland, not recorded in the Vale since the *Flora*, another official injurious weed, collected by Gosselin. The *Naturalists Journal* for 1894 reported 'a bicoloured thistle has been taken by Mr Bougourd – one side was white, the other the usual colour'. J common. A occasional. S occasional. H local .

CREEPING THISTLE *C. arvense* (L.) Scopoli (*Carduus arvensis*) Petit Cardaon. Soudard
A third common injurious Thistle, collected by Gosselin. Var *setosus* C. A. Meyer was noted by Marquand and var *mite* Wimmer & Graebner by Druce in 1907. J common. A common. S common. H common.

DWARF THISTLE *C. acaule* Scopoli (*Carduus acaulos*)
A misunderstanding in Gosselin's List, for what he wrote was 'Dwarf Thistle (Carline)'. There is no other record for the island. J collected 1926. A locally common. S –. H –.

(*C. oleraceum* (L.) Scopoli was collected in 1861 in Jersey, and *C. dissectum* (L.) Hill in 1924/5.)

MILK THISTLE *Silybum Marianum* (L.) Gaertner
The only records seem to be 1892 (twice), 1900 (not 1890) and 1944. J rare. A –. S –. H –.

SCOTCH THISTLE *Onopordum Acanthium* L.
Gosselin's specimen from St Sampson's is the only known occurrence. He called it Cotton Thistle, a much better name. It was given an Award of Merit in 1962. J claimed. A –. S –. H –.

GREATER KNAPWEED *Centaurea Scabiosa* L.
Gosselin's specimen in his scrapbook is a rayed Common Knapweed. This one is noted for St Sampson's by Watson in Babington's own copy of his *Flora*, but there is no specimen. J last collected 1924. A occasional. S –. H –.

(*C. paniculata* L. has been established in Jersey since at least 1858.)

CORNFLOWER *C. Cyanus* L.
There are very few records – Gosselin (who collected it from cornfields and as a medicinal plant), then 1890 (twice), 1893 and 1906 (on a wall) and as a garden escape, with pink flowers too, in recent years. H. Nicolle recollects it as a cornfield weed in the 1920s. J occasional. A rare escape. S –. H –.

BROWN KNAPWEED *C. Jacea* L.
This and the next two taxa, often called Hardheads, hybridise readily and assistance may be needed to determine them. The evidence for the occurrence of this one in Guernsey rests on the expert views of Marsden-Jones and Turrill in their book *British Knapweeds* of 1954, p. 80, where a rayed form is noted from St Saviour's in 1927. The species has been claimed on other occasions, but no vouchers are known. J has occurred. A –. S –. H –.

COMMON KNAPWEED *C. nigra* L. Herbe d' Flon
The usual species, quite frequent, especially in the south, most often unrayed. Gosselin's specimens include both forms. The cream-coloured var *pallens* Koch has been collected several times near Le Gouffre. J occasional. A frequent. S common. H –.

SLENDER KNAPWEED *C. nemoralis* Jordan
Not reported pure by Marsden-Jones and Turrill, but rayed plants are to be seen which would seem to belong here, in so far as this and the last species are separable. Doubt on this was cast by a paper in *Watsonia* in July 1972. J ? A 1958. S 1958. H –.

HYBRID KNAPWEED *C* × *Moncktonii* C. E. Britton (*C. Jacea* × *C. nemoralis*)
The only definite record is from Grandes Rocques in 1958, named by Marsden-Jones as *nemoralis* with a few genes of *Jacea*. J –. A –. S –. H –.

HYBRID KNAPWEED *C.* × *Drucei* C. E. Britton (*C. Jacea* × *C. nigra*)
Listed by Marsden-Jones and Turrill from Jersey. Either this or the next might be the basis for Britton's use of the name *C. pratensis* Thuillier, which he records from Guernsey – cf their book, p. 20. Marquand collected an untraced plant in 1890 which he said approached the *C. pratensis* of French botanists. J listed. A –. S –. H –.

HYBRID KNAPWEED *C. nemoralis* × *C. nigra*
Listed by Marsden-Jones and Turrill from the Forest in 1936. J –. A on record. S on record. H –.

LESSER STAR THISTLE *C. diluta* Aiton
A Mediterranean annual which has become frequent in recent years in bird seed. It has been seen thence in 1968 and since, two overwintering plants at Mont Cuet reaching a height of 4 ft. 6 in. J casual. A –. S –. H –.

ROUGH STAR THISTLE *C. aspera* L.
A Guernsey speciality, which has been known at Vazon Bay ever since Gosselin's day (and once or twice rather farther north, towards Port Soif). He sent seeds and dried specimens to Sir J. E. (then Dr) Smith, Founder of the Linnean Society. It seems to have varied in quantity, appearing to be spreading in 1891, but by the 1940s there was just a small area opposite the Martello Tower where it could be seen. There were about ten plants in 1968, but none could then be found, until three were located in 1972/3, when all seemed sterile. J locally plentiful. A rare. S –. H –.

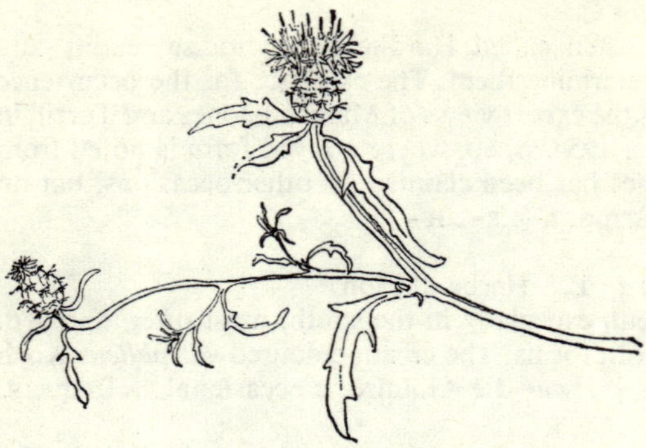

Rough Star Thistle (p. 209) ×½

STAR THISTLE *C. Calcitrapa* L.
Seen only in the 1890s, twice near Vale Castle, and once at Lower Rohais. J last collected 1925. A –. S –. H –.

ST BARNABY'S THISTLE *C. solstitialis* L.
Listed by Gosselin without a specimen. Collected by Hillhouse in 1881 at Mont Cuet; and by Mrs Ryan in 1973 by a Lucerne field at Icart. J last collected 1927. A –. S 1959. H –.

(*C. gymnocarpa* Moris & de Notaris was collected in Jersey in 1925, *C. leucophaea* Jordan claimed in 1858, and *Mantisalca salmantica* (L.) Briquet and Caville (*C. salmantica*) in 1926.)

(Saw-wort, *Serratula tinctoria* L., is locally frequent in Jersey.)

CHICORY *Cichorium Intybus* L. ssp *Intybus* Chicorée
Plants still crop up quite widely but never in quantity. Gosselin's specimens are unlocalised. Its roots and leaves were used herbally in the 18th century. It was recommended as an alternative crop in 1850, although 'the uncertainty of the climate rendered its growth somewhat of a gamble.' Warren tells of a Chicory Factory, the Steam Mill at St Martin's and another near the Château des Marais, early in the last century. J occasional. A rare. S rare. H 1947.

NIPPLEWORT *Lapsana communis* L.
The annotation to Gosselin's specimens implies that it was frequent then: so it is now. J common. A rare. S occasional. J Jethou only.

(Swine's Succory, *Arnoseris minima* (L.) Schweigger & Koerte, was collected in 1926 in Jersey.)

COMMON CAT'S-EAR *Hypochoeris radicata* L.
Common. Gosselin, following Hudson, called his specimens a Hawkweed. J common. A common. S common. H common.

SMOOTH CAT'S-EAR *H. glabra* L.
Probably commoner than it seems, for it is not always noticed, on the south cliffs and in sandy turf. J common. A occasional. S occasional. H frequent.

Spotted Cat's-ear, *H. maculata* L., is one of Jersey's special plants.)

AUTUMN HAWKBIT *Leontodon autumnalis* L.
Widespread and quite frequent. Despite its name it was in flower on 20 April 1957. Gosselin's specimens came from 'pathsides'. J frequent. A common. S common. H listed 1890.

ROUGH HAWKBIT *L. hispidus* L.
Marquand must have muddled this species with the next, with its var *pristis* Druce thought. He called it common on Guernsey, Alderney, Jethou and Crevichon, but from none of these is any specimen known in support from him or anyone else. Gosselin's, from 'meadows, pastures, roadsides etc.', are indeed of the next species. J errors. A errors. S 1953. H errors.

LESSER HAWKBIT *L. saxatilis* Lamarck (*L. nudicaulis. L. taraxacoides. Thrincia hirta*)
Frequent rather than very common, and more on the coast than inland. Druce described his var *pristis* (of *L. nudicaulis*) from Guernsey material, its leaf cutting suggesting a sawfish, which the variously spelt Latin word can mean, and noted also its var *arenaria* (DC) Druce and var *leiolaena* (Bischoff) Druce – cf *Journal of Botany* for 1907, p. 423. J frequent. A frequent. S common. H frequent.

BRISTLY OX-TONGUE *Picris echioides* L. (*Helmintia echioides*)
Local and rare to Marquand, now not infrequent, chiefly in the north and west, but never in plenty. Gosselin's specimens grew in the streets and lanes about the Truchot. A plant with pale lemon-yellow flowers was collected in 1973 from near Fort Richmond. J occasionally plentiful. A frequent. S rare. H –.

HAWKWEED OX-TONGUE *P. hieracioides* L.
This is in Gosselin's List, but the specimen in his scrapbook is Autumnal Hawkbit. J local, A frequent. S –. H 1899.

(Goat's-beard, *Tragopogon pratensis* L., has been claimed from Jersey and Sark, and is rare in Alderney.)

SALSIFY *Tragopogon porrifolius* L.
Marquand called this a casual, and well he might, with only one plant on record. However this came from near Bordeaux, where it seems to have been known ever since, and still is, although never plentiful. It has been seen in St Peter Port, but only as a survivor from a kitchen garden crop. J rare. A last record 1907. S –. H –.

(*Chondrilla juncea* L. was collected in Jersey in 1905.)

PRICKLY LETTUCE *Lactuca serriola* L.
Known, but sparingly, in the area to the south of St Sampson's harbour since 1958, and seen at Bordeaux in 1970. But see also the next species. J –. A –. S –. H –.

GREATER PRICKLY LETTUCE *L. virosa* L.
Mis-claimed in Gosselin's List; claimed by Maj. Smith in the 1850s, who could have been right, unless it was the last species, which was for some time combined with this. Smith wrote 'It is possible the seeds might have been brought among those of clover or grass. Mr Field however found it nearly in the same localities about nine years since.' J collected 1932. A –. S –. H –.

(Wall Lettuce, *Mycelis muralis* (L.) Dumortier, was collected in Jersey in 1928.)

MARSH SOW-THISTLE *Sonchus palustris* L.
In Gosselin's List, but the specimen in his scrapbook so marked is the next species. J –. A –. S –. H –.

CORN SOW-THISTLE *S. arvensis* L.
Widespread and perhaps still not uncommon – 'grows among the corn' wrote Gosselin with his specimens. It was seen with pinkish-grey ray florets at Grandes Mielles in 1958. J frequent. A occasional. S frequent. H rare.

SMOOTH SOW-THISTLE *S. oleraceus* L. Laiträon
Quite common. It sometimes has pale ray florets and mauvish phyllaries. MacCulloch records a saying 'Ou est qu'ell y a du laitron, ch'est le faim' – because Sow-thistles are said to indicate poor land. But they don't. J common. A common. S common. H frequent.

PRICKLY SOW-THISTLE *S. asper* (L.) Hill
Possibly rather less common than the last and rather less inland. J common. A frequent. S common. H frequent.

WALL HAWKWEED *Hieracium sublepistoides* (Zahn) Druce
A form of this with dark phyllaries grows, very sparingly, high on the walls west of Candie gardens and, lusher, in the long ferny bed in the Gardens themselves and in one at the Priaulx Library. It was named by Dr C. West, who has seen all the specimens of C.I. Hawkweeds. J –. A –. S –. H –.

UMBELLATE HAWKWEED *H. umbellatum* L. ssp *umbellatum* (*H.* '*laevigatum*')
This is known from perhaps half a dozen banks, nearly all by roads, from Hommet Paradis to St Peter's. Gosselin's specimens came from roadside hedges at Les Effards and St Sampson's. It has been at Cobo since at least Babington's time. Except for the plant 4 ft. high recorded by Miss Dawber from Ruettes Brayes in 1891, which has not been traced (and may not be of this species), all these are dwarf, hardly exceeding a foot high. Mrs C. Harris reports that these are fertile diploids with $2n = 18$, in common with other material from the south-western parts of the British Isles, and unlike apomictic plants from elsewhere in Britain with $2n = 27$. J rare. A occasional. S –. H –.

ANOTHER UMBELLATE HAWKWEED *H. umbellatum* L. ssp *bichlorophyllum* (Druce & Zahn) Sell & West
This is somewhat commoner than the last, although still scarce, with broader flaccid greener leaves. The earliest specimen is from Royle from a lane near L'Ancresse in 1891. J locally common. A –. S occasional. H –.

(*H. vulgatum* Fries, *H. strumosum* (W. R. Linton) A. Ley and *H. trichocaulon* (Dahlstedt) Johansson have been found in Jersey.)

MOUSE-EAR HAWKWEED *Pilosella officinarum* C. H. & F. W. Schultz (*Hieracium Pilosella*)
This is not common, and never in plenty. Gosselin collected it, and knew it 'sur la rampe' near Bailiff's Cross. It occurs in three forms, which have been called subspecies – ssp *officinarum* with mixed glandular and simple hairs on the phyl-

laries, ssp *nigrescens* (Fries) Sell & West with similar dark hairs and ssp *micradena* (Nägeli & Peter) Sell & West (*concinnata*) with glandular hairs only, which is apparently rare. There is a key in *Watsonia* for July 1970, p. 117, to these and other forms which might occur. J uncommon. A frequent. S occasional H 1958.

SHAGGY MOUSE-EAR HAWKWEED *P. Peleterana* (Mérat) C. H. & F. W. Schultz (*Hieracium Peleteranum*)
Locally common, notably on the south cliffs, distinctive in its stubby stolons upturned at the tip and shaggy leaves. Gosselin collected it, probably at Petit Bot. It occurs in three taxa, which can be hard to tell apart, but have been graded

Shaggy Mouse-ear Hawkweed ×½

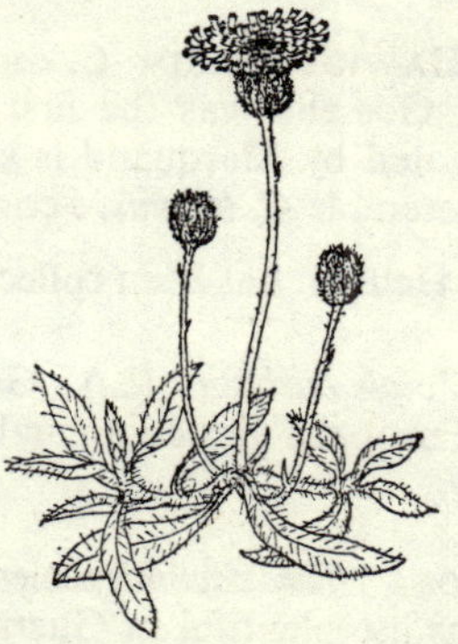

as subspecies – ssp *peleterana*, ssp *tenuiscapa* (Pugsley) Sell & West, and ssp *subpeleterana* (Nägeli & Peter) Sell & West. The first has rather broad leaves and large heads on shortish stalks, the second narrower leaves with smaller heads on taller slenderer stalks, the third calls for specialist measurements. The distribution of these three has not been worked out, but the species in the broad sense was known to Gay in 1832 from St Martin's. J locally common. A occasional. S occasional. H scarce.

HYBRID MOUSE-EAR HAWKWEED *P. × pachylodes* (Nägeli & Peter) Sojak (*P. officinarum × P. Peleterana*)
A specimen collected by Miss Dawber at Pleinmont on 23 August 1893 was detected as this hybrid by Dr C. West, who himself collected it in 1958 between St Peter Port and Fort George. J 2 records. A –. S –. H –.

FOX AND CUBS *P. aurantiaca* (L.) C. H. & F. W. Schultz ssp *brunneocrocea* (Pugsley) Sell & West
This was collected by Piquet in 1854 at St Peter Port, whence came the next record, from a wall at the Grange 107 years later. Ten years after that it was seen on another wall at the Grange. It had been reported from south of the Câtel Church the year before. This is a plant from Central Europe often grown in gardens. The earliest known wild British specimen was collected only the year before Piquet's. This subspecies can be distinguished from ssp *aurantiaca* by its browner flowers and its phyllaries being under 8 mm long. J rare. A –. S –. H –.

BEAKED HAWK'S-BEARD *Crepis vesicaria* L. ssp *taraxacifolia* (Thuillier) Thellung
Marquand muddled this plant, and yet accused Babington of confusing it with the next species (p. 370 of the *Flora*), although Babington corrected the entry on

p. 58 of his *Flora*. Both Marquand's vouchers prove his '*C. biennis*' to be, indeed, the second records for this species, which was then spreading and for long thus muddled. Since then it has spread farther, but is still not very common, although widespread, often on walls. J locally common. A frequent. S occasional. H –.

ROUGH HAWK'S-BEARD *C. biennis* L.
As noted above, both Marquand's records (the first actually came from Miss Dawber) are errors for the last species – see also the comment under the next one. There is no reason to believe this was ever a Guernsey plant. J no specimens. A –. S –. H –.

SMOOTH HAWK'S-BEARD *C. capillaris* (L.) Wallroth (*C. virens*)
Common. Gosselin was the first to collect it. The var *agrestis* Waldstein & Kitaibel noted by Marquand is said by Lester Garland in his *Flora of Jersey* much to resemble *C. biennis*. J common. A common. S common. H frequent.

(*C. setosa* Haller f. has been collected in Jersey in 1858; *C. foetida* L. in 1910.)

TOLPIS *Tolpis barbata* (L.) Gaertner
A South European garden annual collected by a roadside in 1863. J –. A –. S –. H –.

DANDELIONS *Taraxacum* species Plat Laiträon. Hôloges (the fruits)
Dandelions are plentiful in Guernsey – they were used medicinally in the 18th century. All those known here, except one, are apomictic, that is they reproduce themselves identically (in the absence of the rare mutation) from seed without cross-fertilisation. The mutants do the same, hence the multiplicity of different dandelions. These identical microspecies are in effect clones, a fact which their nomenclature ideally should reflect. All the identifications below have been made or confirmed by Dr A. J. Richards, to whom much gratitude is due – but many gatherings proved unnameable. Further details can be found in his *Taraxacum Flora*, a supplement to *Watsonia* in 1972. Our knowledge is too recent and sketchy to assess distribution or frequencies.

DUNE DANDELIONS Section *Obliqua* Dahlstedt
T. platyglossum Raunkiaer L'Ancresse and Port Soif. Basically a northern, Scottish, species. J –. A –. S –. H –.

MARSH DANDELIONS Section *Palustria* Dahlstedt
T. austrinum Haglund. A rarity, but there is quite a patch west of the Grande Mare. J known. A –. S –. H –.

LESSER DANDELIONS Section *Erythrosperma* H. Lindberg f. (*laevigata*)
T. brachyglossum (Dahlstedt) Dahlstedt L'Ancresse, Pezeries and Sausmarez Manor. A non-apomictic species.
T. fulviforme Dahlstedt Mont Saint
T. glauciniforme Dahlstedt Doyle Rock
T. cf *lacistophyllum* (Dahlstedt) Raunkiaer Grandes Rocques, Sausmarez Manor. 'May be hybrid'.
T. laetum Dahlstedt. L'Ancresse. 'May be a hybrid'. This may be a sexual species.
T. rubicundum (Dahlstedt) Dahlstedt L'Ancresse

T. simile Raunkiaer L'Ancresse
J 8 species. A 2 species. S recorded. H 2 species.

RED-VEINED DANDELIONS Section *Spectabilia* Dahlstedt
T. Adamii Claire Château des Marais, Perelle, Kings Mills, Niaulx, Les Lohiers, Les Eperons, Fort George, Caledonia, Government House, Mount Durand.
T. Nordstedtii Dahlstedt Royal Hotel, Château des Marais
T. praestans H. Lindberg f. Grande Mare, Fort George
J 4 species. A –. S –. H –.

COMMON DANDELIONS Section *Vulgaria* Dahlstedt
T. alatum H. Lindberg f. L'Ancresse, Vale Church, St Sampson's Quarry.
T. ancistrolobum Dahlstedt Grandes Rocques, Sausmarez Manor.
T. aureosulum H. Lindberg f. La Porte Hotel.
T. bracteatum Dahlstedt L'Ancresse.
T. cophocentrum Dahlstedt Mare de Carteret, Lower Mount Durand.
T. cyanolepis Dahlstedt Grande Mare, 'Guernsey'.
T. duplidens H. Lindberg f. Mount Durand.
T. expallidiforme Dahlstedt Kings Mills.
T. fasciatum Dahlstedt Grande Mare.
T. hamatiforme Dahlstedt Mare de Carteret, La Houguette, Rue des Bergers, Richmond, Mont Saint, Four Cabot, Fort George, Mount Durand, Fermain.
T. hamatum Raunkiaer Kings Mills, La Houguette, Les Lohiers, L'Ancresse, Mont Saint (?).
T. latisectum H. Lindberg f. La Houguette, ? Contrée des Clercs.
T. lingulatum Markland Mount Durand, Château des Marais.
T. maculatum Jordan Candie, Fauxquets Valley.
T. Marklundii Palmgren (*subhamatum*) St Peter Port, Sausmarez Manor, Ruettes Brayes, Grande Mare, Château des Marais, Mare de Carteret.
T. Sellandii Dahlstedt La Houguette, Kings Mills, Sausmarez Manor, Fort George.
T. subcyanolepis M. P. Christiansen Kings Mills.
T. sublaciniosum Dahlstedt & H. Lindberg f. Sausmarez Manor.
T. tenebricans (Dahlstedt) Dahlstedt L'Ancresse, Les Maingys.
J 27 species. A 1 species. S 4 species. H 1 species.

MONOCOTYLEDONS

Monocotyledones

WATER-PLANTAIN FAMILY Alismataceae

LESSER WATER-PLANTAIN *Baldellia ranunculoides* (L.) Parlatore (*Alisma ranunculoides*)
Always rare in recorded times and now very rare indeed. Gosselin noted it from near the rushes at the Grande Mare and about the Château des Marais, and it was seen in the Grande Mare again in 1971. It was in a now filled-in quarry at Portinfer in 1958. Its only two other records this century were still near Fort le Marchant in 1918 and near Paradis in 1925 – same place? J last collected 1925. A –. S 1909. H –.

COMMON WATER-PLANTAIN *Alisma Plantago-aquatica* L.
Known from the peat at Catioroc and Vazon at a time when opportunities were greater for it, and still in these areas. Gosselin also knew it at the Château des Marais. Recently it has been seen as well in the Vale, St Sampson's, the Mare de Carteret, Footes Lane and by the Reservoir. J frequent. A –. S –. H –.

(The American *Sagittaria latifolia* Willdenow was reported in Jersey in 1961.)

FROG-BIT FAMILY Hydrocharitaceae

FROG-BIT *Hydrocharis Morsus-ranae* L.
Listed by Gosselin as 'dans les Marais'. J last collected 1926. A –. S –. H –.

CANADIAN WATER-WEED *Elodea canadensis* Michaux
This has been claimed for Guernsey on more than one occasion, but the only proven occurrence is from Mont Cuet in 1958. Canadian it is. J extinct. A –. S –. H –.

CURLY WATER-THYME *Lagarosiphon major* (Ridley) Moss
An aquarists' oxygenator from South Africa, which can grow prolifically in goldfish and other ponds, and does. It was first noticed only in 1958, in a pond at the Grange Lodge Hotel, St Peter Port, where it still is, and in a quarry at La Lande. It has been seen in various other such waters since, for example at Candie gardens and Saumarez Park. All known plants in Europe are female. The generic name refers to the very long thin tube of the lower part of the flower. J rare. A one record. S –. H –.

ARROW-GRASS FAMILY Juncaginaceae

MARSH ARROW-GRASS *Triglochin palustris* L.
Scarce, in recent times at least. The only record in the century between Gosselin, who collected it in the Taye Marquand near the ditch on the north side, and Derrick in 1888 is Babington's stating it was common. It is known today by the Vale Pond and in the Grande Mare. J rare. A rare. S –. H –.

SEA ARROW-GRASS *T. maritima* L.
Still only at the Vale Pond and at Pulias. Gosselin's specimens came from the foot of hedges on the Braye du Valle where the sea water had settled. J rare. A –. S –. H –.

EEL-GRASS FAMILY Zosteraceae

COMMON EEL-GRASS *Zostera marina* L. Plise
This is our only genus of salt water flowering plants and this is its commonest species. It was no doubt common for many years. But in the 1930s disease struck the beds of it round our coasts, and it became very scarce. It is now recovering and has been collected growing in several parts; and in addition its long leaves may be seen washed up elsewhere. J frequent. A rare. S 1842, 1872, 1902. H very local.

NARROW-LEAVED EEL-GRASS *Z. angustifolia* (Hornemann) Reichenbach
Claimed, sans specimen, by Marquand from the Grande Havre. Nowadays it is to be seen growing by the Lihou causeway. Prof. Tutin, who named this, says it can be difficult to tell from narrow-leaved forms of the last species from unfavourable habitats. Typically it grows on soft mud exposed at low tide, while the last species is usually always submerged and on a more or less sandy substratum. J 1887 and 1925. A –. S –. H rare.

(Dwarf Eel-grass, *Z. Noltii* Hornemann, is locally abundant in Jersey, and known in Herm.)

PONDWEED FAMILY Potamogetonaceae

BROAD-LEAVED PONDWEED *Potamogeton natans* L.
Usually a common species, but first noted in Guernsey only in 1958. It must have been overlooked before, for it was then in quarries at Mont Cuet, Portinfer and Cobo. Quarries do not stay untouched, and its tenure is uncertain, but it is still to be seen in two or three, most recently at Ville Baudu and La Passée. J rare. A locally plentiful. S –. H –.

BOG PONDWEED *P. polygonifolius* Pourret
There has been no sign of this since the *Flora*. A fruit, which was very likely of this species, was in the peat from Vazon Bay, the area where the plant was last noted. J occasional. A –. S –. H –.

FEN PONDWEED *P. coloratus* Hornemann (*P. plantagineus*)
First collected by Gosselin. Babington got it on 30 August 1837 in damp pits from which peat had been taken at the Grande Mare, and again in 1838. Druce got it in 1877 and F. J. Hanbury in 1884. The only other records, from L'Islet, were during the 1890s. J last collected 1870. A –. S –. H –.

SHINING PONDWEED *P. lucens* L.
Another species first seen, and in quantity, in 1958, at Port Soif. It was still there ten years later. J –. A –. S –. H –.

(*P. alpinus* Balbis was in Jersey in 1907.)

SLENDER PONDWEED *P. Berchtoldii* Fieber
Collected, twice, in the Reservoir in 1961, which was filled only in 1947. It is still there. J –. A 1972. S –. H –.

HAIR-LIKE PONDWEED *P. trichoides* Chamisso & Schlechtendahl
Detected by J. E. Dandy as having been collected in the Reservoir in 1968. Mr Dandy has seen all the known specimens of Guernsey Pondweeds, and greatly helped with them. J –. A –. S –. H –.

CURLED PONDWEED *P. crispus* L. Fane. Vraic du Vivier
The commonest Pondweed in Guernsey, first collected by Gosselin. It is to be met with in various parts of the island, but is not all that common. It too was fished out of the Reservoir in 1961. J occasional. A –. S –. H –.

FENNEL PONDWEED *P. pectinatus* L.
An ancient inhabitant of Guernsey, its fruits in the Vazon peat beds, and collected

by Gosselin. But it has been seen only two or three times since, in the Vale in 1899/1900, and in 1958 in a quarry south of Paradis and in the Mare de Carteret. J last collected 1925. A –. S –. H –.

TASSEL PONDWEED FAMILY Ruppiaceae

SPIRAL TASSEL PONDWEED *Ruppia cirrhosa* (Petagna) Grande (*R. spiralis*)
Collected by Gosselin, Babington (St Sampson's, 24 August 1837), Bailey (neighbourhood of L'Ancresse, 1867), Fraser (Old saltings, 1878), and recently in the Vale Pond. All these gatherings, in so far as they were named, were called *R. maritima* (Babington's as var *spiralis* however), and the correction is due to J. E. Dandy. There remains one unvouched record, by Gay in 1832. J collected 1927. A –. S –. H –.

BEAKED TASSEL PONDWEED *R. maritima* L. (*R. rostellata*)
The only definite records are by Miss Dawber at Cobo on 21 June 1894 and by Gray in July 1894 from 'Canal. Guernsey' (same place?), named by J. E. Dandy. J –. A –. S –. H –.

HORNED PONDWEED FAMILY Zanichelliaceae

HORNED PONDWEED *Zanichellia palustris* L.
Another plant from Guernsey's watery past, fruits having been found in the Vazon peat. But it is scarce nowadays. Records since the war show it still at Vazon in 1947. where it may still be, at the Vale Pond and in the Reservoir at La Vallée, where it still is. J last record 1928. A –. S –. H –.

BROMELIAD FAMILY Bromeliaceae

RHODOSTACHYS *Fascicularia pitcairniifolia* (C. Koch) Mez
An unusual prickly-leaved mat-forming plant from Chile which has settled down and is gently spreading on the dunes at Rocque Poisson; there are also

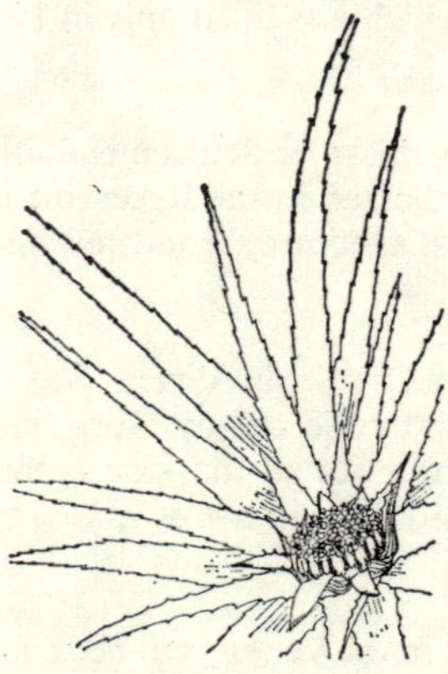

Rhodostachys ×⅙

two patches in the Fermain Valley. Its daunting Latin name, which was confirmed by Dr B. Morley, means the plant growing in little bunches with leaves like those of the genus *Pitcairnia* (named after Dr W. Pitcairn (1711–1791). J –. A –. S –. H –.

LILY FAMILY Liliaceae

RED-HOT POKER *Kniphofia Uvaria* (L.) Hooker
A South African plant which can persist by size and vigour, and has been recorded doing so in at least two places in the south. J –. A –. S –. H –.

(*K. praecox* Baker has persisted on Jersey and Herm.)

DAY LILY *Hemerocallis fulva* (L.) L.
A sterile plant of uncertain origin grown since early times, and now increasingly popular in gardens. Outside them it can also form vigorous clumps, with daughter clumps from wandering rhizomes. It has been seen thus on waste ground in three areas. J –. A –. S –. H –.

NEW ZEALAND FLAX *Phormium tenax* J. R. & G. Forster
Another plant that survives by size – it was particularly called vigorous as long ago as 1826 – and by defying seaside spray and wind. It has been planted for the fibre in its leaves and also decoratively. J planted. A –. S planted. H planted.

(Lily of the Valley, *Convallaria majalis* L., has been claimed from Jersey, and as planted on Alderney.)

GARDEN SOLOMON'S SEAL *Polygonatum* × *hybridum* Brügger (*P. multiflorum* × *P. odoratum* (Miller) Druce)
This is the usual Solomon's Seal in gardens, in various forms. It was found as a waif near a rubbish tip in 1970 by Hon. L. Palmer. J on dumps. A –. S 1957. H –.

(*P. multiflorum* L. was claimed from Jersey in 1962.)

GARDEN ASPARAGUS *Asparagus officinalis* L. ssp *officinalis*
This is the tall cultivated plant which may be bird sown, especially on sandy ground. It has been recorded thus over the years. Curiously, this does not seem to have been derived from the next, prostrate, plant, which has twice the number of chromosomes. Normally cultivated plants have the same or more than their wild counterparts. J occasional. A rare. S –. H –.

WILD ASPARAGUS *A officinalis* L. ssp *prostratus* (Dumortier) E. F. Warburg
This is the prostrate plant, generally scarce, of sea-coasts of south-west Britain. Gosselin collected sterile specimens of it on the Grandes Mielles, and Trevelyan recorded it in 1833 at Pleinmont, but there were no other mentions of it until it was refound there in 1900. In fact there are two or three colonies there, and others are known to the east, at Mont Hérault and Les Tielles. It was reported from La Corbière in 1925, and farther on it is at Jerbourg. Most of these are well down the cliffs, which helps explain their being overlooked. All of which the sex is definitely known are female, except one patch at Pleinmont, which must impede the production of fertile fruits. It is also still known in the north. In 1922 Mrs Hichens re-found it on L'Ancresse, where it is still to be seen east and north of the Club House. Here all the colonies are male. J rare. A –. S –. H –.

BUTCHER'S BROOM *Ruscus aculeatus* L. Prunet. Vaërt
Still quite frequent on the south cliffs, and also to be seen right up to the Vale. Gosselin's specimens are unlocalised. J frequent. A occasional. S rare. H local.

MADONNA LILY *Lilium candidum* L.
A plant of this was collected by a worthy elder botanist up the east path from Petit Bot in 1958. J –. A –. S –. H –.

(*L. pyrenaicum* Gouan occurs in Jersey.)

TULIP *Tulipa* × *gesnerana* L.
A yellow garden throw-out, cultivar name not ascertained, was reported in 1969. J –. A –. S –. H –.

STAR OF BETHLEHEM *Ornithogalum umbellatum* L.
This is the plant known in Britain and in the books by this English name, which in Guernsey is used for *Allium neapolitanum* (p. 225). This one is shorter, with a thicker stem and very narrow flaccid leaves with a central whitish stripe. It was first collected by Dupuy in 1865 and has been recorded over a dozen times in nearly as many areas since. It is usually a garden throw-out, and indeed can survive a while thus, but in Guernsey at any rate usually not for long. J occasional. A locally frequent. S –. H 1937.

(*O. nutans* L. occurred in Jersey.)

AUTUMN SQUILL *Scilla autumnalis* L.
Finlay all but 200 years ago recorded this 'Upon the little hills about the old castle plentifully', and plentiful it still is, from Jerbourg clockwise to St Sampson's locally forming pure turf on its own. Gosselin collected it, noting it first east of the Grandes Maisons at St Sampson's, then at L'Ancresse and on Pleinmont. This is the only plant he ever recorded from St Peter's. 'Autumn', so far as its flowering goes, seems usually to begin in the middle of July. It may occasionally be seen with white flowers. J locally common. A locally common. S common. H frequent.

RUSSIAN SQUILL *S. puschkinioides* Regel
'Grande Havre, Miss Harbord, 1934.' J –. A –. S –. H –.

(*S. Peruviana* L. has been naturalised in Jersey for 50 years. It seeds itself in some Guernsey gardens. Claimed from Alderney in 1958.)

BLUEBELL *Hyacinthoides non-scripta* (L.) Chouard ex Rothmaler (*Endymion nutans*) Côneille
Frequent, and frequently glorious, contributing the rich blue to the gay tapestry of the south cliffs in May. Gosselin collected his plants from the Terres Gosselin. Occasional plants have white flowers, and some pinkish ones, although here hybridity may be suspected with garden ones. Grotesque forms with bracts nearly 2 in. long were collected in 1971 at Jerbourg. J common. A locally frequent. S common. H frequent.

GARDEN BLUEBELL *H. hispanica* (Miller) Rothmaler
In its pure typical form, with thick stems, broad leaves and larger paler spreading flowers with purple anthers, this is rare, for it crosses readily with the last species.

It was first collected by Miss Dawber in 1893 in the Ruettes Brayes. It is native in Spain. J rare. A locally frequent. S rare. H ?

HYBRID BLUEBELL *H. hispanica* × *H. non-scripta*
Wherever these two species come within insect range, fertile hybrids will occur, and hybrid swarms be formed. This has happened in various areas of Guernsey, for example on parts of the south cliffs. The clone 'Bartlett's Pink' began with Bartlett finding an outstanding wild bluebell on the cliffs at Jerbourg. This was planted in his garden and crossed with a pink one and the progeny selected. It was first exhibited to the RHS on 20 May 1947, when it was awarded a certificate of Preliminary Commendation. J occasional. A must occur. S –. H rare.

TASSEL HYACINTH *Muscari comosum* (L.) Miller (*Leopoldinia comosa*)
This is native throughout France and might reach the Channel Islands naturally. But the first record of it was only in 1957, when it was seen scattered over a field south of Mont Cuet. It was still there some years later, and had meanwhile been seen in other places. But it is an uncertain rarity. J rare. A –. S –. H –.

GRAPE HYACINTH *M. neglectum* Gussone ex Tenore (*M.* '*racemosum*')
'A small specimen brought by a school child from St Saviour's. It is doubtful whether it came from a garden or grew wild.' Thus the 1934 Botanical report. No specimen survives and the nomenclature of these grape hyacinths is not easy. Dr D. Stuart's paper in the RHS *Lily Year Book* for 1966, pp. 125–38, discusses them. J occurs. A –. S –. H –.

CABBAGE PALM *Cordyline australis* (Forster f.) Endlicher
This is the very commonly planted New Zealand tree, which helps give the 'sub-tropical' effect beloved of travel writers, and flowers and fruits freely. What is more, its fruits may on occasions be found germinating into seedlings in walls, banks etc., and growing happily. So not all the plants in the island are planted. It is not a true Palm at all. J can seed. A planted. S planted. H planted.

(Meadow Saffron, *Colchicum* sp, was collected in Jersey in 1869.)

SMILAX FAMILY Smilacaceae

SMILAX *Smilax aspera* L.
This thorny Mediterranean clamberer was a nearly ineradicable weed at Vrangue House until 1969. J –. A –. S –. H –.

RUSH FAMILY Juncaceae

SLENDER RUSH *Juncus tenuis* Willdenow
Prof. T. G. Tutin found a large patch of this spreading American species in a quarry near Fort Pembroke in 1949, but only his specimens survive. Its record from the Grande Mare in 1937 was an error for Salt-marsh Rush. J rare. A –. S –. H –.

ROUND-FRUITED RUSH *J. compressus* Jacquin
This can be hard to demarcate from the next species to which every verifiable claim for it for Guernsey, alive or dead, has proved to refer. J errors. A –. S –. H –.

Salt-marsh Rush *J. Gerardii* Loiseleur
This still occurs in several places, some not so near the sea, mostly in lower-lying ground. Norman wrote in 1859 'Two distinct forms grow in the Vale'. There is no knowing what they were, but they might be a basis for the records of the last species. A seed was found in the Vazon peat. J local. A rare. S Brechou only. H –.

Toad Rush *J. bufonius* L. ssp *bufonius* Saie de Trie
Common, its seeds in the peat from Vazon, and Gosselin collected it. The ssp *foliosus* (Desfontaines) Maire & Weiller with dark lines on the perianth segments has been thought more than once to occur, but remains unproven – it was collected in Jersey in 1877. Var *fasciculatus* (Bertolini) Koch was reported by Hurst from L'Ancresse in 1902, but his specimen has not been traced. It could have been similar to dwarf forms with the inner perianth segments hardly longer than the capsule and usually blunt, which come under *J. ranarius* of Perrier & Songeon (an antedated name, and so not the valid one), which could grow in Guernsey in sandy places near the sea. J common. A frequent. S frequent. H common.

Hard Rush *J. inflexus* L. (*J. glaucus*)
Said by Babington to be common, a statement hardly borne out by its never being recorded since. Yet it is an unexpected absentee. J local. A locally common. S –. H rare.

(*J.* × *diffusus* Hoppé (*J. effusus* × *J. inflexus*) was claimed from Jersey in 1933.)

Soft Rush *J. effusus* L. Joncre. Jonc
Common, collected in various forms by Gosselin. J. H. Lenfesty in the *Channel Islands Anthology* 1972/3 says that the stems were used for the Joncquière, the local Green Bed, from the 16th well into the present century. Seeds of this or the next species were abundant in the peat at Vazon. J common. A occasional. S common. H local.

Compact Rush *J. conglomeratus* L.
A species recognised by few recorders. It is probably scarce, but may well have been passed by for the previous species. It has the stem behind the flower-head broadened and brown, instead of equal breadth and green. J frequent. A rare. S last record 1902. H –.

Sea Rush *J. maritimus* Lamarck
The only places this has been seen since the *Flora* are between Port Soif and Vazon and at Bordeaux. It might still be somewhere at the foot of the cliffs, an area not easy to search. J local. A locally frequent. S –. H –.

Sharp Rush *J. acutus* L.
This formidably sharp-leaved plant is still in all the areas recorded for it by Marquand, viz sandy fields from Vazon Bay to the Vale Pond, and at the foot of the cliffs at Petit Port. Gosselin collected it at the Grands-miles. In addition Newbould recorded it at Moulin Huet in 1841/2. J local. A occasional. S –. H common.

Dwarf Rush *J. capitatus* Weigel
The first finder of this miniature was Finlay, about 1780 – the first finder of it anywhere in the British Isles: indeed it was hardly recognised anywhere else for

another 92 years. He described it in detail in Latin in a letter to Sir J. Banks dated 22 February 1787, heading his account '*Schoenus*'. Four of his specimens are in the British Museum, three of them coming from Hudson's estate to Edward Forster. His account ended '***Habitat in Insula Sarnia sed rarissime. In loco infra pagum Bovet dictum inter Fort George et Fernain*** (sic) ***Bay. Floret a medio Maii ad initiam Julii***'. All this, and much of his account, was repeated

Dwarf Rush ×1

verbatim but unacknowledged by T. F. Forster in the Appendix to J. Symons's youthful *Synopsis Plantarum* of 1798, where he described it as *Schoenus minimus nova species*. Sir J. E. Smith in his *English Flora* of 1824 shortened and translated this, and muddled it by calling *Sarnia* Jersey. Indeed the labelling of one of the original specimens has been altered to '*In insula Jersiae infra pagum Bovet*', by the word *Sarnia* being erased and *Jersiae* entered instead. The muddle between these islands and their Latin names is nothing new! But at least Smith was the first to get the identity of the plant right. His error however in attributing it to Jersey lasted through his *English Botany* (Plate 2644), Hooker's *British Flora* and even the early editions of Bentham and Hooker's *Handbook* half a century later. In the course of the inevitable miscopying it became said that Hudson, who was never in the island, found it – even Marquand did – whereas he did no more than possess the specimens for a few years. Babington got it right, in his *Flora* and his *Manual*, right from the start, but no one seemed to take any notice. In Guernsey it is in fact not rare, in the Vale and on the south cliffs, but is elusive and always a pleasure to light on. It can be very small – 3 or 4 mm and is usually in flower by April. J locally plentiful. A occasional. S occasional. H rare.

(*J. subnodulosus* Schrank is rare in Jersey.)

SHARP-FLOWERED RUSH *J. acutiflorus* Ehrhart ex Hoffmann Jonquet
Not common, and only in the north and west. Seeds of it were in the Vazon peat. Gosselin was the first to collect it. J frequent. A frequent. S last record 1892. H local.

JOINTED RUSH *J. articulatus* L. (*J. lampocarpus*) Jonquet
Common in wetter places, and collected by Gosselin. J frequent. A occasional. S occasional. H 1837 only.

BULBOUS RUSH *J. bulbosus* L. (*J. supinus*)
Gosselin's plants and Marquand's from L'Islet in 1891 are this, determined by P. Benoit. No vouchers have been found for Babington's record from the Grande Mare or Marquand's from Fort Doyle. J scarce. A last record 1934. S rare. H –.

KOCH'S BULBOUS RUSH *J. Kochii* F. W. Schultz
Plants of this debated taxon were found in 1971 towards the bottom of Saints

Valley by Mrs B. Garratt and Mrs S. Holland, and named by Mr Benoit. Barton's from Petit Bot in 1914 also definitely belong here. Both species are rare. J –. A rare. S 1953. H –.

HAIRY WOODRUSH *Luzula pilosa* (L.) Willdenow
Reported as new to Guernsey in 1923, but it was in fact a welcome rediscovery of the next species. J last collected 1925. A –. S –. H –.

NARROW-LEAVED WOODRUSH *L. Forsteri* (Smith) DC
Collected by Salwey in May 1848 on top of the made bank in the lane leading from King's Road to Havilland Hall. It was 'rediscovered' in 1923, (as the last species), and again in 1969, and is still there, and there only. J occasional. A – S –. H –.

GREAT WOODRUSH *L. sylvatica* (Hudson) Gaudin
One of the plants which are to be seen in the island only on the cliffs south of Fermain Bay, where it is locally dominant. J local. A –. S –. H –.

GOOD FRIDAY GRASS *L. campestris* (L.) DC Pid d'Alouette
Common. 'Grows in meadows and grass fields and on hedges', wrote Gosselin with his specimens. J common. A frequent. S common. H common.

HEATH WOODRUSH *L. multiflora* (Retzius) Lejeune
Uncommon at best now, scattered over the island. It all seems now to be the var *congesta* (Thuillier) Koch, which has more chromosomes and some rate at least a distinct subspecies. J occasional. A frequent. S scarce. H 1957.

DAFFODIL FAMILY Amaryllidaceae

WILD LEEK *Allium Ampeloprasum* L. Pourraie
This species is assumed to be the wild source of our garden vegetable. The Guernsey variety, var *bulbiferum* Syme, differs in having many good-sized

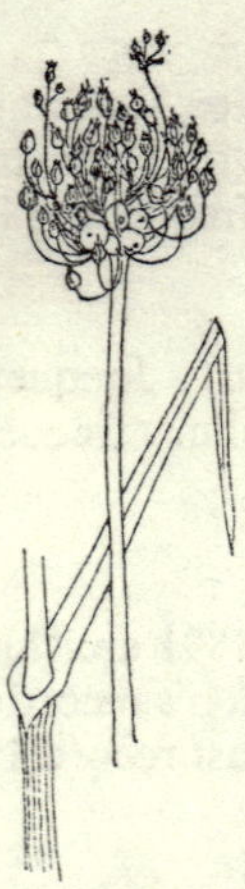

Wild Leek ×¼

bulbils in the inflorescence and, in the words of the *Flora of the British Isles*, 'needs further study'. It has apparently not even had its chromosomes counted, which might help clarify its relationship to the similar *A. Babingtonii* Borrer, a name which has been erroneously used for the Guernsey plant; and some Floras key out the two by saying only that the latter has bulbils – but both may have them! Syme's views on pp. 205–6 of Volume 9 of the 3rd edition of *English Botany* may be consulted. The bulbils of course reproduce the plant identically. Babington himself was the first to collect it, on 26 June 1838 on the cliffs at Fort George – he called it 'my leek', but it was known there to the locals before ever the Fort was built, which was started in 1780. Before that, the area had been uninhabited from time immemorial. And there it continued to be found, and collected, by a stream of visitors for over a century – Druce opined in 1906 that it was then more frequent. Yet it was recorded nowhere else – and it is as obvious a plant as one could wish, first with its lush early green shoots, so like a pale garden leek, and later, when they have withered, with its thick globular heads of flowers waving above a hedge or tall herbage. The first note of it occurring away from Fort George – where it was still very fine in 1958 – was in 1927 from above Rocquaine Bay. But no more was heard until after the war, when it was impossible not to notice it, not only in several hedges in St Peter's, but in various places farther north along the west coast, by the cliff at Icart, at Petit Bot and in a few places inland. It seems still to be spreading. J collected 1878, 1924. A –. S –. H since 1904.

(*A. sphaerocephalon* L. just survives as one of Jersey's rarities. There are records from Jersey of *A. oleraceum* L. and of *A. ursinum* L. the latter probably in error. *A. Moly* L. is said to be established there.)

CROW GARLIC *A. vineale* L. Ail
No longer very rare, but scarce and always in small quantity. It is still where Marquand knew it at Vazon, and farther in at the Grande Mare, and it has also been seen recently at Kings Mills, at Footes Lane, near Port Soif, La Passée, Rousse, Mont Saint and Mouilpied. All seem to be the var *compactum* (Thuillier) Borrer with bulbils and no flowers in the head, and so all of one clone. J locally common. A very rare. S 1956. H –.

GUERNSEY STAR OF BETHLEHEM *A. neapolitanum* Cyrillo
This is a taller laxer plant with a larger flower-head than the true Star of Bethle-

Guernsey Star of Bethlehem ×⅓

hem, *Ornithogalum umbellatum* (p. 220). It was once grown for the cut-flower trade, and has made itself at home in hedges and banks. The earliest specimen is in Dupuy's herbarium dated 1864, and Royle had it in 1890. It was not collected again until 1923, and reported in 1934 from Grande Havre, and in 1938. After the war it was soon realised it was in several places. It has recently been recorded from Fort Richmond and Talbots Valley to Fort Doyle and occasionally elsewhere, and always gives pleasure with its grace and, some detect, its fragrance. It is Mediterranean. J local. A 1962. S –. H 1952.

ROSY GARLIC *A. roseum* L. ssp *bulbiferum* (DC) E. F. Warburg
Dr H. Bowen was the first to notice this charming plant, on the dunes at Les Dicqs in 1957. This colony has happily prospered and now numbers many hundreds. In 1970 a few plants were found a mile away by the road at Portinfer and, a day or so later, by the car park by the Odeon Cinema in Town. It comes from the Mediterranean, and is garden-worthy, but it has not yet been noticed in a garden. J rare. A –. S –. H –.

Rosy Garlic ×⅓

Stinking Onions ×⅓

STINKING ONIONS *A. triquetrum* L. Bllanche Côneille
Marquand was right that the first record of this now abundant plant in Guernsey was from Salwey in 1847. But he in no way looked behind the bald note he came across of this fact, the first record of it for the British Isles, and indeed it was reported from nowhere else for another 16 years. Salwey wrote, 'I cannot make out this *Allium*' (no wonder!); it was 'abundant in the hedges all over Guernsey'. He also wrote that it grew 'in many shady lanes about the Town, particularly (if I remember right) in the narrow lane leading from the Planque into the Couture Road, through which a little stream runs.' He drew a map which showed it also in the south corner of Saumarez Park. Shortly after, other visitors were also calling it common or abundant. The inference is that it was in the island at Cast ten years before Salwey's report, and therefore in the time of Babington, learré, Lukis (who collected it in 1855) and other good observers. It does vanish quickly when it has finished flowering, and might have been almost gone by the time, late June, when Babington arrived. But it is not rare to see flowers in July and some observers were Guernsey residents. Possibly the reason they did not mention it was just because it was common, or that it was still in some way considered a garden plant; for there is a widespread reluctance by many people

to consider gay plants as wild. It comes from the Mediterranean and may well have been brought into some garden, perhaps Saumarez Park, where it rapidly showed how well it was adapted to life in Guernsey. It is probably even commoner now, thanks to the use of herbicides on road verges, to which its bulbs seem immune. Plate 1539 of the 3rd Edition of *English Botany* was presumably drawn from a Guernsey specimen. J common. A common. S common. H frequent.

RAMSONS *A. ursinum* L.
Known for some years by Miss W. Holliday as growing at the top of the Val des Terres. J –. A –. S –. H –.

HONEY BELLS *Nothoscordum inodorum* (Aiton) Nicholson
Another plant which seems to have been advantaged by the use of roadside chemicals, for the same reason as the last species. Its first record was in 1930 by Mrs Hichens from the Vale Pond (labelled, by an expert, *Allium roseum*, an error corrected only in 1957). There were no more until 1958, since when it has been noted in something like a dozen different areas, usually at the foot of walls;

Honey Bells $\times\frac{1}{3}$

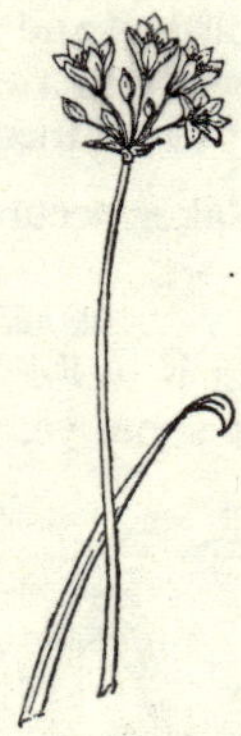

but it can also be a weed in flower-beds, e.g. in the Candie Gardens, as it is in many Botanic gardens. It produces plentifully fertile black seeds apomictically, for it has the drawback of a chromosomal complement of 2n = 19, so Dr P. E. Brandham reports. It is called *inodorum* because it lacks any garlic scent; its flowers in fact have a delicious fragrance, hence its English name. It is North American. J rare. A –. S rare. H rare.

SPRING STAR-FLOWER *Ipheion uniflorum* (Graham) Rafinesque
A South American garden plant which was recorded from the east side of the Vale Road in 1969. J rare. A –. S –. H –.

AFRICAN LILY *Agapanthus praecox* Willdenow
Odd plants of this South African have been recorded, more or less established, in very recent years from half a dozen places, but there is no sign of natural regeneration. Hon. L. Palmer, to whom so much is owed by gardeners for his development of this genus (and much else), said they were of Miss F. M. Leighton's taxon *orientalis* of 1938 and 1968 – she actually called it first a distinct species, later a subspecies. J garden escape. A –. S –. H –.

(The Peruvian Lily, *Alstroemeria aurantiaca* D. Don, successfully persisted for a while outside the garden on Brechou.)

SUMMER SNOWFLAKE *Leucojum aestivum* L.
This used to be grown for the cut-flower market, and a plant or two may be still seen in fields or waste places. Most have been of the earlier and sparser-flowering taxon which R. A. Salisbury called *L. pulchellum*. J rare. A 1962. S –. H –.

SNOWDROP *Galanthus nivalis* L.
Ansted's *Channel Islands* records that this was rare and a doubtful denizen – Gosselin had noted in his garden list that it grew under trees. The only other claim for it as a naturalised plant in Guernsey is from a neglected garden near Les Fontenelles, Forest, where single and double ones look after themselves. J local. A –. S –. H –.

STERNBERGIA *Sternbergia lutea* (L.) Ker-Gawler ex Sprengel
Metman, then Secretary of the Botanical Section, wrote in 1912 that he had known this yellow autumn-flowering Mediterranean plant for at least seven years near the Hougue du Pommier on the Grandes Rocques Road, and that it seemed quite established and spreading. But there seems no sign of it nowadays. In 1969 J. Flint reported two plants close by Cobo church, but rubbish was subsequently dumped on them. J rare. A –. S –. H –.

(*Crinum Powellii* Baker occurs as a garden throw-out in Jersey.)

BELLADONNA LILY *Amaryllis Bella-donna* L.
This South African is well-known in gardens in autumn, but can also do well outside them. For some years it has been coming up strongly and strikingly

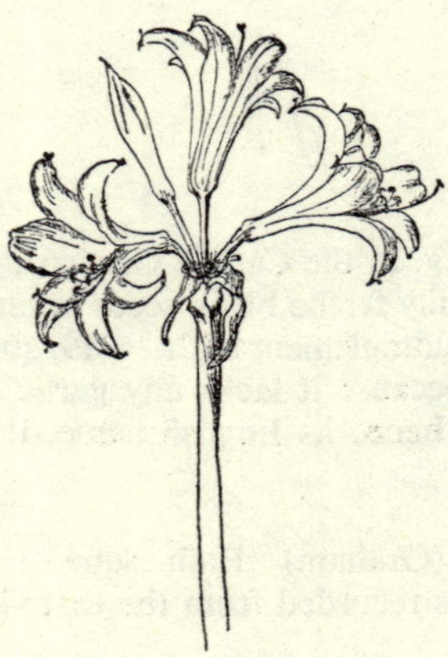

Belladonna Lily ×½

through the brambles etc. on the north side of Fort Saumarez, and it does the same on the cliff at Cobo. It is in two hedges in the Câtel and in a thicket near Les Dicqs. Gosselin was growing it in 1767. It received the Award of Merit in 1934. J –. A –. S –. H rare.

[GUERNSEY LILY *Nerine sarniensis* (L.) Herbert
'*Habitat in Japonia, nunc in Sarniae insula Angliae*' wrote Linnaeus in 1753,

when he formally gave this plant its Latin name, under *Amaryllis*. The reference here is to the story first put out by Morison at the end of the 17th century. He said that bulbs of this plant brought from Japan were thrown on to the sandy shore of Guernsey as a result of the shipwreck of a vessel that had them on board. Here they were driven by the strong winds into the Marram on the shore, where

Guernsey Lily ×⅓

they were soon covered with sand. After some years, to the great amazement of the inhabitants, there suddenly appeared ample elegant red flowers. The species is in fact South African, and it is highly improbable that any such bulbs could survive a drenching in salt water and naturalise themselves. Yet this story has been repeated time and time again right down to the present day.

The facts about the 'Belle Garnsey' have been fascinatingly unearthed thanks to the industry of Dr L. Frost in the *Gardeners Chronicle* for 14 December 1963, and to Miss R. de Sausmarez in the *Review* of the Guernsey Society for Autumn 1970 (which has been reprinted separately more than once). See also the *Countryman* for Winter 1972, and the *Transactions* for 1973. The truth would seem to be that a ship ran on shore, probably in the early 1650s, and the sailors gave some bulbs to the local landowner who befriended them until it was refloated. There is the embellishment gleaned by Knowlton that these were planted and remained for four or five years at least before a flower sprang up among the weeds which, being discovered by his servant, was gathered and brought to him. He then recollected how they were given to him. Another version is that the bulbs were kept for many years but never flowered, so he ordered them to be dug up and thrown away on to a corner of his garden, where in a little time they appeared in the most amazing beauty. But the story got so quickly known, that the name of Guernsey Lily had been used in print by 1664, just 30 years after the bulbs had first flowered in Europe, in Paris: they may have reached Parkinson from there in 1631. In subsequent years this plant was grown in often great quantity in the island, but today it is found difficult, and it is rare in cultivation anywhere. Miss Mary Dobree in 1703/4 'found in a highway some few Guernezeys', the first record of a garden escape in the island. These in 22 years produced in her father John Dobree's garden, not only a good stock of plants, but 1300 at a time were sent in bloom to friends in England. Their culture was described in detail by Knowlton in 1726, who said that often no more care was taken of them than of common flowers such as daffodils etc. Yet in 1677 it was said 'they will not prosper scarce one in twenty of them', so the difficulties must have been soon overcome; if not permanently, at least for well over a century, so much so that Rees' *Cyclopedia* in 1802 said the plant had long been naturalised in Guernsey. A writer of 1748 said 'To see the buty of them, 'tis by looking close to them on a dry day, when ye sun shines upon them: they then ressemble a tissue of gold.' The species normally has 2n = 22. Its derivative 'Glory of Sarnia' (*N. sarniensis* 'Corusca Major' × *N. Fothergillii* 'Major') has 2n = 33, like both its parents, and got an Award of Merit in 1931.]

DAFFODILS *Narcissus* Pouorriaön

The earliest mentions of Daffodils in Guernsey seem to be Knowlton implying they were common in 1726 and Gosselin's 'Daffodils, Narcissus, Double Jonquils and white yellow Cup single flower'd Narcissus' in 1767. The Bulb and Flower Industry, P. J. Girard records in his *History* of it in 1967, started from a single consignment of daffodils sent to the London Market by C. Smith of the Caledonia Nursery in 1864 – before any had been sent from either Jersey or the Scillies. He had a large collection in 1886, and in 1898 the industry was said to be growing every year. At least ten of their introductions from 1907–1910 are in the official RHS list, and eleven from C. B. Blampied of La Fosse, St Martin between 1926 and 1929 and two from E. H. Wheadon & Sons in 1916. But no *Narcissi* are native in Guernsey; those grown, whether in gardens or commercially, are all basically cultivars, identical stock of complicated or often unknown parentage, propagated vegetatively from off-set bulbs. These erstwhile cultivated plants, after being neglected or thrown out as diseased, can settle down and flourish freely and gaily in fields, meadows, woods and cliffs. Furthermore they continue to reproduce identically as the cultivars, clones, they are, with the result that those that bedeck the spring scene are a living museum of varieties grown in times long, or not so long, ago. In most years very few indeed produce any good seed – their flower stems usually wither well before the leaves, and even the rare fat capsules are often empty, false pregnancies. Temperature at critical times influences the insects that might effect fertilisation and the production and ripening of seed, but little if any of what there is seems to germinate, or the seedlings manage to grow on. Since therefore there are no, or hardly any, free breeding populations, only identical spreading clumps, a botanical classification is inappropriate: they should be named as clones. There is a note on the subject in the RHS *Daffodil and Tulip Year Book* for 1971 headed 'The Purity of Naturalised Narcissi, with special reference to those in Guernsey'. Uncertainty in naming Narcissi, which has so long prevailed in works on British wild plants, is nothing new. Parkinson wrote in his *Paradisus* 'There hath beene great confusion among many of our modern [in the 1620s!] Writers of Plants in not distinguishing the manifold varieties of Daffodil'. One cause has been the aversion of most field botanists to studying garden or naturalised plants – Linnaeus wrote in 1737 '*Ego solum creata omnipotentis rimare studio*', as though the Almighty had no hand in the production of cultivars! Salisbury was wiser, and bold for his time, declaring in 1812 'That new species of vegetables may be produced by human art, equally distinct and fertile with those previously in existence, I have not a shadow of doubt: all are alike the works of God, whether he ordains the unconscious foot of a bee or the skilful hand of man to be his agent'. It has not been possible to do more than estimate the frequencies of the various cultivars, nor is it likely that all have been found – some which have been collected lack a name. It has indeed been postulated that practically all the old varieties will survive somewhere, for good commercial ones need to be vigorous. Those so far noted are listed below in the sequence of the Divisions of the RHS Classification of 1950, except for those in their Division X 'wild species and forms', which are put where they belong, as the clones they are in the island, rather than normal wild plants. Those so treated are indicated by having their Latin names from Division X added in brackets. A few others have been given Latin names, but these are best disregarded for present purposes. Local Guernsey names are put in inverted commas. Baker's subdivisions of the Tazettas have been added in Division VIII. An indication of the age of each variety is given by the date of its recorded introduction or first mention, or by that of its highest award from the RHS if that was made reasonably soon after its introduction. Many thanks are due to several growers and others for help naming the plants, notably R. J. Falla, P. J. Girard, Mrs N. Jee and H. Nicolle, who is the sole authority for some of the records.

TRUMPET DAFFODILS. Division I

a. Perianth coloured, corona coloured, not paler than the perianth.

'Achilles'. Originated in Guernsey, probably wild collected, before 1876. Very rare now.

'Dutch Master'. AM 1948. Occasional. In Guernsey in 1938.

'Emperor'. Raised in the 1860s. Not uncommon.

'Flower Carpet'. Post last war. Rare.

'Golden Harvest'. Dates from between the two wars. Rare.

'Golden Spur' ("Spur"). Discovered about 1880. Common.

'Henry Irving' ("Irving"). FCC 1886. Named for Sir H. Irving, *né* Broadribb (1838–1905). Rare.

'King Alfred'. FCC 1899. The first tetraploid Daffodil 2n = 28. Frequent.

'Spurius' (*N. Pseudonarcissus* L. ssp *major* (Curtis) Baker var *spurius* (Haworth) Fernandes). Grown before 1884. Rare.

'Tenby' (*N. obvallaris* Salisbury (*N. lobularis*)). The Latin name was given in 1796, but the plant was possibly known nearly 200 years earlier – see pp. 6–7 of T. A. W. Davis's *Plants of Pembrokeshire* 1970. It has been grown commercially since the last century, but is now rare. In the *Gardeners Chronicle* for 24 April 1886, both 'Tenbys' and *N. lobularis* are listed as being grown by the Caledonia Nursery, but they were probably identical. Compare M. Jefferson-Brown's article in the RHS *Daffodil Year Book* 1971, pp. 180–1. The connection with Tenby had started by 1825. In 1973 it received an AM.

b. Perianth white, corona coloured.

'Empress'. As old as 'Emperor' and also grown commercially since at least the 1890s. Not uncommon.

'Grandis'. AM 1897. Very rare.

'Horsfieldii' (a form of N. *Pseudonarcissus* L. ssp *bicolor* (L.) Baker). Raised by John Horsfield (1793–1854) about 1845. Not infrequent.

'Lent Lily' (*N. Pseudonarcissus* L.). Derrick's record from 1890 was not this, but perhaps 'Princeps'. The true plant was however probably collected near Kings Mills in 1969, and may have been of good seeding stock and no clone. But it has not been seen since. Gerard in 1597 called this *Pseudonarcissus anglicus* and said it was 'so well knowne to all that it needeth no description'. It is native in Jersey.

'Princeps'. Named in print in 1837. Grown since about 1880. Common.

'Silver Spur'. Pre-first war. Just survives.

LARGE-CUPPED NARCISSI. Division II *N.* × *incomparabilis* Miller

a. Perianth coloured, corona coloured, not paler than the perianth.

'Carlton'. FCC 1939. Not infrequent.

'Cheerio'. AM 1941. Rare.

'Croesus'. FCC 1912. Rare.

'Fortune'. Exhibited 1915, FCC 1924, when it fetched £25 a bulb: £5 a bulb was paid when it first reached Guernsey. Frequent.

'Helios'. AM 1912. Rare.

'Scarlet Elegance'. Pre-last war. Uncommon.

'Sir Watkin' ("Watkin"). Discovered 1868, FCC 1884. Named after Sir Watkin Williams-Wynne Bt. MP. (1820–1885). Frequent.

b. Perianth white, corona coloured.

'Celia'. Pre-first war. Local.

'Mrs Langtry' ("Lily Langtry"). Since her heyday: she lived from 1853 to 1929. Occasional.

'Stella'. A century old. Scarce.

SMALL-CUPPED NARCISSI Division III. *N.* × *Barrii* Baker

a. Perianth coloured, corona coloured, not paler than the perianth.

'Barri Conspicuous' ("Barri"). FCC 1886. Commemorates P. Barr (1826–1909), who once visited Guernsey. Occasional.

'Bath's Flame'. AM 1915. From R. H. Bath Ltd. of Wisbech. Rare.

'Edward Buxton' ("Buxton"). AM 1933. Presumably named after E. N. Buxton (1840–1924), the discoverer of *N.* × *Buxtonii* K. Richter, or his son, the third of the same name (1894–1953). Occasional.

b. Perianth white, corona coloured.

'Evangeline'. AM 1913. Very local.

'La Riante'. Pre-last war. Rare.

'Seagull'. Since the 1890s. Rare.

c. Corona white, not paler than the perianth.

'Lady Backhouse'. Occasional.

DOUBLE NARCISSI' Division IV

'Butter and Eggs' ('Poached Egg'). An old favourite. Rare.

'Campernellii'. See division VII.

'Cheerfulness'. FCC 1939. Rare.

'Codlins and Cream' ('Sulphur Phoenix'). Since the 1880s. Rare.

'Eggs and Bacon' ('Orange Phoenix'. "Fried Eggs". Oeue fricachi, a name also applied to similar doubles). Painted by G. D. Ehret (1708–1770). Grown in 1886. Rare.

'Van Sion' ('Telamonius Plenus', the Guernsey Cabbage Daffodil, a double form of *Narcissus Pseudonarcissus* L.). This was illustrated by Parkinson in 1629 as *Pseudonarcissus aureus anglicus maximus*. He wrote that Vincent van Sion 'borne in Flanders . . . a worthy lover of faire flowers . . . cherished it in his Garden for many years without bearing of any flowers untill the yeare 1629.' It was in the first consignment of daffs sent to England in 1864. It varies somewhat in the details of its flowers, and other double forms have been known as long or longer. It is not infrequently naturalised.

JONQUILS Division VII

'Campernellii' (*N.* × *odorus* L. *N. Jonquilla* L. × *N. Pseudonarcissus* L.). Known in gardens since the 16th century, but nowhere wild. It is sometimes single, sometimes double. Rare.

TAZETTA NARCISSI Division VIII

a. *Bicolores* Baker. Perianth white, corona orange or yellow.

'Biflorus' (*N.* × *medioluteus* Miller. *N. biflorus. N. poeticus* L. × *N. Tazetta.* (L.) DC. Primrose Peerless. "Double Roman"). Said by Gerard in the 16th century to be 'generally knowne everywhere'. Frequent in the trade by the 1880s. The 'Primrose' of the name alludes to the flower colour. Occasional.

'Geranium'. Bred between the wars. FCC 1952. Rare.

'Grand Monarque' ("Monarch"). Listed in Miller's *Gardeners Dictionary* in 1759, possibly much older. Quite frequent, Often confused with the next, but this has been checked with Dr L. S. Hannibal of California – compare his articles in the RHS *Daffodil Year Book* for 1964, pp. 136–8, and in the *American Horticultural Magazine* for Jan. 1966, pp. 137-40, which are also relevant to other varieties in this division. It makes few offsets, but has fertile pollen and breeds true.

'Grand Primo' ("Primo". Quezettes). In existence by the end of the 18th century. A ton of bulbs sold for £2 10s. 6d. early in the present century. It is sterile, but produces numerous offsets. Common.

'Minor Monarque', with narrow slender perianth segments, named by Dr Hannibal. Sterile. Rare.

'Saint Agnes'. AM 1926. Rare.

b. *Albae* Baker. Perianth white, corona white.

'Paper White'. Cultivated in Italy for centuries. Exported from Guernsey before the end of the 19th century. A well-known Christmas flower. The only Tazetta whose pollen will strike and set seed at temperatures below 65°F. Rare.

"White Pearl". Known for well over a century and grown commercially in Guernsey by 1890. Its name has lately been taken over by a large-cupped cultivar introduced about 1900. Occasional.

c. *Luteae* Baker. Perianth yellow, corona yellow.

'Grand Soleil d'Or' ("Sols"). In the first edition of Miller's *Dictionary* in 1731, but very likely much older. Another favourite Christmas flower. Rare.

PHEASANT'S EYE NARCISSI Division IX

'Actaea'. From between the wars. AM 1950. Frequent.

'Ornatus' (*N. majalis* Curtis. A form of *N. poeticus* L. ssp *radiiflorus* (Salisbury) Baker var *exertus* (Haworth) Fernandes). Of uncertain origin. Early to flower, with a yellow-based corona. In general cultivation by the mid-1890s. Occasional.

'Ornatus Maximus'. A less scented form of the last with a larger rounder flower. Pre-last war. Rare.

'Ornatus Praecox'. Despite its name, this flowers later than the last two. Rare.

'Pheasant's Eye' (*N. poeticus* L. ssp *poeticus* var *recurvus* (Haworth) Fernandes). The latest to flower of this division, an old fragrant friend, with a green-based corona, well-known in the trade by the 1880s. The now familiar English name originated very shortly before. Scarce. J locally plentiful. A occasional. S occasional. H occasional.

Agave Family Agavaceae

Century Plant *Agave americana* L.
A large-scale plant, often miscalled Aloe, with a rosette of large stout leaves with stiffly and sharply toothed edges and flowers high up a tall bare stout stem. These do not appear every year but hardly, as fable has it, only once in every century. Its rosettes throw offsets, which enable it to continue where it was once put, as on the north slope of Fort Saumarez – for the main rosette dies after flowering. It was first planted in the island in 1778, flowering 36 years later in 1814, when it was 21 ft. high and lasted from August to the end of November. Already by 1826 it was reported to be propagating itself with great vigour even in stone walls. One report in 1859 claimed Carré had two plants of 40 ft. upwards at Valnord, while a third in St Andrew's was 25 ft. with 43 ramifications and more than 300 flowers – there was an engraving in the *Illustrated London News* in August 1859. Victor Hugo had one plant 25 ft. high in his garden in Town in 1878, which was by no means the largest ever seen. At that time it was said to be common in the island: it is now uncommon. J recorded. A –. S recorded. H rare.

Iris Family Iridaceae

The Fire-engine Plant *Sisyrinchium* sp
This was found in 1970 by Mrs Ryan on a rubbish tip at Icart, where it had recently been run over by a fire-engine engaged in quenching a cliff fire. It was propagated thence and is now in several gardens. It was then called *S. iridifolium*, whose portrait in Loddiges *Botanical Cabinet* of 1833, Plate 1979, it matches, but is not the true plant of that name. J grown. A –. S –. H –.

Gladdon *Iris foetidissima* L.
Gosselin grew this in 1767, and later, after he had moved, collected it from his orchard at L'Hyvreuse, marking it a Plante Suspecte. It is quite frequent on the south cliffs, occasional elsewhere. J uncommon. A occasional. S common. H common.

Yellow Iris *I. pseudacorus* L. Gllajeur
Happily, still frequent in wet places. It is recorded that it was in full blow on 10 October 1912. Derrick reported a leaf of this in the peat at L'Ancresse in 1897. Andros in the 16th century recommended chewing its root to remove bad smells from the mouth. Gosselin collected it, listing it from marshy places. J common. A occasional. S occasional. H planted.

Dutch Iris *I.* × *hollandica* Tubergen (*I. tingitana* Boissier & Reuter × *I. Xiphium* L.)
The blue sterile 'Wedgewood' (2n = 31) is the most frequently cultivated of all the bulbous Irises. It is not therefore surprising that it has occasionally been seen flowering where it has been thrown out. It was introduced to the island about 1930 by R. Falla. J –. A –. S –. H –.

(*I. germanica* L. is an occasional garden throw-out in Jersey.)

Purple Crocus *Crocus purpureus* Weston
This must have been long naturalised in the fields at Courtil Rozel, Mount Durand, but Mr and Mrs Allan there pointed it out only in 1968. It grows similarly across the road in the grounds of Government House. J occurs. A –. S –. H –.

(Autumn Crocus, *C. nudiflorus* Smith, is given erroneously for Jersey in the Atlas.)

Sand Crocus *Romulea Columnae* Sebastiani & Mauri (*Ixia* '*Bulbocodium*'. *I. parviflora*. *Trichonema Columnae*) Gênotte
This delightful speciality of the Channel Islands bespangles the cliffs of the south and the sandy turf of the north on sunny spring days. Marquand gives the first record as Gosselin's list published in 1815, but there are many earlier references. It will be what Knowlton saw on Monday 6 June 1726 in two or three places in

Sand Crocus ×1

the island, mentioning Fermain, but 'always upon the highest part of the rocks'. It was in fruit when he found it, and the nearest he could get to its name was *Bulbosa juncifolia*, which was what Ray's *Synopsis*, the book he quotes, uses for *Lloydia serotina*, then recently discovered on Snowdon. He brought back 'many roots and seeds' of which Mr Fairchild (a well-known nurseryman) and Dr Douglas (author of *The Guernsey Lilly*) had a good quantity. This is quite its earliest record in the British Isles. Over half a century later Finlay, who was in Guernsey between 1779 and 1782, wrote to Sir J. Banks, in February 1787, that it grew copiously on dry grassy hillocks, most copiously near Irwin's Redoubt, a habitat that got copied for many decades afterwards in varying versions. He went on to describe the plant in great detail in Latin, but gave no measurements. He used similar words with the specimens he sent to Banks, now in the British Museum. He also sent specimens to Lightfoot, calling it, significantly, var *minor* of *Ixia Bulbocodium*. Gosselin will have known it perhaps rather later. It is in his early List begun in August 1788 as growing on 'Banques de la Ville, L'Ancresse ou Jaones, Moulin des Monts'. His herbarium and second List record it on a hillock to the east and near the house of the Mare de Carteret and on the Hougue à la Père and in the field to the east of the Taye Marquand and Tower fields next to it, furze fields, Windmill Hill, L'Ancresse. His specimens are very fine with two flowers to each corm and one specimen over 7 in. high. But he was not always sure of the plant. In a letter to Sir J. Banks dated 29 November 1790 he wrote 'I waited until the time you mentioned on the *Ixia*'s making its appearance being over, and I am very sorry not to have succeeded in my researches after it. I returned from England at the beginning of June, and as I knew that the flower lasts only a few days, I have ever since been regularly once or twice a week to two places about four miles from home, where I had before seen that plant on the sunny side of a small rocky hillside in a very light soil: I have besides searched everywhere in similar places, but to no purpose. Unfortunately I do not recollect at what time of the year I had seen them but unless you are certain that they blow late in the year, it might perhaps be before June, and I see by the Botanical part of the *Encyclopedia* that some flower in the spring. I shall be glad to know the exact time of their blowing, in order to endeavour to be more successful next Season; if that plant is mentioned in Mr Findlay's (sic) Catalogue of Guernsey plants, he might perhaps recollect *when* and *where* it is to be found, he is in the Duke of Richmond's office – When I found them first, I transplanted some to my garden but they have disappeared.' On 8 April next, he is writing to Banks 'I never was happier than the other day when I found out again the *Ixia*, three of which I send. The reason of my missing them was looking at the improper season; having the idea of their flowering early, I was resolved not to miss them if possible and I found them blown the 1st of April and still continue.' Later he was sending corms to Sir J. E. Smith in a frank via William Smith, MP.

There can be little doubt that Curtis in the text to the *Botanical Magazine* in 1794 was really referring to this species; and that Martyn in his edition of the *Gardeners Dictionary* in 1807 was under the same misapprehension. Plate 2549 of the First edition of *English Botany* which is dated 1 July 1813, beautifully disproves its being what we now understand by the name of *Ixia Bulbocodium*, which it is given by Smith in the text. But, as is said under the next species, this epithet was used for the Guernsey plant for over a century. Smith's text recorded that 'wild specimens of this plant from the Isle of Guernsey were sent long ago by Mr Gosselin to Mr Dickson; and bulbs transmitted by that same accurate observer to Sir J. Banks last year'. Smith repeats these details in his *English Flora* of 1824, and in Vol. 36 of Rees's *Cyclopedia*, but there under *Trichonema Bulbocodium*. This latter volume is dated 1819, but was in fact out in 1817, and there is internal evidence (see *Ixia*) that this section was written by 1814. The story of how the name of this plant came to be clarified is under the next species. But an overlooked reference is to Salisbury's calling it *Ixia parviflora* in his *Prodromus* of 1796 adding 'Sponte nascentem in Insula Jersey, legit R. Finlay', which, with the eternal confusion between the two islands could refer to either. F. Columna (1567–1640) of Naples, who is commemorated in its epithet, called this *Sisyrinchium Theophrasti*. Plants have been noted with white flowers. The corms were eaten by children until at least comparatively recent times. They have a small crescent-shaped ridge at their base with minute fibrils on the ridge, which helps distinguish them from Onion Grass. J common. A common. S common. H common.

GREATER SAND CROCUS *R. Bulbocodium* (L.) Sebastiani & Mauri
(*Ixia Bulbocodium. Trichonema Bulbocodium*)

The specific epithet *Bulbocodium* was used for nearly all the early records for the last species, i.e. by Finlay, Lightfoot, Gosselin, Curtis, Martyn, Smith, and on through Lindley, MacGillivray, Baxter, Mrs Loudon, Bentham in the early editions of his *Handbook* down to 1866 and even in the posthumous reissue of Johnson's *British Wild Flowers* in 1894. This last although Salisbury had indicated the distinction between the two species a century earlier; and, once more, Babington had been right, in his *Flora* and *Manual* in 1843, and Deakin in 1844. The same epithet was used for the Jersey plants and for those from Dawlish Warren, the only place where it grows other than in the Archipelago. But there are indications that true *Bulbocodium* might have been the species intended. One is Curtis's Plate 265 in the *Botanical Magazine* dated 1794, which is obviously of this species, and its text says 'It is said to have been found in Guernsey'. The other is the specimens distributed by J. Dickson in No. 18 of his *Fascicles of British Plants* in 1802. These are definitely labelled as coming from Guernsey, and are undoubtedly of this species – R. D. Meikle at Kew has kindly confirmed this. Furthermore there is a specimen of this species from Guernsey at the British Museum in the herbarium of F. J. Hanbury which came from G. Lyon, but Mr Meikle conjectures that it came from a Dickson *Fascicle*. Now Dickson was a man of 'spotless integrity' and Curtis was as honest. Perhaps they were confused because both these species were then known under the same name, and neither of them had seen the plant wild. Dickson must in fact have used, in all innocence, some finer specimens from farther south, not appreciating the difference, and Curtis did the same. Indeed the fact that Plate 2549 in *English Botany* is correct and was based on specimens from Gosselin, and the Latin name is wrong, supports the likelihood of this explanation. The superb artist P. J. Redouté (1759–1840) on Plate 88 of Vol. II of his *Liliacees* dated 1805 shows both these taxa, as *parviflora* and *grandiflora*, under *R. Bulbocodium*.

The history of the name is that both species were originally called *Ixia Bulbocodium*. In 1802 J. Gawler (1764–1842) – who himself changed his name two years later to Bellenden Ker – created the genus *Trichonema* for this and some related species. This generic name was first used for the Guernsey plant by Smith in Rees's *Cyclopedia* and continued to be used into the present century. The current name of the undoubted Guernsey plant, *R. Columnae*, was proposed by Mauri in his *Flora Romana* in 1818, where he clearly differentiated the two species. Sir W. J. Hooker first took up this epithet and in the 3rd edition of his *British Flora* of 1835 changed it from the *Bulbocodium* he had used hitherto, saying 'It is doubtful which (species) Linnaeus had in view or whether he had not both, when he described the plant in the *Species Plantarum* for he refers in one synonym to the large-flowered kind, the *T. Bulbocodium* of our gardens, and of Curtis's *Botanical Magazine* and also to *Columnae*, which is our small-flowered plant'.

It is not out of the question that this larger species might occur in Guernsey, and it has been known in La Vendée, but it is more probable that all the records in fact belong to the last species, the small one. All Romuleas, Dr M. P. de Vos of Stellenbosch writes, are thermonastic, opening only when the surrounding atmosphere reaches a certain temperature. They can be made to open in pitch darkness if the temperature is high enough. J similar confusion. A –. S –. H –.

ONION-GRASS *R. rosea* Ecklon

There is a stretch nearly 100 paces long of the albino form of the var *australis*

Onion-grass ×⅓

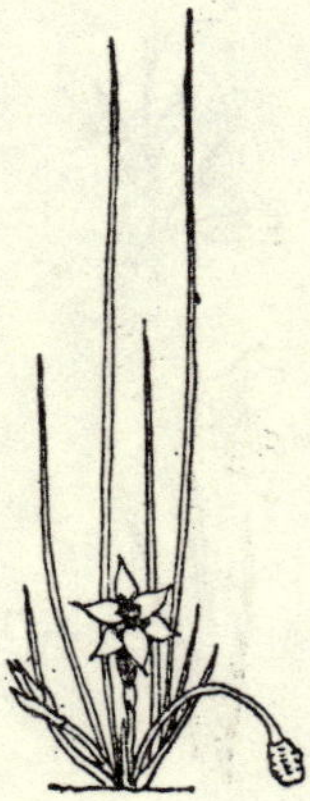

(Ewart) de Vos growing at the foot of a low roadside wall at Cobo and more in thin grass, or dry gravel near by. Its occurrence here is referred to in the *Supplement to the South African Journal of Botany*, 1972, pp. 255-6. This is a stout South African plant, there called Froetang, which is not known now to be in cultivation in the northern hemisphere, but is naturalised in Australia, St Helena and Tristan da Cunha. But not only has it got here, it has thrived, with plants of all ages from seedlings upwards in quantity. It must have been here for many years. It was found by P. Girard in 1969. Its corms too are eaten in South Africa, by humans as well as by baboons. Children eat the capsules when the seeds are still soft and have a sweetish taste, Dr de Vos writes, adding that its corms are distinctive in splitting at the base into rather long pointed teeth which are bent towards one side. J –. A –. S –. H –.

[Ansted records 'In the genera *Sparaxis*, *Babiana* and *Tritoma*, the seed plants itself and the plant becomes naturalised. So, also, the *Ixia longifolia* and the hybrids derived from it, have become weeds difficult to eradicate, owing to the rapidity with which their bulbs multiply and the power they possess of vegetating although buried to a great depth below the surface.']

MONTBRETIA *Crocosmia × crocosmiflora* (Lemoine) N. E. Brown
(*C. aurea* Planchon × *C. Pottsii* (Baker) N. E. Brown)
These are the descendants, which first flowered in 1880, of a cross between two South African species made in France about 1877. They can do very well on their own outside gardens, and so they do in several places in Guernsey, but not yet at any rate, with the exuberance they exhibit in some other parts. It is another gay garden plant which certain people feel 'can't be wild'. Maybe this is why its first record was made only in 1953. It received the AGM in 1973. J frequent. A occasional. S occasional. H occasional.

GLADIOLUS *Gladiolus byzantinus* Miller
Here is another gay plant which must have been looking after itself in Guernsey for many a long year, but was recorded as wild only in 1957, when it was said to be common on roadsides in the L'Ancresse district. But it is to be seen in many places elsewhere, although usually only a few plants at a time. It was once cultivated as a cut flower, but it has been largely superseded by modern cultivars

Gladiolus ×½

with less harsh colouring – this one is Ruby Red HCC 827/3. It could be what was recorded in 1924, sans specimen, as *G. communis*, a much misused name. It will also almost certainly be the *G. italicus* (*G. segetum*) of other observers, another much misclaimed species which A. P. Hamilton says has never definitely been found in the British Isles. This one was grown by Gosselin in the mid-18th century as the Constantinople Corn Flag, following Miller, although it is unknown wild or naturalised anywhere in the Aegean area – it comes nearest this in North Africa. It is an unstable near-sterile triploid with 2n = 90, whose rare seedlings are likely to have different chromosome numbers – more information from Mr Hamilton. J occasional. A rare. S rare. H rare.

COLVILL'S GLADIOLUS *G.* × *Colvillii* Sweet (*G. tristis* Curtis × *G. cardinalis* L.)
A sterile chimaera 2n = 30 – whose parents are both South African. It was 'raised in 1823 in the Nursery of Mr Colvill from seed of *G. concolor* (*G. tristis*) that had been fertilised by the pollen of *G. cardinalis* . . . which confirms our belief', Sweet wrote in describing it 'that the number of species of plants are (sic) daily increasing in the same manner by natural means even as we are increasing them by artificial ones'. The white mutation called 'the Bride' was widely grown in the last century, but only a single example has been collected 'wild' – from a rubbish tip at Mont Cuet in 1971 by J. R. Palmer. A. P. Hamilton named it and produced much of the information about it. J –. A –. S –. H –.

(*G. illyricus* Koch has been claimed from Jersey.)

CAPE TULIP *Homeria Breyniana* (L.) Lewis
Collected by Dr H. Bowen in 1957, one plant outcast by a wall near Rousse. It comes from the Cape. J –. A –. S –. H –.

FREESIA *Freesia refracta* (Jacquin) Klatt
Freesias have been grown commercially in Guernsey since the early days of the trade. In the natural course of events plants get thrown out, and some survive to flower on waste ground etc. Some may even persist in warm sandy soil. But there are very few such records, considering how many greenhouses are full of these plants. They also are South African. They were depicted on a 1/6d. stamp in 1970 to represent Guernsey horticulture. J ? A –. S –. H –.

YAM FAMILY *Dioscoreaceae*

BLACK BRYONY *Tamus communis* L. Bryaonne
This is indeed a scarce plant in Guernsey yet it is surprising that no one noticed it before Marquand in 1893. For it can quite readily be seen, nowadays anyway, in its very limited area south from Fort George down to the Bec du Nez. It was reported in 1958 from between Portelet and the Petit Gouffre, but never proved. J rare. A –. S –. H –.

ORCHID FAMILY Orchidaceae

MARSH HELLEBORINE *Epipactis palustris* (L.) Crantz
'Specimens are still preserved' of this, but nothing has been seen of it since Marquand's day. Nor is there much chance of its reappearing, for the habitat has

changed too much, above all at Grandes Rocques and the Mare de Carteret. Even at the Grande Mare conditions do not look quite right now. No doubt this is what Derrick, there in 1882, called Purple Helleborine. J very rare. A –. S –. H –.

AUTUMN LADY'S TRESSES *Spiranthes spiralis* (L.) Chevallier (*S. autumnalis*)
Still to be seen in many places, most on the coast – it was said to be abundant on L'Ancresse in 1930. But it does adapt itself to the mown turf of garden lawns and there are at least four inland records of it from these in recent years. J locally frequent. A frequent. S occasional. H last record 1930.

SUMMER LADY'S TRESSES *S. aestivalis* (Poiret) Richard
Once one of the prides of Guernsey, not seen since 1914. In 1906 it was said to be quite rare, and no wonder. The number of complete plants from the Grande Mare pulled up tuber and all, dried and killed, in herbaria is an utter disgrace to the unthinking cupidity of collectors, all of whom had to have at least a sheet of

Summer Lady's Tresses ×¼

it for themselves. Such overcropping combined with the drainage and the shrinkage of the suitable ground must have been too much for it. There is in fact still a small area of sphagnum bog in the Grande Mare which has been diligently searched on several occasions, but in vain. The earliest collector was not Babington, who found all the other special plants of this area (and indeed first found it in the British Isles, in Jersey in 1837), but perhaps his friend Haslam in 1855, the year before he died. Thereafter collectors raided the spot – or spots? – at least twelve times before the 1891 that Marquand gives as the first record – Blow had reported it as in abundance in 1876 to the Botanical Record Club to which Marquand belonged at the time, and he himself had written in 1890 that it was plentiful. Perhaps the modest Newbould should have the credit of first finding it, for there is an undated record of his – presumably 1841/2 – from 'St Martin's Parish' if this is not a slip. But Beevor listed it about 1898 from St Martin's, and Wolsey and F. A. Hanbury recorded seeing it 'at an unpublished locality' in June 1862. There is an article on this orchid in *Country Life* for 11 July 1968, p. 73. J last collected 1926. A –. S –. H –.

TWAYBLADE *Listera ovata* (L.) R. Brown
Babington recorded this plant from the Grande Mare, but nobody else mentioned it, until Marquand said it was scattered all over the marsh, nor has anyone

reported it since. Miss Guille had however collected it in 1846 at Archers, St Andrews. And that is all. J last collected 1923. A –. S –. H –.

(Lesser Butterfly, *Platanthera bifolia* (L.) Richard, was last collected in 1926 in Jersey, and Greater Butterfly Orchid, *P. chlorantha* (Custer) Reichenbach, claimed there in error.)

BEE ORCHID *Ophrys apifera* Hudson ssp *apifera*
In miniature, one of our exotic-looking plants, holding on in varying quantity – plentiful in 1870, vanished in other years. It has been known as a Guernsey plant since Gosselin collected it in the Portinfer area, which seems to have been its headquarters, and where it still is. In 1965 it was 'rediscovered' there, when it was thought extinct, as a result of a colour transparency of it taken by Mme Berliet. In days gone by it was also known from the Bec du Nez, Petit Port and the cliffs between Mont Hérault and Les Tielles, and Dupuy collected some very fine specimens near Richmond in 1864, but these localities have not been found. Against this however it has been seen in recent years, and apparently gone, from Grandes Rocques, from the south-east corner of L'Ancresse and from Vazon Bay. Here it appeared from time to time from 1928 until at least 1966, and the ground is still suitable. Its photo is on the *Transactions* for 1963, p. 434. J last seen 1946. A 1949. S –. H –.

(Early Spider Orchid, *Ophrys sphegodes* Miller, Lady Orchid, *Orchis purpurea* Hudson and Lizard Orchid, *Himantoglossum hircinum* (L.) Sprengel were in Jersey until respectively 1929, the end of the war and the late 1960s. The record for the Military Orchid, *O. militaris* L., there is an error.)

GREEN-WINGED ORCHID *Orchis Morio* L.
Another vanished Guernsey orchid. Its first record was only in 1890 by Marquand. He then found it however in considerable quantity near the watchhouse at Pleinmont, and in 1894 a little to the south-east. In the 1890s it was also seen at Pezeries, by the Imperial Hotel, and between Pleinmont and Mont Hérault, and plentifully between there and Les Tielles. In the 1896 report it was said to range over a much larger area than had previously been known. But since those days, there is only one record, from Pleinmont in 1924. Is this another example of how this species is getting scarcer everywhere? Gosselin claimed it in his List calling it Female Fool-stones, but it seems he was muddling it with the next species. J locally frequent. A rare. S –. H 1922.

LOOSE-FLOWERED ORCHID *O. laxiflora* Lamarck Pennecoûte
A rich glory peculiar to Guernsey and Jersey in the British Islands, and there is far more of it in Guernsey. Its first collector was Gosselin. In 1890 Marquand wrote that it was common in moist meadows in all parts of the island, but especially in the middle of the north and western sides: fields were quite purple with it – and he repeated this ten years later in his *Flora*. In 1905 he was saying that the marshy meadows in the low-lying parts especially about Vazon and Cobo were purple with them. Only one small colony is now known at Cobo, and the main concentration is in St Peter's, where the first actual record seems to have been only in 1957 – except for one at L'Erée, where it has not been refound. In the days after the last war it was a notable sight by the Grande Mare in the central reserve for the Whitsuntide horse races (its Guernsey-French name means Whitsuntide). A specimen collected in 1859 is labelled 'St Andrew's Valley', but this could be a slip by the visitor concerned – there are no other definite records

Loose-flowered Orchid ×⅙

for the five eastern and south-eastern parishes, except for Marquand's general statement. A count made by Mrs Burridge in 1972 showed some 14,428 plants, scattered from L'Ancresse down to St Peter's, where the majority were – over 7,000 in square 43; this despite regular encroachment on its preserves. But it remains important that the areas for this lovely Guernsey heritage be known, and cherished. It has been reported with rose-coloured flowers and white ones – at least one, photographed, albino has been seen each year lately in the Grande Mare. The species was depicted in 1972 on the Jersey 7½p. stamp. J very locally plentiful. A –. S –. H –.

SOUTHERN LOOSE-FLOWERED ORCHID *O. palustris* Jacquin
The story of how this closely related species came erroneously to be claimed as a Guernsey plant is told in the *Journal of Botany* in 1873 and 1875. J –. A –. S –. H –.

HYBRID ORCHID *O.* × *alata* Fleury (*O. laxiflora* × *O. Morio*)
Collected at the Grande Mare in 1949 by N. D. Simpson, a quarter of a century after the last record for its Green-winged parent. J very rare. A –. S –. H –.

EARLY PURPLE ORCHID *O. mascula* (L.) L.
Now thoroughly rare, and indeed it has been reported from only three places since the *Flora*. Miss Elliott in 1966 knew it in two spots in the Fort le Marchant area, and shortly after J. Bichard photographed it on the bare cliffs opposite the Pea Stacks, where it still grows with white flowers. In 1972 Mrs Mackay found it in a wood of hers towards Jerbourg Point. Dupuy knew it in St Saviour's. Gosselin's specimens are unlocalised – he called it Male Foolstones, Hudson's name, which goes back to the 15th century, male, Grigson tells us, because the tubers were larger than those of the female, the Green-winged Orchid. J rare. A –. S 1896. H 1955.

COMMON SPOTTED ORCHID *Dactylorhiza Fuchsii* (Druce) Soó ssp *Fuchsii* (*Orchis* '*maculata*')
Scattered and never in quantity, now at any rate. One of Gosselin's '*Orchis*' specimens is of this species. J occurs. A rare. S –. H –.

Heath Spotted Orchid *D. maculata* (L.) Soó ssp *ericetorum* (E. F. Linton) Hunt & Summerhayes (*Orchis ericetorum*)
Knowledge of this close relative of the last species arrived just in time to be mentioned in Marquand's *Flora*. It also is now uncommon, but rather less so. It is Gosselin's Female-handed Orchis, a name Hudson and his predecessors took from Gerard – because its roots are 'branched . . . like a hand', like those of the Marsh Orchids, the stouter Male counterpart. It is on a 2½p. stamp of 1972. J occurs. A –. S rare. H rare.

Hybrid Spotted Orchid *D. Fuchsii* × *D. maculata*
Occurs by the Rue des Vicheries, St Peters. J on record. A –. S –. H –.

Early Marsh Orchid *D. incarnata* (L.) Soó (*Orchis incarnata*).
Four records – Grande Mare and Rocquaine 1899, N. D. Simpson 1923 and A. J. Wilmott 1928. No specimens have been seen. J error. A error? S –. H –.

Southern Marsh Orchid *D. praetermissa* (Druce) Soó (*Orchis 'latifolia'*)
No longer common, but still to be met with in various parts. Gosselin was the first to collect it. J local. A rare. S –. H –.

Hybrid Orchid *D. Fuchsii* × *D. praetermissa*
Collected in the Grande Mare in 1923 by T. J. Foggitt and N. D. Simpson and seen by the Rue des Vicheries in 1973. J on record. A –. S –. H –.

Hybrid Orchid *D. maculata* × *D. praetermissa*
Collected three times in the 1920s in the Grande Mare, and also seen by the Rue des Vicheries in 1973. J on record. A –. S –. H –.

(Pyramidal Orchid, *Anacamptis pyramidalis* (L.) Richard, grows rarely in Jersey and Alderney.

Man Orchid, *Aceras anthropophorum* (L.) Aiton f., was collected in 1926 in Jersey.)

Arum Family Araceae

Sweet Flag *Acorus Calamus* L.
A water plant with aromatic rootstock and leaves, these distinctively wrinkled down one side, which reached Europe from Turkey in 1557 and England by the 1590s. It is probably a native of India. Since those days it has managed to get well naturalised, even though it never ripens fruits anywhere in Europe. Its flower-spike comes as a surprise to most people, and can be seen most years by the pond in Saumarez Park, where the colony was first noted only in 1958. Yet it will have been there very much longer. J one planted locality. A –. S –. H –.

(*Lysichiton americanus* Hultén & St John, which has come to be miscalled Skunk Cabbage, was recently in Jersey. In Guernsey it is at present only in gardens.)

Lords and Ladies *Arum maculatum* L. Couaille de Pretre
Quite common, in the west and the south at least. The form with spotted leaves, the source of its specific epithet, seems scarce. Yet Gosselin's specimens included it, and Marquand implied it was as common as the unspotted var *immaculatum*

(Reichenbach) Mutel. It occurs with both yellow and purple spadix. This is one of the fascinating, improbable, plants of Britain and nowhere is its amazing story better told than in Dr C. T. Prime's monograph *Lords and Ladies* of 1960. J frequent. A –. S frequent. H error.

LARGE LORDS AND LADIES *A. italicum* Miller
Dr Prime's book deals just as absorbingly with this species too, and he and his colleague O. Buckle have paid several visits to Guernsey to learn more about it and its distribution. In October and November it is easy enough to see where it grows, for its leaves are then well above ground, whereas those of the last species do not appear until about Christmas time. Marquand was surely wrong in calling it rare, and certainly in claiming to have been the first to find it. The earliest specimen noted dates from 1870, from Wood from St. Martin's, and other visitors got it in 1871 and regularly after 1884. It does seem to be rather local, and mostly in the southern parts of the island, but keen eyes in late autumn should be able to add to the list of its whereabouts. There are two extremes of leaf markings, one with all-green leaves which has been called, first a variety, *neglectum*, by Townsend in 1883 and then a full species under this name by Ridley. The preferred grade now is usually subspecies, but it may be little more than a form; and there are intermediates linking it to the decorative taxon with creamy veins, the 'Pictum' of gardeners. Such forms are very scarce in Guernsey, and never very well marked. The spadix is sometimes purple. J common. A rare. S rare. H rare.

HYBRID LORDS AND LADIES *A. italicum* × *A. maculatum*
This is not at all easy to tell, especially when it is between immaculate forms of the species, as it will almost invariably be in Guernsey. Yet it must surely exist less rarely than the only record shows, from a well mixed colony in St Peter's, collected in 1971, and vetted by Dr Prime. J occurs. A –. S –. H –.

DRAGON ARUM *Dracunculus vulgaris* Schott
A striking Mediterranean plant occasionally to be seen in gardens, and occasionally successfully planted outside them. It has been seen thus in one or two shady places in Guernsey. J rare. A –. S –. H –.

ARUM LILY *Zantedeschia aethiopica* (L.) Sprengel
This familiar 'Lily' comes from South Africa and not from Ethiopia at all. It can do quite well on its own in ditches in warmer parts, and is well established in the lower reaches of the Fermain Valley, where it has been since before the war. It has also been noted elsewhere, but only as a throw-out. J one planted locality. A –. S –. H –.

DUCKWEED FAMILY Lemnaceae

GREATER DUCKWEED *Spirodela polyrhiza* (L.) Schleiden (*Lemna polyrhiza*)
This was listed by Babington, collected in 1881, and said in the *Flora* to be plentiful by the Château des Marais. Its pool at Spur Point has been filled in, and there has been never a mention of it since. J last collected 1926. A –. S –. H –.

Ivy-leaved Duckweed *Lemna trisulca* L.
Gosselin listed this from a horse pond at Les Villets in the Forest, its only record. J rare. A locally abundant. S 1872. H –.

Common Duckweed *L. minor* L. Herbe à piraettes
Frequent now rather than very common. The pollen and the fruit nearly a millimetre long of a *Lemna* were found in the Vazon peat, but cannot be named to the species. Gosselin collected it twice, once inadvertently in the roots of Water Dropwort. J common. A occasional. S occasional. H rare.

Fat Duckweed *L. gibba* L.
Andrews' unvouched record from the Château des Marais in 1900 is still the only one. J last collected 1926. A –. S –. H –.

Bur-reed Family *Sparganiaceae*

Branched Bur-reed *Sparganium erectum* L. ssp *oocarpum* (Celakovsky) Domin (*S. ramosum*)
Specimens from the St Sampson's Marais, near the bird-ringing hut, were ascribed to this subspecies by Prof. Cook. This is at present the only place known for any Bur-reed, although there is a report of it by the Reservoir; and this is the only gathering with fruits well enough developed to ascertain its subspecies. Bur-reed pollen is in the peats of the west coasts. J aggregate occasional. A aggregate rare. S –. H rare.

Beeby's Branched Bur-reed *S. erectum* L. ssp *neglectum* (Beeby) Schinz & Thellung
No voucher has been traced for the only record, by Andrews, from St Andrew's church. J –. A –. S –. H –.

(Small Bur-reed, *S. emersum* Rehmann, was collected in 1928 from Jersey.)

Reed-mace Family Typhaceae

Great Reed-mace *Typha latifolia* L. Pavie
This is the plant so often miscalled Bulrush, a name which belongs to the tall leafless Poolrush, *Scirpus* species. Its history in Guernsey is rather a puzzle. It was there in early times, for its distinctive pollen and fruits are in the Vazon peat. Gosselin collected it near St Saviour's church. Babington listed it from the Grande Mare and Ansted included it. Yet in the *Flora* Marquand considered it extinct for at least thirty years. But had it been? The story restarts with a delighted Marquand himself finding a large patch in a quarry east of the Vale church in 1904. The next record however was not until 1933, when Mrs McCrea found plenty in a pond on L'Ancresse. After the last war, and especially in the last dozen or so years, it has been found in many places, the Vale Pond included. The most remarkable site is just west of the Château des Marais. Here there are masses of it which, on the evidence of someone who has lived close by for forty years, have been there in that quantity as long as he can remember. Could Marquand and all his collaborators have overlooked so much? But whatever happened to it during Queen Victoria's reign, it is now to be seen by several

watery places, all but one in the northern half of the island. J frequent. A rare. S extinct. H –.

LESSER REED-MACE *T. angustifolia* L.
The pollen of this species is also listed from the Vazon peat. It too was noted by Babington and Ansted, and then vanished. However it too has managed to reappear – or persist – in one or two quarries near Paradis, at St Sampson's, near the Vale Pond, at Grandes Rocques and, in the south, near La Vallée. J very rare. A –. S –. H –.

SEDGE FAMILY Cyperaceae

COMMON COTTON-GRASS *Eriophorum angustifolium* Honckeny (*E. polystachion*)
Gosselin collected this, so did Babington on 15 June 1838, at the Grande Mare, where Marquand thought it in danger of being lost. It is a marvel that it is not, although there is only a small quantity left. Watson collected it near Petit Port in 1852, surprisingly, and Marquand recorded it on east L'Ancresse, but no one else has seen it in either of these places. J rare. A –. S –. H –.

SEA CLUB-RUSH *Scirpus maritimus* L.
This still occurs in about five places down the west coast – it has not been noted from the Château des Marais since the *Flora*, where the waters are no longer brackish. A patch below the hotel at Pleinmont has very long flower spikelets. Similar ones from the Mediterranean have been referred to f. *macrostachys* (Willdenow) Visiani, but the Pleinmont plant is still exceptional – the spikelets are slender and can reach 2 in. long. This was found by Mrs Ryan in 1971. At the other extreme, the singular-looking f. *monostachys* (G. F. W. Meyer) Junge with only a single spikelet has been twice reported. Gosselin was the first collector of the species. J rare. A rare. S –. H –.

(Clustered Club-rush, *S. Holoschoenus* L., was collected in Jersey in 1923 and 1931.)

SHARP BULRUSH *S. americanus* Persoon (*S. pungens*)
There is a specimen of this species labelled from Guernsey collected by Green in 1890. But he himself later said he had collected it in Jersey and did not remember seeing it in Guernsey – cf *Journal of Botany*, 1931, p. 157. J last seen *c.* 1969. A –. S –. H –.

BULRUSH *S. lacustris* L.
This was listed by Gosselin and said by Salwey to be in the Grande Mare and other wet places. But neither of them mentioned the next species, which was grouped with this one by some authors, such as Hudson. But it seems odd it does not occur in the Channel Islands. J error. A –. S –. H –.

GREY BULRUSH *S. Tabernaemontani* C. C. Gmelin
Of the four places for this plant recorded by Gosselin with his specimens – Taye Marquand, Clôture, Moulin de Haut and the foot of Les Vardes, and Marquand's four, only the Grande Mare and Grandes Rocques seem to survive, But quite early on – by 1962 – it had found its way to the Reservoir, where it is

on both the north and south sides. Its use in saddles is referred to under Galingale. J rare. A last record 1900. S –. H –.

BRISTLE CLUB-RUSH *S. setaceus* L.
Possibly less scarce than it seems, because it can easily be overlooked. All Gosselin's specimens under this name are of the next species. J occasional. A locally frequent. S occasional. H rare.

SLENDER BRISTLE CLUB-RUSH *S. cernuus* Vahl (*S. Savii*)
Apparently scarce. Too few observers have been sure of knowing this and the last species apart – the smooth matt fruit is the surest character. This one was collected by Gosselin and listed by Woods on 18 July 1836 before Babington ever arrived. J local. A local. S occasional. H 1837.

FLOATING SPIKE-RUSH *S. fluitans* L.
A sterile specimen in Gosselin's scrapbook is thought by J. E. Dandy to be of this species. J rare. A –. S –. H –.

NEEDLE SPIKE-RUSH *Eleocharis acicularis* (L.) Roemer & Schultes (*Scirpus acicularis*)
Recorded erroneously in 1922 and 1923 from L'Ancresse. The plant was *S. cernuus*. J last collected 1928. A –. S –. H –.

FEW-FLOWERED SPIKE-RUSH *E. quinqueflora* (F. X. Hartmann) Schwarz (*Scirpus parviflorus*)
Recently collected in all three localities mentioned by Marquand. Specimens from the Grande Mare were up to 17 in. long. J rare. A rare. S –. H –.

MANY-STALKED SPIKE-RUSH *E. multicaulis* (Smith) Smith
Noted since Marquand's days only on the eastern side of L'Ancresse; and in addition it had reached the Reservoir by 1961. J scarce. A very rare. S –. H –.

COMMON SPIKE-RUSH *E. palustris* (L.) Roemer & Schultes ssp *vulgaris* S. M. Walters
Now inevitably less common, but not infrequent. Gosselin was the first to collect it. J fairly frequent. A locally plentiful. S occasional. H local.

(*E. uniglumis* (Link) Schultes was collected in Jersey in 1951.)

FLAT-HEADED SEDGE *Blysmus compressus* (L.) Panzer ex Link
The record in Gosselin's *Flora Sarnica* is supported by a specimen in his scrapbook. J –. A –. S –. H –.

GALINGALE *Cyperus longus* L. ssp *longus* Han
Not Gosselin (who collected it in a meadow behind Blancbois), but Yalden, by 1774, seems to have been the first person to mention this. He wrote that it grew in such plenty that Cart Loads of it were used by the Inhabitants to make Saddles with. Yet it has been so plentiful – and still is locally, chiefly in the west – and so much used, that surely there must be earlier references somewhere. Later on it is often referred to. A complete set of articles made with it was at the Great Exhibition in 1851, such as farm saddles, mats, footstools and bullocks' and horses' collars. At the Great Paris Exhibition shortly after, unbleached paper was

Galingale ×$\frac{1}{6}$

exhibited made from this plant, according to a patent taken out by Dr Hoskins. A visitor in 1862 recorded it was also cultivated for commercial purposes. In 1868 Bailey was saying that farmers left patches of it unmown in the meadows in order that it may be gathered in the autumn for making into cordage. He added that the fishermen considered that ropes made from this plant were much better in the sea than the ordinary ones. In 1870 Thistleton-Dyer, later Director of Kew, was in Guernsey and wrote 'I heard that native-made saddles and mats were occasionally brought into St Peter Port from the distant parts of the island . . . One of the saddles . . . is now in the Economic Museum at Kew. The main part is simply made of the plaited stems of *Scirpus Tabernaemontani*. The inside is partly lined with *Cyperus longus*, but in its natural state, merely dried . . . I noticed that bands of the *Cyperus* were used in tying up sheaves of barley'. It was also recorded as being twisted rope-fashion and fastened from leg to leg of sheep. As late as the 1920s P. Girard helped his grandfather twist it to bind corn sheaves. J common. A occasional. S rare. H rare.

GREEN CYPERUS *C. Eragrostis* Lamarck (*C. vegetus*)
A South American plant, which has been listed by nurserymen for many years, yet is only very rarely to be seen in any garden, but has been on the R. Loire since 1909. It already extended over 200 yards on the north bank of the Reservoir by 1961 and lost little time in crossing to the other side of the dam. It is now to be seen in plenty on its shores. By 1968 it had reached Grandes Rocques and Saumarez Park. Its arrival in the new Reservoir in Jersey also in the 1960s –

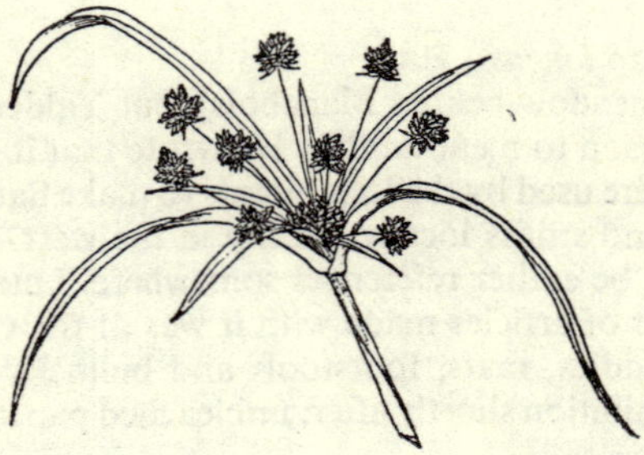

Green Cyperus ×$\frac{1}{4}$

from Guernsey? – is referred to by Dr M. Gillham on p. 95 of the *Flora of a Changing Britain* 1970. J rare but increasing. A –. S –. H –.

BLACK CYPERUS *C. fuscus* L.
There is a specimen dated July 1866 collected by Roseveare in 'Guernsey'. Was this another error for Jersey? J last collected 1928. A –. S –. H –.

BOG RUSH *Schoenus nigricans* L.
Still in the Grande Mare, at Cobo and Grandes Rocques – rather to the surprise of some visitors. Gosselin recorded it from Rocque Hyvreuse field, at the Grande Miles and moist spots near Hommet. J rare. A locally common. S –. H –.

FEN SEDGE *Cladium Mariscus* (L.) Pohl
Pollen of this has been seen from the middle peat beds of Vazon Bay. J St Ouen's Pond. A –. S –. H –.

SMOOTH SEDGE *Carex laevigata* Smith
There are two sets of records. The first in the Talbots Valley in 1888 and by a footpath between Les Paysans and the Coudré Mill in 1894. The second in 1970 when fine plants were found in a wet pasture at Sous l'Eglise by Lady Emma Tennant, and the very next day in two other places, near the Route de Cantereine and in the Ruette des Norgiots. There have been no other claims even. In the Channel Islands this does not grow in woods. J local. A –. S –. H –.

DISTANT SEDGE *C. distans* L.
This has been collected at intervals ever since Gosselin's time, and is still to be seen, but is uncommon. J rare. A rare. S rare. H –.

DOTTED SEDGE *C. punctata* Gaudin
This too has been collected at intervals, indeed has been a special quarry for many visitors. Gosselin got it, so did Babington, his specimen being confirmed by the American Sedge specialist F. M. D. Boott. These and others in that century went to the Grande Mare for it. Blow in 1876 wrote that it was confined to one spot (sic!) about an acre in extent, where the rare orchid grew; and Druce the next year reported it to be in tolerable plenty. Marquand in his *Flora* said it was scattered all over the marsh, but thinly. Today it is at best very thinly spread, and needs some finding, and being sure it is not the last species. The *Flora* extended its localities to Icart, where it still was in 1936, to the upper Moulin Huet Valley with *Gunnera*, where it could still be, to the Claire Mare, where it has not been reseen, to the Jaonnet Valley east of Petit Bot and the shore of a bay west of it, where it was seen in 1968. The following year it was found low on the cliffs at Jerbourg and at the Bec du Nez. So it may be found elsewhere by those who venture low. J local. A –. S 1902. H –.

(Moor Sedge, *C. binervis* Smith, is local in Jersey, and rare on Herm.)

COMMON YELLOW SEDGE *C. demissa* Hornemann (*C. 'flava'*)
Apparently unrecorded from the Grande Mare since Marquand's day, but seen recently at both ends of L'Ancresse, at Rocquaine and at Saints Bay. J frequent. A occasional. S occasional. H rare.

LONG-STALKED YELLOW SEDGE *C. lepidocarpa* Tausch
This was claimed by Marquand in 1891, but the record was later withdrawn. J collected 1925. A –. S –. H –.

SMALL YELLOW SEDGE *C. serotina* Mérat (*C. 'Oederi'*)
Druce was the first to collect this, in 1877 from the Grande Mare (where no one else has noticed it), his specimens confirmed by Trimen. It is still on L'Ancresse. J collected 1928. A –. S 1902. H –.

SALTMARSH SEDGE *C. extensa* Goodenough
This is still by the Vale Pond, but its main habitat – where it is nevertheless scarce – is at the foot of the south and south-eastern cliffs, on the rocks above high-water line, from La Bette Bay to the Fort George area. J local. A rare. S –. H –.

WOOD SEDGE *C. sylvatica* Hudson
First recorded only in 1958 at Fort George, where it still is, and in 1968 from Les Vauxbelets, its only stations in the Channel Islands. J –. A –. S –. H –.

(Hop Sedge, *C. Pseudocyperus* L., grows by St Ouen's Pond in Jersey.)

BLADDER SEDGE *C. vesicaria* L.
Marquand recorded this from a lane side at the Grande Mare 'but hardly typical'. Druce claimed it in 1907 from what may have been the same place, between the Mare and the Rue d'Enfer (now Rue des Bergers). That is all. No specimen of either survives. J –. A –. S –. H –.

GREATER POND SEDGE *C. riparia* Curtis
Seen since the days of the *Flora* only by the Château des Marais, the Grande Mare and the Rue des Vicheries. J St Ouen's Pond. A –. S –. H –.

DROOPING SEDGE *C. pendula* Hudson
Marquand claimed to be the first discoverer of this relatively large and obvious species, when he saw several clumps at the base of the cliffs in Fort Bay where at least one plant still was in 1958. He had no doubt whatever it was originally planted. So indeed it can be, and since his time it has been seen, for example, at Sausmarez Manor and Vimiera clearly spreading from planted plants. But it is in other places, such as the Vale Pond, Saints Bay, Petit Bot and the Talbots Valley, where it looks natural enough; and finally the first record, also from Fort George, was 44 years earlier, by Salwey. But why did no one else note it in the Victorian era? J local. A local. S –. H –.

(*C. pallescens* L. was collected in Jersey in 1925. The record for *C. filiformis* L. there is an error.)

CARNATION SEDGE *C. panicea* L.
The only records since the *Flora* at all recent, are from La Grève and Hougue Patris on L'Ancresse, from the Grande Mare/Kings Mills area, from La Bette Bay and Saints Bay. J local. A occasional. S –. H –.

GLAUCOUS SEDGE *C. flacca* Schreber (*C. glauca*)
Apparently rather scarce now, and unrecorded in the south-east. Gosselin collected it. J local. A frequent. S occasional. H frequent.

HAIRY SEDGE *C. hirta* L.
All the records are still from the central parts of the island, recent ones between the levels of the Fauxquets Valley and Port Soif. This is the type species of this huge genus. J frequent. A common. S –. H –.

PILL SEDGE *C. pilulifera* L.
This is another plant not first recorded by Marquand, but by Newbould in 1841/2 from St Martin's. But it is still very scarce. Its only localities since the *Flora*, all recent, are between Fort Doyle and Fort le Marchant, Hommet Paradis, Pleinmont and the Fauxquets Valley. J occasional. A –. S occasional. H 1957.

SPRING SEDGE *C. caryophyllea* Latourette (*C. praecox*)
Widespread, but now either rather scarce or overlooked. Gosselin gives no locality for his specimens. J rare. A rare. S occasional. H very rare.

(*C. acuta* L. grows rarely in Jersey.)

COMMON SEDGE *C. nigra* (L.) Reichard (*C. vulgaris*)
Scarce, in widely separated localities. J local. A –. S –. H –.

TUSSOCK SEDGE *C. paniculata* L.
Seen recently in eight squares from the Grande Mare area down to Petit Bot, including Rohais where Gosselin (and Babington) collected it – he also got it farther north, at the Taye Marquand. J rare. A occasional. S –. H –.

FOX SEDGE *C. Otrubae* Podpera (*C. 'vulpina'*)
Collected first by Gosselin: probably the most frequent Sedge in the island. J local. A –. S rare. H occasional.

AXILLARY SEDGE *C.* × *pseudaxillaris* K. Richter (*C. Otrubae* × *C. remota*) (*C. axillaris*)
Not noted since Marquand got it in 1890 in Footes Lane and at Pont Vaillant. J –. A –. S –. H –.

BROWN SEDGE *C. disticha* Hudson
First found by Williams in 1930 by the Mare de Carteret, where there is still a good patch, its only locality in the Channel Islands. J –. A –. S –. H –.

SAND SEDGE *C. arenaria* L.
Still quite frequent, noted recently from Fort Doyle to Pleinmont and at Saints Bay. Gosselin had it from the parapet along Belgrave. J common. A common. S 1902. H common.

(*C. divisa* Hudson grows, rarely, in Jersey.)

GREY SEDGE *C. divulsa* Stokes
There are two records, the first by Watson in 1852 from between St Peter Port and St Sampson's, the other by Marquand in Footes Lane in 1891. J rare. A rare. S occasional. H –.

SPIKED SEDGE *C. spicata* Hudson (*C. 'muricata'*)
This is difficult to tell from the next species, but convincing specimens have been collected by the Grande Mare during and since N. D. Simpson's visit in 1923. J –. A –. S –. H –.

LESSER SPIKED SEDGE *C. muricata* L. ssp *muricata* (*C. Pairaei*)
Not rare, and well distributed over the island. Gosselin's specimens came from

beyond the brick fields near Fort George. J locally frequent. A rare. S frequent. H occasional.

(*C. muricata* L. ssp *Leersii* Ascherson & Graebner (*C. 'polyphylla'*) has been known from Alderney and Sark.)

STAR SEDGE *C. echinata* Murray (*C. stellulata*)
Still in the Grande Mare, but not seen elsewhere since Marquand's time. J rare. A rare. S –. H –.

REMOTE SEDGE *C. remota* L.
In various places in the central parts of the island, but not at all common. Gosselin's specimens came from the Douit behind the Vrangue, Moulin Huet and the foot of the Varde near the Paumier. J rare. A –. S –. H –.

OVAL SEDGE *C. ovalis* Goodenough
Another plant first found long before Marquand, indeed by Gosselin, unwittingly, and then by Newbould in 1842 at Moulin Huet. It is rather scarce. It was measured at 37½ in. by the Grande Mare in 1968. J occasional. A scarce. S rare. H –.

FLEA SEDGE *C. pulicaris* L.
Happily still in the Grande Mare, where alone it has been noted: Gosselin's specimens are unlocalised. According to Ray, its English name was given it by Goodyer 'because the seeds (which turn downwards on the Stalk) do in shape and colour resemble Fleas'. J rare. A rare. S –. H –.

GRASS FAMILY *Gramineae*

REED *Phragmites australis* (Cavanilles) Trinius ex Steudel ssp *australis* (*P. communis*) Ros
Presumably because this is so ordinary a plant, no one seems to have noted picking it between Gosselin about 1790 and Pierre Girard, great-grandfather of the present Peter from the Grande Mare on 24 October 1900, presumably for thatching. It is still widespread, including low on the cliffs, even though wet places are much less common. It was noted in 1967 with runners 18 ft. long on bare mud at the Claire Mare. J common. A locally abundant. S rare. H local.

PAMPAS GRASS *Cortaderia Selloana* (J. A. & J. H. Schultes) Ascherson & Graebner
This is in effect a dioecious grass, and it is the female which is usually grown for its long silky plumes. Alone, all it can do, and it does it, is to fatten its own clump, until a male or hermaphrodite plant comes within reach. But the odd plants outside gardens in Guernsey seem all to have been female. It is South American. J rare. A –. S –. H –.

PURPLE MOOR-GRASS *Molinia caerulea* (L.) Moench ssp *caerulea*
Still rare. The only localities noted since the *Flora*, all recent, are the Garennes d'Ancresse and d'Anneville, near the Château des Marais and in the Grande Mare, still. J locally frequent. A –. S –. H –.

HEATH GRASS *Sieglingia decumbens* (L.) Bernhardi (*Triodia decumbens*)
Apparently only local now – or overlooked? It was seen 29″ tall in 1968. J local. A occasional. S last record 1897. H local.

FLOTE-GRASS *Glyceria fluitans* (L.) R. Brown
Still quite frequent. First collected by Gosselin. J common. A occasional. S last record 1892. H rare.

SWEET-GRASS *G. plicata* Fries
Marquand's records are the only ones proven – his specimen from the Château des Marais was confirmed by Dr Melderis. Much effort has been made to refind this, in vain. J last collected 1925. A occasional. S –. H –.

SMALL FLOTE-GRASS *G. declinata* Brébisson
Similarly, Marquand's specimen from St Helena in 1891 is the only, verified, record. J rare. A very rare. S 1928. H –.

(*G.* × *pedicellata* Townsend was collected in 1897 on Jersey, and in 1953 on Alderney. Great Water Grass, *G. maxima* (Hartman) Holmberg, was collected in 1928 on Jersey.)

MEADOW FESCUE *Festuca pratensis* Hudson (*F.* '*elatior*')
Apparently scarce.
J rare. A –. S –. H –.

TALL FESCUE *F. arundinacea* Schreber
Here and there in the north and west. J locally frequent. A rare. S –. H –.

RED FESCUE *F. rubra* L. ssp *rubra* (incl. *F. oraria*)
This is still a common, and very variable, grass to which various varietal names have been given. Gosselin collected it, as *Poa setacea*, from the Terres Gosselin. Its var *pruinosa* (Hackel) Howarth with glaucous leaves is a plentiful mimic on the south cliffs for the true Glaucous Fescue and occurs elsewhere; var *glaucescens* (Hegetschweiler & Heer) Richter has hairy spikelets as well as glaucous foliage. Var *grandiflora* (Hackel) Howarth with lemmas 6–6.5 mm and leaves 5–7 nerved approaches *F. juncifolia*. The species was recommended for lawns in the 18th century. J common. A common. S common. H common.

CHEWINGS FESCUE *F. rubra* L. ssp *commutata* Gaudin
Collected by Dr C. E. Hubbard in 1953 from Vazon and no doubt missed by the less expert both before and since, who have not marked its tufted habit with no rhizomes. Mr Chewings first sold its seed in New Zealand. J –. A –. S –. H –.

RUSH-LEAVED FESCUE *F. juncifolia* St-Amans
Detected after careful measurement by Dr Hubbard from a gathering he made from L'Erée in 1953. Its lemmas are at least 8 mm long and its leaves can have up to 13 ribs. J collected 1925. A –. S –. H –.

SHEEP'S FESCUE *F. ovina* L. ssp *ovina*
This variable species has not been properly sorted from the next taxon, but one or other or both occur widely. Search should also be made for the variations recorded in Brittany, one of them as a distinct species. This one was recommended for lawns in the 18th century. J common. A common. S common. H common.

FINE-LEAVED SHEEP'S FESCUE *F. tenuifolia* Sibthorp
Undoubtedly occurs, but its awnless lemmas have been noticed by very few. Its very narrow leaves can also make it look different at a glance. J occurs. A occurs. S ? H ?

GLAUCOUS FESCUE *F. glauca* Lamarck (*F. cinerea*) (*F. caesia*)
The first definite record of this came from the visit of Dr Hubbard in 1953, when he got it at Jerbourg on the south cliffs, and it has recently been seen farther west, for example at Portelet, Saints Bay, Icart, Le Gouffre and Pleinmont and maybe elsewhere. But it has been much confused with the glaucous varieties of Red Fescue, which are common there. Even its green-leaved forms can be told

Glaucous Fescue ×½

by their closely tufted habit, without rhizomes or sprawling growth, and by the youngest leaf-sheaths being silvery and hairless (as opposed to brown and pubescent), the innermost open to the base, one margin folded over the other, as in the last two species, not split, or open just at the top only – details which come from Drs Hubbard and Melderis. It is sometimes used as an edging in gardens. J 1968. A –. S on record. H –.

HYBRID FESCUE × *Festulolium loliaceum* (Hudson) P. Fournier (*F. pratensis* × *Lolium perenne*)
There are two specimens of this sterile hybrid, and no other records. The first is from Gosselin in the 18th century, the other from Osborn in 1851 in J. C. Melville's herbarium at Harrow School (where Melville was a pupil). J 1837, 1851, and 1961 A –. S –. H –.

(*Festuca arundinacea* × *Lolium multiflorum* was collected in Jersey in 1924.)

HUBBARD'S HYBRID FESCUE × *Festulpia Hubbardii* Stace & Cotton (*F. rubra* × *Vulpia membranacea*)
This short-lived perennial of varying stature was first noted for the British flora only in 1954. But it had in fact been collected earlier in Guernsey – indeed Gosselin's specimens are probably the oldest known, and F. J. Hanbury in 1884, F. Druce in 1928 and Dr Hubbard in 1953 also got it – cf *Proceedings* of the BSBI for July 1955, pp. 390–1, and May 1967, pp. 387–8, and Watsonia, July

1974. It has been gathered since, always serendipitiously, purposeful searching seeming always to fail. It is probably scarce as well as elusive, since no one plant will survive for more than a year or so, and new ones must then be bred. J –. A 1933. S –. H –.

PERENNIAL RYE-GRASS *Lolium perenne* L. Raie-grasse
Common and variable, both naturally and sown. J common. A frequent. S common. H common.

ITALIAN RYE-GRASS *L. multiflorum* Lamarck (*L. italicum*)
An Italian species unknown to either botanists or agriculturists in Britain until after 1831, but now abundantly sown and well able to persist or spread for at least a while thereafter. The account of this species in the *Biological Flora*, No. 131, may be consulted. J common. A occasional. S occasional. H occasional.

SHORT ROTATION RYE-GRASS *L.* × *hybridum* Haussknecht (*L. multiflorum* × *L. perenne*
This fertile hybrid arises readily, and here belong some of the agricultural forms which are sown in leys and appear also near by. J occurs. A –. S –. H –.

WIMMERA RYE-GRASS *L. rigidum* Gaudin
Collected at Mont Crevelt in 1958. This is a Mediterranean grass imported into South America and Australia, which did particularly well by the Wimmera River in Victoria, where the rainfall is only 15 in.–20 in. J 1968. A –. S –. H –.

DARNEL *L. temulentum* L.
Collected by Gosselin and listed by Carré in Babington's *Flora*. There are no other records, even from bird seed. J casual. A 1838. S 1874. H –.

DUNE FESCUE *Vulpia membranacea* (L.) Dumortier (*Festuca uniglumis*)
Still quite frequent on the dunes but no longer, apparently, nearly as far south as Rocquaine. J locally common. A frequent. S error. H –.

SQUIRREL-TAIL FESCUE *V. bromoides* (L.) Gray (*F. sciuroides*)
Frequent. The strange-looking plants Marquand found in 1890 at Mont Saint and thought possibly were hybrids with the next species have not been traced. J common. A common. S occasional. H common.

RAT'S-TAIL FESCUE *V. Myuros* (L.) C. C. Gmelin (*F. Myuros*)
Very scarce, but has continued to be collected ever since it was noted by Babington. J occasional. A 1838. S –. H –.

BEARDED FESCUE *V. ambigua* (Le Gall) More
First spotted by Druce and Marquand in 1906 and 1907, at L'Ancresse and Grande Havre, then by Dr Hubbard in 1953 at the latter, where he said it was frequent. It has eluded all other searchers. J rare. A 1906. S –. H –.

SPHENOPUS *Sphenopus divaricatus* (Gouan) Reichenbach
Plants collected by the redoubtable Lady Davy in July 1930 and published as this Mediterranean species, were large Fern-grass. Dr Melderis unmasked this misidentification, which had had the apparent consent of leading contemporary botanists. J –. A –. S –. H –.

COMMON SALTMARSH-GRASS *Puccinellia maritima* (Hudson) Parlatore (*Sclerochloa maritima*)
Marquand noted this only from the eastern side of Cobo, and it was claimed from Fort Hommet in 1968. He implied he did not know it from the area of the old Braye du Valle, where it must have been plentiful, and indeed he knew Gosselin and Babington collected it; and there it still is, by the Vale Pond, and, until 1972, where there was a pond at Les Dicqs. J rare. A –. S error. H –.

REFLEXED SALTMARSH-GRASS *P. distans* (Jacquin) Parlatore (*Sclerochloa distans*)
Marquand knew this from Bordeaux, but implied it died out there. So it was satisfactory when it was reported from there again in 1968. It has also been twice reported from Albecq since 1958, but possibly one of the forms of the last may have been mistaken for it. J rare. A –. S –. H –.

(*P. fasciculata* (Torrey) Bicknell was gathered in 1928 in Jersey.)

PROCUMBENT SALTMARSH-GRASS *P. rupestris* (Withering) Fernald & Weatherby (*Sclerochloa procumbens*)
This was collected by Babington on '6/23/1838', as he used to put it, near the Bouet and by Watson at the Braye du Valle in 1865. It was claimed from the Vale Road in 1902, and from the Route Isabelle in 1941. The latter was in fact the next species, a mistake which has been made since, nor is any voucher known for the former, by Hurst. However Dr Bowen had it from made ground at St Sampson's in 1968. J collected 1928. A –. S –. H –.

FERN-GRASS *Catapodium rigidum* (L.) C. E. Hubbard (*Sclerochloa rigida*)
Certainly not rare, which is how Marquand assessed it, but locally common. Curiously no one had collected it, or even mentioned it, before he got it in 1890, so perhaps it is spreading. it varies much in stature (it has been measured at 19 in. high) and how widely the panicle branches. The large forms have been variously called variety or subspecies, *majus* (*patens*). Such can be striking and are locally frequent at the foot of walls, and puzzle visitors used only to the usual tight wiry form – one got called *Sphenopus* (q.v.). But in Guernsey there seems no dividing line to separate off these imposing and decorative plants, so perhaps they should be rated as no more than a form. J common. A occasional. S –. H occasional.

DARNEL FESCUE *C. marinum* (L.) C. E. Hubbard (*Sclerochloa loliacea*)
Not so frequent as the latter, with which it sometimes grows – when the hybrid between the two might be found. So far it hasn't. J common. A common. S common. H common.

ANNUAL MEADOW-GRASS *Poa annua* L.
'Grows everywhere' wrote Gosselin on the folder of his specimens. So it does. A perennial form was collected in Cambridge Park in 1973. J ubiquitous. A common. S common. H common.

EARLY MEADOW-GRASS *P. infirma* Kunth (*P. remotiflora. P. exilis*)
A Channel Islands speciality, which Burkill collected unwittingly at Icart Point in April 1891 (74 years before he died), for it was not described as a British plant until August 1914, in the *Journal of Botany*, pp. 193–6. But even then people

Early Meadow-grass ×1

were slow to recognise it, which does need practice; and only in quite recent years has it been realised how locally plentiful it is all over the island; and how every trace has vanished by late spring. In the field, its pale whitish green colour and erect, never deflexed, panicle branches with scattered spikelets and very small anthers help to tell it. J locally common. A frequent. S occasional. H frequent.

HYBRID MEADOW-GRASS *P. annua* × *P. infirma*
On 19 February 1954 A. Nygren wrote to Dr Hubbard 'Last summer you were kind enough to send me some seeds of *Poa annua* and *P. infirma* from a hybrid population in the Normandie islands . . . We have obtained chromosome numbers between 2n = 14 and 2n = 21 for most plants. We have some plants with the number 2n = 14 and 2n = 21 which so far as I can see are *P. infirma* and its hybrid with *annua*. The plants we have with 2n = 16, 17, 19 and so on seem to be the offspring from the previous hybrid, which should thus be partly fertile.' These seeds in fact came from Guernsey, and Dr Hubbard kindly allowed this interesting letter to be quoted. In his invaluable Pelican of 1968 *Grasses* he says a hybrid of 2n = 21 has been found in Guernsey. But no one has yet successfully collected the hybrid in the field. There is a photo of it in *Watsonia* for August 1957, opposite p. 5, and a description on p. 7; and a note on it in *Hybridization and the Flora of the British Isles*. J –. A –. S –. H –.

BULBOUS MEADOW-GRASS *P. bulbosa* L.
The discovery of this was the skilful achievement of A. Copping on 20 April 1969. There was only a small patch of it, on typical open turf west of the La Varde dolmen, and it was too young to have any stalk, let alone flower. Yet he recognised its bulbous stem bases, and by growing them on proved them to be of the normal form, and not the viviparous one also known in Jersey. But despite much effort, no one has managed to see it since. He suggests it may have been introduced. J locally plentiful. A –. S –. H –.

WOOD MEADOW-GRASS *P. nemoralis* L.
G. Morgan was, unknown to himself, the first finder of this grass in Guernsey, in 1951 – on a roadside just south of the Village de Putron. It was seen in Fermain Lane in 1958 (in which area it still is), and has been claimed from Les

Vauxbelets in 1968 and from La Haye du Puits and the Vale, sans specimens. It is sometimes introduced with shrubs. J rare. A –. S –. H –.

FLATTENED MEADOW-GRASS *P. compressa* L. ssp *compressa*
The only time this has even been claimed was when N. D. Simpson collected it on a wall at Câtel Hill in 1968. J collected 1924. A –. S claimed 1872. H –.

SMOOTH MEADOW-GRASS *P. pratensis* L.
In recent years this species has tended to be split into three, with the next two taxa, but few have distinguished them. Their comparative frequency is therefore a matter for investigation, but plants of the group are common. For the distinctions between them, see the *Proceedings* of the BSBI for May 1967, pp. 262–4 and for all grasses, Dr Hubbard's *Grasses*. Dr Hubbard in 1953 collected at Perelle an unusual form 70–80 cm high with relatively flat and long leaf-blades and large loose panicles 15 cm long. J common? A common? S common? H occasional?

SPREADING MEADOW-GRASS *P. subcaerulea* Smith (*P. irrigata*)
A specimen of this is in Gosselin's herbarium, and Marquand knew it, but did not note it for Guernsey until 1906. Yet it seems to be frequent. Tell it by the hairy edge to its young leaf blades and acutely acuminate, relatively broad 3-nerved glumes (or lower 1-nerved), and generally stocky appearance. It is discussed in *Watsonia* for April 1962, pp. 162–73. Dr Hubbard in 1953 found a variant frequent in loose short grass near the sea. J recorded. A recorded. S recorded. H –.

NARROW-LEAVED MEADOW-GRASS *P. angustifolia* L.
This has been satisfactorily collected (named by D. M. Barling) three times since Dr Hubbard first gathered it in 1953. Its short ligule helps tell it from the larger *P. trivialis* – see *Watsonia* for November 1959, pp. 146–68. It is probably not rare. A specimen in Gosselin's scrapbook may be of this species. J recorded. A ? S ? H ?

ROUGH MEADOW-GRASS *P. trivialis* L.
Frequent, or indeed common. Gosselin's specimens labelled *P. pratensis* are this. J common. A common. S frequent. H occasional.

(*P. palustris* L. has been twice recently collected in Jersey. *P. Chaixii* Villars (*P. sudetica*) was recorded from Alderney in 1900.)

(*Eragrostis pilosa* (L.) Beauvois (*E. parviflora*) has been established in Jersey since 1961. *E. minor* Host was collected there in 1898.)

WHORL-GRASS *Catabrosa aquatica* (L.) Beauvois
Collected by Gosselin in the 18th century – very fine specimens – and by Marquand a century later, in three places in the centre of the island, but never even reported since. J collected 1926. A very rare. S –. H –.

COCKSFOOT *Dactylis glomerata* L.
All over the place, as Gosselin's specimens imply it was in his time. Dwarf plants from the cliffs and dunes have been called var *abbreviata* Bernhardi, var *collina* Schlechtendahl and ssp *hispanica* (Roth) Nyman. They are being grown and studied. J abundant. A common. S abundant. H common.

CRESTED DOG'S-TAIL *Cynosurus cristatus* L.
Gosselin collected this, which very few others have done – and mounted it on the same sheet as the next species. But it is not very common, and presumably sown from time to time. J common. A frequent. S frequent. H common.

ROUGH DOG'S-TAIL *C. echinatus* L.
This may crop up almost anywhere, but seems to persist most in the L'Ancresse, L'Erée and St Sampson's areas. It is now scarce rather than rare. J locally common. A –. S –. H –.

(*Lamarckia aurea* (L.) Moench was collected in Jersey in 1929.)

QUAKING-GRASS *Briza media* L.
This was first collected only in 1906 in a 'rich meadow by the Grande Mare', hardly an unvisited area. Since then it has spread but little. Was it introduced? J collected 1924/5. A occasional. S –. H –.

LESSER QUAKING-GRASS *B. minor* L.
Marquand called this rather rare; it is now quite frequent, but perhaps not in the south-east. There is a specimen of this plant at Kew in Lightfoot's herbarium collected by his friend Yalden by 1774, and a note in his copy of Hudson's *Flora Anglica*: 'In the borders of ploughed fields in the Island of Guernsey going

Lesser Quaking-grass ×¼

from the Town to the Little Vale Church'. Gosselin collected it not long after, and wrote it grew among the corn, particularly at St Sampson's. It is quite a speciality of the island. J rare. A –. S rare. H –.

GREATER QUAKING-GRASS *B. maxima* L.
This seems indeed to have been first recorded by Marquand on 20 May 1889, who called it rare and an alien. Rare it is not now, occurring in several places, and especially on the sunny dry south-facing cliffs. It is still in his place on the Dôs d'Ane, and well naturalised, if indeed it did come originally from gardens. J locally common. A –. S 1892. H –.

UPRIGHT BROME *Bromus erectus* Hudson
One clump was seen by Dr Hubbard at Cobo in 1953. J collected 1927. A –. S –. H –.

(*B. inermis* Leysser was collected from Jersey in 1926.)

BARREN BROME *B. sterilis* L.
Frequent in waste places. J common. A common. S last record 1897. H occasional.

COMPACT BROME *B. madritensis* L.
In scattered localities and not at all common. It occurs with hairy (var *ciliatus* Gussone) or hairless spikelets. The *Flora* records for 'var *rigidus*' belong here, and not to the next species. J rare. A rare. S rare. H –.

RIPGUT BROME *B. rigidus* Roth
A much misunderstood plant, none of the Guernsey claimants having long enough awns, on short rough stalks. They all belong to the last species. J local. A –. S 1839. H –.

(*B. rubens* L. was recorded in error from Sark.)

GREAT BROME *B. diandrus* Roth (*B. maximus*)
Very rare to Marquand, nowadays local, mostly in the north. It is to be found on dunes as well as in waste places. J locally plentiful. A locally common. S rare. H rare.

(*B. tectorum* L. was last collected in Jersey in 1926.)

SOFT BROME *B. mollis* L. (*B. hordeaceus* L. ssp *hordeaceus*. *Serrafalcus mollis*)
Gosselin commented with his specimens that this species grew among other grasses in fields and meadows. It is still probably common, but too few are competent to differentiate it from the other Soft Bromes. It could well be that this and the next three should all be considered as forms of this species, for they all seem to cross freely and blur what distinctions there are. Dr P. Smith calls the first two subspecies, but he agrees his key in *Watsonia* for June 1968 pp. 327–44 contains uncertainties, which is symptomatic of the difficulties. J common. A common. S common. H common.

LEAST SOFT BROME *B. Ferronii* Mabille
Apparently always on the coast and never a weed: to be told by its strongly outward curving awns. It was first collected only in 1928, by Wilmott. J occurs. A frequent. S occasional. H occasional.

DUNE SOFT BROME *B. Thominii* Hardouin
This dwarf taxon, as segregated by Dr Smith, was confirmed by him from specimens from dunes in the north-west collected by Gosselin, and in 1971. All other records under this name belong to *B.* × *pseudothominii*. But he agrees it is difficult to separate this from depauperate examples of *B. mollis*. The reason is that all populations on the dunes are heterogeneous. They will certainly not have originated from single colonisations and, with the prevalent selfing, many diverse types would have come to have a superficial similarity owing to their dune adaptation. This species should have lemmas 6.5 to 7.5 mm long: *B. mollis* has them 8mm or more. J occurs. A occasional. S –. H ?

SLENDER SOFT BROME *B. lepidus* Holmberg
The only certain record is by Dr Hubbard in 1953. J rare. A –. S –. H rare.

LESSER SOFT BROME *B.* × *pseudothominii* P. Smith (*B. lepidus* × *B. mollis*)
Here belong the, few, old records for *B. Thominii*, the first only in 1906 and 1928. It seems an uncommon weed, but is too rarely recognised. For comments on, and a key to, this and the following species, see Dr Smith's paper in *Watsonia* for July 1973. J occurs. A occasional. S Brechou. H –.

SMOOTH BROME *B. racemosus* L. (*Serrafalcus racemosus*)
No doubt uncommon, but very few people have collected it. J has been collected. A –. S 1872. H –.

MEADOW BROME *B. commutatus* Schrader (*Serrafalcus commutatus*)
Another little collected and probably scarce Soft Brome. Dr H. Scholz in *Willdenowia* for 1970, Vol. 6, pp. 139–59, illustrates how the hairs on the sheaths of this species (and the last and the next) differ from those in the *mollis/lepidus* group by being thicker and stiffer and spreading instead of soft and more or less appressed. But this does not always seem clear. J last collected 1936. A 1906. S 1907. H –.

RYE BROME *B. secalinus* L.
First collected by Druce in 1906, and little since. It would seem to be uncommon. J last collected 1926. A –. S –. H –.

FIELD SOFT BROME *B. arvensis* L. (*Serrafalcus arvensis*)
At one time much overclaimed, because this was the name Bentham and Hooker used for all the Soft Bromes. However both the Guernsey records are vouched, and the vouchers expertly passed. They are from Noirmont House, Vale in 1892, and from Moulin Huet in 1925 by Miss M. Cobbe. J collected 1926. A –. S –. H –.

(*B. lanceolatus* Roth (*B. macrostachys*) was collected in Jersey in 1928.)

RESCUE-GRASS *B. Willdenowii* Kunth (*Ceratochloa unioloides*)
A fodder grass of South American origin, first collected by Miss Cobbe near Bordeaux in 1925, then by Dr Bowen in 1957, and again in 1968, near Capelles, where it was abundant in a field. J locally plentiful. A rare. S –. H –.

SLENDER FALSE BROME *Brachypodium sylvaticum* (Hudson) Beauvois
Common. J locally common. A rare. S frequent. H common.

(*B. pinnatum* (L.) Beauvois was collected in Jersey in 1931: and was found established in Alderney in 1973.)

BEARDED COUCH *Agropyron caninum* (L.) Beauvois (*Triticum caninum*)
Another possibly mislabelled plant in Melville's herbarium, collected by Osborn in 1851. The only other record is Gosselin's, but his specimen is of the next species. J –. A –. S –. H –.

COMMON COUCH *A. repens* (L.) Beauvois (*Triticum repens*) Bâs
Generally common. It occurs in a variety of forms, which have been given a variety of names by experts. The upper surfaces of its leaves have rounded distant ribs, and its rachis is scabrid on the margins. Dr Melderis has given much patient help with the Couches. J common. A common. S occasional. H rare.

SEA COUCH *A. pycnanthum* Grenier & Godron (*A. littorale. A. 'pungens'*)
Quite frequent on the low coasts, and also variable. It too has a scabrid rachis, but the leaves are hairless with wide flattened close ribs. J locally frequent. A occasional. S –. H rare.

(*A.* × *Oliveri* Druce (*A. pycnanthum* × *A. repens*) was collected in Jersey in 1924.)

SAND COUCH *A. junceiforme* (A. & D. Löve) A. & D. Löve (*Triticum junceum*)
Local on the looser sand. Gosselin collected it first. It has a smooth rachis and rather close rounded, minutely and densely hairy ribs to the leaves. J local. A locally frequent. S –. H local.

HYBRID COUCH *A.* × *laxum* (Fries) Tutin (*A. junceiforme* × *A. repens*)
Unless this was Newbould's *T. laxum* from Vazon Bay in the early 1840s (a record repeated in print in 1851) this was first claimed only in 1907 by Druce from the Grande Havre, but his specimens are now thought to belong to the next taxon. It was however collected in the Albecq area in 1958, but will surely be passed by, except by the very knowledgeable. J occurs. A 1958. S –. H –.

Crested Sea Couch ×⅓

HYBRID SEA COUCH *A.* × *obtusiusculum* Lange (*A. junceiforme* × *A. pycnanthum*) (*A.* × *Hackelii*)
Collected by Gosselin, Syme in 1843, Ley in 1885 and claimed on various occasions since from the western dunes. But too little is known of these hybrids to be sure of their frequencies. The broad-spiked 'Cristatum' ('*pycnanthum*') has been known at Vazon and Albecq since Gosselin's time and was collected at Grande Havre in 1906. It needs, and is receiving, study. It may be endemic to Guernsey. J occurs. A scarce? S –. H –.

(*Aegilops cylindrica* Host was collected in Jersey in 1901.)

LARGE SPELT *Triticum Spelta* L.
There is a single record of this grain plant, in 1899. J –. A –. S –. H –.

BREAD WHEAT *T. aestivum* L. Bllaie
May be seen on rubbish heaps etc., nowadays, no doubt usually from bird seed,

and by field edges. It was reported in 1757 that a single grain of Wheat sown by John Tupper produced 142 ears from 3 in.–6 in. long and the product of those ears was 5,600 grains. J casual. A –. S –. H –.

RYE *Secale cereale* L. Seigle
At one time this was grown: it still is mixed with grass leys, but it is also a grain casual. It was noticed in 1968 and 1972, but is unrecognised by most people. It has much narrower glumes than Wheat and is of a typical glaucous colour. It is also the only self-sterile cereal. Consequently one seedling alone cannot produce a colony. J –. A –. S –. H –.

LYME-GRASS *Elymus arenarius* L.
Claimed for Guernsey by Ansted, but never proved. Linnaeus's specimens under this name are of *Agropyron caninum*, so it will need to be altered. J collected 1840 and 1911. A –. S –. H –.

MEADOW BARLEY *Hordeum secalinum* Schreber
First found by Druce in Marquand's company on 10 July 1906 near Perelle, collected there by Dr Hubbard in 1953, and rather to the north at Le Gelé in 1968. It was unknown elsewhere until noted by E. Milne-Redhead near the Château des Marais in 1971. J 1958. A –. S –. H –.

WALL BARLEY *H. murinum* L. Herbe sorchière
Quite common. Collected by Gosselin. J common. A occasional. S rare. H occasional.

SEA BARLEY *H. marinum* Hudson (*H. maritimum*)
There are the following records for this species. First by Babington from L'Erée and the Braye du Valle, but he did not collect it from the latter, likely, locality. His specimen from the former shows it to be of the next species, which is very easily confounded with this one. Next was Druce, who claimed it from St Sampson's in 1877 sans specimen, but he could have been right. Then came Marquand, who recorded it from L'Erée and from the quarry heap near the Vale Castle, a prolific source of casuals. There is no specimen from the latter, but his from L'Erée, in 1890, is, again, the next species. Dr. Melderis has seen all the vouchers. J error? A –. S –. H 1837.

MEDITERRANEAN BARLEY *H. geniculatum* Allioni (*H. histrix*)
This differs from the last in having both its outer glumes bristle-like. Since it is basically a Mediterranean plant, it is interesting that it seems to have survived in the L'Erée area for at least 68 years from 2 July 1838 – see the comments under the last species. But it has not been noted since 1906. J –. A –. S –. H –.

TWO-ROWED BARLEY *H. distichon* L. Orge
A grain casual first reported from Vazon in 1928 by Williams, and very occasionally since. Barley was once much grown, in Orgeries, used chiefly for bread for the poor, but also by maltsters. J casual. A Burhou. S –. H –.

(*H. vulgare* L. is on record as a casual from Jersey.)

CRESTED HAIR-GRASS *Koeleria cristata* (L.) Persoon
Still rather surprisingly local, from Cobo to L'Ancresse. This polymorphic species has not been studied in Guernsey. J local. A frequent. S –. H –.

FRENCH OAT *Gaudinia fragilis* (L.) Beauvois
This has an interesting history and status in Guernsey. It is a Mediterranean species, but is to be found, if rarely, right up to the opposite coasts of France. It was first noted, and collected, by Wilmott and Williams in 1928 from south of the Grande Mare in quantity. There is no note of anyone looking for it subsequently, but Dr P. Macpherson and Mr and Mrs G. Wheeldon lit on it in the same area in 1970. In 1971 it was found to be in the hayfields there, as indeed it

French Oat ×⅓

is in the Isle of Wight across the Channel, and in southern Ireland – see the records in *Watsonia* for July 1972, pp. 143–6. In these areas it seems to have been introduced with agricultural seed and persisted, and there is no reason to doubt its having been similarly in the Grande Mare meadows for over forty years. 1970 was memorable also in that a day or two later, this grass was found by Mrs B. Garratt in apparently native turf south of the Doyle Rock on L'Ancresse. This is a well-botanised area, but the grass is short, and so is this species there, which does not stand out at all, and by early July is worn away. But whatever its source or the length of time it has been there, it is at least well entrenched. The *Armorican Flora* records it as a spreading adventive. J 1954. A once local, now established in one area. S –. H –.

YELLOW OAT *Trisetum flavescens* (L.) Beauvois
Another grass, the only record of which is due to Dr Hubbard's perspicuity on shelly sand behind the sea wall at Cobo in 1953. J last collected 1925. A occasional. S –. H rare.

WILD OAT *Avena fatua* L. Avenon
Collected from Gosselin's time onwards, and recently listed in 22 squares. J casual. A occasional. S very rare. H –.

WINTER WILD OAT *A. Ludoviciana* Durieu
Two casual records, both in 1958 from St Sampson's and from Albecq, both duly vetted. J 1927 and 1963. A 1963. S –. H –.

BRISTLE OAT *A. strigosa* Schreber
This was first recorded by Major Smith in a field near Cambray, St Saviour's, in the middle of the last century. Marquand got it in 1892, and there have been two

records since, in 1969 and 1970. It is a grain casual. J last collected 1929. A 1900. S –. H –.

SLENDER OAT *A. barbata* Pott ex Link
Astutely spotted by A. Leslie, and later recognised by A. Silverside, from L'Erée in 1970. Also doubtless a grain casual. J –. A –. S –. H –.

ANIMATED OAT *A. sterilis* L.
Collected in 1958 at St Jacques by M. English. This could come from grain, but it is sometimes grown in gardens for its fine spikelets, whose awns twist and turn with varying humidity and so give the plant its English name. The Latin epithet is, of course, quite erroneous, but can never on that account be changed. J –. A –. S –. H –.

CULTIVATED OAT *A. sativa* L. Avogne
To be seen on dumps etc., often very likely from bird seed. It is in Gosselin's second list from fields at Mont Plaisir. But there is a pencilled comment, bracketed with the entry for the next species, 'not certain of these'! J casual, A occasional. S 1902. H 1958.

(*Helictotrichon pubescens* (Hudson) Pilger grows locally in Jersey and Alderney. *H. pratense* (L.) Pilger was collected in Jersey in 1925.)

FALSE OAT *Arrhenatherum elatius* (L.) Beauvois ex J. & C. Presl
Tchen d'Dent
A common grass, usually with the bulbous stem base, which gives it the name of Onion Couch, the var *bulbosum* (Willdenow) Spenner. J common. A common. S common. H common.

YORKSHIRE FOG *Holcus lanatus* L. Molle Herbe
Common. Gosselin implies in the notes with his specimens that it was so in his time. J common. A frequent. S occasional. H frequent.

CREEPING SOFT-GRASS *H. mollis* L.
Not so common. J frequent. A rare. S occasional. H –.

TUFTED HAIR-GRASS *Deschampsia cespitosa* (L.) Beauvois
Found by Sir H. de Sausmarez in his grounds at Sausmarez Manor in 1925, where it might have been put, or introduced with shrubs. No one has found it since. J rare. A –. S 1902. H –.

WAVY HAIR-GRASS *D. flexuosa* (L.) Trinius (*Aira flexuosa*)
Two records, one by Babington in the late 1830s, the other by his pupil Hillhouse in 1881. No specimens. J very rare. A –. S 1838. H –.

SMALL HAIR-GRASS *Aira praecox* L.
Frequent. One of Gosselin's specimens survives, in the folder for another species. The one marked *A. praecox* contains *Mibora*. J common. A common. S common. H common.

SILVER HAIR-GRASS *A. caryophyllea* L. ssp *caryophyllea*
Quite common. Large open forms resemble ssp *multiculmis*, but have florets over, and not under, 2.5 mm. J common. A common. S frequent. H common.

(*A. caryophyllea* L. ssp *multiculmis* (Dumortier) Ascherson & Graebner was collected in Jersey in 1881.)

GREY HAIR-GRASS *Corynephorus canescens* (L.) Beauvois
Claimed by Newbould in the 1840s, but his vouchers are all from Jersey. But there are specimens loose in Gosselin's scrapbook. J locally plentiful. A –. S –. H –.

MARRAM *Ammophila arenaria* (L.) Link (*Psamma arenaria*) Milgré
Not very common now, and only from Grandes Rocques to L'Ancresse. Its first record is as *Sparta marina*, by Morison in telling his fable of the Guernsey Lily's shipwreck, which he wrote about 1680. But he was never in the island, so this can be no more than invented local colour. J locally common. A locally abundant. S –. H common.

BUSH-GRASS *Calamagrostis epigejos* (L.) Roth
First found by Babington on 23 July 1838 on the St Martin's cliffs beyond the Artillery Barracks; and it is still at the Bec du Nez where it was originally specifically noted in 1899. Marquand knew it at Les Gigands in 1891; and it has been claimed without proof from above, east of, Petit Bot, a much visited area. It was however discovered in some quantity by Lady Anne Brewis under conifers just north of the Reservoir in 1969. J rare. A –. S –. H –.

VELVET BENT *Agrostis canina* L. ssp *canina*
This has been so little recognised that it is not possible to be sure of its frequency, but it is probably no longer common. J rare. A rare. S 1902. H –.

BROWN BENT *A. canina* L. ssp *montana* (Hartmann) Hartmann
Even less recognised than the last, but it does occur. J –. A –. S –. H –.

COMMON BENT *A. tenuis* Sibthorp ssp *tenuis* (*A. vulgaris*)
Common. J common. A common. S common. H common.

BLACK BENT *A. gigantea* Roth
Collected unawares by Marquand, but first noted in the field only in 1958, when it was described as frequent in the St Sampson's area. It has since been found in various places and seems to be not uncommon, typically as a weed of arable. But it too is unrecognised by most people, or miscollected for stout forms of the next species. This one has underground, not overground, runners, an open panicle which does not contract in fruit, and florets with 3-nerved lemmas. J Confirmed only in 1885. A rare. S –. H Jethou 1838.

WHITE BENT *A. stolonifera* L. (*A.* '*alba*') Bllue Herbe Trainaïn
Common, to be seen locally in lawns. The stout Marsh Bent, var *palustris* (Hudson) Farwell, has been collected on several occasions in recent years, and has been taken for the last species. It was recommended for lawns in the 18th century. The *Armorican Flora* records ssp *maritima* (Lamarck) P. Fournier for Guernsey and Alderney. J common. A common. S common. H common.

WATER BENT *A. semiverticillata* (Forskål) C. Christensen (*A. viridis*)
In some parts this is a common grass, especially by roadsides, and is probably on the increase. It was first spotted only in 1906, by Druce, a discovery then new

to the British flora, which was reported to the Linnean Society on 7 March 1907; compare also the *Journal of Botany* for 1906, p. 320, and other contemporary references. However it had been collected earlier, at Bordeaux Quarry on 3 July 1897 by Gray, who had called it *A. palustris/alba*. It presumably reached Guernsey not much earlier, or it eluded many good botanists. It was found at Brest in 1878/9, the first record for the shores nearest the Channel Islands – it is really Mediterranean. It is now common there. J scarce. A frequent. S –. H –.

HYBRID BENT *A. semiverticillata* × *A. stolonifera*
Collected at Grandes Rocques twice, independently, in 1953 and 1958. But it would doubtless be missed by most people. The same is true of other hybrids in this genus which must surely await local discovery. J –. A –. S –. H –.

(*A. nebulosa* Boissier & Reuter has been twice collected in Jersey.)

PERENNIAL BEARD-GRASS × *Agropogon littoralis* (Smith) C. E. Hubbard
(*A. stolonifera* × *Polypogon monspeliensis*) (*Polypogon littoralis*)
Marquand knew of two records for this rarity, and rejected them both. But there is no doubt that it once grew in the saline marshes of St Sampson's and at the Château des Marais as well. The earliest record is indeed Major Smith's, which appears in both his annotated copy of Babington and in the short extract of his lost List. Wolsey, who will have known Smith, also reported it from the Château des Marais and is as reliable an observer. The only specimen is from Watson in August 1858 from the marshes inland from St Sampson's and the Braye du Valle. Druce remarked that he could not find it in 1877, which implies it had then recently at least been a recognised Guernsey plant. J –. A –. S –. H –.

ANNUAL BEARD-GRASS *Polypogon monspeliensis* (L.) Desfontaines
This was at the Braye du Valle while salt marshes still existed there. Babington was the first to collect it, on 14 August 1837, and again in July 1838. Miss Guille got it in 1850, Bailey in the 1860s and it was at least locally very abundant in 1877. It was last collected there in 1886, eighty years after the channel was drained. It too seems to have been in the marshes near the Château des Marais, which must have been brackish then – Wolsey had it from there in 1862 and 1863, and it is marked on Guérin's map of 1888. The only time Marquand saw it was as a casual at Vale Castle in 1889. Nothing more was then heard of this erstwhile native for another eighty years, when a fine, but dead, tuft was found, inexplicably, alone in a pot behind some greenhouses in St Peter's. Next year and in 1971, several plants were seen on the floor of a quarry at Mont Cuet, source unknown, but habitat not all that wrong. J –. A –. S –. H –.

SILKY BENT *Apera Spica-venti* (L.) Beauvois
A lovely grass listed by Ansted in 1862, very likely correctly, although Marquand did not think so, who was unaware of the sound bases for his lists. There have been three records since, in 1942, 1950 and 1958, all as casuals. J last record 1947. A 1966. S –. H –.

EARLY SAND-GRASS *Mibora minima* (L.) Desvaux
A speciality of the Channel Islands, of which Finlay wrote in 1787 a long description in Latin to Sir J. Banks ending '*habitat in pascuis aridis ad Jerbourg copiose*'. About the same time Gosselin collected it from the east or sunny side of the parapet beyond Hougue à la Père. It is in fact locally frequent on the cliffs and

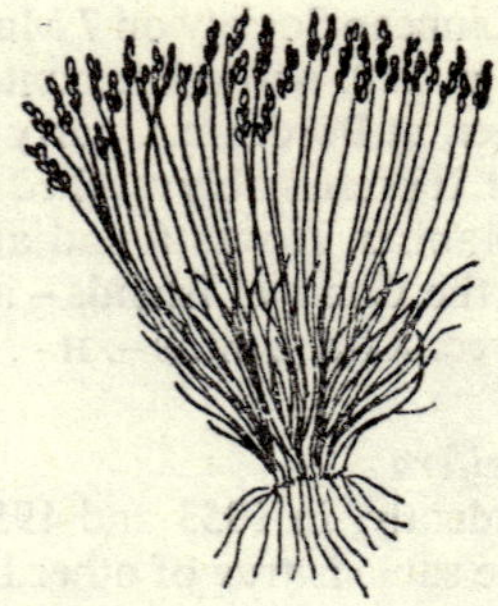

Early Sand-grass ×1

sandy coasts, but has not been noted inland. It can be very small, and soon dries up and is therefore often missed by visitors. J locally common. A –. S 1903. H frequent.

NIT-GRASS *Gastridium ventricosum* (Gouan) Schinz & Thellung (*G. lendigerum*)
Probably always scarce, although Gosselin's are lush plants and Newbould called it common when he collected it in St Andrew's. Others have remarked how there were only single plants (although there are two on Marquand's sheet from Torteval, where in the *Flora* he says there was only one). The extreme south-west seems to have been at least its main area since the end of the last century, for its only other records were from St Peter's in 1928 and 1947. This last came from a garden at Le Douit, where the plant was again seen in 1972. In 1971 it was found by Miss Caddick in the Rue du Gain, three-quarters of a mile to the south, and two days later a single plant by St Peter's Post Office, by Dr Tayler. Its only other collection this century was from a completely new area, Les Ammareurs on west L'Ancresse, by Dr J. Mason in 1965. J error. A –. S rare. H –.

HARE'S-TAIL GRASS *Lagurus ovatus* L. Pousse d'banque
One of our most attractive grasses, its bobbles bespangling the dunes, lovely, both fresh and be-anthered, and dried, naturally, for the winter. How long it has been in Guernsey is a matter for conjecture. '*Nuper inventa fuit in Insula Sarnia a D. Finlay* 1787' in Lightfoot's copy of Hudson's *Flora Anglica* suggests one first record. So does the text to the illustration in *English Botany*, Plate 1334, dated 1 July 1804, 'We have received this from Guernsey. It was first observed there by Mr Gosselin, who sent specimens to Mr Dickson'. Dickson

Hare's-tail Grass ×½

included it in No. VII of his *Fascicles of British Plants* in 1794. Gosselin sent it to Sir J. Banks on 8 April 1791. His own herbarium notes it on the Jaones on L'Ancresse, at the Vazon and near Pulias. Gay got it south of the Vale Church in 1832 and it has since been well known on the dunes of the north and west down as far as Richmond, where Dupuy gathered it in 1864, and it still is, and at one time Rocquaine, where Hillhouse had it in 1881. Guérin's map of 1888 marks it for Cocagne. Marquand called it abundant in 1890 and common in his *Flora*, but it is definitely local now, great stretches of dunes having none. It is perhaps best in the area by Pembroke Bay. In Black's *Guide* for 1873 it is called Guernsey Grass. But is it native? Probably not.

First take its history in Jersey – it is practically unknown in the other islands. Here, as Marquand relates, and *pace* the *Atlas*, many attempts were made to introduce it, before Piquet succeeded in the 1860s – the earlier Jersey specimens will have come from these earlier attempts. But nowadays who could guess that it had been in St Ouen's Bay for a mere century or so, who did not know of Piquet's well-known action? Its locality at Dawlish in S. Devon dates back only to 1930. On the proximate coasts of France it was in Victorian times very rare. Lloyd in his *Flora of the West* mentions it only in his Supplement for 1878/9, when he comments that it had got going at one spot in the Loire Inferieure, mentioning also that it was cultivated everywhere for dried bouquets. So it did, and so it was; rare at the turn of the century in the south, almost unknown in the north, but now locally plentiful in the Armorican peninsula. Previously it had been frequent only as far north as the estuary of the Gironde. It is known that there was considerable trade in the early Middle Ages between Guernsey (and not Jersey) and this region, no doubt often for its wines. The main Guernsey anchorage in those days was the hence-named Grande Havre, in the midst of the north-west sandy coasts. Is this perhaps how it got to Guernsey? – an idea originating with Mrs le Sueur. J locally abundant. A 1951. S 1892. H 1902.

SMALL TIMOTHY *Phleum Bertolinii* DC

Potentially native, although unmentioned by Marquand, but also a relic of sown leys. Both Timothies exist in many agricultural strains. J rare. A 1969. S –. H –.

TIMOTHY *P. pratense* L.

This has been found over the years in various parts of the island, but it is likely always to have been introduced with seed mixtures for agricultural purposes. Once having got in, it seems capable of remaining for at least a while, and perhaps, locally indefinitely. But it is still not common. At Port Soif some plants had spikes 7½ in. long. Timothy was Timothy Hanson, an emigrant to America in the early 18th century. There is an account of him in *Companion to Flowers* of 1966, pp. 181–2. J common. A rare. S –. H 1889.

SAND CAT'S-TAIL *P. arenarium* L.

Known to Gosselin, Gay and Babington in the early days, but now not as frequent as one might have expected. J locally common. A common. S –. H common.

(*P. phleoides* (L.) Karsten was recorded from Jersey in error.)

BLACK GRASS *Alopecurus myosuroides* Hudson (*A. agrestis*)

The first record for this agricultural weed was Carré's in Babington's *Flora*. Shortly after, Newbould got it in St Peter Port. A century later it was in a garden in St Peter Port along with Silky Bent. Twenty-nine years after, in 1971 came the only other records, both apparently mere waifs, by Miss Sturdy at Fort George and Mrs Garratt at Vazon. J rare. A –. S –. H –.

MEADOW FOX-TAIL *A. pratensis* L.
Still in every parish, but rather scarce, and doubtless often sown. It was measured 5 ft. tall in 1968. J occasional. A rare. S occasional. H –.

MARSH FOX-TAIL *A. geniculatus* L. Herbe pointue
Quite frequent in wetter places. Its first record was when Gosselin sent specimens to Sir J. Banks in 1791 – others survive in his herbarium. J common. A rare. S rare. H –.

BULBOUS FOX-TAIL *A. bulbosus* Gouan
A grass which must have been among the salt-marsh vegetation of the Braye du Valle, but was first collected by the Vale Pond, which is on the site of the Braye, only in 1958. There it still is, its only locality in the islands. J –. A –. S –. H –.

DWARF MILLET *Milium scabrum* Richard
A supreme Guernsey rarity, a native plant never recorded anywhere else in the British Isles, and for many years thought no longer to grow there at all: the *Transactions* for 1940 said just that. The trouble started when the original finder, Andrews (on 17 April 1899), forgot where he had collected his specimens, but

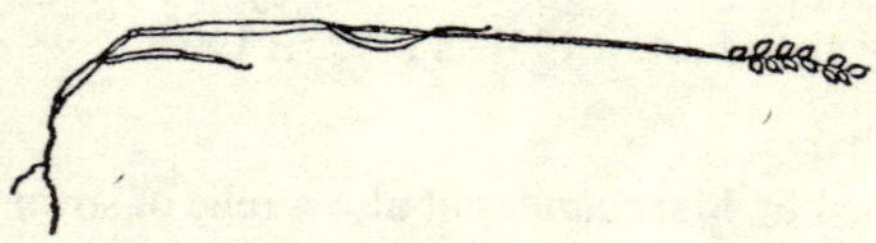

Dwarf Millet ×1

thought they came from the cliffs at Petit Bot. Hither went streams of hunters, bottoms up, but none could see it. The reason, we now know, was not just that it is small, prostrate and unobvious, but that it was probably not on the south cliffs at all that Andrews got it, but on the dunes in the north-west, which are after all its normal habitat. Here anyway was where Prof. Tutin and J. Raven turned it up in 1949 – see the paper in *Watsonia* for December 1950, pp. 345–8, where there is also a photograph of its chromosomes – it has the unusually low number of $2n = 8$. They record that it grew abundantly though usually in small patches, and also at Vazon Bay. But no one lately has managed to see it other than at the western end of L'Ancresse, and even there it is in very small and elusive quantity. J error. A –. S –. H –.

(*M. effusum* L. was recorded in error from Jersey.)

(*Oryzopsis miliacea* (L.) Bentham & Hooker ex Ascherson and Schweinfurth is naturalised in Jersey. *O. virescens* (Trinius) G. Beck was collected there in 1930.)

SWEET VERNAL-GRASS *Anthoxanthum odoratum* L.
Common. Gosselin's specimens are unlocalised. J common. A common. S common. H common.

ANNUAL VERNAL-GRASS *A. Puelii* Lecoq & Lamotte
The only record is by Rogers in 1897 from the Common near the Vale Church. No specimens of his have been located. J 1879. A –. S –. H –.

REED-GRASS *Phalaris arundinacea* L.
One would have thought this would have been at least a frequent grass in the more watery Guernsey of the past. But the only mention of the normal form was by Babington from the Grande Mare; and no one else reported it from this well-botanised area until Cdr Annett got it on the east side in 1968. In the same year it was seen by the stream in Saumarez Park, in marshy ground above Saints Bay, and reported from the Ruettes Brayes and the Reservoir. It is hard to think of an explanation for this sudden apparent resurgence. The var *picta* L., the striped 'Gardener's Garters', may grow too well in the border and get thrown out, when it may go on growing well for a while at least. It has done so in Guernsey, apparently since Babington's day, who says he saw it with the usual form in the Grande Mare. J rare. A –. S error. H –.

CANARY-GRASS *P. canariensis* L.
This is the supreme bird food plant, regularly to be seen on tips or where birds have been fed. Gosselin was the first to collect it. J casual. A rare. S 1902. H 1894 and 1959.

GUERNSEY CANARY-GRASS *P. minor* Retzius
Another Guernsey speciality, collected by Gosselin, and doubtless in the island

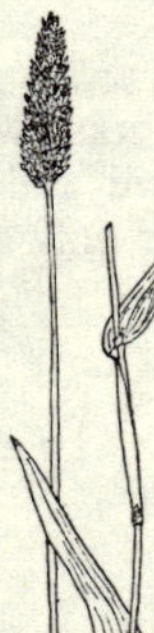

Guernsey Canary-grass ×⅓

much longer. Yet no one noted it between his time and 1899 – see Andrews's paper in the *Journal of Botany* for 1900, p. 33. It is now quite frequent in the north, less so in the west, and apparently not in the south-east. Gosselin's specimens are of two sorts. Some are typical and robust with cylindrical flower-heads; the others are very slender, small and branched with globular heads, which he sent under a manuscript name to Sir J. Banks on 8 April 1791. It was Dr Melderis who eventually recognised these as depauperate *P. minor*. J now casual. A locally frequent. S 1909. H –.

AWNED CANARY-GRASS *P. paradoxa* L.
The only record is among grain casuals in St Peter Port in 1900. J –. A –. S –. H –.

SEA HARD-GRASS *Parapholis strigosa* (Dumortier) C. E. Hubbard (*Lepturus 'filiformis'*)
Collected by Gosselin, and much more often seen – or less overlooked? – now than when Marquand wrote. It is plentiful behind Rocque Poisson, the old Mare Hailla, still at the Claire Mare and Grande Mare, seen at Albecq since at least 1913 and still at Pulias and the Vale Pond, and is by Mont Cuet. On the other side it has been seen near Fort Doyle for at least 45 years and was at St Sampson's in 1953. Newbould got it at Portinfer in 1841, and no doubt there was plenty by the Braye du Valle, where Babington saw it. J rare. A 1969. S –. H –.

CURVED HARD-GRASS *P. incurva* (L.) C. E. Hubbard
This has been claimed on several occasions, but has always proved to be the last species. Yet it could occur. J locally common. A rare. S –. H –.

MAT-GRASS *Nardus stricta* L.
A third grass collected in 'Guernsey' in 1851 by Osborn, and claimed by no one, or practically no one, else. J rare. A –. S –. H –.

CORD-GRASS *Spartina maritima* (Curtis) Fernald (*S. stricta*)
This surely unmistakable grass was included in Derrick's List of Plants in 1888. Marquand gives no reason for ignoring the record. J last collected 1924. A –. S –. H –.

(*S. anglica* C. E. Hubbard was in Jersey from 1958 to 1970.)

BERMUDA-GRASS *Cynodon Dactylon* (L.) Persoon
A perennial fingered grass widespread in warmer regions, which has been at Vazon Bay since Carré and Haslam reported it to Babington in the 1830s. Marquand knew it for only a hundred yards there, but it can now be seen for

Bermuda-grass × ¼

nearer six hundred, although still thickest opposite the Martello Tower, and is as far south as Fort Saumarez. In 1950 J. E. Lousley found it extended to Portinfer, and Dr Bowen got it at Grandes Rocques in 1968. N. D. Simpson collected it from L'Ancresse in 1922. J local. A rare. S –. H –.

COCKSPUR-GRASS *Echinochloa Crus-galli* (L.) Beauvois
Curiously rare. The only records are in 1900, 1925, 1950, 1967 and 1973. J locally common. A one plant 1900. S –. H –.

CRAB-GRASS *Digitaria sanguinalis* (L.) Scopoli
An annual fingered grass, taller than Bermuda grass, surprisingly not reported before 1904. It is now to be seen in several parts of the island, chiefly in the north, especially at the foot of walls, when the road tidiers allow. J common. A –. S rare. H –.

GREEN BRISTLE-GRASS *Setaria viridis* (L.) Beauvois
A casual with fewer records than might have been expected, the earliest in 1893, followed by about nine others, the last in 1925 and 1971. J scarce, A –. S –. H –.

ROUGH BRISTLE-GRASS *S. verticillata* (L.) Beauvois ssp. *verticillata*
First reported by Mrs McCrea in a tomato house at Grandes Rocques in 1932, but then not again until 1950. Since then there have been about half a dozen records, some in greenhouses, and the plant has been noticed persisting between flagstones at the La Porte Hotel. J casual. A –. S –. H –.

YELLOW BRISTLE-GRASS *S. lutescens* (Weigel) Hubbard (*S.* '*glauca*')
Three records in the 1800s, two in 1911/12, then 1958, 1968 and 1973. It is not known to have persisted, although there were in 1958 'a dozen or more lusty plants'. J casual. A –. S 1961. H –.

FOX-TAIL MILLET *S. italica* (L.) Beauvois
A common bird seed plant bought for its fat curving bunches of seeds, which surely will have appeared on rubbish tips etc. long before its first record in 1967. Fanciers call it Panicum or Chinese Millet. J casual. A –. S –. H –.

COMMON MILLET *Panicum miliaceum* L.
Another common bird seed plant, first noted in 1925 and misleadingly rarely since, except in very recent years, which show it to be as frequent as would be expected. It is the Plate Yellow Millet, or White Millet, of the Fancy. It is also called Proso Millet. J casual. A –. S –. H –.

(*P. capillare* L. has appeared as a casual in Jersey.)

SORGHUM *Sorghum saccharatum* (L.) Moench
Yet another bird seed plant, recorded so far only twice, in 1967 and 1973, but which must have cropped up in other years. It is a polymorphic species, one form being known as Dari. MacCulloch reported in 1826 that 'a species of *Panicum*, the Guinea Corn' had proved hardy and 'sprang at once in the open air from imported seeds, producing its own seed'. It is also recorded as being introduced

to the island in the 1850s by G. Foote, yields reaching 30 tons per acre for fodder. It received a prize, as 'maize' in 1858 from the RASG, who reported in 1860 that one perch sown on 1 June and cut on 22 August yielded at the rate of 26¼ tons per acre. J casual. A –. S –. H –.

MAIZE *Zea Mays* L.
Used for chickens as well as pet cage birds – and by humans and stock, and increasingly grown for cattle feed. Yet it has been reported as a casual only in 1967. J casual. A –. S –. H –.

(Job's Tears, *Coix Lacryma-jobi* L., was collected in Jersey in 1927.)

METAKE *Arundinaria japonica* Siebold & Zuccarini
The commonest, and dowdiest, bamboo in Guernsey, but invaluable as a windbreak. It is a good persister, and may indeed spread by its usually short rhizomes, as it has on the slopes above Portelet Harbour, where there are small thickets. It may be found showing the odd flower in many years, but so far no seed. A remarkable example of injury apparently bringing on flowering occurred in Saumarez Park in the 1960s. Two or three clumps got burned down to the ground. Next year, these came into luxuriant flower, none of the others in the Park, even adjoining ones which were presumably of the same clone, showing any flower at all – see *Journal* of the RHS for December 1967, p. 524. These clumps are still the only ones in full flower. The species comes from Japan. J frequent. A planted. S planted. H planted.

NARIHIRADAKE *A. fastuosa* (Mitford) Makino
The native name for this, and most others, is hardly as well known as the one for the last. But it seems the only one to use, following Mitford in his classic *Bamboo Garden* of 1896 and others, and as it is for Japanese Cherries. This is another Guernsey stalwart, although not far outside gardens, where it is used for tall hedges. Unfortunately for their effectiveness, this species came into full flower about 1960, possibly as early as 1957, and some clumps are still showing flower, putting out fresh inflorescences and stamens twelve months in the year, year after year non-stop. Admittedly this bout seems to be slowing down, and the damage will be naturally repaired, but in the meantime some hedges have been grubbed up as at least unsightly, and apparently dead. But in fact few plants died completely and those that have been left have nearly all thrown up fresh shoots, soon of full vigour. No seed has been found anywhere, so this is just as well for the continuance of the species. It received an Award of Merit in 1953. J –. A –. S –. H –.

ANCEPS BAMBOO *A. anceps* Mitford
This comes from north India and is one of the most graceful species, but also one with strong running roots. It was seen in flower at the Caledonia Nursery by 1966, and soon after at Les Fontenelles, Côte des Vardes, Mouilpied, Les Granges and near the Vale Church – but this is hardly surprising because these plants will have come from Caledonia. Here too flowering continues, on a few plants only, but apparently without causing any setback to the canes. But only one seed has been detected. There are one or two thickets in the island. J local. A planted. S –. H –.

OROSHIMA-CHIKU *A. disticha* (Mitford) Pfitzer
A dwarf Japanese bamboo rare in cultivation, which was one of the survivors

of the fine collection made by Lord de Sausmarez with Lord Redesdale (Hon. A. B. Freeman-Mitford, who originally named many of these species) and Mr de Putron at Saumarez Park. This species suddenly shot into full flowering in 1970, just after its first flower in England had been discovered. Next year all the shoots had died except a very few, which still bore flowers, but by summer they too had died. No seed could be found, and there seems no sign of these plants having survived at all or left any seedlings, a rare occurrence among bamboos in the British Isles. J –. A –. S –. H –.

OKINADAKE *A. variegata* (Siebold ex Miquel) Makino (*A. Fortunei*)
This dwarfish Japanese bamboo with its leaves striped longitudinally is the variety of the species usually cultivated. It grows, grew, untended with the last species in Saumarez Park and also at Caledonia, good patches in each. J –. A –. S –. H –.

(*A. Simonii* Rivière occurs in Jersey, and *A. viridistriata* André (*A. auricoma*) in Sark.)

CHIMAKIZASA *Sasa palmata* (Burbidge) E. G. Camus
This broad-leaved species from Japan is not at all common in Guernsey. There is a thicket of it at Sausmarez Manor, and the odd clump elsewhere. It has been in continuous flower in the British Isles since the early 1960s, but this may soon be finished, leaving the clumps looking very untidy with many stems dead. But the rhizomes are not, and fresh shoots will soon cover them. There was very sparse seed at Sausmarez Manor, but no one has yet succeeded in germinating any. J occurs. A –. S –. H –.

KUMAZASA *S. Veitchii* (Carrière) Rehder
This species, also from Japan, has leaves which go white at the edges shortly after they have emerged, ramps much less than the last, and is usually dwarfer. There is a colony of it along a bank of Valnord Lane. J –. A –. S –. H –.

MADAKE *Phyllostachys bambusoides* Siebold & Zuccarini
There are good clumps of this Chinese bamboo beyond the lake at Sausmarez Manor. Its cultivar 'Castillonis', Kimmei-chiku, is well established in the wetter parts of the Caledonia Nursery, where it grows very tall. It flowered generally from about 1962 for at least six years. Some clumps did die, but those at Caledonia were in such vigorous health that they pulled through. No seed has been found anywhere in Britain. J ? A ? S ? H ?

HA-CHIKU *P. nigra* (Loddiges) Munro
There are some fine specimens at Les Granges Manor and down the Fermain Valley, which might be due to flower soon. J –. A –. S –. H –.

(Other bamboos surviving untended long after they were planted at the Caledonia Nursery or Saumarez Park include *A. Falconeri* (Hooker f. ex Munro) Gamble, which died slowly after glorious flower in 1967/8, leaving seedlings; *A. marmorea* (Mitford) Makino, in flower by 1967; *A. Murieliae* Gamble; *A. nitida* Mitford; *A. pumila* Mitford; *A. vagans* Gamble; *Phillostachys pubescens* Lahaie 'Heterocycla', the Tortoiseshell Bamboo, and *P. viridiglaucescens* (Carrière) A. & C. Rivière. In the naming of all these, the essential help of Dr Hubbard is most gratefully acknowledged.)

Bibliography

THE existence of N. D. Simpson's comprehensive *Bibliographical Index of the British Flora* of 1960 (privately printed at Bournemouth) makes a full set of references supererogatory. Pages 83–5 are particularly devoted to Guernsey. To them may be added the following printed sources.

Bichard, J. D. & McClintock, D	1975	*Wild Flowers of the Channel Islands.* Chatto & Windus.
De Garis, M.	1967	*Dictiounnaire Angllais-Guernesiais.* Société Guernesiaise, St. Peter Port, 2nd Ed 1968, *Supplement* 1973.
des Abbayes, H.	1971	*Flore et Végétation du Massif Armoricain*, Vol. 1. St Brieuc.
Jee, N.	1953	*Flowers of the Guernsey Cliffs*. Q. Jnl. Guernsey Soc. 3–5.
	1957	*Flowers of the Sand Dunes. ibid* 23–5.
	1960	*Guernsey's Garden Weeds. ibid.* 1–3.
	1967	*Guernsey's Natural History.* Guernsey Press, St Peter Port, 2nd Ed 1972.
McClintock, D.	1968	*The Plants of Guernsey*. Gardeners Chronicle, 29 March, 5 and 12 April.
	1975	*Guernsey's Wealth of Wild Flowers*. Country Life, Jan.
	1975	*Early Records of Guernsey Plants*. Channel Islands Anthology No 3. Toucan Press.
MacCulloch, J.	1815	In Quayle, T., *A General View of the Agriculture of the Islands*, Appendix *List of the Flowers of Jersey and Guernsey*. (cf. p. 26)
	1826	*On the Naturalisation of Plants with Remarks on the Horticulture of Guernsey*. Q. Jnl. of Science, July.
Perring, F. H. & Walters, S.M.	1962	*Atlas of the British Flora.* Nelson. 2nd Ed. David & Charles 1973.
Perring, F. H. & Sell, P. D.	1968	*Critical Supplement to the Atlas of the British Flora.* Nelson 1968.
Stace C. A. (Ed.)	1975	*Hybridisation and the Flora of the British Isles.* Academic Press.

Accounts of the field meetings in 1969–71 are to be found in *Watsonia* and the *Wild Flower Magazine*; and of that of the British Pteridological Society in 1971 in their *Newsletter* for November 1971.

Clues in the indexes and elsewhere to the *Gardeners Chronicle*, *The Garden*, the *Journal of the Royal Horticultural Society*, and to many other similar horticultural, botanical and island publications have been followed up. It has not been possible to go through the files of the island's daily newspapers.

References for individual plants are given under the plants in question.

Appendix

Sources of Data on Other Features of the Island's Natural History

The *Transactions* are those of the Société Guernsiaise. The *Flora* that of Guernsey by E. D. Marquand, 1901.)

Climate

Climatological summaries have appeared in the *Transactions* since 1893.

Geology

Plymen, G. H. 1932. The Geology of Guernsey. *Transactions*, pp. 301–18.

Roach, R. A. 1965. Outline and Guide to the Geology of Guernsey. *Transactions*, pp. 751–75.

Lower Plants

MOSSES

Marquand, E. D. 1901. *Flora*, pp. 216–29.

Rhodes, P. G. M. 1909. Notes on Mosses, Hepaticae and Lichens from the Channel Islands. *Transactions*, pp. 88–91.

LIVERWORTS

Marquand, E. D. 1901. *Flora*, pp. 230–3.

Rhodes, P. G. M. 1909. *loc. cit.*

Paton, J. A. 1969. The Hepatic Flora of Guernsey. *Transactions*, pp. 375–82.

LICHENS

Marquand, E. D. 1901. *Flora*, pp. 278–302.

Rhodes, P. G. M. 1909. *loc. cit.*

FUNGI

Marquand, E. D. 1901. *Flora*, pp. 234–77.

ALGAE – *fresh water*

Marquand, E. D. 1901. *Flora*, pp. 215, 321–4.

ALGAE – *marine*

Dixon, P. S. 1961. List of Marine Algae collected in the Channel Islands . . . Sept. 1960. *Br. Phycol. Bull.* 2, 71-80.

Lyle, L. 1920. Marine Algae of Guernsey. *Journal of Botany*, Supplement II.
— 1925. Some further additions to the Marine Algae of Guernsey. *Transactions*, p. 490.
Marquand, E. D. 1901. *Flora*, pp. 303–20.
Van Heurck, H. 1908. Prodrome de la Flora des Algues marines des Iles Anglo-Normandes. Société Jersiaise.

DIATOMS

Marquand, E. D. 1901. *Flora*, pp. 325-44.

Animals

MAMMALS, REPTILES AND AMPHIBIANS

Brehaut, R. N. 1962. List of Mammals, Reptiles and Amphibians. *Transactions*, pp. 295–300.

BIRDS

Carey, C. C. 1961. A list of the Birds of the Channel Islands. *Transactions*, pp. 103–18. (Revised April 1965.)
Dobson, R. 1952. *The Birds of the Channel Islands*. Staples, London.

FISHES

Sinel, J. 1905. The Fishes of the Channel Islands. *Transactions*, pp. 56–65.
(An updated account is kept by R. Brehaut, La Canurie, Collings Road, St Peter Port.)

PROTOCHORDATA

Brehaut, R. N. 1964. The Protochordata of Guernsey. *Transactions*, pp. 545–8.

ECHINODERMATA

Brehaut, R. N. 1966. The Echinodermata of Guernsey. *Transactions*, pp. 54–7.

SPIDERS

Bristowe, W. S. 1929. A Contribution to the knowledge of the Spiders of the Channel Islands. *Proceedings of the Zoological Society*, Pt. 2. Reprinted in *Transactions*, pp. 407–15.
(An updated account is available from J. Guerin, Shenfield, Les Hurettes Lane, St Martin, Guernsey.)

INSECTS

Last, H. R. 1966. The Coleoptera of Guernsey. *Proceedings S. London Entomological . . . Society*, pp. 101–15.
— 1970. ditto. *Proceedings British Entomological . . . Society*, pp. 1–2.
Luff, W. A. 1904. The Fauna and Flora of the Sarnian Islands. *Transactions*, pp. 402–5. (Summary of papers to date on all subjects.)
— 1905. The Aphides of Guernsey. *Transactions*, pp. 82–9.
— 1907. The non-British Insects of the Sarnian Islands. *Transactions*, pp. 349–54.

— 1909. The Pezomachi (Ichneumonidae) of Guernsey. *Transactions*, pp. 97–8.

Shayer, C. J. 1966. List of Butterflies of the Guernsey Bailiwick. *Transactions*, pp. 28–9.

CRUSTACEA

Norman, A. M. 1907. Notes on the Crustaceans of the Channel Islands. *Annals and Magazine of Natural History*, Ser. 7, Vol. XX, pp. 356–71.

Sinel, J. 1906. A Contribution to our knowledge of the Crustacea of the Channel Islands. *Transactions*, pp. 212–25.

Walker, A. O. & Hornell, J. 1896. Report on the Schizopoda . . . and Amphipoda of the Channel Islands. *Journal of Marine Zoology and Microscopy*, 2(7), pp. 49–55.

MOLLUSCS

Gosselin, J. 1812. Conchologia Sarniensis. Cf. p. 25.

Marquand, E. D. 1894. Land and Freshwater shells of Guernsey. *Transactions*, pp. 356–9.

— 1896. Additional ditto. *Transactions*, pp. 111–12.

— 1901. Marine shells of Guernsey. *Transactions*, pp. 70–86.

Tomlin, J. R. B. & Marquand, E. D. 1902. Land and Freshwater Shells of the Channel Islands. *Journal of Conchology*, pp. 285–97.

(An updated account – some 400 species – is available from R. Brehaut.)

ANNELIDA, NEMERTEANS AND PLATYHELMINTHES

Lankester, E. R. 1866. Annelida and Turbellaria of Guernsey. *Annals and Magazine of Natural History*, Ser. 3, Vol. XVII, pp. 388–90.

COELENTERATA

Mabbs, R. C. 1906. The Sea Anemones of our shores. *Transactions*, pp. 231–3.

Marquand, E. D. 1906. The Zoophytes . . . of Guernsey. *Transactions*, pp. 164–76.

(Up-to-date records, believed to be comprehensive for sea anemones, but possibly incomplete for hydroids, are kept by R. Brehaut.)

SPONGES

Sharp, E. W. 1918. The Sponges of Guernsey. *Transactions*, pp. 110–14.

(Ideas on sponge taxonomy have altered so drastically that the early references have little value today. Modern records are confined to the relatively small number of recognisable species.)

PROTOZOA AND FORAMINIFERA

Halkyard, E. 1891. A comparative list of the recent foraminifera of the islands of Guernsey, Herm and Jersey. *Transactions and Report of the Manchester Microscopical Society*, pp. 18–28.

R. Bréhaut, and N. Jee have greatly assisted in the compilation of this appendix.

Index of Plant Names

INDEX